Motoring My Way

MOTORING MY WAY

Stanley Sedgwick

B T Batsford Ltd · London

First published 1976
Second edition 1991
© Stanley Sedgwick 1976, 1991

Typeset by Servis Filmsetting Ltd, Manchester
and printed in Great Britain by
Courier International Ltd, East Kilbride,
Scotland

Published by B.T. Batsford Ltd
4 Fitzhardinge Street
London W1H 0AH

A catalogue record for this book is available
from the British Library

ISBN 0 7134 6976 5

Acknowledgments

The majority of the photographs in this book are
from the author's own collection – for those
which are not the author gratefully acknow-
ledges their use as follows; Richmond Pike for
illustration 9, Jean Sejnost, Nice, for illustrations
27 and 28, *Diamond Fields Advertiser*, Kimberley, S.A., for illustration 32, Chris Posnett for
illustration 33, 'Ace' Rosner for illustration 35,
Michael Cooper for illustration 59, Louis Kle-
mentaski for illustration 76, Studio 3 for illustration 137, and *Motor* for the drawings on
page 149. Thanks to my daughter Carol Salter
who processed my words, and my thanks, too, to
Timothy Auger and Elizabeth Radford of Batsford for their expert and patient guidance, from
typescript to the printed word.

Dedication

I humbly dedicate this book to the late Walter Owen Bentley – the man whose products and achievements captured my imagination from boyhood.

I was not among those fortunate enough to have witnessed the Bentleys racing in their heyday, but the Bentley tradition was well established when I left school. For me there was only one motor car – the Bentley. W.O. was an enigmatic, unknown figure whose name ranked in one's teenage hall of fame with Louis Armstrong, Jack Hobbs and the like. Little did I dream when I gazed in awe upon the great green Bentleys that one day I would come to know their legendary creator – indeed to number myself among his friends and to be privileged to drive thousands of miles in a variety of cars with him as a contented passenger.

When I met W.O. for the first time after the war and told him that I was helping to revive the Bentley Drivers Club, it was clear to me that the idea of encouraging ownership and preservation of the old Bentleys was an enterprise which he regarded with little enthusiasm and considerable misgiving.

W.O., disillusioned by the adversities which he had endured in the thirties, was in no hurry to reopen a chapter of his life which he had tried to forget, but in due course he accepted the Club's invitation to become Patron and as the Club grew and grew, so blossomed its association with W.O. His attendance at sporting and social gatherings up and down the country, always accompanied by his wife, Margaret, was a source of pleasure to all concerned.

The cottage at Shamley Green was the Mecca of Bentley enthusiasts who beat a path to his door from all corners of the globe. He was too kindly a man to turn away even the most importunate visitor.

Humility and a sense of humour were, perhaps, his most endearing attributes. He could never understand the hero-worship apparent at gatherings of Bentley owners and was embarrassed when those meeting him for the first time thanked him for the pleasure he had brought into their lives. He was a man who never sought the limelight and would never make a speech in public. To have insisted on his doing so would have spoiled his enjoyment of the occasion, but it is characteristic of him smilingly to have found refuge in his later years in the philosophy that people would have been disappointed if he had changed his Trappist image. Nevertheless, overcoming his natural shyness, he yielded to pressure to appear on television and radio programmes on several occasions and proved himself a match for the most experienced interviewers.

W.O. was held in high esteem far beyond the immediate circle of Bentley owners. The French Minister of Youth and Sport conferred upon him the Mérite Sportif Français on the occasion of the Silver Jubilee Celebration of the marque at Le Mans in 1969. There are many who consider that the honour bestowed upon W.O. by a grateful Government at home was less than his due; that he merited the accolade no less than many of his contemporaries.

Few people are known widely by their initials alone. Those of W.O. will long be remembered, and his memory is enshrined in the cars which bear his name and show every sign of sharing the longevity of the man who conceived them.

W.O. said that the pleasure he derived in the post-war years from Club activities; from making new friends among its members; and from seeing the loving care bestowed upon 'his' cars, had more than compensated for all his earlier disappointments. I count myself fortunate in having played some part in creating the opportunities for this great man to enjoy a belated sense of fulfilment.

Preface to first edition

Only those who have undertaken a similar task can know the sheer hard work and application involved in writing a book of this kind in one's spare time.

I do not think I could have embarked upon the job at all if it had not been for two things – firstly, my penchant for hoarding piles and piles of papers, notes, magazines, letters and suchlike just in case I should need them for reference and, secondly, the vast accumulation of self-processed photographs lying about in my study. I have thus been able to draw freely upon my writings in a variety of motoring periodicals over the years and to dig out sufficient source material to enable me to cover subjects and episodes not before recounted.

My reward has been the pleasure derived from reliving my motoring life in retrospect. I do not flatter myself that readers will share every moment with me – indeed one colleague who kindly read the manuscript said that some people would be exhausted merely by reading of some of my more marathon exploits – but I hope that everyone will find something to their liking.

It will be found that I enjoy driving alone, but most of my experiences have been shared with other like-minded enthusiasts. I gratefully acknowledge my indebtedness to all these friends for their co-operation and partnership. My thanks go to my niece, Anthea, who typed the book from very messy manuscripts; to John Croxson who undertook the unenviable task of suggesting deletions to meet the publisher's length limitations and succeeded without impairing our long-standing friendship; and to Hugh Young who also read the manuscript and painstakingly checked the proofs.

I have given this book to the custodians of The W. O. Bentley Memorial Fund and, therefore, unashamedly express the hope that in so doing I have done the right thing – in other words, that the book will sell well.

Preface to second edition

You may ask, 'Why have a second edition in which three-quarters of the material is virtually a reprint of the first edition?' I offer two reasons: firstly, the original edition has been out of print for many years and many enthusiasts have asked me where they can get a copy; secondly, others who have enjoyed the first edition have been kind enough to enquire, 'When are you going to write another book?' My reply has been that I do not have enough to write about to justify another book.

Then it dawned on me that I have experienced quite a lot of motoring in different cars in different countries during the intervening sixteen years and to produce this edition would, hopefully, satisfy both those who had been unsuccessful in obtaining a copy of the 1976 edition and those readers of that edition thirsting for more of the same. So I started work again, going through my files, records and photographs, and this is the result.

I have enjoyed writing the new text in this book as much as I did the original version and *if* any surplus is realized over the costs of publication and distribution it will follow the net proceeds of the 1976 edition into the 'W.O. Bentley Memorial Fund'.

Stanley Sedgwick

Contents

Appreciation

This autobiography would be incomplete without an expression of appreciation of the immense contribution which my understanding wife, Con, has made to my enjoyment of motoring.

Herself a keen driver, preferring open cars, she took her driving test on my 4½-litre Bentley and failed because an ill-informed examiner could not understand how or why she changed gears without using the clutch – a procedure which I had taught her because she found it an uncomfortable stretch to depress the pedal fully. There was a bright side, however, for Con's father bought her a second-hand TC MG as a more suitable car in which to take her test. She did indeed throw away her L plates as soon as a new test could be arranged, and her liking for the marque was to continue through The TD, TF, MGA and MGB series, then superseded by an Alfa Romeo 1750 Spyder and a 2000 Spyder. For the last six years her choice has been a 280SL Mercedes-Benz.

Con has shared in many of my motoring adventures and has tolerated my idiosyncracies when I took off on long-distance solo ventures. By reason of my involvement with motoring clubs and organizations, she has borne with fortitude unconscionable intrusions upon our domestic life at all times of day and night. Con, too, has shared the many treasured friendships formed throughout the world and feels rewarded, as I do, for the thought and effort devoted to motoring activities of one sort or another.

2 *Con with her 280SL Mercedes-Benz*

Mainly about Bentleys

The 3-litre Bentley

I can remember that during my schooldays there existed for me only one make of car; it was, of course, the Bentley. When I left school at sixteen I vowed that I would never own a car until I could afford a Bentley and twelve years passed before I became the owner of a Bentley – and could not afford it! During the war, I bought a 3-litre 'Red Label' unseen through the post from an RAF officer, one John Stone stationed near Dundee, for £150. Some will deem such an incautious procedure a clear manifestation of my youth and inexperience, but I have no regrets and remained on speaking terms with the previous owner. Owing to petrol restrictions and the exigencies of the Service it was not possible for the Bentley to be driven to Surrey from Scotland. It was, therefore, entrusted to the railway, which conveyed it on a flat truck for a sum approximating one-sixth of the cost of the car. My eyes first fell upon my new acquisition as it stood in the cattle yard at King's Cross. A quick survey showed that it had not been damaged in transit. Then followed an inspection of the unfamiliar controls and a final study of the vendor's instructions on how to start the car. A veil must be drawn over the drive home to Cobham – it would have taken something much more substantial to muffle the noise which issued from the protesting gearbox. On arriving home the 3-litre was put on blocks until more propitious times permitted it to be put on the road once more. This car gave me two years of uncomplaining service. Very little had to be spent on maintenance once the ravages of war-time hibernation had been dealt with. The gearbox was soon mastered, and indeed I have yet to meet a Bentley owner

3 *The author's first car, a 1925 3-litre Bentley, as it arrived home in June 1942. Note the wartime masks on the headlamps*

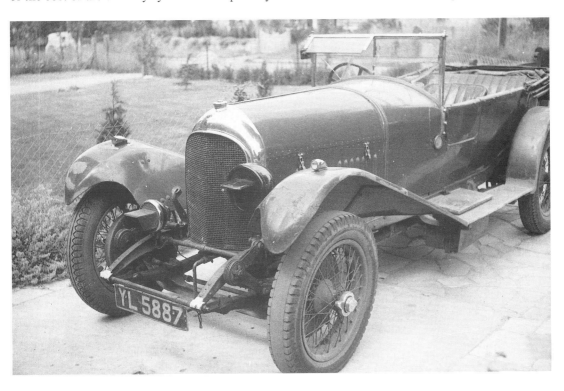

who does not admit to causing horrible noises once in a while!

I enjoyed many thousands of miles of motoring in this 3-litre. Many were the convoys of Bentleys I led to Prescott at speeds of up to 80 mph in those post-war days when opportunities to indulge one's interest in motor sport were few indeed.

A 3-litre owner's greatest problem is the ever-present ambition to own a 4½-litre and, as so many others have done before and since, I eventually succumbed to temptation. The 3-litre is now owned by a young enthusiast living only ten miles away and is unquestionably in better condition than when I parted with it over forty years ago.

The 4½-litre Bentley

The 4½-litre which I was able to acquire fortuitously in November 1947 was quite well known amongst Bentley enthusiasts before the war when owned by Roddy Seys, and became available only as a result of his untimely death on active service. (It was featured in the *Autocar* 'Talking of Sports Cars' series on 14 March 1941.) When I first saw this car, it was looking rather bedraggled through being laid up for several years but a short run confirmed the impression of good, sound motor car underneath the surface shabbiness. This was as it should be, for the Bentley had been cared for by L.C. McKenzie, known to all vintage Bentley enthusiasts as the 'high priest'.

It was one of the very few TT Replicas. The compression ratio had been raised by milling 6 mm off the cylinder block; twin sloping SU carburettors, which are reputed to give 6 bhp more than the vertical type, were fitted, and special ribbed brake drums, manufactured in high-carbon steel by Krupps at Essen, had been substituted for the standard type.

This car was driven home with great pride and new-found pleasure in the additional horses under the bonnet. Alas, ten days after taking delivery, misfortune overtook the 4½. Returning home in the early hours from a BARC dance in London, I was driving along the Kingston Bypass when I noticed a haystack on fire in a field alongside the road. Glancing back at this disturbing sight I saw sparks in the road behind me which I thought to be strays from the burning stack. Another look revealed a trail of sparks behind the car, and I realized at once that my Bentley was on fire. My cry to Con, who had been asleep, that the car was on fire was met with a sleepy enquiry as to whether she should get out – needless to say full consciousness returned rapidly and was followed by a speedy exit. This car had a stoneguard on the petrol tank in the form of wooden slats strapped on over felt. Flames were coming from this stone-guard underneath the tank, and I can only conclude that war-time storage had resulted in the tank becoming perforated, impregnating the felt with petrol. One of the leather retaining straps had broken and, possibly, a spark from the buckle trailing on the road had started the fire. Frantic efforts to tear off the stone-guard with bare hands and to smother the flames with a rug were of no avail. The fire-extinguisher that I had observed on the car when I bought it proved to be empty. It seemed hours before a car came into sight and the flames were really getting a hold by the time the driver of this car brought his extinguisher to bear. The fire was now too fierce to be doused by ordinary methods and the good Samaritan went off to call the fire brigade from Esher. They arrived in a creditably short time though it seemed an age, and were soon at work on the flames, which by then were twenty feet high from the bulkhead to the back of the car. We gratefully accepted a lift home from the driver who had come to our assistance and reached home in a very depressed state, having left the erstwhile beautiful Bentley a smoking, soaking wreck at the roadside.

Next day, the wreck was towed to McKenzie's workshop by the 'high priest' himself, while Avery, his foreman, choked by wind-blown

4 *The 1925 3-litre Bentley still going strong 48 years later. Still owned by Roy Baker of Guildford*
5 *The 4½-litre Bentley one week after acquisition*

6 *The 4½-litre Bentley after the burn-up on the Bypass*

ash and cinders, steered the burnt-out remains.

The next six months were occupied by The Great Rebuild, not the least difficult part of which was the search for replacement parts. Fellow Bentley enthusiasts were most helpful; such things as a prop-shaft, bulkhead, Autovac, instruments and steering column were soon acquired, and advantage was taken of an opportunity to instal a 'D'-type gearbox in place of the original 'A'-type. The chassis and engine were not damaged, but the body was a complete write-off. Mac fitted a Borg & Beck clutch and lightened the flywheel considerably.

It was clear that the biggest headache was going to be finding a new body. The one which had been destroyed was a Vanden Plas open four-seater, but it was different from the body usually fitted to Bentleys in that the rear panel swept inwards at the bottom to make room for the 25-gallon petrol tank. It was, in fact, a replica of the one fitted to the car driven by Humphrey Cook in the TT. Then a million-to-

one stroke of luck came my way – Bill Shortt presented me with the body which came off the actual Humphrey Cook car! I collected my prize from a grassy grave and delivered it to the coachbuilders, who stripped off the rotted fabric, replaced rotten timber, mounted it on the chassis and re-covered the body with leather inside and out. That doyen of Vintage Bentley owners, the late Forrest Lycett, gave me a windscreen from an earlier version of his 8-litre, which required little alteration to form an admirable fold-flat screen for the rapidly forming 'new' 4½-litre Bentley. Hood and tonneau cover were added – mercifully the hood irons were not beyond repair after the fire. A coat of green paint, new tyres, new electric wiring, windscreen wiper driven by a motor under the scuttle and the car was ready for the road once again.

It was indeed a case of an ill wind, for the 4½ was now in far better shape than when I had bought it and the insurance company had contributed more than half the cost of the rebuild.

I collected the car in Putney at the end of May and next day left for a 2,000-mile Continental tour with four up and luggage.

Novice abroad

This was to be my first venture by car on to the Continent of Europe and I was pleased to have the guidance and, for part of the trip, the company of Johnnie Green in his open Vanden Plas 3-litre Bentley. We joined Johnnie at Dover on 20 May 1948 to catch the midnight ferry to Dunkerque. Here we met Gerry Crozier – destined to become one of my closest friends but, alas, no longer with us – driving his 38/250 Mercedes-Benz drophead coupé. This car had the biggest petrol tank I have ever seen – 50 gallons, I think – and, despite the thirsty engine, he expected to reach Italy without having to replenish the tank.

The first day's driving brought us to Paris. The following afternoon we all went to the Paris Grand Prix at Montlhéry, but my enjoyment was marred by having damaged the $4\frac{1}{2}$ earlier in the day in a collision with a taxi near the Opéra – the result of my unfamiliarity with the operation of the priority from the right rule when bowling down a wide boulevard. The race, though almost a procession, was very enjoyable, and it was grand to be on a real race track once again. P.A.T. Garland was placed fifth in his Delage and because he was a lone hand from England we found him afterwards and went driving through Paris streets straight off the track, sans silencer, sans licence, sans number plates, sans almost everything except a terrific performance. The gendarmes couldn't have cared less and waved us on with a welter of Citroëns and Renaults. It was through Garland that I was fortunate enough to meet Henri Trillaud and his partner, the racing-driver Albert Divo, who immediately undertook to straighten the frame of the $4\frac{1}{2}$ and render it mobile once again. It turned out that three new spring main leaves had to be made. In view of the indefinite

delay in prospect, Con and our two friends went on to Interlaken by night train. The 3-litre and the Mercedes also went on their way to Interlaken, having very sportingly delayed their departure until it was certain that the $4\frac{1}{2}$ was under treatment.

The springs were fitted by Divo and I collected the car three days later, setting off for Switzerland in pouring rain. After a brief stop at Barbizon for an excellent dinner at Les Pléiades, I pressed on to Interlaken on a non-stop run of 350 miles. It rained all night, and two incidents have stuck in my mind. The first was when I turned left with the road in Auxerre only to find myself right in the middle of a conglomeration of railway tracks. I was so surprised that I stopped, until it soon struck me that it was not such a very good idea to remain there. The second moment was when, climbing over the mountains to Pontarlier in thick mist, the first streaks of dawn just appearing, the road surface became so bad that I thought I had left the road and entered a farm. After reversing downhill for half a mile I noticed no side turning and that the telegraph wires followed the supposed road, so I went ahead again. This atrocious road went on for some miles, and then suddenly broadened out into a good metalled surface as if it had never been anything else.

After a couple of hours sleep our reunited party left to keep an appointment in Bern with a great enthusiast Ditlev Scheel, then a junior diplomat and now retired in Canada after a number of ambassadorial posts. On the way we met Johnnie in the 3-litre; he had trickled down from Paris via Dijon and Ouchy. We drove round the Bremgarten circuit already being prepared for the Swiss Grand Prix, and then partook of a sumptuous repast at the home of the Scheels. We still talk about the vast quantities of strawberries and cream which came as a revelation to us rationed Britons.

The Merc. had now arrived at Krebs Hotel in Interlaken and the convoy went out pass-storming the next day. The Susten Pass was climbed to within a mile of the summit at which point it was blocked by snow. As the Grimsel and Furka were also impassable, the journey next day to Lugano necessitated a detour via Lucerne and a climb over the St Gotthard Pass. Lugano was reached before dinner, and the next morning we spent looking round and buying lire and French francs with our surplus Swiss currency – a highly recommended piece of arbitrage at the time.

After lunch we parted company with the 3-litre and the Merc. and left for Italy. Como and the Italian customs behind us, we entered the autostrada for Milan and covered 30 kilometres in just under 15 minutes, an average speed of 75 mph. This road was not then twin track, the surface had not been touched since the war, and it was pretty busy with heavy commercial traffic. We arrived in Milan somewhat buffetted from the fast run with screen flat, and were circling the square outside the Cathedral looking for a car park when an HRG wearing GB plates shot across the square, the owner (Charles Meisl) shouting some crack about it being '. . . the only time you get enough petrol, Sedgwick.'

After tea we set out for Genoa without knowing where we would spend the night. Hunger forced us to stop for a meal at a roadside service station where our lack of knowledge of Italian was only partly overcome by mime, for we thought we had ordered chicken, but were served up with a poached egg in soup! Genoa was reached at 11 pm and a wrong turn landed us in the dock area.

Now whether it was the darkness or the ignorance of the language I do not know, but everything looked sinister and menacing. It appeared to us as if a revolution might start at any minute as we prowled around looking for a hotel at which to spend the night. We did not find anything in that district and left on the road to Ventimiglia. After some miles we stopped in a small watering-place to debate our plans; we were almost reconciled to spending the night in the car by then. It appeared, however, that we were outside a hotel and some Italians – presumably acting on the mad-dog-the-Englishman-theory and not in the least surprised to find four people in an open car long after midnight – guessed we wanted to sleep and knocked to awaken the porter without further ado.

Then followed an altercation which appeared to be concerned with finding a garage to house the machine. The porter, who had dragged a pair of trousers over his pyjamas, mounted the step of the $4\frac{1}{2}$ and directed us half a mile down the road to a garage which was definitely shut. The original locals again appeared and the knocking business started again – this time it was poor Ricardo who was being called from his bed. The car garaged, the procession returned to the albergo on foot with all the luggage, and a very comfortable night – or what remained of it – was spent.

It was not until after breakfast that we found out the name of the village; it was Arenzano. A short delay to complete certain petroleum transactions and to convert into French francs enough lire notes to paper a bathroom and we set off along the coast road for Nice.

We stayed on the Côte d'Azur a day longer than planned which made it necessary to attempt the run to Paris – over six hundred miles – in one day. We left Nice at 7 am, planning to arrive in Paris at midnight. After an hour, however, a headlamp post was seen to be leaning drunkenly inwards and investigation showed that the universal on the perrot shaft operating the front brake had given up the ghost – a latent defect as a result of the prang in Paris, now just showing itself. An hour's delay proved that nothing could be done about it, so we continued to limp on our way using only the hand-brake. Lyon was reached at 6 pm, where tea was taken, petrol vouchers converted into coupons, another 100 litres of petrol taken aboard and all set for the second 300 miles. A further delay occurred when a back tyre punctured and necessitated a wheel change. A belated dinner of Lucullan description was taken at 9.30 pm at the Hôtel de la Poste at Saulieu. We left there for Paris at 10.30. Incidentally, only one headlamp was working and as no relief driver was in the crew three short naps had to be taken before we eventually reached Paris just as the street lights went out at 4 am. On checking in at the hotel we were informed that the Merc. was within, but that the 3-litre had not yet reported.

After lunch the following day we left, with the Merc., for Le Touquet. Here we found the 3-litre outside the hotel, but the owner was out and we did not see him again until the following day on the dockside at Calais. A pleasant crossing, tea with friends in Folkestone, a fast run up the London road (how smooth after those on the Continent), a quick cup of coffee at the home of Bill and Marion Cook – always a recognized staging-post when going to, or returning from, the Continent – and the final lap of Cobham concluded a most enjoyable holiday. By this time I had become very adept at progressing quite rapidly with only the hand-brake working, a skill which was to stand me in good stead in later years.

We had covered nearly 2,300 miles and, believe it or not, the *net* cost of petrol was 7s. 6d. (37½p) per head! My first motoring holiday on the Continent truly had been an exciting experience. The two passengers – the late Edgar Baker and his wife – who covered the whole distance (including the Nice to Paris in a day effort) in the back of the 4½ with the luggage, bought a 3-litre Bentley soon after their return to England. Whether this was because they were so impressed with vintage Bentley motoring or whether, as some unbeliever suggested, they were determined never to ride in the back of one again, I never knew for sure.

It is not easy for those accustomed to the autoroute era to visualize road and traffic conditions in France and Italy in those early post-war years. There were few bypasses, and one had to drive through village after village – often behind a crawling camion – on road surfaces still bearing the ravages of armoured vehicles and almost total war-time neglect. Average speeds achieved on long drives considered to be very creditable in those days would now be regarded as a snail's pace.

Across France in a day

May 1950 saw the 4½ once more heading across France towards the Mediterranean, this time in the company of two more 4½-litres belonging to Geoffrey Kramer and Harry Kemp-Place; the former being the Pacey-Hassan in its then two-seater road-going guise and surely having the least ground clearance of any vintage Bentley.

It had been decided to go away towards the end of May with the object of including visits to the Grands Prix of Monaco, Monza and Bern which were to be held on three consecutive weekends.

We planned to go to the same places and hotels at more or less the same time, but each car was to be a law unto itself. The Kramer and Kemp-Place équipes, each having only one driver, arranged to take two days to cross France and accordingly took the Dover to Dunkerque night ferry on Thursday, 18 May. They were delayed on arrival while the customs officials had breakfast but reached Dijon before nightfall, and pressed on to Monte-Carlo next day, reaching their destination at 11.30 pm. Geoffrey and Anne bore physical and psychological signs of the unremitting battle between the low hard-sprung 4½ and the pavé. The car had shed a headlamp and broken a spare-wheel mounting bracket.

I took the opportunity of fulfilling a wish of long-standing to cross France in one day. Co-driver Bob Gregory and our wives were talked into this marathon run and we left England on the night ferry 24 hours behind our colleagues. We were fortunate in clearing customs at Dunkerque without delay and at 5.05 am turned the Bentley's radiator southwards determined to see the Mediterranean before we slept again. The first 200 miles were covered in pouring rain in five hours, including stops totalling 25 minutes. Only another 560 miles to go! Our route lay through Péronne, Soissons, Sézanne, and Troyes to Dijon, where we partook of our first French meal at the Hôtel du Nord. We were informed that two other Bentleys had spent the night there and left early that morning. The 'others' had, indeed, selected the same hotel by coincidence for an overnight stop. We were still less than half-way and left almost $1\frac{1}{2}$ hours later for Mâcon, Lyon and points South. The 25-gallon tank, which was filled with rationed petrol at Dover to save precious currency, became empty at Mâcon (400 miles) and received its first dose of 'super-carburant'. We resumed our journey through Lyon, Valence and Avignon, stopped for dinner just after leaving Avignon and continued in darkness grateful for the unaccustomed warmth now making itself felt in the air. Through Aix-en-Provence to Fréjus, we then took the road over the hills to Cannes and the coast road to Nice and beyond.

The Bentley came to rest, after a trouble-free run, at 2 am outside the Beau Rivage Hotel – alas, since replaced by an apartment block with the same name – overlooking Monte-Carlo harbour and we retired to bed having ascertained that the other two Bentleys and their crews were safely within. We were delighted to learn that Johnnie Green, 3-litre and parents were there also. We had covered the 760 miles in 21 hours including stops; nothing outstanding, but an ambition, however senseless, achieved.

Next morning we awoke to eat a late breakfast on our bedroom balcony, while watching final preparations for the world-famous Monaco Grand Prix. We strolled round the town before lunch, running across other Club members and British drivers, then we took up positions on our respective balconies ready for the Race of a Thousand Corners.

The pack of cars arriving at the first corner after the start took our breath away and we were agog to see them re-appear along the harbour's edge. They came, and then the disaster struck. Farina spun round and the following eight cars telescoped into each other. Seen from our vantage point it seemed like a dodgem track. Each driver bounced up into the air when his car collided with the one in front and was then bounced again as another car hit him in the back. It looked as if the race was washed out, but some of the drivers managed to stop before the wreckage and remained there blipping until a gap was made to allow them through. The field was halved and much of the interest went out of the race but we enjoyed seeing Fangio drive through to win on an Alfa Romeo, and it was a pleasure to see Bob Gerard acquit himself so creditably with a car so much slower than the leaders.

Much of the rest of that week was spent in idleness. One day spent crossing the hills to Grasse for lunch and Castellane for tea, a trip prompted by a desire to see if the road really was as bad as it had appeared under sheet-ice during the Monte-Carlo Rally, and also by the reference to the Grand Canyon du Verdon in Rodney Walkerley's book. We left Castellane after tea to do the circular tour recommended by R.L.de B.W.; although it seemed a long time before we reached the gorge, the grandeur revealed at our first glimpse took our breath away. The road climbed higher and higher along the side of the canyon – sometimes on a ledge, sometimes in a tunnel – and every minute the view became more and more awe-inspiring. The route lived up to its reputation and the scenery equalled any I had seen in Switzerland.

To the regret of the sea-bathers and sun-worshippers, departure day came all too soon, and three heavily-laden Bentleys departed eastwards. Our route lay along the coast road to Genoa – where my $4\frac{1}{2}$ fractured a lamp bracket and shed the headlamp – and then via the Autostrada to Milan. We were headed for the fabulous Villa d'Este at Cernobbio on Lake Como. We were able to stop at this palatial hotel only by reason of a personal introduction by Club member Max Colombi, Banqueting Manager of 'The Dorchester', to M. Willy Dombré, the owner, who gave us luxurious rooms at incredibly low charges. Nevertheless, our stay here made a considerable dent in our currency allowances; we could not afford to dine in the hotel but were otherwise monarchs for a day.

Early next morning, the five males clambered into my Bentley and we were soon back on the Autostrada for Milan. We visited the Alfa Romeo works and were made most welcome. Dr Alessio, the Managing Director, allowed us to examine closely one of the racing cars (the one driven by Reg Parnell a fortnight earlier at Silverstone) and the prototype of the new production 2-litre 100 mph saloon. While we were climbing in and out of the cockpit and poking about in the engine-room of the Type 158, workers in the factory crowded round the door outside to catch a glimpse of the racing car. Dr Alessio placed at our disposal a chauffeur-driven Alfa Romeo and arranged for the Export Manager, Tony Compari, to accompany us to Monza to see the practice for the next day's Grand Prix of the Autodrome.

Early next morning we left Cernobbio for breakfast with Count Lurani at his villa at Cernusco. I was in front and put up a black by leading the convoy through villages where Dunlop (or even Pirelli) tread had never been seen before. Before regaining the correct road we had squeezed by bullock carts and left entire populations speculating upon our passing. Eventually, the three 4½s swept into the drive at Cernusco where we all tucked into breakfast with several of Johnny's friends assembled for the racing. The menfolk found it hard to tear themselves away from the famous garage where the white-washed walls were covered with the autographs of dozens of racing drivers and personalities. We were privileged to add our own signatures in black chalk and noted

7 *Havoc at the Tabac – the first lap pile-up when Farina spun in the Monaco Grand Prix of 1950*

other familiar names – Pomeroy, Lycett, Nockolds, etc – among the famous Caracciola, Nuvolari, Varzi and a hundred more.

The convoy then left for Monza – three 4½-litre Bentleys sandwiched between a couple of 1500 cc Fiat saloons and Johnny's new 1100 cc model. The gatekeeper at the track was overwhelmed by the heavy metal and the Bentleys were soon parked alongside the course in the Paddock.

I was invited to lunch by the President of the Automobile Club of Milan and met several prominent figures in the Italian motor-racing world; all were unanimous in their sincere desire to have the BRM offer some worthwhile opposition. When I sat down to lunch our proposed itinerary was to take us to St Moritz that evening, back into Italy over the Bernina

Pass the next day and thence to Innsbruck via an, as yet, undetermined route. When I arose to resume watching the racing, the plot had undergone a complete re-routing, chiefly at the instance of Signor Lombardini, Racing Manager of Pirelli's. On the back of a menu was drawn a route considered to be far more worthwhile than our original itinerary – and so it turned out.

After the racing we returned to Johnny's place, and left, not for the Maloja Pass, but for Gardone on Lake Garda. One of Johnny's friends conducted us some miles on our way to point out the gorge which formed the background in the classical painting 'La Gioconda'. Thereafter, we traversed some 15 miles of second-class road towards Bergamo. Hermetically sealed Aprilias and Pinin Farinas may have been all right off the main roads in Italy but not open cars such as ours – unless one liked to be enveloped in choking white dust and enjoyed surfaces on which the pavé of northern France had nothing. We arrived, very dirty and tired, at the Grand Hotel Fasano on the shores of Lake Garda in good time for a meal before turning in.

Following the recommendations of our Italian friends we then drove northwards on the road built by Mussolini along the steeply rising banks of Lake Garda and at the northern extremity turned south following the other shore of this beautiful lake. The leisurely progress round the lake soon gave way to a rapid run along the Autostrada to Venice. We obtained rooms and set out to explore the famous city. Some time was spent next morning in further exploration, but we were not sorry to leave Venice on this occasion. Beautiful as the city undoubtedly is, we found our nasal reactions outweighed visual appreciation. At one time it seemed likely that one, if not two, of the ladies, suffering from food-poisoning, might not be fit to travel, and it was a thankful group of fellow-travellers who lunched at a roadside restaurant overlooking the Lake of S. Croce on the road to Cortina

8 *The 4½-litre Bentley at Johnny Lurani's home at Cernusco*

d'Ampezzo. After passing through Cortina we turned westwards to drive over the famous Dolomiti Road to Bolzano and Austria.

At the top of the first of three passes, the Falzarego, we stopped to play with the first snow we had encountered. We then proceeded to climb the Pordoi Pass. I was driving at the time, in front of the other two Bentleys, thoroughly enjoying the prospect of a long climb of countless hairpins. Inexcusably, I looked upwards to trace the zigzag path of the road over the mountainside.

As my eyes returned to the road I saw that I was running on to the grass verge on the near side. I corrected, but not in time to prevent the front hub hitting the end of a rock wall holding up the mountain. Then things began to happen with astounding rapidity. The steering-wheel was wrenched out of my hands, the suitcase secured to the near-side step disintegrated as it, too, hit the wall; then the back wheel hit as well. This last impact flung the back of the car across the road, and it came to rest at right-angles driving its nose into the wall. I stopped the engine and got out thinking 'This can't happen to me'. But it had. The passengers were shaken but fortunately unhurt. Not so the poor $4\frac{1}{2}$. She was lying there looking to my inexpert eyes a complete write-off. The other two Bentleys arrived and none of us could really believe our eyes. The front axle was pushed back about five inches, having sheared the dowel-pin; the back spring had been broken clean off at the front end, and the rear axle had moved back and split the petrol tank; both off-side wheels were bent beyond use and the tyres and tubes were torn into shreds; the dumb iron was considerably bent; and the wings were creased, and there was other subsidiary damage.

I could not have wished to have the help of more able or willing chaps than Bob, Harry and Geoffrey who proceeded to tackle the problem without delay.

The two spare wheels were put on; the car dragged sideways by means of a tow-rope; the front axle was unbolted from the spring and refixed nearer to its correct location; the back spring was sledge-hammered roughly into place so that the free, repeat free, end of the main leaf was bearing on its bracket; and the back brake was disconnected to prevent braking torque from dislodging the spring from its temporary resting place. A trial proved that the car could be driven under its own power in spite of its crippled condition – the back and front axles were eight inches out of track. It was decided to limp on, so somehow we transferred part of our luggage and both Con and Marjorie Gregory into the other Bentleys – a rearrangement which caused much discomfort to all concerned. The convoy then went up and up to the summit of the pass, where we stopped to see how the car was faring. A leak manifested itself

in the radiator; it was running out of the honey-comb like a tap. All stocks of radiator panaceas were put in to no avail.

We reached a village as darkness was falling and Bob and I persuaded the rest of the party to press on to Bolzano for a meal and thence to Innsbruck where we had reservations at the Maria Theresia Hotel. As their tail-lights disappeared up the street I think we felt something like Edge and Jarrott must have felt when trouble overtook them during the famous inter-city races of long ago. Neither of us spoke a word of Italian and we were in a village which rivalled any Balkan ditto in the crudity of its amenities. The radiator continued to empty itself, and we dared not tackle the Costalunga Pass without means of replenishing the cooling water. After protracted negotiations with the local motor repairer through a semi-intoxicated native who spoke an obscure French patois, I found a jerrican in a shed and purchased it for a bag of gold. Thus armed we set off into the night. A book could be filled with the diverse methods by which we procured water that night. Suffice it to say that the radiator had to be filled every 10 kilometres and was boiling almost continuously. We were thankful that we were in a country full of streams, springs and pumps. Eventually we pulled into a petrol station in Bolzano just as the others were preparing to leave after a meal. We left before the other Bentleys, took a wrong turn in the town, and the other cars passed on before we regained the main road. We heard afterwards that they drove fast to catch us, but after some time concluded that we just could not have gone that fast and must have run out of road into a ravine. Actually we slogged on with countless stops for water, climbed the Brenner Pass, crossed the frontier into Austria in the small hours and reached Innsbruck just as it was getting light at 4 am.

Noon found us at a radiator repairer's workshop where we were told that the hole would be repaired by 6 pm. The springs had remained in place and, as the car seemed no worse for its journey after the accident, we decided to go on to Interlaken, where we were to stay for a few days, and to have the springs fixed and the chassis straightened in Switzerland. We left Innsbruck at 6.30 pm, some six hours behind the other two Bentleys, and headed for the Arlberg Pass. For some reason the battery had run down and we had to resort to second gear to get sufficient current to light the headlamps. It seems incredible now, but we negotiated the Arlberg Pass with the aid of a torch shone upon the trees lining the road. At midnight, we parked above the Walensee and picnicked – this was the first stop, apart from the frontier, since leaving Innsbruck. After another couple of hours we decided that it was useless to go on with virtually no lights when it would be daylight in half an hour or so. Once again we stopped and all went to sleep in situ. Con awoke to find four mystified Swiss faces peering out of a cottage window at the strange sight of an open car full of sleeping bodies. We reached Krebs Hotel at Interlaken at 9 am in time for breakfast and only 12 hours behind schedule.

The $4\frac{1}{2}$ had survived nearly 400 miles since the prang – I venture to think that only a vintage Bentley would perform thus. The Kemp-Places were at the hotel, but the Kramer outfit had not turned up. To everyone's relief Geoffrey and Anne arrived during the morning; unhurt, but the $4\frac{1}{2}$ had suffered damage. The sprag – as we called the protruding end of the hand-brake lever – had inevitably grounded and resulted in a split brake drum. The front brakes were therefore disconnected. While cautiously descending the Arlberg Pass the rear brakes were insufficient to bring the slowly moving car, confronted with a road blocked by two parked lorries just round a hairpin corner, to a standstill. Geoffrey had aimed the expensive parts through the inadequate gap between the two vehicles, and wings and windscreen were torn adrift. They had decided, not surprisingly, to call it a day and spent the night in the next

village completing the journey into Interlaken the next morning.

I snatched a few hours sleep and at lunchtime drove the $4\frac{1}{2}$ into the Bahnhof Garage where Herr Zimmermann and his staff set to work to straighten out the Bentley. They worked with a will and skill refreshing to behold. A new spring leaf was made; the chassis, track-rod and front-axle – the latter found to be slightly bent when dismantled – were straightened, the damaged wings roughly beaten out and painted; and the car was ready for the road at 6 pm two days later.

On Sunday Geoffrey left for Paris, conscious of his poor brakes, and the rest of us went into Bern to witness the Swiss Grand Prix. In addition to the Alfa Romeos of Farina, Fangio and Fagioli fighting it out, we saw the Heath/Abecassis team of H.W.M.s acquit themselves well in the Formula II event and the British motorcycles do well in both solo and sidecar races.

How different were those Grands Prix to the 'slot racing' between Armco barriers to which we have now become accustomed. If a driver left the road and hit a bank at Monte-Carlo it tended to be Barclays, and big solid trees bordered much of the Bremgarten Circuit at Bern. How long will it be before driverless cars are radio controlled from the pits?

The next day we left early for Paris 390 miles away. Motoring steadily all day, we reached the capital in time for dinner. The Kramers had arrived the previous evening, and had experienced only one bad moment on the way when an approaching camion driver had apparently fallen asleep while overtaking another camion – Geoffrey meanwhile had come to a standstill and was looking for reverse. When only twenty yards or so away the driver was roused by his mate and the camion scraped by without touching the Bentley.

The next morning was spent shopping; it was always a good plan to visit Paris at the end of a trip so that the available balance of currency could be calculated with an accuracy all too real. After lunch, we gazed into the windows of the motor accessory shops in the Avenue de la Grande Armée and left Paris at 6 pm for Dunkerque and the night ferry. We dined royally at the Maison Godbert in Amiens – another Walkerley recommendation – and did not leave that town until 10 pm. Then the headlamp which had been temporarily remounted became loose upon its pillar and swung round to the right. It was secured with insulating tape, but this broke several times and we drove with the light shining at right angles to the road for the last 20 miles. As we threaded our way through the docks at Dunkerque midnight chimed, and the Bentley was garaged on board.

So ended a memorable holiday and a hundred and one unrecorded incidents now crowd into my mind: innumerable, seemingly interminable, settlings-up ('I have paid the hotel bills, that's 22,195 lire including 15% service; deduct the extra eggs Bob had for breakfast, Jack's doctor's bill, and Geoff's drinks; that leaves 18,215 lire divided by five, but I paid for that last lot of petrol in Swiss francs and Harry owes me 1,000 French francs for his window at the Monaco Grand Prix and I don't want Austrian schillings if they are not convertible into Swiss francs, so if Bob gives me £2 when we get home and Geoff pays 50% of all our lunches at Innsbruck we shall be all square if Harry buys the programmes at Bern, etc, etc.'); . . . Con swigging Chianti out of a litre flask on the beach at Ventimiglia; heady waves of oleander perfume sweeping across the road; the Mille Miglia Ferrari on show in Milan; being shadowed and taken for fire-raisers when out for a stroll late at night in Interlaken; the Union Flag hoisted when Fergus Anderson won the motorcycle race at Bern; Geoffrey running his $4\frac{1}{2}$ on the ferry alongside the trains because his 'sprags' wouldn't let him up the car ramp . . . and so many other things which served to whet the appetite for the next time.

Two trips on the Continent and two accidents

was not a record to be proud of. I must have learnt my lesson, for in thousands of miles driving over there in many different cars since those days I have had only three traffic brushes – one with a Swiss army truck when my car was stationary; another with an improvised agricultural snowplough meandering across an ice-bound road, again in Switzerland; and a ding from a Toyota at traffic lights in Germany.

More Continental motoring

The year 1951 was a very busy one for me. I had taken on the editorship of a new glossy motoring magazine, *Autocourse*, which was to be published quarterly in four languages. This was the first time that an effort had been made to report in depth on a regular basis the Grand Prix races counting towards the World Championship and certain other important races. This involved personal attendance at nearly all of them (fortunately most Grands Prix took place within the confines of Europe at that time), and afterwards the production, analysis and interpretation of charts showing the relative positions at the end of each lap, and the lap times for every lap, of every competitor. These were compiled from the official time sheets obtained from the race organizers and I must draw a veil over the number of inaccuracies therein that I found necessary to correct in order to make sense of them.

Most of the travelling was done by air, but I did take the Bentley to Spa, Reims and Le Mans on consecutive weekends, leaving it in a hangar at Le Touquet during the intervening weeks and flying to and fro to collect it. These trips, too, had their highlights – as do all Continental excursions by road – and I call to mind the lap of the Reims circuit, on the eve of the race, when the $4\frac{1}{2}$ took exactly twice Fangio's time even though she was doing just under 'the ton' down the straight; a 10 minute run on the Jabbeke-Aeltre road at an average speed of $87\frac{1}{2}$ mph by kilometre stones and stopwatch; the thrill of the 24 hour race 'from the outside';

and searching for a hotel on arrival in Reims and finishing up over a dance-hall in most unusual circumstances (all the bedrooms had red doors!).

At the end of August we set off again in the 4½ for a Continental holiday, this time accompanied by Horace Wilmshurst in 'Bluebell', the 4½-litre Bentley built by Mac, the 'high priest', for his own use in hill-climbs, and owned after the War by Gordon Alexander, then Bill Cook and now Tim Llewellyn.

We crossed the Channel by the now familiar Dover-Dunkerque midnight ferry, pleased to find a new ship, the 'Saint Germain', in service, and were off the boat very early the next morning. It was raining (I had yet to leave Dunkerque on a fine day). Our destination that evening was Interlaken, some 510 miles away, and our route lay via Arras, Reims, Châlons-sur-Marne, Chaumont, Besançon, Pontarlier and Bern. Geoffrey and Anne Kramer were travelling in my car as far as Bern, thence by train to Geneva to stay with friends until we picked them up on our return from the South of France a fortnight later. Geoffrey wondered, 'A 1150-mile hitch – is this a record?'

We pressed on in the rain with hoods up until we stopped at Laon at 8.45 am, having covered 147 miles. Oh, yes – there was one stop before this and it had the makings of being a permanent one. I had just crossed one of those nasty wooden-surfaced, hump-backed temporary bridges which abounded at that time in northern France and noticed too late that I should have turned immediately right. I stopped and backed up a bit, ready to take the correct course, when I perceived the other Bentley crossing the bridge. Horace braked, ready to follow me to the right, but all four wheels locked and the car slid on the slippery wood straight towards me, without any perceptible deceleration. Mercifully, there was three yards of pavé between the end of the wooden bridge and my car, and the front tyres of the approaching 'Bluebell' found some adhesion and came to rest

less than an inch from my rear lamps. Having revived the fainting bystanders . . .!

After breakfast and refuelling 'Bluebell' – whose four SUs demanded a gallon every 12 miles and whose tank limited the distance between fill-ups to about 150 miles – we continued our journey, still in the rain, straight through Reims, resisting the temptation to race round the Grand Prix circuit just outside the city. We stopped in Châlons to lower hoods, the rain having ceased at last, and left for Chaumont. Here both cars were refuelled, coats were shed and windscreens lowered; at last we were beginning to realize that our holiday had really started. It was our intention to travel via Besançon, but we missed the left turn south of Langres, and consequently decided to go on through Dijon and lunch at the Hôtel du Nord, which we did.

We continued on and just before entering Pontarlier, a majority vote called for a cup of tea and out came the stove and kettle. The interval was enlivened by 'Bluebell's' ammeter needle disappearing on the discharge side while a wisp of smoke from under the dash promised an incipient fire if ignored. The fault was traced to the cut-out, temporarily rectified, and the journey continued through the customs and into Switzerland. As we came within striking distance of Bern it occurred to me that if we hurried it would be possible for the Kramers to catch the 7.22 pm train to Geneva; and so it turned out. The last few kilometres into the centre of Bern will long be remembered by those concerned, and probably also by those residents of Bern who saw two Bentleys dash to a stop outside the station, all the passengers and luggage disgorge on to the road, and two people hurriedly disappear into the station. Passengers and luggage caught the train with less than a minute to spare – not bad after nearly 500 miles. Then on to Interlaken in time for dinner at Krebs Hotel, where Bentley owners are always welcome. If perchance you should visit this hostelry, ask to see the visitor's book for the early '50s.

The next day included a short run up to the top of the Susten Pass, and a visit to the Aar Gorge and the Reichenbach Falls. The following day we all piled into my car and went shopping in Bern before a rapid run down to Lausanne for lunch at the Château d'Ouchy, overlooking Lac Léman. The return to Interlaken, after a visit to the Château de Chillon at Montreux, was made via the Col du Pillon.

We were to leave Interlaken the next day, Friday, August 31, intending to cover half a dozen of the highest passes in Europe on the way to Innsbruck. An early start was made, overcast skies and a promise of rain replacing the customary hot sunshine. The first pass negotiated was the Grimsel, and as we reached the first dam the rains came. It poured and poured for the rest of the day. We were very wet before we abandoned the hope that 'it was only a shower' and put up the hoods. The Furka Pass was climbed in a thunderstorm, and we decided to curtail our proposed 'pass-storming' route and settle for the Oberalp and Arlberg Passes. (This was the third occasion on which my desire to climb the Stelvio had been foiled and another 27 years were to pass before I fitted it into a tour.)

After crossing the Austrian frontier, we stopped for a meal at a pleasant-looking gasthof – this was, I think, the only bad meal we had during that holiday – and then came round a bend to see a fellow countryman making fruitless efforts to extinguish flames under the bonnet of his elderly Austin. Horace put the fire out with one squirt from his 'Pyrene', and we moved on to reach Innsbruck at 10.15 pm. Imagine our surprise and anger when we were told by the manager that, as we had not arrived by 9 pm, he had let our rooms! He was unrepentant and maintained that this was an accepted practice. I pointed out that I had made similar reservations the previous year and arrived at 4 am to find the rooms still available, and what the hell! All he could or would do was offer us one large double room with three beds. Eventually, tired and dispirited, I told him to push in another bed and we all four shared the one room that night. I still like this hotel, but really . . .

The next morning we made a pre-arranged call at the B.P. depot to collect some benzole awaiting our arrival, and at lunch-time left for Salzburg via the southern tip of Germany near Berchtesgaden. This in spite of the fact that one of my magnetos had ceased to function. I put this down to failure of the insulation and steeled myself to cover the remaining 2,000 miles on one mag. – if it lasted – and, if necessary, have another flown out.

Hotel accommodation in Salzburg was at a premium, but we found satisfactory rooms at the fifth attempt and then repaired to the Goldener Hirsch for dinner. Afterwards, we went up to the castle to a folk-dancing and yodelling concert where a real live Austrian zither player played the very popular 'Harry Lime Theme' to the obvious satisfaction of all present.

The next day, after a visit to the mirth-provoking Schloss at Hellbron, we turned southwards over the famous Grossglockner Pass to Cortina d'Ampezzo. My $4\frac{1}{2}$ did this trip, including the 8,438-ft climb, on one mag., and Horace streaked up the beautifully-engineered Grossglockner road as if at Prescott.

We left Cortina next morning to traverse the well-known Dolomiti Road (on which I had disgraced myself the previous year by driving the Bentley into the mountain side) over the Falzarego Pass, the Pordoi Pass and the Costalunga Pass to Bolzano, and then down to Fasano on the shore of Lake Garda. This was to prove an eventful day. The clouds were low and much of the beautiful scenery was obscured. While descending the first pass, Horace discovered, as a result of a door that refused to shut, that his chassis had cracked on the left side just behind the rear engine bearer. His wife transferred herself to the back seat of my car, and Horace decided that he would drive on slowly into civilization. The roads were under repair in parts and there were many miles of very bad surface indeed. We all felt every bump and jolt, and before long the crack developed into a clean break. The radiator trunnion clamp was removed to obviate the possibility of the flexing chassis splitting the matrix, and the magneto advance and retard control was disconnected. We eventually arrived at Lake Garda with no further worsening of this state of affairs.

A telephone call to Count Maggi, the man behind the Mille Miglia, sent us scurrying next morning to Brescia and the garage of the Lancia agent, Cantoni. Willing hands set to work on our arrival at 10.20 am and the job was finished at 3 pm, the frame member having been welded and boxed. Meantime, 20 minutes work on my ailing magneto by a Marelli mechanic cured the fault. Immediately, we headed for the Autostrada to Milan and arrived at Johnny Lurani's home at Cernusco in time for tea. Less than an hour later we were on our way to nearby Monza, where to our delight we found Farina indulging in some brake tests in a G.P. Alfa. He lapped consistently in 1 min. 57 secs. – well inside the lap record and a whole minute less than Horace in 'Bluebell' later in the day. We then did a lap in a new experimental 1900 Alfa Romeo with lights on and Guidotti driving. We were impressed more than somewhat. Then back to Johnny's house, where he had kindly invited us to spend the night.

Next morning was spent in Milan, and after lunch we turned south for Genoa and the Mediterranean. After a very pleasant drive along the coast road through Alassio, we reached Monte-Carlo in time for dinner; a visit to the Casino, of course, to add a modicum of our currency allowance to the coffers of that establishment; a visit to the Sporting Garage for benzole and a much-needed 'lavage de route'; then, along the coast to Juan-les-Pins where we anticipated four days of lazy bathing and generally taking

things easy. We were all very disappointed in both the town and the hotel. The hotel had very small bedrooms, and only one bathroom in commission for those unfortunate enough not to possess the not inconsiderable means to pay for a room with bath. We coped with the town by leaving it every morning for a secluded beach near Antibes.

Telephone calls to and from a fellow Bentley enthusiast, Arnold Stenhouse, at Ste. Maxime, and artist Roy Nockolds at St. Jean Cap Ferrat, resulted in a run down to Ste. Maxime, where a most enjoyable swimming party took place.

Tales of bad weather at home made us reluctant to leave the almost too hot weather of the South of France, but the end of our stay approached. We left Juan-les-Pins at 7 am on Monday, September 10, and went via the Route Napoléon to Geneva, breakfasting in Castellane and lunching in Grenoble. At Geneva we were met by the Kramers, who had made reservations for us at the then new and highly satisfactory Hôtel du Rhône.

Early next morning we left for Paris and, thanks to the Michelin Guide, partook of an excellent lunch at Vieux Morvan at Rouvray, just north of Saulieu – the Omelette Meringué really was something! Resuming our course at a steady pace, we approached Paris rather more slowly than usual – the effects of the lunch, I think – and on reaching our destination parked the Bentley outside the Hôtel Continentale (now the Inter-Continental) in Rue Castiglione.

We had but 24 hours to spend in Paris and proceeded to make the most of it. After the lengthy ablutions which naturally follow a day's run in an open car on the Continent, we all six piled into the four-seater Bentley and went to eat at La Grenouille, or 'Roger the Frog's' as it was known to its habitués. The Michelin Guide described this eating place as 'Fantasie et bonne humeur – au coude à coude', and was quite right. The menu was scribbled in chalk on a blackboard and you were handed a pair of opera glasses to read it; the place was a series

9 *The 4½-litre Bentley in Vintage Sports-Car Club driving tests at Slough, December 1953*

of small rooms surrounding the kitchen; ancient theatre posters and odd souvenirs decorated the walls and waiters were, to say the least of it, less formal than usual. Our waiter talked one of the girls in our party into having a sweet called 'Maison de Chef' – suffice to say that it was a confection of ice cream and fruit in a form which reduced all within sight to helpless laughter, but which in London (at that time) would have left the most broad-minded Watch Committee at a loss for words.

About six o'clock the following evening we reluctantly left Paris to catch the night ferry at Dunkerque – or so we thought. During dinner at the Moderne in Arras an old friend on his way to Monza told us of floods in south-east England and broken dock gates at Dunkerque. This chance encounter and a subsequent telephone call to the RAC Port Officer at Dunkerque from the police station at Béthune, saved us a fruitless journey to Dunkerque for a non-

existent ferry-boat and sent us beetling off to Calais from which the 'Dinard' was making a special trip in the small hours. During the latter part of this trip I passed a car of the 'tin-box' variety with British plates and, thinking that it was probably heading for Dunkerque, slowed down alongside and called out to the driver that the lock was 'out' and that we were being diverted via Calais. Far from a word of thanks for this friendly act, the driver of the termite reacted as if I personally had run into the lock gates.

So back to England, many pounds poorer, but richer in experience, and having thoroughly enjoyed yet another spell of Vintage motoring on the mainland of Europe. We had covered 3,106 miles in the course of which some 240 gallons of petrol had been used.

The next year (1952) I clocked up over 2,500 miles on the 4½ in France and Switzerland, including a visit to Le Mans for the 24 Hour Race

– the latter trip enlivened by the presence in the back seat of cartoonist Russell Brockbank.

I had the 4½-litre for a few more years, enjoyed every mile in it and took part in many rallies, sprints and driving test competitions with it, but at the end of 1952 I acquired 'for business purposes' another car – a Rolls-Royce Phantom III of which more later – and tended to use this for Continental journeys. In addition, my health began to deteriorate, as a result of which I spent six months during the winter of 1955/6 in a sanatorium with T.B., which effectively curtailed my motoring activities for a spell.

I sold my 4½ to David Braxton in August 1956, but not until I had my sights firmly on the next step up the Vintage Bentley ladder – a 6½-litre; specifically, the unique Speed Six belonging to John Norris.

The Speed Six

Thus, I graduated from the ruddy thump of a four-cylinder to the smoother torque of a six – but what a six!

My first ride, not drive, in a Speed Six – indeed in any Bentley – was during World War II when a G/Capt. E.M. Jones very kindly took me some miles up and down the A5 in his Barker-bodied boat-tailed 6½-litre with torpedo running-boards and matching mudguards. At the time, this trip was a highlight in the midst of gloom and I hardly dared contemplate whether such opportunities would still arise when Peace broke out.

'AC 260' – my Speed Six – was often referred to by its registration number and will always be remembered for its battleship grey four-seater body (the rear two seats being in a tonneau-covered hole); for its five carburettors; and for its two large headlamps mounted close together in front of the radiator.

John Norris had owned AC 260 since 1945 when he acquired it from John Morris. The latter, who held a senior position with SU

Carburetters, devised and installed a five-carburettor lay-out which worked extremely well. Five carburettors for a six-cylinder engine sounds crazy until it is realized that there are three small carburettors which function all the time, and two large ones, which only come into operation when the throttle pedal is pressed beyond a certain point. The effect is not unlike the blower coming into operation on the 38/250 Mercedes-Benz. John Norris drove the Speed Six with zest on the road and in competition during his leave periods in the U.K. His eyes sparkled as he told of 100 mph plus over Salisbury Plain at dead of night, and he once put it alongside Mavrogordato's Birkin Blower (now in the Sears' collection) and offered to toss him 'double or quits' – the winner to take both cars! His 1957 home leave coincided with the period of petrol rationing imposed upon us as a result of 'the Suez business', so he turned to his other love, sailing, and sold the car to me.

Would-be 'record-breakers'

It was in November 1957, when glancing through a copy of the V.S.C.C. Bulletin, that I was reminded of Tom Plowman's magnificent 106.9 miles in an hour at Montlhéry in August 1953, in his 30/98 Vauxhall. To me and many other Bentley enthusiasts this was a performance which could not forever remain unchallenged, and having recently acquired the Speed Six – not a fair comparison with a 30/98, I know – my thoughts turned to the possibility of my car, and perhaps Forrest Lycett's famous 8-litre, putting rather more than a hundred miles into the hour at Monza. At this stage it was only a pipe-dream, and not until I broke a connecting rod in my 6½-litre during the Lagonda November Handicap Rally, thus making an engine overhaul necessary earlier than previously anticipated, did I seriously consider the project.

My Bentley was towed to Hofmann & Burton's works at Henley-on-Thames and whilst being driven home afterwards by George Burton

I gave him an inkling of my plot, and as a post-script asked him if he would like to bring his 4½ as well. He said 'Yes' just like that, and within 24 hours I was in a flurry of letter-writing and telephone calls making preliminary investigations as to the practicability of the operation. When should we go? Would the track be available and, if so, how much would it cost to hire for a day? Would the right kind and size of tyres be available? A host of other problems had to be settled before any real steps could be taken.

I called a meeting at my house of all concerned. Geoffrey Kramer agreed to join the party as Assistant Chef d'Equipe and Gerry Crozier, one-time owner of the Barnato-Hassan, agreed to drive my Speed Six – family and business considerations deterring me from doing the job myself. Don McKenzie found himself in the party committed to take part with his 3-litre Bentley, once owned by Forrest Lycett. Forrest Lycett, after careful consideration, decided not to participate in the venture. An

invitation to Stanley Sears to join in with his beautifully rebuilt supercharged 4½-litre Birkin Team car was reluctantly declined by the owner, who, understandably, hesitated to expose such a precious possession to the risk of breakage or damage.

And so the party comprised three Bentleys – my Speed Six to be driven by Gerry Crozier, George Burton's 4½-litre and Don McKenzie's 3-litre.

An exchange of letters with Johnny Lurani and Mr. Bacciagalupi, Track Manager at Monza, revealed that the 'Circuito di Velocita' could be hired for Wednesday, 9 April, at a figure which looked astronomical in lire, but less frightening when converted to sterling. The date was cunningly chosen so that a 10-day trip bracketing the Easter week-end would mean the loss of only four working days. Meantime, Norman Freeman of Dunlops had started enquiries about the availability of suitable tyres. It turned out that special racing covers would have to be made for the project – *if* the moulds were still in existence. Many years had passed since there had been a demand for tyres for 18-inch and 19-inch wheels to carry cars weighing nearly two tons at over 100 mph. After several panic periods, during which Harold Smets and Dick Jeffery acquired not a few grey hairs as first one and then another size was eliminated when old plant proved to be unusable, Dunlops turned up trumps and produced sufficient 6.00×19, 7.00 and 6.50×19 covers to make the venture possible. These covers were buffed at the Works, reducing the tread-depth by 3 mm to lessen the likelihood of thrown treads.

All three participants were meeting the cost of preparing their own cars, sharing the hire of the track and paying all their own expenses throughout the venture. The idea was to chalk up one more prestige performance for the Vintage Bentleys – in other words, we were doing it for the hell of it. Nevertheless, we wished to reduce the cost to ourselves if at all possible. Esso, very sportingly I think, agreed to supply the oil and petrol needed for the journey out and home and for the high-speed runs at Monza. Silver City Airways made a special reduction in the cross-channel air ferry charges, and Lodge provided suitable plugs. I think that all this co-operation was forthcoming because the Vintage Bentley was (and still is) held in high esteem everywhere.

The problem of finding a suitable vehicle for the transport of wheels, tyres and spares was solved when Roney Messervy of Rolls-Royce Motor Car Division secured for us the loan of a brand-new Commer 30 cwt van.

Each month there was a 'Monza Meeting' at my home, when all the problems – administrative, technical and logistic – were fully discussed. The party was joined by Derek and Mary Waller, who were to do the lap-scoring and timing; Bob Gregory and Fred Hofmann, who were to drive the van carrying the spares; and John Tate and Ivor Kramer, who were to make a film of the whole thing. Bill Cook came along to assist generally, and his 300 SL Mercedes-Benz gull-wing coupé acted as a surprising 'tail-end Charlie' for many miles in trek across Europe.

The Speed Six engine was rebuilt with modified exhaust valves and lighter pistons. The chassis was 'gone over', all steering parts crack tested, and a 2.8 rear axle fitted, giving 34 mph per 1,000 rpm with 6.50×19 tyres.

The $4\frac{1}{2}$-litre of George Burton had distinguished itself at the hands of its owner at race meetings, sprints and hill-climbs up and down the country, and was undoubtedly one of the three fastest $4\frac{1}{2}$s in existence. The power behind the disarming 3-litre radiator had shaken more than one driver of a modern sports car. Each winter had brought its quota of 'mods.' and it is not surprising that the suspension and road-holding were selected for particular attention during the winter of 1957–8. I was surprised, however, to learn that George proposed to convert the rear of the $4\frac{1}{2}$ to De Dion suspension of his own design using mainly Bentley parts. This conversion was carried out using Bentley springs and differential unit (now containing a 2.8 ratio lent by Forrest Lycett for the occasion). The De Dion tube was of mammoth proportions and the whole thing proved to be a most workmanlike job. There are those who will disapprove of this modification to a Vintage Bentley and regret yet another departure from the original design. This viewpoint is certainly a valid one, but it is extremely difficult to know where to draw the line, to decide when a Bentley is not a Bentley. Is the internal modification of the engine more open to criticism than the fitting of hydraulic brakes? Is the use of wheels smaller than those originally fitted (21-inch!) more anachronous than an oil cooling radiator? Whatever one's view, the fact remains that a De Dion type rear end is almost as old as motoring itself and, in this case, it worked extremely well.

Don McKenzie, with the smallest Bentley in the party, was faced with the most difficult

11 *The author at the wheel of the Speed Six
in touring trim*

12 *Don McKenzie's 3-litre circulating at Monza*

problem of all: how to make a 3-litre in more or less touring trim cover 100 miles in the hour. It was asking a lot from a car which had left the factory 31 years previously. What combination of axle ratio and tyre size would enable the car to maintain its peak revs for one hour? There were many problems arising from sustained high-speed motoring which could not be resolved until we reached Monza, as we were to find out to our cost.

To my lot had fallen the task of making all the arrangements connected with the movement of the party to and from Monza. This involved a considerable amount of work. Few would relish the problem of finding hotel accommodation for single nights for 18 people along a 700 mile route across Europe during the Easter holidays. Other things, too, occupied my mind. Obtaining a currency allowance from the Bank of England;

French and Italian petrol coupons; a permit to drive a van through France; lots of copies in English and French of the formidable list of spare parts to be taken, showing the value of each item (ever tried to translate 'rear-axle pinion-sleeve securing bolt' into French?); personal accident insurance; and a great deal of other paper work inevitable before a convoy of six cars and a van could set forth on such a Continental foray.

At last the day of departure arrived and Good Friday saw the three Vintage Bentleys, my Mark VI Bentley (which was to be a maid of all work) and the DB2/4 Aston Martin of our film unit, assembled at Lydd for the cross-channel flight to Le Touquet. The Commer was crossing by the Dover-Boulogne boat accompanied by the 300 SL, and bore a vast quantity of spares. It is said that the unfortunate customers of Hofmann & Burton and McKenzie Motors could hardly get a plug changed during 'Monza week' as the stores were very bare indeed while the gaffers were away. Some wag, seeing the pile of 17 wheels in the van, made an uncalled-for remark about customers' cars being jacked up for a fortnight.

The whole party joined up at Reims for the first night, and left next morning for Lucerne. This day's run was enjoyed by everyone, not the least amusing feature being the faces of the astonished Frenchmen, who saw first one Vintage Bentley, then another and finally a third pass through their village in thunderous procession.

Passing motorists, cyclists and pedestrians stared in wonder at the phalanx and Bill Cook, taking up the rear had to take many an avoiding action to preserve the lives of absent-minded road-users still wondering if the Paris-Madrid was on again. Many times did Russell Brockbank's famous cartoon, 'Citron Pressé', come to life, hard-pressed DS 19's giving up the unequal struggle as, one after the other, the three Bentleys thundered by. The only incident of note was the collapse of one of the rear wheels on the Speed Six – a 'slave' wheel not rebuilt for the occasion – which proved to have 27 broken spokes when inspected as a slight wobble became a formidable one.

At Lucerne next morning the cars were lined up outside the Schweizerhof Hotel prior to departure, and quite a crowd gathered to gaze at the cavalcade. Just as we were about to leave for Milan, George Burton came up to me and said: 'I've just pressed my starter button and all I got was an ominous clonk. I think I'm in trouble.' So, instead of making an impressive departure, we slunk one by one to the back of the hotel to investigate the trouble. Someone had commented during the previous day on the steam issuing from the $4\frac{1}{2}$'s exhaust, but only when the removal of a plug from No. 1 cylinder produced a veritable fountain of water was the possibility of a leak into the cylinder fully realized. George motored apprehensively on three cylinders to a nearby garage, where a large quantity of a well-known crack filling preparation was poured into the radiator.

By lunch-time it had been decided that the 3-litre and Speed Six, accompanied by the DB 2/4 and the 300 SL, should press on, whilst I should stay behind in the Mk. VI to cope with the problems arising from the $4\frac{1}{2}$. Fortunately, the Commer had not made an early start that morning and was standing by the disabled Bentley. It soon became evident that the cylinder block was well and truly cracked internally and that nothing short of a proper welding job would yield results – and perhaps not even that. It was decided that the van should tow the $4\frac{1}{2}$ to Monza so that the car would be on the spot and in a place where work could be carried out in comfort, within reach of adequate engineering facilities. So we started off towards Göschenen to board the train through the tunnel to Airolo.

As we neared the mountains the road surface became badly pot-holed and the gradient steeper. The Commer made light enough work of towing the $4\frac{1}{2}$, but its speed was considerably

reduced on these gradients, and George in the Bentley could not see the holes in time to avoid them. Time was passing and the prospect of a long tow in the dark in this terrain was not without its hazards. We decided, therefore, to entrain the $4\frac{1}{2}$ and its occupants at Erstfeld, some 14 miles before Göschenen, the van going on ahead to board a train at Göschenen and to wait for the $4\frac{1}{2}$ further on at Airolo, where it would arrive at 6.10 pm.

Having seen the $4\frac{1}{2}$ safely on to its wagon – arranged by the Swiss Railway with no advance notice – I left to catch the van. The Mk. VI and the Commer took the same train through the tunnel and, whilst awaiting the arrival of the $4\frac{1}{2}$ at Airolo, I enquired if the train to which the wagon was attached was going any further. It was, so I decided to make arrangements for the disabled car to continue its journey by train to Chiasso and again sent on the van to await its arrival. When George and Margaret stepped out of the train at Airolo, I told them what I had done and to get back into the train. Just then a booking clerk came running up to say that he had made a mistake and that the train went only as far as Bellinzona. Then, as he rushed away with all the tickets to get different ones, George dropped the bomb-shell that he had left his wallet containing carnet and nearly everything else on the station at Erstfeld.

The train was held up while the station-master telephoned to arrange for the portfolio to be sent on the next train to the frontier station of Chiasso. The booking clerk came running back with the tickets and a refund, and George and Margaret got back into the train. I then set off in the Mk VI in an attempt to overtake the Commer before it reached Bellinzona, for otherwise the towing vehicle would be well on its way to the Italian frontier to wait for the arrival of the $4\frac{1}{2}$. Of course, I didn't overtake the van before Bellinzona – although I did beat the train by twenty minutes – and it was now well and truly dark. What was to be done now? I went to the station-master and explained the position in my halting French. The train was due in a few minutes. Could he attach the wagon with the $4\frac{1}{2}$ to another train leaving for Chiasso that evening? It was now 7.45 pm. Yes, he would send it on a train leaving at 8.50 pm, due at Chiasso at 10 pm. Good, I thought, and asked him to telephone to his colleague at Chiasso to tell him what was happening and to say that if two Englishmen turned up asking about the $4\frac{1}{2}$ to tell them it would be in at 10 o'clock. This done, I once again went to greet the Burtons as they stepped from the train – this time to whisk them into the buffet for a meal during the shunting operation.

Hunger satisfied, I left for Chiasso and drove as fast as conditions permitted. I was amazed on arrival at the station there to find no trace of the van nor of the portfolio, which should by then have arrived from Erstfeld! Once again I had arrived before the train and found that the station authorities did not know that the car was on the train now due in seven minutes' time. It seemed that the telephone call from Bellinzona had coincided with a change of shift, and Bob Gregory (as I discovered later) was told that the $4\frac{1}{2}$ couldn't arrive until the next morning. Thus misinformed, he crossed the frontier and high-tailed it for Milan, intending to return the next morning for his tow. Immediate arrangements were made for the $4\frac{1}{2}$'s wagon to be shunted to a siding where the car was off-loaded by pushing. At this moment, the missing portfolio was found by a luggage clerk, but we were still not in the clear for we had no towing vehicle. Fortunately, the tow-rope was still attached to the $4\frac{1}{2}$, so I fixed the other end of it to the rear bumper of the Mark VI and drove to the frontier about 100 yards away, where I fervently hoped to find the Commer. It was not to be. I was told that it had waited for some time and then departed southwards.

I decided that the Mk VI could tow the $4\frac{1}{2}$ the 30-odd miles into Milan, and after many minutes on the telephone filled with 'Prontos'

I was able to tell Geoffrey Kramer at the hotel in Milan that I was bringing the $4\frac{1}{2}$ and expected to arrive at 12.15 am. Thus I left the Customs driving the Mark VI, which carried five passengers, a boot full of luggage, four suitcases on a roof-rack, and a $4\frac{1}{2}$-litre Bentley containing two persons and their luggage on a rope behind. The car went remarkably well and barely seemed to notice the added load. At the entrance to the Autostrada I asked George if he would be all right if I went a bit faster. He said 'Yes.' The night was clear. The Autostrada was deserted. The speed crept up. I could see the line of road-side reflectors and an empty road for miles ahead. The 50 mph I had had in mind was soon reached and, as speed is always relative, a mile-a-minute seemed a mere crawl after a short while. Much of the Autostrada was covered at 70 mph and there was a sustained 80 on the clock on more than one occasion. The Burtons stepped out of the car at the end of this stage without any visible signs of wear, George remarking laconically about the Mk VI: 'These cars really are a magic carpet, aren't they?'

We arrived at the hotel on time and were welcomed by the whole party, for everyone had stayed up to greet us. And so we were all in Milan on schedule. And here a brief tribute to my long-suffering passengers would not be out of place – Con and daughter Carol, Marjorie Gregory and Anne Kramer – who had borne the day's activities with fortitude and good temper. (I soon learned that, provided they were regularly 'fed and watered', they would put up with almost anything.)

The $4\frac{1}{2}$ was towed to Monza next morning by the Commer, and the block lifted to reveal a T-shaped crack which ran for almost one inch across the top of No. 1 cylinder and about the same distance downwards between Nos. 1 and 2 cylinders. It was Easter Monday and nothing in the way of welding could be done until the block could be taken to a welding wizard the following morning.

Meanwhile work proceeded on preparing all three cars for the high-speed runs. We intended to do the runs in touring trim, but decided to remove lamps, mudguards and full-width windscreens for reasons of safety. Apart from this, the cars ran in the same trim in which they had been driven from England.

Dunlop's fitter, Sid West, supervised the fitting of the wheels with the racing covers, and arrangements were made to obtain a supply of Esso Extra from the pumps at the track. The Speed Six and the 3-litre were almost ready for the fray before the $4\frac{1}{2}$-litre's block came back from the welding shop. All hands set to work at tea time, on the day before THE day, to reassemble the $4\frac{1}{2}$ engine. This was completed in a few hours and the car was left standing overnight whilst we all kept our fingers crossed hoping that yet another tin of magic would complete the sealing operation. It was not to be, however, and next morning George made repeated efforts in the Paddock to get the engine to fire on all four cylinders whilst the other two cars were completing their qualifying laps.

Every driver using the 4.25 kilometre banked circuit at Monza was required to do 10 laps at gradually increasing speeds up to 70 per cent of the target speed set for the actual record attempt or high-speed trial. These familiarization laps were undoubtedly of great value, even to experienced racing drivers who had not before driven on a banked circuit. Both Don McKenzie and Gerry Crozier confessed that an increase of only 10 mph on the lap speed gave one quite a different impression of the circuit. The Speed Six and the 3-litre, having completed their qualifying laps, put in a couple of fast ones for Dunlops, whose French Racing Manager, Henri Lallement, had flown down from Paris to pass judgment on tyre temperatures. The cool weather no doubt contributed to the happy verdict that no speed limitation was to be imposed. Nevertheless, the 50 lbs pressure insisted upon gave the drivers a very bumpy ride indeed, and on the worst parts they bounced six inches off their seats.

Poor George came out of the Paddock on three cylinders to do his qualifying laps, hoping that No. 1 cylinder would 'chime in' when he really got going. He did his first two qualifying laps on three cylinders in second gear to keep the revs up but he was out of luck, and also caused some consternation by having greatly exceeded his qualifying speeds. The timely intervention of Johnny Lurani averted the imposition of a 5,000 lire fine. George then went out to do one fast lap for Dunlops and all four cylinders were in for part of this lap; his lap speed was 110 mph. His luck was right out, however, and further work on the car being of no avail he was forced to abandon the attempt.

The Speed Six had now started its Hour Run. After four laps at just over 118 mph Gerry Crozier came in because he had lost all his power quite suddenly and suspected the need for hotter plugs. Whilst the plugs were changed – no speedy operation on the inlet side – Don McKenzie took out the 3-litre on its One Hour Run. It was now 3 pm and less than three hours of track time remained available. He lapped consistently for 40 minutes at nearly 98 mph, then our hearts sank as he came low off the banking and headed for the pits. As he came to a stop the engine sounded uneven, but his real complaint was that he had no clutch and no brakes. A cursory inspection revealed that the pedal cross-shaft had come adrift at one end, and a glance under the valve cover revealed that a valve had broken. The Speed Six was now ready for another go and Gerry set off once more whilst Don, not one whit daunted, proceeded to take the block off the 3-litre to replace the broken valve, hoping that no further damage had been done.

The $6\frac{1}{2}$-litre sounded and looked magnificent. The first four laps were covered at over 118 mph, the next two a good deal slower, and we feared the same trouble had recurred. However, the engine picked up and seemed to be going well until Gerry brought the car in after 12 laps with a most uneven beat. Further examination revealed that an inlet valve had broken, thus putting paid to the Speed Six's effort. It was great while it lasted and we couldn't forget the wonderful sight and sound as it came past the pits at over 120 mph. Its fastest lap was 119.4 mph and it had covered 50 kms at 110.3 mph.

Don's valve job was progressing apace with the assistance of Fred Hofmann, who had left his fruitless labours on the $4\frac{1}{2}$. At 5.30 pm Don was back on the starting line, having changed the valve, fixed the loose pedal-shaft and re-fuelled in $1\frac{3}{4}$ hours. We wondered if this augured new piece-work rates at Thornton Heath.

It was now a case of all our hopes resting on Don McKenzie's shoulders. He soon got his lap time down to a steady 1' 39.6" (96.5 mph). When complimented on his consistent lappery at the end of his first attempt, he replied that there was nothing to congratulate him about; it just wouldn't go any faster, it was flat out all the time.

The tension built up among those of us standing at the pits as Don circulated, and time never went so slowly. Lap after lap went by. Then, with only 10 minutes to go, he came past a minute late and more slowly; the engine sounded a bit rough. Two slowish laps later he stopped and said, 'It's happened again. I've broken another valve. I don't think it will drop in so I think I'll go on and finish the Hour on three cylinders.' And so he did. He covered 89.19 miles in the hour and had covered 100 kilometres at a speed of 96.54 mph before his engine blew up. His fastest lap was 98.63 mph. For sheer grit and determination, Don's work at Monza on that day took a lot of beating.

We all returned to Milan feeling disappointed about the day's happenings – indeed more than one of the womenfolk had shed a tear – but there was not the overwhelming sense of despair which might have been expected with the prospect before us of all three Vintage Bentleys lying out of action in garages at Monza.

It was agreed that the Aston Martin and the Mercedes-Benz should leave for Lausanne during the morning according to plan. The blocks were to be lifted off the Speed Six and the 3-litre and new valves fitted and if no further irreparable damage was discovered they would start for Lausanne later in the day. Bob was to make a solid tow-bar to couple the $4\frac{1}{2}$-litre to the back of the Commer. The van had to be loaded and the wings and lamps put back on the Bentleys. I left Monza in the Mark VI at 2.30 pm and after a miserable three hours spent before, in, and after, the Simplon Tunnel, checked in at the Château d'Ouchy in Lausanne about 11 pm. It was bitterly cold and snowing part of the way. We felt really sorry for those in the open Bentleys, especially for George and Margaret Burton, faced with a tow all the way home without any engine heat and, of course, no hood or sidescreens.

The van and its tow left Monza at 5 pm and reached Lausanne at 2.30 am. On arrival at Lausanne I had received a message from Geoffrey Kramer at Domodossola that the Speed Six and 3-litre were on the last train through the tunnel and they hoped to be in by 3 am, this after having worked on their engines for five or six hours. They arrived at 4 am and were frozen; it had been snowing most of the 100 miles from Brig and to cap it all, they had missed a badly placed diversion sign in Brig. It was some time before they realized that the fallen trees, rocks and snow drifts were not meant and that they were in fact climbing the closed Simplon Pass back into Italy. The necessary reversal of direction was a hazardous business undertaken on a narrow precipitous road, made none the more pleasant by Fred Hofmann's assertions that a Bentley exhaust could easily start an avalanche. Over a very early morning cup of tea in the hotel kitchen, we decided that we would make for Paris the next day as planned, but would defer our departure until lunch-time.

Again the Aston and the Mercedes went ahead with a request to confirm the room reservations at the Hotel Continental, the rest of the convoy leaving about mid-day. Everybody was in good heart, especially the Burtons, for whom our admiration grew as they progressed on their long 'graunch' home behind the Commer. We found snow on the roads in the Jura Mountains and there was a bitterly cold east wind blowing all day. Suffice to say we all reached Paris, the van arriving at 2 am.

The next day was spent resting, and in the evening we dined at the Lido. When more comely chassis were not demanding our attention, we were having a technical post-mortem. It was the considered opinion that there must be some peculiar valve-spring period at sustained peak revs which led to the valves breaking, for all three valves (two in the 3-litre and one in the Speed Six) were made from KE 965, though by two different manufacturers. We recalled the similar trouble experienced by W.O. with the streamlined 3-litre at Montlhéry in 1926. It was gratifying to those responsible for preparing the cars that these breakages were of new components of standard design and could not possibly have been foreseen.

It was then that I heard somebody say, 'If we go again, we must do so and so.' Later on the tone of the conversation changed to *when* instead of *if*. George, the most unfortunate of us all – he had had the devil's own luck and not even one really fast lap of Monza – then said, 'I regard this as "unfinished business". I, for one, will return again next year or the year after.' Don said he was sure he could make his 3-litre do the 100 in the hour. It was as if the underlying enthusiasm which had made the whole thing possible in the first place had risen like a phoenix from the table and, though not yet home from the current venture, possible dates for the next attempt were being mentioned before we went to bed that night.

The journey from Paris to the Channel coast was uneventful; damned cold, but uneventful. It is ironical to record that Bob Gregory, after having driven with Fred Hofmann in the Commer all the way from Monza with the $4\frac{1}{2}$ on tow, was warned for speeding near Leatherhead. The boys in blue must have wondered if they were having their legs pulled when told that the van had towed the Bentley all the way from Italy in three days!

The party disbanded at my house as the clock neared midnight, the Burtons cheerfully facing the last 25 miles of their 860-mile tow. Monza to Maidenhead ten feet behind a Commer van. Is this a record? Incidentally, even after this George couldn't tell us the number of the van!

We had not achieved what we set out to do – over 100 miles in the hour with each car – but we had proved to ourselves that each of the cars was indeed capable of such a performance. We learned a lot, mostly the hard way. George confirmed he would go again; the magic '100' was within Don's grasp and he, too, could not resist having another go. It was taken for granted that the Speed Six would be there again, and it was assumed that I would once again undertake the organization and administration.

And so we retired to lick our financial wounds and to let the boffins solve the valve trouble before returning to the fray. (We took our problem to Terrys – the spring people. They set up a bench rig and ran tests which confirmed the diagnosis. A spring with different characteristics was specified and, as an additional safeguard, stronger valves were made and fitted.)

Flying Kilometres and a reconnaisance of Montlhéry

During the winter we discussed the possibility of using the Montlhéry track, just outside Paris, for the next sixty-minute 'blinds'. We had chosen Monza the previous year because it was a relatively new circuit and we reckoned it would, therefore, be much smoother than the old Montlhéry piste. The Monza track, however, was quite bumpy and subsequent enquiries led us to believe that the French track might be no worse, although it was a much 'tighter' circuit with a lap distance of about 1½ miles compared with the 3½ miles of Monza. The advantages of being able to play at record breakers so much nearer home were apparent, but we did not feel happy about mounting another full-scale 'Monza-type' operation on hearsay alone; some sort of reconnaisance at racing speeds seemed advisable. I was arranging for a party of enthusiasts to be timed in their Bentleys over a measured mile, and kilometre, in Belgium – myself in the Speed Six included – and decided to go on afterwards to try out the Montlhéry track. This coincided with Gordon McDonald's avowed intention of improving upon Tom Plowman's 30/98 Vauxhall performance in his 4½-litre Bentley. Thus, I found myself organizing a two-pronged foray to the continent in 1959.

The idea entered my head sometime before Christmas that it might be possible to arrange for the well-known Jabbeke-Aeltre stretch of the Ostend-Brussels autoroute to be closed for the purpose of timed runs over a measured kilometre and a measured mile. The late Forrest Lycett had been there in 1950 by courtesy of 'Goldie' Gardner – making record-breaking attempts there with his MG – and set up new National Class 'B' Records for the Flying Kilometre and Flying Mile of 134.755 mph and 133.828 mph respectively in his famous 8-litre now in the Sears family collection. That Forrest Lycett joined us was, in his words, '. . . solely due to the benevolent yet persistent importunity of Stanley Sedgwick, President and Good Shepherd of the Bentley Drivers Club for, truth to tell, I had been but lukewarm at best.' We were anxious to see the 8-litre take back the honours from Maurice Trintignant, who had improved on the 8-litre's 1950 speeds in a Facel Vega, achieving 139.895 mph and 140.186 mph for the kilometre and mile respectively.

Forrest's last defences were breached when I secured from Dunlops an undertaking to build special tyres for the 8-litre and to guarantee

them up to 150 mph, so he 'phoned Don McKenzie, son of 'Mac' who had built the car, and gave him carte blanche to go through it from end to end with a view to making it faster than it had ever been before.

Permission was sought from the Belgian Government to close the Jabbeke road, but this was not forthcoming as it was now part of the completed and very busy autoroute joining the capital with the coast. Through the good offices of Mr. de Harlez of the RAC Belgium, the Government agreed to place at our disposal a completed stretch of a new motor-road in the course of construction between Antwerp and Liège.

It was an optimistic and dedicated band of Vintage Bentley enthusiasts that gathered on Sunday morning, 24 May 1959, to drive their cars on to the ferry at Dover. They comprised at least one Vintage Bentley of each model except the 4-litre. David Llewellyn was to uphold the honour of the 3-litres, Don McKenzie having a full-time job ministering to the Lycett 8; Harold Pounds and the late Harry Rose took their 4½-litres and George Burton again appeared in his 4½; Stanley Sears, accompanied by son Jack and Tony Townshend, was giving an airing to his 'Birkin Blower'; the Speed Six (ferried by Hugh Young) was mine, and Oliver Batten's 8-litre was company for its distinguished fellow. Eight competing Bentleys, plus a back-up of helpers. I took my Mk VI as a maid of all work. The spares van, was driven on this occasion by Fred Hofmann and Peter Corney. Bill and Marion Cook came along in their Phantom III Rolls-Royce, which also did its share of 'to-ing and fro-ing'. Dunlop produced the necessary tyres and honoured us by sending D.J. MacDonald (Dunlop Mac) to keep an eye on them; and Esso provided petrol and oil.

At Ostend the cars were lined up and various petrol tanks were drained of their Golden Esso (unobtainable in Belgium) to be reserved for Forrest Lycett's 8-litre which pinked badly on petrols of lower octane. This completed, the journey to Antwerp began, the Mk VI leading with the P III bringing up the rear, Bill Cook thus resuming his Monza role of 'tail-end Charlie'. The van was left to pursue its own leisurely course.

On the Monday morning at 10.30 am the the convoy set off to explore the stretch of road which was to be our testing ground. It will not be difficult to imagine the amazement of the townsfolk to see a line of Bentleys rumbling and roaring over the pavé, down narrow streets, twisting round trams and in and out of the traffic. Ten kilometres later we had reached the Autoroute, stretching as far as one could see with only one very slight curve, and a gentle gradient at one end. I led the way in the Mk VI at between 95 and 100 mph and a never-to-be-forgotten sight in the rear-view mirror was a column of flying Vintage Bentleys in pursuit, their spinning locking rings sparkling in the bright sunlight. Soon after, I made a run in the Speed Six and managed a sustained 125 mph, a gratifying come-back after the disappointment of Monza.

The party then adjourned for lunch and spent the afternoon removing wings, lamps and screens in readiness for the following day. This was a safety precaution but would also make quite an appreciable difference to maximum speed. Tyre sizes were varied and pressures checked regularly, Dunlop Mac unobtrusively picking his way from car to car armed with the biggest tyre gauge under the sun. By this time, a number of passing motorists had pulled up to admire these gleaming monsters from a foreign land. Harry Rose expressed himself well satisfied with just under 110 mph. David Llewellyn, however, was overgeared and went into a further huddle over the tyre sizes. There was some concern, too, for Forrest Lycett who found the 8-litre to be decidedly faster than it had been for years, but taking too long to reach 130 mph. Don McKenzie worked late that night and happily rounded up the missing

horses, as the results of the next day proved beyond doubt.

THE day started with a 5.30 breakfast in Trappist-like silence and a procession to arrive at the motor-road at 6.45 am. Our side of the twin-track highway was closed to public traffic from about 8 am. The cars were parked in echelon at the roadside, and it looked as if a Le Mans start was the order of the day! The weather was ideal: cloudy, bright, cool and a slight breeze. The RAC of Belgium were on duty to record the times electrically; the Belgian police were there to direct traffic and generally control matters.

The rules governing records require the distance to be covered in both directions within an hour, and it must be the same piece of road. Thus, when a mile and kilometre are being timed it is usual to measure off the mile and then place the kilometre at one end of, and within the mile. Flying runs can thus be timed over both the mile and the kilometre on a single run; this is so in both directions. There are strict limitations as to permitted gradients at each end of the measured distances which themselves have to be level within very small tolerances. At Herentals – the village nearest to the stretch of road we were using – there was a 3 kilometres run-in at one end of the measured mile and 5 kilometres at the other, and so everyone had ample opportunity to wind up their Bentley to maximum speed before entering the timed distances – and ample distance for slowing down on completing the mile.

Most of the entrants were pleased with the outcome of their endeavours, with the exception of George Burton, who seems only to have to cross the Channel with 'NPA 83' to take aboard unsuspected gremlins. The $4\frac{1}{2}$ could run week-end after week-end in competitions in England, but after Monza – Antwerp! With characteristic zeal George tackled the job of dismantling his engine – lifting the block at the roadside – when he clattered to the end of his very first run over the mile. The evidence was all too damning; the cylinder liner had dropped on No. 3 and lay in fragments in the sump. Nothing could be done to enable further competition driving, and once again George Burton was cheated of the opportunity to show the paces of his car under controlled conditions. Let it be said that the failure in the engine was no part of the work done by George himself. The block which failed on the way to Monza had been sold for 6d ($2\frac{1}{2}$p) and a replacement block – which had appeared to be 100 per cent – was used instead.

Stanley Sears' blower car looked and sounded magnificent and did just about what its owner and Tony expected – 125.304 mph for the mile and 125.599 mph over the kilometre. It was refreshing to find that this car (and Harry Rose's $4\frac{1}{2}$) which habitually won Concours d'Elegance was expected to provide continental transport for its owner and also to acquit itself commendably in competitive motoring – a welcome contrast to some of the cotton-wool concours-only cars of all makes with which we are all familiar.

Harold Pounds' speed over the mile so exceeded his expectations – over 119 mph with an unblown $4\frac{1}{2}$ – that he called it a day. His unbridled pleasure at his car's performance delighted everyone, not least Dunlop Mac who said that in all his experience he had never seen anyone so enthusiastically overjoyed over the performance of a car.

David Llewellyn's efforts to achieve an average speed of 100 mph using Don McKenzie's 'Monza' 3-litre engine borrowed for the occasion, were unsuccessful but $98\frac{1}{2}$ mph was no mean performance.

Oliver Batten's 8-litre, with its home-made body in one of its characteristically ugly forms, averaged 123.587 mph over the kilometre despite an unintended air-brake. As soon as he took off on his first flying run the boot lid of his car – about 4 ft square – came unlocked. Hinged at the top behind the seats, it flapped up and down all the way, rather like a rapidly reversing hungry whale. Oliver was completely unaware of the sheet metal jive going on just behind but was surprised that he was several hundred revs down on his expected performance.

I was delighted with the Speed Six and with my average speed over the two-way mile of 127.818 mph. It reflected great credit on Fred Hofmann and George Burton and their merry men at Henley that this car, which was not greatly modified, should have been made to go so fast. Its 128 mph was within striking distance of the speed attained by Forrest Lycett's 8-litre at Jabbeke in 1950. To me, driving at that speed in the ideal conditions of the day was out of this world. The car felt very steady and it was exhilarating in the extreme. It brought home to me the vast difference between 100 mph and 125 mph in a Vintage car.

I had planned to borrow George's 700×17 tyres for the standing start runs, but when I went to get them off his disabled car – feeling rather like a corpse-robber – someone else had been there first. The $4\frac{1}{2}$ was jacked-up on the roadside minus engine and front wheels. I used the next best size available, 700×18, but the overall ratio thus obtained was hopelessly high for sprints.

The cynosure of all eyes was, of course, Forrest Lycett's 8-litre. During a 15-mile warm up he found that Don had indeed breathed effectively upon the works and the car had been transformed overnight.

The time of his first run went unrecorded, but the 8-litre made several runs through the measured distances. The lack of a communication system between the timekeeper and competitors meant that such times as reached the drivers did so spasmodically and were, to say the least, unofficial. We had heard that the 8-litre had improved on the Facel Vega's time, but did not know by how much, and, in view of the limited time available and the number of cars to be timed it was not possible to hold up proceedings to find out. I asked Forrest Lycett if he would like to have one more pair of runs over the flying mile before we started the standing runs for the other cars. He decided to do this, but expressed a doubt as to whether he had enough petrol for a flying distance, although he had sufficient for a standing start attempt. But off he went. I had not seen any of the Bentleys flat out on the measured mile, so Bill Cook took me down the parallel track in the PIII to see the 8-litre on the return run.

This was not to be as the engine blew up on the first run. Our alarm at the rush of police and officials towards a cloud of smoke in the distance was relieved when we perceived the 8-litre at rest on the grass verge Forrest Lycett surveying the scene. Thus did the 8-litre experience its first ever blow-up through fuel starvation, the resultant weakened mixture burning a hole in a piston crown. Poor Don had spent the morning driving up and down the parallel track with a supply of fuel, only to be passed by the 8-litre going the other way, or to arrive at the turning-point just as Forrest Lycett took off in the other direction. It was unfortunate that the car became hors de combat before covering a standing kilometre in both directions. Equally unfortunate was it that the timing apparatus failed to record the 8-litre's first pair of runs over the mile for, as the rev counter clearly showed, the first of these was marginally the best run of the day.

The average speeds of the two pairs of runs which counted for the flying kilometre and mile Belgian National Class 'B' Records were 141.131 mph and 140.845 mph respectively; (these comparing with 139.895 mph and 140.186 mph by Maurice Trintignant on the Facel Vega the previous November and with Forrest Lycett's own speeds of 134.755 mph and 133.828 mph in 1950 at Jabbeke). The best recorded run was 141.667 mph over the kilometre.

Forrest Lycett had been an enthusiastic owner of Bentleys for over thirty-five years and during that time devoted much thought and not a little money to improving his Bentleys. The fruits of such experimental work thus carried

out by 'Mac' have benefitted all owners of Vintage Bentleys. I had known Forrest Lycett personally only since the war, but my impression of his agelessness was borne out by those who had known him much longer than I. That Forrest Lycett continued to enjoy driving his 8-litre in competitions – in which success can be made or marred by fractions of a second gained or lost in gear changes – in spite of the physical discomfort caused by arthritis in his hands was illustrative of the courage of the man. It was characteristic of him that he said nothing at Antwerp of the pain he was suffering whilst driving. Forrest Lycett's performance in his 8-litre would have called for the highest praise if he had been young and in robust health; as it was, it was magnificent. There is not a member of the Bentley Drivers Club who would not count himself fortunate indeed to be able to drive nearly as well at an age many years his junior. Outside immediate Club circles the fact that an elderly gentleman could drive an elderly car at such a speed was considered little short of miraculous and evoked the highest admiration. (It was not generally known that he bore a substantial part of the cost of closing and policing the road for the benefit of all.) Forrest Lycett not only owned the fastest vintage Bentley in the world, but could justly have claimed to be the only septuagenarian in the world to have been timed at over 140 mph.

At the end of the morning's proceedings I towed Forrest Lycett's 8-litre, with my Mk VI, back to the garage in Antwerp. I decided to leave it on the ground floor, as I was not keen on towing it up two steep ramps to the second floor where we had a large garage to ourselves. Imagine my surprise, on returning to the garage after a brief visit to the hotel, to find that Hugh Young had leapt into the Mk VI, romped up the ramps with the 8-litre on tow and thought nothing of it.

By 1.15 pm the Government were given back their road and we returned to lunch, followed by a post-mortem of the morning's activities conducted concurrently with the mounting of wings, etc. Forrest was mobile again by early evening, Don having removed the valve gear from No. 2 cylinder to relieve the compression, the 8 motoring home quite happily on five cylinders. By now, George had removed No. 3 piston, con rod and valve gear (not forgetting to seal off the oil hole in the crank journal); and had the sump replaced before sunset. After a little persuasion and some hearty pushing the $4\frac{1}{2}$ came to life again. Inevitably she was hardly smooth on three cylinders, and the general effect on George was that of undergoing vibro-massage treatment. However, it was decided that she was fit to run to Paris on the following day, for George was going to drive the reconnaisance laps in the Speed Six at Montlhéry in place of Gerry Crozier, who had not been well enough to accompany us.

Perhaps the most noteworthy feature of this effort was the wonderful spirit of co-operation and sportsmanship that characterized the whole venture. The way in which a number of chaps of widely differing temperaments, ages and means worked together as a team without any ructions is a tribute to the single-mindedness imbued in enthusiasts by the Vintage Bentleys. An outsider would never have known, for instance, that the cars had been prepared by three different firms specializing in Vintage Bentleys and that the proprietors and brains of all three firms were in the party. Their knowledge, effort and tools were pooled for the good of all and the owners of all the participating cars were the first to give credit to the chaps concerned: Burton, Hofmann, McKenzie and Townshend.

On Wednesday morning the party split up, the 'mile and kilometre only' contingent returning home whilst the Montlhéry party, comprising my two Bentleys, the spares van and the lame $4\frac{1}{2}$ of George Burton set off for Paris. The van crew, who had left Antwerp well in advance, were held up at the frontier for an hour-and-a-half explaining how they came to have one more spare tyre on board than listed

13 *George Burton in the Speed Six passing the pits at 120 mph plus, Montlhéry 1959*
14 *The Speed Six engine after the fire at Montlhéry, May 1959*

in the inventory.

The sight of the Speed Six in my rear-view mirror was a stirring one and the driver, Hugh Young – then owner of a very nice Speed Six of more pedestrian aspect – was thoroughly enjoying himself. As darkness fell, he discovered that the Speed Six rear lights were not operative and, being somewhat fatigued stopped at 10.20 pm and booked a room in an all-night café 60 miles north of Paris. No sooner had he registered than in walked George to book another room, with the news that a second liner had gone and he was leaving the $4\frac{1}{2}$ to the tender mercies of the AA for shipment back to England. Hugh and luggage were transferred from the Speed Six to the Mk VI which then continued to Paris, leaving George

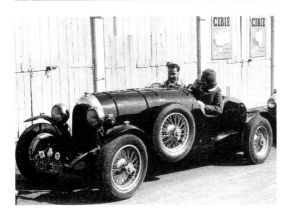

15 *Bill Cook in his 300 SL Mercedes and the faithful Mk VI at Montlhéry, 1960*
16 *Gordon McDonald arriving at Montlhéry en famille*
17 *Don McKenzie arriving at Montlhéry in the 3-litre*

and family to follow on the next morning in the Speed Six.

The following morning we set off for Montlhéry, some 15 miles south of Paris, first calling at Orly to pick up Geoffrey Kramer who had flown from England to assist with lap-scoring and time-keeping. Gordon McDonald and family were already at the track, his $4\frac{1}{2}$-litre stripped down to racing trim. No serious attempts were contemplated until the following day, but Mac put in several trial laps at between 105 and 112 mph before lunch, to familiarize himself with the steeply banked concrete circuit, and made the rather disconcerting announcement that he had felt something 'pick-up' – the compression was down on No. 4. It sounded like a piston ring playing up, but oil applied through the carburettor air intakes appeared to ease the situation.

The afternoon was sunny with a slight breeze blowing when Mac took off again, but the over-cooled engine (58° C) was not giving its best performance. Part of the radiator was blanked off, and a fair quantity of summer grade oil drained from the sump and replaced with SAE 30 in the search for higher working temperature, better upper-cylinder lubrication, and another 200 rpm.

Three more laps were then reeled off, two of them at over 110 mph but the $4\frac{1}{2}$ was still running cool, and was brought into the pits for further blanking off. It was now time for the Speed Six to have a run and Fred Hofmann introduced it and himself to the circuit with four laps, gradually increasing the lap speed from 110 mph to 118.75 mph on the fourth circuit. Returning to the pits, Fred announced that the throttle had been nowhere near fully open. When asked by Geoffrey Kramer, 'Why not?' the answer was, 'I'm not a bloody racing driver.'

The visit to Montlhéry had a two-fold objective as far as George and I were concerned: to see if the valve trouble experienced at Monza had been overcome, and to compare the tracks from a speed potential point of view. It was not

18 *Gerry Crozier prepares for his first run at Montlhéry, Easter Monday 1960*

intended to attempt an hour's run with the Speed Six. It was only when Fred's reconnaisance produced a lap within one mile per hour of the best lap at Monza the previous year that our fear that the roughness of the track might not permit the Bentleys to be driven at their maximum speed was dispelled and, as the Speed Six was going like a train, it was decided to run it for an hour next day.

Friday, THE day, was cool and cloudy with a slight breeze, ideal conditions for the work in hand. Speed Six and 4½ both had their final goings over, petrol pumps, distributor caps and ignition leads being taped up, and were then driven round the circuit for a few check laps to ensure that all was well. George put in one lap at 123.9 mph (3,550 rpm) on 700×19's and pronounced both car and driver to be very happy. An extra turn was given to the shockers to cope with the petrol load for one hour, the tyres checked by Dunlop Mac for the *n*th time, and all was ready. Like Fred, George's hoof

was not right down on the floorboards, but he was going 'almost as fast as I can drive it'. Mac had reached 114 mph at 3,700 rpm with an occasional 3,800 on 700×17's against the 19's of the previous day. There was now no more to be done to either car.

Accordingly, the Speed Six set off at noon, followed after several laps by the 4½. The two made a handsome high-speed couple, Mac dropping down the banking to allow George to pass when necessary. For about 35 minutes the Speed Six circulated steadily, lap after lap, running very sweetly and going like hell. Then for four or five laps it had a tendency to misfire and George eased back from the 122 mph mark down to 116 mph thinking, as we all did, that it was a spot of plug trouble. For three or four laps after that she picked up again and everyone heaved a sigh of relief. However, Fate was to be agin us again, and the misfiring recurred. As George came past we could see a lick of flame from the left side of the bonnet. We did not

19 *When a Speed Six swallows a valve!*
Portrait of Geoffrey Kramer through a piston.

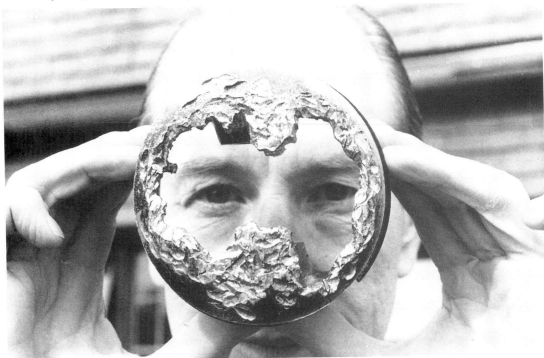

know whether he knew the car was on fire and stood by with fire extinguishers ready to signal him to stop. George had seen the flames and maintained speed in the hope that the rush of air would subdue them until he reached the pits. Once at a standstill, the flames leapt up round both sides of the bonnet and down into the under-tray. The sight of a gallant Bentley in flames is one which would grip the heart of the most hardened individual. The fire was soon extinguished, thanks to prompt attention and quick thinking, and no serious damage was done except to petrol connections, plug leads, and the paint work on the bonnet. The main thing was that George was OK and unharmed, having abandoned ship with some agility.

It did not take long to discover the cause of the trouble: a carburettor float chamber had worked loose due to the rough surface of the track, the loss of petrol resulting in a lean mixture which caused flames to spit back through the air intake and so start the fire. Another carburettor

float chamber was also found to be loose, yet the securing nuts had been checked and tightened only a short time before the start of the run. Here I think we should pause to pay tribute to W.O. for designing all his Bentleys with the exhaust system on the opposite side of the engine to the carburettors. Petrol streaming from a carburettor on to a hot exhaust manifold would have produced effects ten times more serious. Some strong elbow grease by Geoffrey Kramer during the remaining hours restored the blackened engine to its former condition and, with new connections and leads fitted, there was very little to show what had happened, especially as no mechanical defects had been incurred.

Meanwhile, Mac had been pushing steadily on round the track averaging about 110 mph (21 laps at over 114 mph and a best lap at 116.8 mph) but again cruel Fate stepped in after 40 minutes of magnificent driving. As Mac came off the banking and into the pits, I think his worries of the previous day were in everyone's mind. A nasty metallic sound and loss of compression on one cylinder had caused the pit stop and it was unpleasantly obvious from the engine note that the trouble was serious. The block was lifted and examination revealed that the gudgeon pin on No. 4 had failed, probably due to the piston seizing, and the 'blower' con rod was twisted and bent. The piston crown was wedged hard up against the valve heads, the skirt being in pieces down in the crankcase.

McDonald had failed to complete the planned one-hour high speed run. Nevertheless, out of adversity came not despair, but determination to tackle the problem with renewed vigour the following year and to put into practice many lessons learnt the hard way. In the outcome, the temporary repairs effected to the $4\frac{1}{2}$ did not survive another week's holiday-making and this car, too, returned to England by train.

As for the Speed Six, the reconnaisance turned out to be an attempt to run for the hour which terminated after 45 minutes. Its performance had, nevertheless, exceeded all expectations and demonstrated that it was capable of lapping Montlhéry at a sustained average speed in excess of 120 mph, its best lap being 123.38 mph. Not only did the reconnaisance satisfy us of the suitability of Montlhéry for these high speed runs in Vintage Bentleys, but it proved conclusively that the Monza valve troubles had been solved, no tappet on the Speed Six having varied by more than one thou. after 45 minutes of hard thrashing at Montlhéry and several miles flat out at Antwerp, which would have played hell with the Monza valves.

So ended our dual-purpose venture into high-speed motoring for 1959. Could we leave it at that – 'No.' All were agreed that our seeking after the 'Elusive Hour' must be continued the following year.

That elusive hour – the third attempt
And so once again the convoy of would-be record-breakers and their support group crossed the Channel and headed for Montlhéry where the track had been booked for part of the day on Easter Monday, 1960.

Esso and Dunlop were again playing their full part and RR had again lent us their Commer van for the transportation of spares.

The cars to be driven in anger at Montlhéry were the three which had been to Monza two years earlier – my Speed Six, George Burton's $4\frac{1}{2}$ and Don McKenzie's 3-litre – plus McDonald's $4\frac{1}{2}$ which had shown such promise at Montlhéry the previous year. The support team had been augmented by Michael Ford, an official RAC timekeeper, and several other willing helpers. The faithful Mk VI was again in attendance as was Bill Cook in his 300 SL Mercedes, specifically adding pit signalling to his role of 'tail-end Charlie'. Optimists all, we had raised our sights considerably for the larger cars. It was no longer 100 miles in an hour, but 120 miles for the Speed Six, 114 or thereabouts for the $4\frac{1}{2}$s, and still 100 for the 3-litre. Our high spirits were damped on the Sunday by the sad news of Forrest Lycett's death – knocked down by a taxi near his home in Kensington.

A certain amount of preparatory work was done on the cars on Sunday. George Burton's $4\frac{1}{2}$ had a new body, still a family-carrying four-seater, but all accessories being quickly detachable to meet the needs of competition motoring. McDonald's $4\frac{1}{2}$ was in good shape, with lowered compression ratio and 700×18 tyres. His run from the coast had been interrupted when, cruising along at 80–85 mph, a hub race broke up and rather surprisingly locked the offside rear wheel. Thinking a tyre had burst, Mac refrained from using the brakes; and a brand new racing cover was worn down to the canvas before the $4\frac{1}{2}$ came to rest. The skid mark, as spotted clearly by us on the way to Beauvais, several days later, was surely the longest in history.

A glance under the bonnet of the Speed Six revealed that everything which could be wired up had been so dealt with. This time Hofmann and Burton had made up special flanges which had been brazed to the float chambers of the two large carburettors and shaped round the air intakes, being secured thereto with jubilee clips. This idea proved very successful in the ensuing runs and is a very positive method of combining immobility with detachability. The three smaller carburettors were amongst the numerous other parts which were well and truly wired on. Happily, Gerry Crozier was fit again and looking forward to putting the $6\frac{1}{2}$ through its paces on this new (to him) track.

Mercifully, the weatherman produced a sunny, dry day on Easter Monday, but there was, nevertheless, a fairly fresh wind blowing. Slowly the minutes ticked away until at midday Gerry took out the Six for a few preliminary laps to check plugs and generally warm up the oil. There was a very slight leak from one of the rivets on the petrol tank, not serious enough to worry about at this stage. Gerry pronounced himself quite happy with the car and the uneven track, which he preferred to Monza, as it 'has a different kind of bump!'

He was then despatched upon his attempt to complete an hour's run flat out. It really was flat out. The lap times varied scarcely one-fifth of a second as the Bentley raced round – a never-to-be-forgotten sight and sound – at over 120 mph. The circuit measured 1.583 miles, so that a car lapping at 120 mph came past about every 47 seconds. The minutes (surely the longest minutes in the world) dragged by: 15 minutes and still going like a train, 30 minutes and all's well, 45 minutes, then 100 miles completed. Dare we uncross our fingers? No; the engine makes an odd noise and the car comes low off the banking next time round to stop at the pits. A gallant effort, during which the speed of the car for 50 minutes never dropped below 120 mph, had ended. It was soon found that the centre of an inlet valve cap had broken off, but fortunately the valve hadn't dropped in and there was no further damage. Geoffrey Kramer and Fred Hofmann started work at once to replace the valve cap in readiness for another go later in the day.

Meanwhile, Don McKenzie had started his run and was circulating consistently at around 97 mph. The aim of 100 miles in an hour for a 3-litre Bentley was indeed an ambitious one and would have daunted lesser mortals than Don. He was not one to under-estimate the task and had gone to great lengths in matters of weight saving, wind cheating and friction-reducing to attain his ends. It was one of these 'modifications' which was to prove his undoing – he had fitted only two rings on each piston and had assembled the engine with generous clearances. The outcome was a voracious appetite for oil which proved beyond the capacity of the comparatively small sump to supply. Thus, after 40 minutes of very creditable motoring indeed, Don had to give up with non-existent oil-pressure, there being no oil to pump. Slide rules and mental agility showed that if he stopped during the course of an hour's run to replenish his sump then, on his previous showing, he could not hope to improve upon his performance at Monza. With the best possible good nature Don called it a day, in the sad realization that his gamble had availed little – and had certainly not brought the elusive 'ton' within his reach.

Neither Gordon McDonald nor George Burton were ready to commence their runs in time to complete them within the allotted spell during the lunch break, and had to wait until 6 pm before tackling the job. Gordon, having made a few practice runs in the middle of the day, was sent off to start his hour at 6 o'clock. George Burton was not immediately ready to start, his carburation not being au point – of which more anon. McDonald's $4\frac{1}{2}$-litre was surely the most versatile of cars. He had left home for France with his wife in the front seat and two of his children in the back – goodness knows where he put the luggage – and was combining a fortnight's holiday in the Château country with his run at Montlhéry. On arrival at the circuit, the family debouched from the car, the wings and other bits were stripped off and he was ready for the 'Hour'. The hands of the clock went never more slowly as the $4\frac{1}{2}$-litre covered lap after lap and the nearer the end of the hour approached the greater became the suspense. At last Michael Ford told me that the hour was up and I unfurled the chequered flag for the first time. As McDonald crossed the line there was a most un-Bentley-like noise under the bonnet; fortunately it was only two exhaust pipes which had broken away at the manifold. The car had survived its hour without any harm and had covered 111.18 miles. And so the Famille McDonald put on the wings and went off to resume their holiday. A truly remarkable performance.

Whilst McDonald was doing his stuff, George Burton was endeavouring to get his carburation right. He, and the resident mechanic Repain tried everything, but each time the car went out for a practice spin it was clear that there were a lot of horses missing. Now this $4\frac{1}{2}$ had a very much raised compression ratio and was always run on 100-octane fuel in England. In France the Octane value of fuel was Government controlled, and the Esso Super available in France was 94 Research Method. We had taken some Golden Esso in cans from England and this was used to lace the local brew. However, the Burton gremlin was still in attendance and after the first few laps of the attempt at the hour the car 'blew-up' and came to rest followed by a cloud of blue smoke. There was a hole in a piston and that was that. George had not succeeded in 'avenging' the Monza misfortune, but he removed the rockers from the offending cylinder, fixed the valves in the closed position, and continued his holiday with Margaret and his two children on three cylinders, returning home a week later with no further damage.

About 6 pm Gerry took out the repaired Speed Six and soon got going at her morning speed of 121 mph. The McDonald $4\frac{1}{2}$ and the Speed Six circulating together again created a memor-

able sight and sound, especially when Gerry went high on the banking to overtake the smaller car. This happy situation prevailed for some time and slowly the minutes passed. After 32 laps Gerry gave his now familiar thumbs up sign, but he was not to experience the onlookers' growing concern for the petrol tank leak, which appeared to be growing worse. After 30 minutes I was considering flagging him in as by then there was a definite increase in the amount of petrol spraying from the leak and one back-fire from the exhaust might have started a blaze. At that moment, however, there came a crackling noise from the engine and the Speed Six came slowly back to the pits. Possible petrol shortage came to mind, but two steady streams on to the concrete from the leaking tank dispelled this theory.

Examination of the engine revealed that the gaps had closed on one magneto, but that otherwise everything was in order for another go. It was by then too late for further operations at Montlhéry that day and arrangements were made to use the track for a short time the following day. Then we came upon a real snag.

Sid West of Dunlops had to tell us that there was now insufficient tread left on the big (7.00×19) tyres for another hour – and to think of all that lovely tread buffed-off at Fort Dunlop! I had to decide whether to give up the attempt or to fit smaller wheels (6.50×19) and allow Gerry to use more revs. Knowing that this was to be our last visit to Montlhéry, I decided to take the calculated risk of blowing up the engine in an attempt to cover the 120 miles in an hour. Off went Gerry and succeeded in lapping at just over 120 mph, but not ten minutes had passed before the engine swallowed a valve and the Speed Six's indigestion became acute. A valve had broken and gone through the crown of a piston after dancing a tattoo in the combustion chamber to no mean effect. The car was attached to the Commer with a bar and returned to England with Fred Hofmann and Peter Corney taking turns in the warm comfort

20 *Charles Mortimer drives away in his new acquisition, the Speed Six*

of the lorry and the unheated Bentley.

Looking back upon our venture I feel that the performances recorded were praiseworthy indeed. We had not achieved all we had set out to do, but I think Con summed up the situation when she said, 'When you first started this business you wanted to do 100 miles in an hour. Now you have done it in fifty minutes and you are disappointed.' As Fred Hofmann said, a sustained speed of 120 mph for a prolonged period such as 50 minutes, in a Bentley which was not by any means an out-and-out track car, would have been an achievement worthy of note some 30 years previously when the car was new. I felt that, having chalked up a measured mile at 127.818 mph and 100 miles at 120.62 mph, AC 260 had really done more than one could reasonably expect and had earned its retirement from such strenuous activities – a prospect which also appealed to my pocket, for there is a limit to which one can indulge one's hobby.

It seemed likely that the thunder of Vintage Bentley exhausts had been heard for the last time on the pistes of Europe, but our regret was tempered by the tremendous amount of enjoyment all concerned derived from those efforts to record yet more meritorious achievements in the annals of Bentleys, undertaken by enthusiasts just for the hell of it.

In due course the Speed Six was once more sorted out at Henley and had a less demanding life for another 18 months before I decided to part with it – or 'her', as I prefer to say, for she had become a personality in the Sedgwick family – and to venture for the first time into Veteran car ownership.

After a short spell in Charles Mortimer's ownership it was bought by Lord Weir.

We were very sad to see the Speed Six go; this particular car was – and still is – Con's favourite of the Vintage Bentleys we have owned. Nearly ten years were to elapse before another 'W.O.' Bentley graced our garage. It was then owned for a time by Victor Gauntlett before returning to Surrey where it is now in Ronnie Frost's collection.

21 *Although the 8-litre radiator is five inches lower than standard, the bonnet is just level with the roof of a Daytona Ferrari. Alongside Jack Durlacher's car at Eze*

One in a hundred – the 8-litre

Although the first production model 8-litre was delivered in October 1930 and thus fell within the accepted definition of a Vintage Car as one manufactured before 31 December 1930, not all the hundred 8-litres built were finished by that date. Nevertheless, the Vintage Sports-Car Club has granted a dispensation whereby all 8-litre Bentleys, including those completed in 1931 and 1932, are classified as Vintage cars on the grounds that the component parts were probably manufactured in the relevant period.

I first saw my 8-litre in 1946 at a meeting of the Bentley Drivers Club in Kensington Gardens and at once rated it the car I would most like to own. A pipe-dream then, even though prices at the time were expressed in hundreds rather than hundreds of thousands of pounds, and I little thought that UL 7 would become my very own 25 years later.

The chassis, a long wheelbase one (13 ft), with a 3.78 axle ratio, left the Bentley Works on

4 February 1932 for the Northampton coach-works of Arthur Mulliner where a Sedanca de Ville was mounted for its first owner, who took delivery of the completed car at the end of April, 1932.

A year later, having covered only 5,000 miles, it passed into the ownership of Mr Willie Evans of Hendon who kept it over three years before it was bought by Mrs Nea Vivien Flemmich of Grosvenor Square. The Service Department record shows a mileage of 64,014 on 4 March 1935, indicating that Mr Evans was a 30,000 miles-a-year man. It seems likely, therefore, that the mileage was approaching 100,000 when Mrs Flemmich acquired it in mid-1936. Anyway, this lady sent the car back to Bentleys for a complete overhaul and a new body. The wheelbase was shortened to 12 ft and practically every part replaced with new parts. A Barker Sedanca de Ville was built on the car – described by McKenzie as '. . . the most terrible body I have ever seen, the back consisting mostly of a glass box to carry two large

22 *The 8-litre Bentley – handsome from any angle*

23 *The 8-litre Bentley – the rounded tail a tribute to the panel-beater's craft*

dogs.' (A strange contrast this to the writer who won't have any dog in any of his cars!) The total bill is said to have been about £4,000, an almost unbelievable sum in those days, and this seems to have impressed the Works sufficiently to justify an entry in the Service Record to the effect that the car was *re-delivered* to Mrs Flemmich on 31 December 1936.

Twelve months later the 8-litre was obtained by 'Mac' for Mr A.C. Clark, of Sherborne, with only about 4,000 miles on the clock since the rebuild. On Mr Clark's instructions the 'High Priest' then went to work and, in his own words, '. . . altered nearly everything to produce the nicest one I ever built intended for fast and comfortable Continental touring.' The modifications included the lowering of the scuttle and radiator by 5″. Three SU carburettors and two Autopulse electric petrol pumps were installed – the Autovac being retained as a stand-by – and a complicated set of pipes, junctions and taps devised to change over from one fuel feed system to the other. The coil was dispensed with and two magnetos running at three-quarters engine speed installed, as were pistons of 'Mac's' own design, weighing 6 ounces less than the standard ones, raising the compression ratio to about 6 to 1. A 3-in diameter exhaust pipe was used with the object of recouping some of the 28 bhp said to be absorbed at 3,000 rpm by the standard 2-in system. The fitting of 19″ wheels with 7.00×19 Dunlop 90 Fort tyres lowered the whole car another inch. (Even so, the bonnet line was just about level with the roof of a Daytona Ferrari.) New hypoid bevels were made to raise the axle ratio to 3.3 to 1 which gave 110 mph at the now permissible 4,000 rpm. Large black-dialled AT speedometer and rev-counter directly in front of the driver convey the message in this respect.

The relatively new body was discarded and replaced by an open four-seater tourer built by Corsica. Well, there are certainly four comfortable seats, but I sometimes wonder if this wasn't the original 2 plus 2, for the foot-wells in the rear compartment were certainly not meant to take normal adult male feet. There are raised wind-deflectors on the scuttle – rather like the TC MG – and a single fold-flat screen. The rounded tail is as good an example of the panel-beater's craft as I have ever seen; it conceals a first-class hood which is comparatively easily raised by sliding forward the whole frame and fixing the hood-iron pivots in this new position.

Mr Clark drove the reconstructed 8-litre about 16,000 miles, the intervention of World War II doubtless curtailing his plans. Oliver Goodwin bought the car in April 1945, in memory of his son who had introduced him to the Vintage Bentley cult before being killed in a Services flying accident. 'Bertha' – as Oliver and his wife, Helen, called the 8-litre – was their pride and joy for many years and they put in a big touring mileage before Oliver's failing health severely limited its use. They took part in the Swedish Rally to the Midnight Sun in 1950 which involved vast distances in quite a short time, and there is a plaque on the side of the bonnet marking this venture.

I was not the only one to approach Oliver during his lifetime with a view to staking a claim to consideration should he ever decide to sell the car, but it was not until two years after his death that I wrote to Helen enquiring if she still had the 8-litre and, if so would she consider selling it. After conversations in which it was apparent that the finding of a good home for the cherished Bentley took precedence over seeking the highest price in the open market, I bought the car in April 1971 and counted myself privileged to have become the owner, even though the price had 'grown another nought' since I was first captivated by its functional beauty.

After a once-over at Hofmann & Mountfort to remedy the obvious deterioration during 2 years of standing and a look-round to ensure that the car was a safe and efficient means of transport, Con and I set off for a short holiday in the South of France to include the Monaco Grand Prix. At the southern end of the Autoroute du Sud oil spray on the passenger's windscreen foretold of internal troubles which had not earlier manifested themselves. The oil pressure was normal, but the engine and nearly everything under the bonnet was covered with oil. It seemed to be coming from the front end where the water pump shaft emerges from the cam cover. I tightened a few nuts and continued at reduced speed with one eye glued to the oil pressure gauge. The leakage persisted and it was a case of adding oil at frequent intervals until we reached our hotel where I parked the car under the trees, but not before depositing an appreciable pool of black oil on the pink forecourt before the eyes of an unappreciative management. (On subsequent arrivals at this hotel I have been met laughingly with a bucket of sawdust, shovel and broom!)

I contacted local Bentley Drivers Club member, Michael Glass, who very kindly asked his mechanic, John Sands, to work on my car and, with the aid of several telephone conversations with Basil Mountfort back in Henley, proceeded to diagnose and cure the trouble. Investigation showed that at some time in its life the inside of the rocker-box and cam-cover had been treated with a red anti-corrosive paint. During the period of lay-up, the treated parts had been high and dry and this, combined with the 'action' of the Elektron alloy, caused the paint to flake off when the engine came to life again. The resultant 'goo' progressively blocked the drain tubes from the rocker chest to the sump, until the surplus oil up top found its way out of a relief hole designed into the system, and thence everywhere under and around the bonnet. After a thorough clean-up and refill of fresh oil – 5 gallons at French prices! – the journey home through Italy and Switzerland was trouble-free and we enjoyed many miles of cruising at about 85 mph, in company with Bill and Marion Cook in their

300 SL Mercedes-Benz convertible. On my return home H. & M. examined the engine and made sure that any remaining paint was removed from the system. My oil leak problems were by no means over, however, as a good deal of oil was getting out of the joint between the iron cylinder block and the Elektron crankcase – a constant niggle to most 8-litre owners. It wasn't the cost of keeping the sump full which worried me, but the unsightly oil-streaked engine on display whenever the bonnet was raised and the tell tale drips in the car park which did not exactly 'go with the car.'

Eventually, after the 1,000 mile run described elsewhere, I accepted the need to lift the block if any real improvement was to be achieved and again headed in the direction of Henley-on-Thames. It did not take long to discover a slight lack of flatness in one of the mating faces. This was hand-polished appropriately, restoring oil-tightness so far as was humanly possible, but still leaving a trace of weep. But the story doesn't end there . . .

Whilst the car was on test, following reassembly of the engine, two rear pistons 'picked up', with consequent loss of compression. The reason for the 'pick-up' was inexplicable, as everything appeared normal and the engine was not unduly tight. Time was important, so Basil doctored the affected pistons to the best of his, or anyone else's, ability and reassembled the engine after checking one or two possible causes. However, as was expected, the piston slap on the two rear cylinders was excessive. Acceptable on a racing engine, but not for a touring car such as UL 7.

A serious problem now had to be faced. New pistons were definitely called for, but virtually unobtainable, being of a special type. The alternative was a complete engine strip, rebore and the manufacture of new pistons, a very expensive procedure merely to cure a bit of piston slap! By a tremendous stroke of luck, Don McKenzie whose father had built the car, unearthed a pair of pistons identical to those

24 *The 8-litre on a typical French road – with the extension of the autoroute system one sees fewer and fewer stretches like this*

figures (over 20 years ago!), and without drastic operation of the 'Old Pal's Act', and the sheer luck in finding the two pistons, it would have been very considerably more.

I am inclined to think that probably it would have been better in the long run – and not much more expensive – to have faced up to a complete engine overhaul at the start. It is a good thing that appreciating values nowadays absorb the high cost of maintaining these cars in the manner to which they are accustomed, for make no mistake, it is an increasingly costly pastime. Not only is it necessary to manufacture specially more and more replacement parts, but not nearly enough youngsters are learning to follow in the footsteps of the decreasing number of skilled and experienced craftsmen to whom we owners of old cars owe so much.

Thus the 8-litre went back into service, hopefully with many thousands of trouble free miles before it. But it was not to be; 'Lady Luck' was not riding on my radiator cap.

In June 1974, Con and I spent a most enjoyable week in the car accompanying the tour of the UK organized by the Bentley Drivers Club for visiting Overseas Members, which included, among other diversions, visits to the National Motor Museum at Beaulieu; the Concorde factory at Filton; the restoration job to end all restoration jobs, the SS 'Great Britain', at Bristol; and a foray into Snowdonia to witness a spectacular start-up of the restored World Speed Record car, 'Babs', in which Parry Thomas had been killed on Pendine Sands. We decided to leave the Scotland-bound tourists after the Vintage Sports-Car Club race meeting at Oulton Park and to spend a few hours at the International Balloon meeting at Cirencester on the way home after an overnight stop at Bourton-on-the-Water. We bowled happily southwards on M5 in glorious sunshine, the combination of sustained speed – well, 70 mph – and high ambient temperature keeping the rather tired radiator busy. (From time to time since I had bought the car, it had been neces-

required. So once again the block was off and this time, while he was at it, Basil decided to strip thoroughly the whole block to ensure no further trouble ensued. Fortunately so, as the reason for the 'pick-up' came to light. The front alloy water jacket plate had badly corroded and broken up, and – possibly whilst the block was on end during the hand scraping operation on the base – the broken-up bits had found their way down the internal water gallery, effectively blocking the feed to the two rear cylinders and causing serious overheating. A few other matters were attended to and the whole lot reassembled.

The moral of this cautionary tale is that with the very best of intentions all round, a job which started as an oil leak ran into four

25 *The piston looked as if an angry giant had taken a bite out of it and then gnashed his teeth on the top!*

sary to discourage leaks with that most effective preparation known as 'Barsleaks'.) However, the needle – which for some time used to pass the 100° Centigrade mark and start going round the dial again when crawling along in heavy traffic – kept the right side of 90; the 8-litre was going in the manner to which it had been designed to become accustomed. With a final burst of speed, a mite over the limit, I signalled a left turn for the Cheltenham Exit and lifted my foot, when it happened! A loud bang and clouds of smoke from under the bonnet. Not again, I thought, as I switched off and coasted to a standstill off the motorway. A peek underneath revealed no pool of oil on the road; a stare under the bonnet showed the crankcase to be intact; turning the engine (switched off) with the starter did not result in any abnormal noises, but the tell tale puffs of smoke from the oil filler indicated a holed piston. That put paid to the plan to visit the Balloon Club gathering and after arranging for the

Bentley to be collected by the Car Recovery Service Club and transported to its second home at Henley-on-Thames, we repaired to the Queen's Hotel for the night. We returned to London by the scheduled motor coach service and finished the last lap home in a borrowed Silver Shadow.

The prospect of more expensive repair work was not pleasing, but was overshadowed by anxiety lest the job should not be completed in time to participate in the Monte-Carlo Rally for Old Cars, which started two weeks later and to which I had been looking forward immensely. Hofmann & Mountfort pulled out all the stops and lifted the block to ascertain the extent of the damage. Sure enough, the rear piston looked as if an angry giant had taken a bite out of it and then gnashed his teeth on the top for good measure. The reciprocating remains had scored the bore but not to the extent that it required machining. Again there was no obvious single cause for the collapse of this piston. It seemed that the clearance had been, perhaps, a little less than it might have been in the quest for silence, and that the continuous running in the heat had contributed to the seizure. In the course of the work it was discovered that the petrol tank was bone dry – shades of Forrest Lycett's spectacular blow-up at Antwerp – an oversight which almost certainly weakened the mixture with disastrous results. Fortunately, Don McKenzie again turned up trumps and produced a replacement piston which was fitted with a greater than standard clearance, all concerned counselling the acceptance of a bit of slap in the interests of longevity. By dint of assiduous labour, the work was completed and the 8-litre brought over to Cobham the day before I was due to leave for my chosen starting-point of John o'Groats. The only problem I expected to encounter was possible boiling of the less than perfect radiator in the mountains, but a large bidon of water and some reserve tins of Barsleaks would cope with any difficulties which might arise.

Now about this rally. The announcement of a Monte-Carlo Rally for Old Cars in July in connection with the 25th Anniversary of the Accession of Prince Rainier whetted my appetite for a midsummer Continental run of a mildly competitive nature.

The Automobile Club de Monaco invited entries from owners of cars built between 1923 and 1939 and offered a choice of seventeen starting points ranging from Oporto to Athens, and Stockholm to Palermo. I was delighted when my 8-litre Bentley was accepted as a starter from John o'Groats and pleased that Hugh Young agreed to accompany me as co-driver.

In the event, indisposition prevented me from driving the 700-odd miles to the John o'Groats starting point, and I was allowed to join the London starters two days later. Thus, at five o'clock of a July morning we reported to the RAC in Belgrave Square where our fellow-competitors were gathering. Peter Rae and Douglas Macfarlane in the former's 1925 3-litre Bentley and Anthony Heathcote in his 1938 25/30 Rolls-Royce with 'Skit' Poulter, arrived on time with over 700 miles already to their credit after a foul-weather drive from John o'Groats. The other London starters were Nicholas Harley (1926 H6B Hispano-Suiza), Peter Bone in the Craven Foundation (of Canada) 1930 Model 'A' Ford and Peter Kendall-Torry's 1937 4¼-litre Bentley.

The regulations called for an average speed of only 25 kph as far as Annecy, where all the routes from the various starting-points converged, and thereafter it was increased to 35 kph over the hills to the Riviera. Our route took us to Dover; across the Channel to Calais; thence via Time Controls at Reims and Besançon to Annecy. The regulations indicated that there would be Controls of Passage in Rouen, Chalon-sur-Saône and Bourg, but these did not materialize and the choice of route between Time Controls was entirely free, despite contrary instructions emanating from Officials en route.

I realized that quite unhurried driving would take us from Calais to Reims in less than 5 hours, so I reserved a room at the Novotel just outside Reims to secure some rest. The skies looked threatening as we disembarked at Calais, and we erected the hood and a couple of side-screens. On arrival in the 'Champagne Capital' we drove round the disused Grand Prix circuit – rather a depressing experience this – and checked into the hotel at 6 pm. We were due to check in (and out of) the Control at the Automobile Club at 10.54 pm, so we had a meal and went to bed for a couple of hours. On the way to the Control we filled up with petrol and, after a welcoming glass of champagne, checked out. Much to the surprise of fellow competitors setting off through the night for Besançon, we went back to the hotel to bed, registering a wake-up call for 1 am. At this time the sky was clear and the moon shining brightly, so the hood was furled and at half-past one we set out for a leisurely drive on deserted roads. After a to follow the circuitous route via Chalon-sur-Saône and Bourg, possibly to fulfil advance indications for publicity purposes. I decided to rely on a telex message sent by the Automobile Club de Monaco to the RAC in London stating that the choice of route between Controls was at the competitors' option. We pursued a leisurely course by the shortest route through Lausanne and Geneva. My insistence on turning left on leaving the Control car park, when everyone else turned right, caused some confusion among the marshals and gendarmerie. We stopped in Pontarlier to replenish the petrol tank and seized the opportunity to have the car washed using a do-it-yourself installation of Swiss manufacture called 'Hypromat', in which device each franc inserted produced a sequence of high-powered sprays of hot water, soapy water, steam, rinsing water, etc. through a fish-tailed hose. It was a hot, sunny day and motoring along the Autoroute from Lausanne to Geneva above the lake in the sparkling open Bentley was very pleasant. At 3 pm we drove into the parc fermé on the lakeside in Annecy. I counted 99 Rally cars including now some classic American cars – Packard, Pierce-Arrow, Marmon. The Bugattis, of which there were 28 in the Rally, belied their reputation for unreliability, all reaching this point without penalty. Especially creditable, in my view, was the performance of the four Bugattistes who had started from Athens, led by Philippe Vernholes in his Type 44 and shepherded by a tender vehicle of the French Bugatti Club. (Some competitors thought this set-up rather like a 'works' operation, but I considered it a praiseworthy Club effort.)

We enjoyed a full night's rest at Annecy before tackling the mountain route to the south. This common route took us over the Col de Leschaux and Col du Frêne, through Grenoble to a Time Control at Aspres-sur-Buëch; thence by Sisteron and Digne to Grasse. This was effectively the end of the controlled road section, for the run-in to Monte-Carlo had

26 *Hugh Young securing the hood for the wet run across northern France on the first day of the Rallye Monte-Carlo des Voitures Anciennes*

couple of hours the first streaks of dawn appeared and we switched off the lights just after 4 am in Chaumont, a short night's motoring indeed. The water temperature was steady at 70° and oil pressure, at 2,000 rpm, was 60 psi. Arriving in Besançon in time for an early breakfast we became aware of strange old cars appearing from different directions. In the Control we found starters from Sweden, Denmark, Germany and Austria gathered in the sunshine. It was a fine cross-section of desirable pre-war cars – Bugattis, Hispano-Suizas, Rolls-Royces, Bentleys, Mercedes, Alfa Romeos and several examples of makes not frequently encountered. The next Time Control was at Annecy where competitors from the remaining starting-points would join us. The misinformed Officials at Besançon were telling competitors been neutralised. A good job, too, for the traffic congestion was terrible.

The Automobile Club de Monaco, assisted by the sponsors of the Rally (the manufacturers of Chesterfield cigarettes) did everything possible to make it an enjoyable experience from the moment competitors entered the Principality. The Finishing Control outside the Casino was similar to that set up each year for the 'real' Monte-Carlo Rally. A large crowd lined the approach to the Control, and there were the customary official greetings, photographs and a loudspeaker commentary. We walked across to our prepaid lodgings – in l'Hermitage, if you please – and from then on enjoyed a lavish social round of lunches and dinners culminating in a Gala affair at the recently opened New Sporting Club.

The day after our arrival in Monte-Carlo was to include a highlight of the event: a speed hill-climb in the centre of the town! The course was about a kilometre long and one's climb started in the Avenue Princesse Grace facing west. After a hundred metres or so one turned sharp right up the hill towards the old station hairpin, now driving on the Grand Prix circuit but in the opposite direction to the race. After negotiating the hairpin one continued climbing, sweeping to the right, then left up the hill below the Metropole Hôtel. A straw bale chicane stuck out into the road from the left-hand side just outside the Wagons-Lits office. One then turned left in front of the Café de Paris negotiating another chicane before streaking round the gardens in front of the Casino to the Finish line below the terrace of the Hôtel de Paris. All this on a Saturday afternoon in July! The road was closed to traffic, but crowd control and protection were at a minimum – a few straw bales which spectators used as grandstands; no crash helmets required, and passengers carried. Arrangements conceived no doubt as fitting for a lot of old cars grinding up a hill but, in practice exciting in the extreme for drivers, passengers and spectators alike in

the case of the more potent Vintage sports-cars. I enjoyed the climb in the 8-litre immensely, made more demanding by the presence of a chicane which had not been there in the morning when I had walked the course. Hugh had been enjoined to brace himself in the passenger seat with the ciné camera set to run continuously, to glue his eye to the view-finder and to film the road ahead from start to finish. This he did with satisfactory results, except for a momentary lapse when the unexpected chicane appeared from nowhere calling for a sharp tack to port when he had expected to proceed straight for the Casino. The Bugattis raced round the Casino gardens with élan to the accompaniment of screeching tyres, and the sight and sound of Von Raffay's supercharged 'S' Mercedes completing the climb is something I will never forget. Fastest time was set up, not surprisingly, by a 1937 Type 328 BMW.

The next day's activities included a procession of all the competing cars to the Palace in Monaco, in front of which the prize-giving was to take place. The square, full of beautiful 'classic' cars, was a sight to behold. The outright winner was a 1926 Hispano-Suiza H6B saloon which had started from Athens. The owner, Modeste Trehin, collected some impressive silver-ware and a cheque for 10,000 francs for his pains. Second, third and fourth places were filled by Bugattis, Types 37, 44 and 57, respectively, the highest placed British (Scottish) entry being Peter Rae's 3-litre Bentley in 9th position.

The method of marking penalized the relative youth of the 8-litre and the relatively short distance from London, and we were unplaced. The Rally was a great success and we greatly enjoyed it.

The 8-litre had run beautifully and overheating had been experienced only occasionally in traffic, and not at all in the mountains. Oil consumption had been nil and petrol consumption had worked out at 9.9 mpg overall for the 1,000-mile trip.

27 *Negotiating the chicane outside the Casino in the speed hill-climb in the Monte Carlo Rally of 'Voitures Anciennes' – July 1974*

Hugh readily agreed to my suggestion that we should start the return journey early on the day after the Rally ended and follow the A8, A7 and A6 autoroutes without commitment as to the journey's end that evening.

We left Monte-Carlo at 7 am and stopped after 90 miles at Brignoles for breakfast. The radiator was seen to be leaking rather badly and in went a couple of tins of Barsleaks which did the trick. The weather was fine, but a very strong cross wind was blowing. The mileage recorder was checked against kilometre markers and found it to be accurate within 1/10th of a mile over a distance of 125 miles! We refuelled at Montélimar and continued our leisurely progress – about 70–75 mph – pleased to find that the autoroute now went past Vienne on the opposite bank of the Rhône, avoiding the single track overpass in the town. After lunch at the International Motel at Dardilly, north of Lyon, we set off again at 1.42 pm. Ten hours actual driving time saw 500 miles behind us and as we reached the Paris end of the autoroute just before 6 pm I said to Hugh, who was driving at the time, 'How about going straight through to Dunkerque?' He responded with a laconic 'It's OK by me.' We negotiated the Boulevard Périphérique to the accompaniment of Gallic gestures from fellow motorists at the steam issuing from below, and ate just north of Paris at 7 o'clock; truly a leisurely progress this, for the day's stops had reached the unprecedented total (for me) of 2 hours 44 minutes. We reached the Motellerie at Dunkerque – which had seen the start and finish of our run across France and back in a day in the Rolls the previous year – at 11.10 pm, the day's distance being 773.7 miles (point-to-point average 47.8 mph; and driving average speed 57.6 mph).

By the time I reached home at Cobham the round trip mileage amounted to 1,889.7; $190\frac{3}{4}$ gallons of petrol had been converted into energy and exhaust gases at the rate of 1 gallon every 9.9 miles. A couple of pints of oil restored the oil level to full and the radiator leaked no longer.

In the footsteps of Napoléon
For the second year running, in the summer of 1975, the Automobile Club Dauphinois, based in Grenoble, organised a three-day Rally for old

cars, following the Route Napoléon to the Riviera. I decided to enter the 8-litre and take a week's holiday on the Côte D'Azur before driving home. Con opted to come with me – despite being a self-confessed non-starter when it comes to map-reading and timekeeping – a decision not unconnected with reports of my doings with Hugh Young on the Monte-Carlo Rally in the previous year.

The 8-litre's radiator was obviously getting tired and leaked between periodic doses of Barsleaks, so I had it rebuilt with a new core by Serck during the winter. Frankly, I was disappointed with the result during the week or so I was able to test it before our departure for France. It didn't leak, of course, but the water temperature was consistently higher than I had expected and it boiled in London's rush-hour traffic. There was no apparent reason for this and Serck were baffled. I decided to see how it behaved on the 2,000 mile run on the Continent.

Just as we were about to leave home for Newhaven after breakfast on Thursday, 29 June, 1975 in the heavily loaded 8-litre, a neighbour told us that all the French Channel ports were closed due to a strike. I headed for Dover in the hope of securing a place on a boat leaving for Ostend, although the latter would be an inconvenient landfall for our night-stop destination at Fontainebleau; and we were lucky to leave on the 12.30 pm service, nearly an hour late. There our luck ended as far as this Belgian ferry was concerned, for my ciné camera was stolen from the Bentley during the crossing. *Very* annoying, as I planned to make my customary film record of the Rally for the vicarious pleasure of like-minded enthusiasts.

The 8-litre had a very good-looking and practical hood, which stowed out of sight behind the back seat. It was easily erected, but rarely used. However, when the back seat was to be loaded with luggage before a long day's motoring, it was advisable to decide before starting whether or not to put up the hood. On this occasion, before the day was out, we were very

thankful that threatening skies had induced me to raise the hood.

We left Ostend at exactly 5 pm and made for Paris by autoroutes – first towards Brussels then turning westwards at Ghent to join the A1 at Lille. I was pleased to try out the then new access to the Boulevard Périphérique, by leaving the A1 about 5 kms after passing under the runways of Charles de Gaulle airport at Roissy following signs to *Paris Est* on B3 and then A3. This route joined the Boulevard Périphérique at the Porte du Bagnolet and was 3 miles shorter than the hitherto conventional approach via the Porte de la Chapelle. (More importantly, it just about halved the distance to be driven on the ring road.) We joined the Boulevard at 8.40 pm, having covered 215 miles non-stop since leaving the boat. As we turned south on to the A6 at the Porte d'Italie it was getting dark and the rain was belting down. Inefficient wipers and blinding rain made driving very trying and unpleasant. We pulled up at the Novotel at Fontainebleau/Ury at 9.35 pm, having driven $359\frac{1}{2}$ miles since leaving Cobham, and feeling satisfied that we were back on schedule despite the Channel ports strike.

Next morning I took a chance on improving weather and stowed the hood. Filling the tank to the brim with 128.3 litres of Super showed that the consumption over the 305.2 miles since the previous fill-up at Dover was 10.8 mpg. Our route was southwards on the autoroute to Lyon and then eastwards to Chambéry for a night-stop at the Hotel Ombremont at Le Bourget du Lac. It was raining again when we reached our destination, but was fine the next morning. I spent a couple of hours washing the Bentley so as to arrive spick and span for scrutineering in Grenoble 40 miles away. As I loaded the luggage it started to rain and we postponed our departure, hoping for sunshine, but it was not to be, and we left at noon with the hood up, the result of two hours labour being nullified in a few minutes.

On arriving in the Rally car park at Grenoble I was cheered by the sight of a well-turned out $4\frac{1}{2}$-litre Bentley – also with hood up – which I did not recognize despite its English registration number.

We went into the adjacent supermarket for a snack lunch and you could have knocked me down with the proverbial feather when I perceived the not insignificant frames of Colin Crabbe and Tim Howkins coming through a check-out counter with Fiona, Colin's wife. Clearly these were the occupants of the $4\frac{1}{2}$ and their extrovert enjoyment of the Rally was to add zest to our own pleasure. Back in the car-park we encountered George Oks, a BDC member resident in Paris, who was taking part in the Rally in his 1936 $4\frac{1}{4}$-litre Bentley.

On registering our arrival we were given Rally plates with plywood cut-outs to be mounted fore and aft. The rear one presented no problem as I had a special removable bracket which had been made for the Monte-Carlo Rally the previous year, but the front plate was a different matter. The position of lamps, dynamo, badges and number-plate left little room for fixing a plate 20″ long and 10″ high. Eventually I jammed it in front of the fog lamp and behind the badges and there it remained without budging until the end of the Rally. Looking at photographs of the car taken head-on I now realize how much this plate must have interfered with the airflow to the radiator and thus contributed to its boiling propensities.

There followed a walking-pace parade in pouring rain through Grenoble for publicity purposes, rewarded with a boiling radiator and a bottle of champagne. In the evening we enjoyed(?) a téléférique ride through the fog to the Bastille for a Mayoral reception, and then dinner as the guests of the 'Record 2' supermarket.

It was a bleary-eyed crowd of automobilists and motor-cyclists that was picked up by Rally mini-buses at various hotels at 7 am on a very wet Sunday morning to drive their vehicles out of the overnight garage for an 8 am start in front of the Town Hall. There were 53 starters including a motor-cycle and two cycle-cars. The cars were divided into Veteran (1905–18) of which there

were only three, the oldest being the 1910 Renault belonging to Raymond Mareuse of Monaco, whose be-whiskered countenance earned him the name of 'the Cecil Bendall of France' among the irreverent English contingent. Twenty-one Vintage cars and 26 Classics (1931–45) completed the entry list. The majority (30) of the cars were of French origin and 10 were British makes, including the three Bentleys, a pair of MGs and two Rolls-Royces. There was, however, only one other competitor from the UK – Geoffrey Godber-Ford in his immaculate Jaguar SS 100.

We set out on our 400-km route from Grenoble up into the mountains to the first stop for refreshments in the village of Laffrey. The heavy rain and thick mist slowed the traffic. After an unpleasant uphill crawl the 8-litre was boiling well when we stopped. Even a large umbrella failed to keep one dry when just crossing the road to a café.

Each category's arrival times at Time Controls were calculated on the basis of declared average speeds, and there were random stretches on each section where penalties were incurred for each second off the target. Most cars were controlled through these Regularity sections by a navigator with eyes flashing from stop-watch to distance recorder. My co-équipier being more interested in mountains than mathematics, I had to attempt to maintain an exact 30 kph from the moment of entering a timed section until the flag marking its end. Have you ever tried to keep going up hill and down dale at exactly $18\frac{3}{4}$ mph with the needle habitually swinging through a 5 mph arc? This need to keep down to such a slow speed when climbing hills, placed an added burden on the hard-working radiator, and we had to replenish lost water on completion of the section.

An excellent lunch at Gap and promises of sunshine at Digne cheered everybody, and by the time we checked in at Sisteron in mid-afternoon the sun was drying out both cars and clothing. Here we participated in a Manœuvrability Test consisting of a drive against the clock through a maze of straw bales laid out in the Town Hall square. At Digne the weather seemed set fair and the departure scene on the following morning looked much more like the South of France. We proceeded leisurely, retracing the footsteps of Napoléon – someone said he must have been nuts choosing this route – and passed through more Regularity sections, partook of refreshment at frequent intervals, lunched in Castellane and survived another whirligig driving test on arrival in Grasse. The organizers were hard put to it to find hotel accommodation for a couple of hundred bodies in this small town and we were accommodated several miles out in the country – but on a noisy main road. I managed to extricate the Bentley from the parc gardé to have it washed at a nearby BP station and felt much happier with a shining car in the beautiful weather. The day's

run of 50 miles was a circuitous one, largely on minor roads in the hills around Grasse and terminating at Juan-les-Pins, with a stop in Cannes for an excellent outdoor lunch at the Port Pierre Canto. A most enjoyable day's motoring, everyone lapping up the sunshine and the frequent libations offered us *en route*.

That evening we all turned out for a gala dinner and prize-giving in the Casino at Antibes. There was a large number of really worthwhile prizes. A 1928 Talbot (L. Maldes) won the Vintage class and a 1936 Delage (M. Grosgogeat) topped the Classics. The Howkins/Crabbe 4½ was 10th Vintage out of 18 finishers. I was 10th, and George Oks 16th, out of 25 in the Classic class. (Just a comment here: the 8-litre Bentley is accepted by the Vintage Sports-Car Club as a Vintage car because the design was unchanged after 1930, although some examples were not completed until after that date. My 8-litre did not, in fact, leave the Works until April 1932, and when I give this date as the 'date of manufacture' on Rally entry forms, the car is automatically

28 *Following a circuitous route through the mountains approaching Grasse, in the Route Napoléon Rally – June 1975*

classified as post-Vintage.) In this case, the penalty points I incurred (181) would have placed me 6th in the class had my car been treated as Vintage.

Godber-Ford's SS 100 was a very creditable 3rd in the Classics. There were cups for the oldest driver and co-driver; the youngest ditto; the oldest car; the most unfortunate, and so on. I received a large vase of Vallauris pottery for the BDC as the best-represented foreign club. All the foreign entrants were given a magnum of Moët.

I spoke on behalf of the UK contingent, using my Yorkshire French. I thanked everyone who had worked so hard to make the Rally so enjoyable, and Esso for sponsoring the event – though not furnishing petrol. In passing I said that Mr Esso ought really to be thanking me for entering a car which consumed 28 litres of Super every 100 kilometres.

A big 'Thank You' to Mme Ogier and her colleagues of the A.C. Dauphinois for providing such a rewarding way of completing the journey to the South.

- and the retreat

We spent a week at Cap Estel at Eze-sur-mer, where the 8-litre was a centre of interest, but rented a Renault for local mobility, the Bentley not being ideally suited to holiday traffic on the Corniche, nor the near-impossible parking conditions in Nice and Monte-Carlo.

Instead of my usual dash all the way home on autoroutes I actually allowed myself three days to reach Dieppe, and planned some rubbernecking on the way. We did follow the autoroutes to Lyon, stopping for lunch at Montélimar after a 197-mile run from Nice in 3 hours and 12 minutes. I was cruising at between 2,300 rpm and 2,500 rpm with occasional stretches at 2,800 rpm. The sun was hot and the water temperature varied between 83°C and 90°C. (The Rally plate had been removed and on returning home I decided that the central fog lamp must have constituted a fair wind deflector and removed it to increase the air flow through the radiator.)

Incidentally, checking the distance recorder on the Bentley against the kilometre markers reconfirmed the accuracy of the instrument, which was less than one-tenth of a mile out over a distance of 210 kms.

Our first stop for sightseeing was some 10 miles north of Lyon at Monsieur Henri Malartre's Automobile Museum at Rochetaillée. The cars exhibited in the château were an interesting collection of the early French motor industry, but I found the collection of heavy metal in the new Salle Gordini more interesting. The road from Lyon (D433) to Rochetaillée runs along the Saone valley providing a welcome contrast to the customary autoroute if one is in a meandering mood.

My 'bible' for overnight stops on the Continent – especially in France – is a free booklet published annually by the French Tourist Office and entitled *Relais de Campagne, Châteaux Hotels, Relais Gourmands*. During several years' usage of this guide I have never been disappointed. The selection for this particular night was the Château de Fleurville on the west bank of the Rhône between Mâcon and Tournus and, though somewhat less sophisticated than others in the book, it provided a comfortable night's rest and, Con assures me, an excellent dinner.

Next day our destination was Le Mans, entailing a 150-mile run northwards on the A6 and then another 150 miles to the west on ordinary main roads. Large spots of rain during breakfast persuaded me to raise the hood and we were stuck with it for the rest of the day, although the rain did not persist.

As we joined the autoroute at Tournus a Porsche went streaking past with another car on its tail. Alas, the pursuer was an unmarked police car and not a mile further on the drivers of the two cars were 'in conference' on the hard shoulder. The autoroute speed limit is 130 kph (about 80 mph) and in the course of 500 miles motoring this particular Porsche was the only car we saw exceeding the limit by any appreciable margin. It was a hour-and-a-half before he caught us up and passed – at a more modest pace – but he had had his no doubt expensive fun for the day.

Leaving the A6 at the Courtenay exit we drove the 65 miles along the N60 to the outskirts of Orléans, stopping for lunch at 'La Grange' in St Jean de Braye. After lunch, having returned to the 8-litre in a parking bay on the opposite side of the road, I was unscrewing the radiator cap to top up the water level from my onboard supply when two locals, who had dismounted from their 'Corporation lorry' to gaze in admiration at the Bentley, saw what was afoot. They were galvanized into action and wanted to procure water for me – from, I thought, the restaurant. Imagine my surprise, therefore, when yielding to their obvious desire to be helpful, I saw one go back to the Corporation lorry and produce a hose and bucket whilst his mate removed the cover from a nearby manhole and disappeared from sight. They connected the hose to the underground supply and brought me a brimming bucket with the compliments of the City of Orléans!

The route due west from Orléans to Le Mans was 85 miles on N826 (this road number may have changed since) and N157. This road ran across open agricultural land in long, straight stretches and we saw very little traffic. As we approached Le Mans the placards and signs concerning the 24-hour Race reminded me of many previous visits and this was, indeed, the first day of practice for the 1975 race. I had accepted an invitation from Monsieur Lelièvre, President of the A.C. de l'Ouest to dine with him and watch the practice from his box. We drove straight through Le Mans to Loué, Con having opted for the culinary delights of the Hotel Ricordeau – another from the Relais booklet – where we were to spend the night. I enquired if the Patron was still the same as ten or twenty years ago, for I knew that this place was a favourite with Laurence Pomeroy and Forrest Lycett. The attractive receptionist replied, 'Yes, he is my father'. When I met him his face lit up at the recollection of those motoring connoisseurs

of good living.

I returned alone to Le Mans and got lost at Arnage before reaching the circuit. It was a nostalgic occasion for me to watch the cars streaking past the pits in the dark, and I recalled the years when I was totally involved with the Cunningham team. It was a sobering thought to look across the track from the President's stand to see the memorial plaque to those killed in the Levegh accident, and to realise that it was twenty years ago to the day that I had witnessed that tragedy from the Cunningham pit counter. The most surprising thing about my visit to Le Mans was the almost total lack of Britons. The paddock used to be half full of our chaps, but I met no one I knew, did not hear English spoken and was greeted at the Dunlop van by a fitter whose first words were, 'How nice to meet an Englishman'.

Next day we stopped at Bayeux to see the tapestry, visited the invasion beaches at Arromanches and spent the night 25 miles south-west of Rouen in the village of Le Bec-Hellouin at the Auberge de l'Abbaye – not in the book, but a very pleasant place for an overnight stop. The choice of Le Bec-Hellouin was made to permit a visit to the car museum at the abbey. At that time it belonged to Monsieur de Borredon, a great motoring enthusiast, and was well worth a detour. Among his collection of forty or so cars were half-a-dozen Bugattis and examples of Rolls-Royce, Ferrari, Mercedes-Benz, Delage; and several French makes; all were extremely well-kept and well-presented in a purpose-built building.

Then we made the short run to Dieppe for the midday boat to Newhaven.

Throughout the holiday I had followed my usual practice of filling the petrol tank to the base of the short filler pipe on each occasion and recording the distance covered since the last replenishment, thereby keeping an accurate check on fuel consumption. The tank held $32\frac{1}{2}$ gallons and I reckoned to cover 300 miles or thereabouts before tanking up. I had filled up just after leaving Loué and had done 268 miles by the time I boarded the boat. I wondered if I could reach home at Cobham without stopping for petrol. By Gatwick the needle was firmly on 'Empty', but I pressed on (gently) despite protests from Con, to whom I could give no rational reason for such behaviour. Reigate and Dorking passed, but as I turned off the Leatherhead bypass for Fetcham about 4 miles from home the engine missed and died. I free-wheeled into a car-park and thumbed a lift a quarter-of-a-mile to a garage for a gallon of petrol in a can, leaving a 100-franc note as a deposit in the absence of ready sterling. Con, who had been logging times, distances and petrol purchases for me, took the opportunity whilst waiting for my return to make an unsolicited entry: 'Bloody well ran out! Stupide!'

When I reached home I put in 32 gallons – that is how I know the tank holds 32½ gallons. A full tank of petrol is equivalent to having a 16-stone man sitting behind the rear axle!

The 8-litre converted 211.4 gallons into energy, boiling water and exhaust gases during the 2126.1 mile drive, equalling a consumption of 10 mpg. It would probably have been cheaper to travel by rail taking the Bentley as luggage. Truly, the high cost of petrol and the imposition of speed limits are tending to transform motoring in Europe from a delight to be indulged in by enthusiasts as frequently as possible, to a time- and money-consuming means of transport.

Yorkshire bound

Bentley drivers do not need an excuse to drive their cars, and the touring events organized by the Bentley Drivers Club have proved very popular. Touring in company with like-minded fellow members imbues confidence in the less adventurous, for they can be sure that there are those whose enjoyment would be less than 100 per cent if they were not called upon to perform mechanical tasks in ailing motor cars, often at ungodly hours, in appalling weather, miles from anywhere. These runs afford an opportunity to

drive other peoples' Bentleys; they are a catalyst for new friendship, and a medium for the exchange of experiences and expertise.

It seems to add something to these events if they are linked to an anniversary of some description – perhaps a significant event in the history of the marque or the Company – and in 1977 it was decided to join in the countrywide celebrations of H.M. the Queen's Silver Jubilee.

The '77 Run' was thus planned to take place in May. It was based on a suggested 'spine' route, starting from Runnymede on the River Thames near Staines, and running via Beaulieu, Alveston, the Wye Valley and Newcastle-under-Lyme to Ilkley (yes, that one!) where the headquarters pub was to be the Craiglands Hotel. Participants joined in wherever they chose, and other feeder itineraries originated in Cornwall, East Anglia and Edinburgh, joining the London contingent *en route* or at Ilkley. The plotting of routes had been delegated to the Regional Committees whose areas were to be traversed, with the exhortation to select uncluttered roads passing through scenic countryside.

Con and I took part in this event in the 8-litre, starting from Runnymede on 12 May, and escorted Margaret Bentley being driven by Steve Stone in a T2 Bentley kindly provided by the Company.

Whilst in Yorkshire I took the opportunity to deviate to Huddersfield to see the house where I was born, which I had not seen since the age of eight. The occupants were puzzled by the 8-litre stopping outside their house, but gave their unannounced visitors a real Yorkshire welcome when told the reason for the call.

An unexpected sight on the roadside in North Wales, which created great interest, was Jimmy McAlpine's 8-litre Bentley. It started life as a Thrupp & Maberly saloon with a division, but in 1966 when the present owner acquired it he had a shooting-brake body substituted. This giant vehicle has a compartment for dogs; carries ten passengers and has oil-fired central heating.

The highlight of the '77 Run' was to be the

29 *Jimmy McAlpine's 8-litre Bentley with the ten-seater shooting-brake body – May 1977*

gathering of all the participating Bentleys – and others whose owners cared to attend – at Oulton Park. The sight of nearly 200 Bentleys, of which half were Vintage models, ranked four abreast on the (very long) starting grid will long be remembered. The run culminated with a visit to the Rolls-Royce factory at Crewe, where we were conducted round the works and entertained to lunch, during which we were told by George Fenn, Managing Director of the Motor-car Division, that the Bentley was to be reintroduced into the United States after a break of four years. And to the cheers of the assembled company he said: 'There'll always be a Bentley'.

For us, it was then a drive back to Cobham with another 893 miles of happy Vintage motoring on the clock – at 9.6 mpg.

Le Mans and Aubusson

When someone pointed out that 1980 was the fiftieth anniversary of the last Bentley win at Le Mans it was decided to mark the occasion by another pilgrimage to the circuit. So it was that 98 Bentleys, of which 81 were Vintage models, crossed from Newhaven to Dieppe at the beginning of September that year. I decided to take both my Bentleys – the 8-litre (UL7) being appropriate to the occasion and 'Olga', the R-type Continental, which was the actual car used by Charles Faroux as the Course Car during the 24-hour race in 1952 and which, incidentally, was to provide us with transport on a touring holiday after the conclusion of activities at Aubusson (of which more anon). There was no lack of volunteer drivers to assist me but, not surprisingly, the choice fell upon Hugh Young, my companion on previous trips.

The day before departure I noticed a certain unevenness in the running of the 8-litre engine which, on inspection, proved to be a stripped timing gear in one of the magnetos. Vaughan Davis, then with Hofmann & Mountfort, came over on Sunday morning, the day of departure, and removed the faulty magneto. It was decided to do the journey on one magneto, the other one being repaired and kept ready to be sent out to France in case of need. (It was not required.) Fate had not yet finished – diagnosis of the ignition fault had flattened the battery and the 8-litre had to be given a tow-start by 'Olga'.

The convoy reached Le Mans with no more than the minor inconveniences normally associated with driving old cars. Various parades and touring events took place on the Bugatti Circuit and no one was surprised when some of them turned into flat-out 'blinds'. Interest in these was enhanced by the participation of several Bentleys which had actually raced at Le Mans half-a-century earlier.

Much hospitality was extended to the drivers and their passengers by the Automobile Club de l'Ouest and was reciprocated by a farewell dinner in a nearby Abbaye.

On the next day the Bentleys moved off via Tours and Châteauroux to reconvene at Aubusson for a return visit to Pierre Bardinon's private race circuit at Mas du Clos. My own departure from the hotel in the 8-litre was nicely captured in the words of Hugh Young reporting for the Bentley Drivers Club Review and I quote:

'There are two parking lots at la Seiglière, one higher than the other, and a very long drive sloping gently to the road. The battery of the 8-litre, having been charged overnight in Le Mans, is beginning to get the hang of things, but the remaining magneto is now weakening and requires increasing amounts of advance for starting. The great black car has been turned loose at the top of the slope and has passed the lower parking lot; all conversation

has ceased and a hundred bodies stand transfixed, all facing the gently sloping drive down which the 8-litre now trundles amiably towards Aubusson, its progress marked by a series of fierce reports as the magneto searches desperately for sufficient flux to make something fire. Seen from the upper parking lot, this extraordinary vignette seemed to say it all, whatever it was. At least to us.'

and I crib again from Hugh's account of the next show of temperament on the part of the 8-litre:

'The 8-litre had one last trick up its sleeve, before finally settling down and behaving itself. Stan, starting it in the leafy bower that served as the paddock (at Aubusson), pressed the button. Nothing; not even the click of the solenoid. Nonplussed, we reached across and switched on the sidelights. Graham Woodrow-Hill, standing at the front of the car, said, "Those work. Now turn on the headlights and start it." We turned on the headlights and the engine fired immediately. "I've never seen that

30 *'Olga' and the 8-litre on the Mulsanne straight at Le Mans – September 1980*

particular trick used before", we commented. "Neither have I", replied Graham. He had not meant to be taken seriously! Well it was that sort of affair. Words failed, once more.'

A day of most enjoyable and somewhat unrestrained lappery concluded the organized part of the rally. Con and I continued our holiday in 'Olga' and Hugh Young revelled in a trouble-free and unsupervised (by me) drive homewards in the 8-litre.

Tour of South Africa

As I signed on at the organizer's table in the Elangeni Hotel in Durban and was given a route book, badges, medical kit, T-shirt, windcheater and other goodies, I reflected on all the effort and money expended with the object of getting me and my Vintage Bentley – and 50 other similar partnerships – to this point of departure on a 2,000-mile tour of South Africa.

The idea, conceived in 1975 by Rudi Reitz, was put into cold storage because of the economic climate and petrol rationing, until 1981, when its realization seemed a practicable possibility once again. Plans were made, and enthusiasm to put them into action knew no bounds when the oil company Total South Africa (Pty) Ltd. decided to sponsor the run, not only by supplying free petrol, oil and back-up transportation, but putting a very substantial sum of money at the disposal of the organizing committee.

It was realized from the start that sending a car by sea from the UK to South Africa and back, following in person by air, insuring the vehicle ashore and afloat, insuring oneself against sickness and accident, and paying hotel and living expenses, would be a very costly exercise. With the firm financial underpinning of Total, the organizers (members of the Bentley Drivers Club in South Africa) successfully solicited support from shippers, shipowners, the national airline and others to reduce the outlay. These efforts were rewarded when no less than thirty owners decided to make the trip from the UK – plus one

from the USA and one from New Zealand – and were joined by another twenty from South Africa and Zimbabwe.

Our anticipation of the super motoring which lay ahead was tempered by the news that the 3-litre of John White, Chairman of the Organizing Committee, had been savaged at both ends by the gyrations of a modern car in the hands of a local 'cowboy'. Also, that George Tabbernor was in hospital in Durban having collided with a girder and broken his collarbone when dashing with a fire extinguisher towards my car which was emitting smoke from the short-circuiting of incorrectly disconnected (not by me) battery leads. After a pinning operation he showed great stoicism, completing the whole route as passenger in his own 6½-litre driven by Harvey Hine in an unaccustomed gentle manner.

So it was that 52 Bentleys spanning a decade from 1922 and including all models except the 4-litre foregathered at the Pavilion on the morning of Saturday, 5 March 1983 amid a large and enthusiastic crowd. The heat and humidity was already making itself felt to those of us who had left winter behind at Heathrow and we eagerly accepted the insulated bag of iced Coco-Cola pressed upon us as we left at one-minute intervals on the drive northwards through the sugar belt to the lunch-stop at Mtunzini in Zululand some 90 miles away. Subsequently, drivers were free to choose their starting times bearing in mind the distances to the next meal or night-stop.

The humidity and heat – 102°C in the shade (and there wasn't any) – severely tried the UK contingent, who soon realized why many of the locals had started their journey with their hoods up. Stalwarts, who prided themselves on not erecting their hoods for rain in England, were constrained to put them up as sunshades – and pretty tatty some of them looked, having remained unseen and uncared for in their covers for years. On parking, I decided to put mine up before going in to lunch. This proved to be an unwise move, demanding much exertion moving luggage and stretching material, in blazing sun-

31 *Luggage-porter with a musical bent at the
Zululand Safari Lodge, Hluhluwe – March 1983*

shine, when I was feeling hotter than ever before, with the result that I was almost prostrate with heat exhaustion for the next hour or so. After lunch I recovered and planted a yellow-wood tree at the invitation of local dignitaries to mark our passing, before resuming our drive to Hluhluwe (pronounced something like 'shloo-shloo-ey') where we were comfortably installed in a *ronda-vel* (a round grass-roofed lodge) with all mod. cons. within the game park of the Zululand Safari Lodge. We were greeted on arrival with the sight of a well-endowed, drum-beating, topless Zulu woman (who doubled as luggage-porter) and an ostrich or two wandering in the car-park.

The next day was free and started for us with the sight of a couple of rhinos grazing within 20 feet of our bedroom window, and a zebra sheltering from the sun in the porch of the next-door *rondavel*. Everyone went on conducted tours in the surrounding reserve to see giraffe, rhinos and many other animals in their natural habitat. Drivers were now coming to terms with the heat and coping with problems experienced with their cars in the unfamiliar climate, not the least of which was the manifestation of weak-nesses in tyres. Several cars mounted on beaded-edge tyres had been brought to a halt when the beads came away from the covers, a characteristic, I believe, found only in the then latest Dunlop tyres, on which the beads were attached by adhesive instead of being integral in the manufacturing process. Incidentally, the abrasive surface of the superb South African highways, encountered throughout the tour, rapidly wore down the Dunlops of the UK contingent, a disadvantage not experienced by others using different makes of much harder compounds. Apart from the above-average wear, my own $6.50/7.00 \times 19$ Dunlops, run at 40 psi, carried my 8-litre (weighting $2\frac{1}{4}$ tons) throughout the run with no loss of pressure and no problems from the high temperatures generated.

We studied the route book to see what the morrow held in store for us – a 350-mile stretch to Sandton (Johannesburg) with a lunch-stop at Ermelo. Particular attention was paid to the location of Total filling stations where tanks could be replenished with 93 or 98 octane petrol by courtesy of 'Mr Total'. This sponsor's service van followed the route at the tail-end with trouble-shooter John Ambler aboard, for whose expert advice and work many of us had reason to be grateful at one time or another.

Lunch at Ermelo provided a welcome air-conditioned respite and a chance to replenish our iced Coco-Cola supply. To our relief, the humidity dropped as we climbed into the Transvaal, but we got a soaking when greeted by a violent thunderstorm on the outskirts of Johannesburg. All but one Bentley – the 3-litre of Dick Phillipson, which dropped out with persistent magneto and/or petrol-feed trouble – checked in at the new Holiday Inn at Sandton, and the reception that followed was enlivened by the presence of Giulio Ramponi, then living in Nelspruit, who re-lived his Bentley Le Mans days to the delight of his many listeners.

The following day's optional activities included a visit to the Gold Mine Museum, where we witnessed molten gold being poured into ingot moulds and then went for a walk 700 feet underground. Afterwards we were guests of Grosvenor Motors, the local Rolls-Royce representatives, at a rained-off barbecue lunch that had to be rapidly transferred indoors.

Our departure next morning was made easy by a police escort which whisked us round the outskirts of Johannesburg, holding up cross traffic for our passage, and scarcely dropping below 50 mph until we were well on the road to Kimberley. Halts at Stillfontein for 'elevenses' (called tea breaks in South Africa, not coffee breaks) and at Christiana for lunch relieved our exposure to the extreme heat, but we were settling down to enjoy motoring in wide open spaces, on traffic-free roads running straight across undulating and seemingly uninhabited terrain. The speed limit of 100 kph ($62\frac{1}{2}$ mph) seemed to become the cruising speed for most, with occasional bursts of exuberance, not to mention Len Wilton's indecently high average speed after he found himself in Pretoria before realizing that he should be headed in the opposite direction. It was on this stretch that Ian Thompson's $4\frac{1}{2}$-litre from Cape Town suffered severe internal disorders when big-end bolts let go, necessitating a trailer ride and exit from the tour. Thereafter, no cars fell by the wayside, and all completed the 2,100-mile drive under their own power.

Kimberley had been included in the itinerary because of its association with Woolf Barnato – his wealth, derived from diamonds, certainly prolonged the life of Bentley Motors – even though the withdrawal of his support augured the end of the company. We felt that Speed Six and 8-litre owners owed their prized possessions indirectly to this diamond city. The mayor gave us a reception at the Open Mine Museum where we had an opportunity to gaze into the Big Hole – a long-abandoned diamond working some 1,550 feet across and 1,600 feet deep – for which Barney Barnato (Babe's father) received a cheque for over five million pounds.

As the drive to Bloemfontein next day was a relatively short one of 110 miles, departures were rather more spread out than usual, and I drove 75 miles before seeing another Bentley. The road was straight and invited fast driving, but a kindly

32 *Arrival at Kimberley*

'mole' let us know that the day's speed trap was at Kilometre 60, thus only one driver so far forgot himself as to get caught. The sun was blazing down, and so rare was any shade that road signs indicated the existence of a roadside tree 1 km ahead. Good, one thought, relishing the prospect of a dive into the bottomless Coke bag, only to find on several occasions that all the available shade was already occupied by two or three Bentleys, necessitating a further stretch before the next haven.

In the evening we were taken from our hotel in Bloemfontein to Waldy Greyvensteyn's home for pre-dinner drinks and a long-anticipated visit to his collection of cars, including Bentleys, Rolls-Royces, Bugattis, Alfa-Romeos, an Isotta-Fraschini, a Hispano-Suiza, and many other desirable makes.

From Bloemfontein we headed south for Graaff Reinet, 280 miles away, stopping for lunch near the impressive Hendrik Verwoerd Dam across the Orange River. At this point the Total service excelled itself by transporting and erecting, before we arrived, a mobile, petrol filling station complete with orthodox pumps (supplied from a tanker), forecourt, fencing, and

product stands. It was dismantled when all our needs had been satisfied, and was packed up on the vehicle and on its way as the last Bentley was leaving.

On arrival on the outskirts of Graaff Reinet we were halted at the roadside until quite a number of Bentleys had gathered, and were then escorted into the centre of town by a mounted escort from the local riding-school. After an open-air civic welcome amidst an interested crowd of residents and tourists we dispersed to our hotels with all too little time left to explore this pleasant town.

Southwards again to Port Elizabeth, where the Bentleys were gathered on the city boundary and escorted by motor-cycle police in double file through the busy Saturday afternoon traffic to the beach-front hotel, and then put on display on an enclosed lawn overlooking the Indian Ocean. The highlight of the next free day in Port Elizabeth was a visit to the Aldo Scribante Motor Racing Circuit, where we were allowed to make spirited laps with or without passengers; no racing, of course, but members of local motor clubs certainly enjoyed the sight of Vintage Bentleys being driven in anger. For my part, the day was one of disappointment, for, having elected to forego the lappery in the interest of securing a photographic record of the antics of my fellow-travellers – and some might say thereby taking the more dangerous option – I discovered afterwards that the film had not been winding on! The heat was intense and the wind-blown sand very trying – which reminds me that, in addition to the two questions one is asked everywhere – what is it worth and what will it do? the South Africans asked 'Where are your air filters?'

We were now at the eastern end of the southern coast of the continent of Africa, and looking forward to heading westwards on the famous Garden Route. We were recommended to make a deviation 25 miles out of Port Elizabeth by way of Van Staden's Pass. (The UK drivers, accustomed to pass-storming in Europe, were surprised to find that sometimes one went *down* into a valley to cross a pass in South Africa.) In this case the pass was a stone bridge from which one could look skywards to the new single-span bridge carrying the main road, and downstream at the remains of the old causeway in use at the time our cars were coming out of the factory.

Our first stop on the Garden Route was at Storms River Mouth, a delightful resort in the Tsitsikamma Coastal National Park, approached down a steep and twisty hill which was closed to traffic the next morning to enable us to take part in a regularity hill-climb test. The course, of about one mile, was divided into two equal sections and one was required to cover each half in the same time of one's choice. Those whose philosophy on regularity tests is that the only sure basis for success is to go flat out from the start, were foxed on finding that the second part was a good deal less steep and twisty than the bottom end.

Our enjoyment of this timely break, in beautiful surroundings after 1,600 miles of motoring, was marred when a member's wife, Elizabeth Nutter, was struck by a super-wave and swept off

33 *Storms River Mouth, South Africa*

the rocks from which she was admiring the magnificent rollers. She was thrown about among the jagged rocks and sustained severe lacerations and a cracked skull before being pulled out in a semi-conscious state. She was driven 70 miles over the hilly coastal road to hospital in Knysna, and subsequently taken by air-ambulance to Cape Town. She later flew home where, thankfully, she made a full recovery from her frightening experience.

Drivers were seen to be attending to their Bentleys – changing oil, welding an exhaust pipe, and generally tidying and tightening up, whilst others made a round trip to Plattenburg Bay to swim off the sandy beaches.

We had heard glowing accounts of the passes on the road to be followed on leaving Storms River Mouth, and we were not disappointed. The Groot River Pass and the Bloukrans Pass were a joy to the driver, where one felt dwarfed by nature. Having made an early start, we were able to linger awhile at Plattenburg Bay, where my dynamo ceased charging – not a happy state of affairs in temperatures that demanded my auxiliary Kenlowe fans be in operation when climbing long hills.

The stop at the Knysna Town Hall for 'Elevenses' will be long remembered, for the ladies responsible for entertaining us had excelled themselves in providing home-made confections unequalled on the rest of our trip. After a brief deviation to visit Elizabeth Nutter in hospital, we continued along the Garden Route through Wilderness – where one well-known lady member of the Club is said to have shown a great interest in its attractions as a retirement home.

Having driven over 100 miles of the Garden Route, we turned inland at George for the Outeniqua Pass on the road to Oudtshoorn in the barren Little Karoo country. Famous for its ostrich farms, we heard tales of some hairy rides astride these gigantic birds during the afternoon, but many of us opted for the air-conditioned comfort of the Holiday Inn as a refuge from the searing heat. Late in the afternoon I moved the 8-

litre into the only shade I could find, and borrowed the gardener's hose to wash the car for the only time on the tour. Water restrictions, imposed because of the country-wide drought, were not unwelcome to those of us who do not relish the daily spit-and-polish and, truth to tell, the cars remained remarkably clean. Then, I was fortunate enough to have a knowledgeable member forsake the pool to look into my electrical problem and restore the charging function.

We had covered 1,750 miles by this time and were looking forward with mixed feelings to the next day, which was to see the last leg of our journey – pleasurable anticipation of reaching Cape Town for a few days relaxation, but regret that our fabulous tour was nearing its end.

A very hot drive of 150 miles brought us to Montague for lunch, after which we continued towards our goal over the impressive Du Toit's Kloof Pass and through the wine country. The sight of Table Mountain on the skyline heralded our journey's end, and it was with a sense of achievement and gratification that the Bentleys turned into the pillared entrance of the Mount Nelson Hotel to occupy a whole floor of the multi-storey car-park. It was surely a tribute to these fifty Bentleys which left the factory more than half-a-century ago, and to their owners and drivers, that they had been driven fairly smartly for a total of over 100,000 miles in twelve days without mishap.

The energetic members of our group went on a Wineland tour, by coach (advisedly) the next day; others rode the cable-car to the top of Table Mountain; whilst many sat around the pool unwinding and relishing the prospect of no more early starts. Everyone was on parade on the morrow for the Peninsula trip – a spectacular drive along the rocky coast (reminiscent of the Big Sur road in California) to Cape Point, where the Atlantic and Indian Oceans meet in frothy turmoil.

Saturday morning saw a convoy of Bentleys dolefully driven to the docks to be enshrined in containers for the return voyage to Southampton. Most participants, having seen their cherished carriages firmly tied down, were ferried back to the hotel by local members in time to leave for the airport and the long flight home.

Some – including Con and I – were staying on a few days to enjoy the sunshine and the hospitality of friends. We had been lucky enough to secure a compartment on the famous 'Blue Train' for the overnight journey of nearly 1,000 miles to Johannesburg. The experience lived up to our high expectations, and proved to be a memorable prelude to a tedious flight home via the Cape Verde Islands.

Our holiday in South Africa had been one of the most enjoyable of our lives.

Paris–Deauville Rally

Having heard good reports from fellow-enthusiasts on the annual Paris–Deauville Rally organized by the Club de l'Auto, I decided to enter the nineteenth of these events in October 1985. It entailed a reasonable amount of cross-country motoring and concluded with a *concours d'elegance* judged not only on car and costume, but on a one-and-half-minute presentation of one's own devising. The Rally was open to cars built before World War Two and the entry of 104 cars comprised 59 different makes, ranging from a 1902 Mors to a 1939 Hotchkiss, of which 42 carried GB plates, including four Bentleys. Competitors were required to present themselves on Saturday morning for the start in the Place Vendôme, having reached the capital in their own time by a route of their choice.

Con accompanied me on this occasion and we set off from home just after 9 am on Thursday to cross the Channel from Dover to Calais. Unfortunately, we were delayed for an hour *en route* by a puncture – in a brand-new tyre fitted for the Rally. The result was that we did not leave Calais until 3.45 pm. We had a good run down the autoroute as far as the outskirts of Paris when it seems that our arrival coincided with that of Gorbachev. You can guess who was given priority. My notes on the trip speak for themselves: *From Le Bourget – traffic terrible – stationary and crawling – clutch slipping – car tremendously hot – very hot ourselves – weather really warm.* It was hairy being in the tunnels and approaching upgrades in that congestion without knowing whether I could jiggle the car into moving after an involuntary stop. I missed a turning near the Gare du Nord and aimed down a narrow, one-way street in the general direction of our hotel. Cars were parked on both sides of the road leaving only a single lane for traffic. Just after I had committed myself to this route I saw ahead of me that the road was completely blocked by a crowd of men – perhaps of North African descent – demonstrating about something. I foresaw the possibility of hostile action against the old car and its occupants but, to my surprise, all eyes turned on the Bentley and the crowd parted to allow us to pass amid smiles all round and apparent goodwill. I like to think that the 8-litre had made them forget what they were demonstrating about!

34 *'The Colonel and his Lady' attired in 1930s costume in the Paris–Deauville Rally Concours d'Elegance – October 1985*

I left the Bentley in the garage of British Motors – owned by a motoring enthusiast and collector – and rented an Opel Corsa for more convenient driving in and around Paris the next day – Con's birthday – when I had planned a surprise for her. The surprise was lunch at the Coq Hardy at Bougival, but the icing on the cake was that I had secretly arranged for Carol, our daughter, and her husband Roger, who were staying with friends near Le Havre, to join us there. Altogether a very happy prelude to the Paris–Deauville Rally.

From the start on Saturday morning in the Place Vendôme we followed a picturesque route of some 150 miles, interrupted by an extended lunch-stop at Château de Senneville, arriving in good time to take up our reservations at the Normandy Hotel. The opportunity was taken in Deauville to enlist the practised hand of Bob May – this time in his 1925 Silver Ghost, not his Speed Six – to adjust the clutch properly, after which it behaved impeccably. Everyone's thoughts were now directed towards the manifestation to take place the following afternoon at the famous racecourse of Deauville. It was gratifying to see the trouble owners had taken to present their cars in superb condition and with the occupants attired in keeping with the age of the car. Much ingenuity had gone into presenting the miniature play-acting as the cars stopped in front of the judge's platform. For our part, Con, who really likes dressing up, hired a super black-and-white outfit from a theatrical costumiers, including feather boa, which placed her right in the thirties. As I was the driver, and involuntarily part of the tableau, my usual weekend go-to-Silverstone clothes would have ruined the effect, so I too rented a costume – that of a full colonel in the contemporary British Army. Our scenario was based on the colonel giving preferential treatment to the car, messing about under the bonnet, whilst his lady fumed in the passenger seat with no one to open the door to allow her to dismount and show off her finery.

The evening was marked by a Gala Dinner in

the Casino. As we entered the dining-room we saw a glittering array of prizes, including a Methuselah of champagne which we thought must be top award of the whole rally. (Charles Heidsieck were one of the sponsors.) However, when the results were announced, the outright winner (having the highest aggregate marks for both car and costume), Geoffrey Butcher with his 1910 Hotchkiss, was presented with a huge Louis Vuitton trunk, not the gigantic bottle of bubbly. I was pleased to be placed equal second in the car category and third overall in the combined car and costume markings – and even more pleased when my prize turned out to be the Methuselah (containing the equivalent of eight bottles of champagne). Whilst others went off next day to lunch in Honfleur, we drove home to conclude a most enjoyable weekend, having averaged the customary 10 mpg for the round trip of 616 miles.

Norwich Union–RAC Classic
In May 1986 I entered the 8-litre in the inaugural Norwich Union–RAC Classic Run – which elastic description covered cars built between 1905 and 1966. The earlier date was chosen, apparently, to provide a gentle, cross-country drive for cars not old enough to take part in the Veteran Car Run to Brighton. That it filled a gap in the motoring calendar was quite evident by an entry of 466 cars, including a score of Bentleys. It has grown each year since, and it is said that the organizers are expecting 1,400 participants in 1991.

Ronald ('Steady') Barker accepted my invitation to accompany me as navigator and he would be the first to admit that it was not a demanding task. I chose to start from the RAC Country Club at Woodcote Park, Epsom, from whence we followed a devious route via Brooklands, Luton Hoo and Old Warden Park near Biggleswade, to Silverstone. Other optional starting points included Bath and Nottingham.

One thing indelibly impressed upon my memory was the (relatively) tiny roundabouts at every intersection in Milton Keynes, where there was a Control of Passage, and the physically exhausting effort involved in hauling the 8-litre three times from lock-to-lock at the end of every block.

Silverstone Circuit was indeed full of cars by the end of the afternoon, and lasting signatures made in oil on the track marked their presence. On a fine day, this event offers an excellent way of sharing one's enthusiasm with like-minded fellows – on a wet day, well. . . !

The M25 Fun Run
The M25 motorway, or – to give its correct title – the London Orbital motorway, opened completely in 1986 with the aim of easing the flow of traffic from one side of London to the other. It has since become notorious for the inadequate planning which failed to provide enough lanes to accommodate the volume of traffic making use of it. It is 119 miles long and gives direct access to motorways leading away from the capital – the M1, M3, M4, M11, M20, M23, M26 and M40 – and provides a motorway link between London's two main airports, Heathrow and Gatwick. As with all motorways in the UK, there is no charge for vehicles using the M25, except for a toll if the Dartford Tunnel is used.

During rush hours, and at other times when there has been any incident or accident to cause an obstruction, the congestion and delays have become a talking-point among motorists and a butt for comics – 'largest car-park in the south-east', etc. It is not surprising, therefore, that when I suggested a 'Fun Run' round the M25, for the Bentley Drivers Club, several Committee members thought it was a contradiction in terms.

And so it would have been, on any day other than the one chosen for this outing, namely the 'fourth' day of Christmas – Sunday, 28th December 1986. On that particular day many were seeking something to do following a surfeit of food and drink. The notion of a leisurely mile-a-minute cruise for a couple of hours round the Metropolis in the company of like-minded Bentley drivers clearly met that need. The idea was that one could join the junction nearest to one's home and circumnavigate the motorway in either direction, returning to the same point in one's own time.

Two factors – one anticipated, and one hoped for but fortuitous – contributed to its successful execution. The first was the complete absence of commercial traffic, and the second was the beautiful weather. The sun shone brightly; a bonus much appreciated at the time, and even more so in retrospect as the following Sunday was wet and foggy, and the one after that found the country in the grip of snow and ice.

So it was that, driving my 8-litre, I joined 25 other Bentleys gathered at the Seven Hills Hotel in Cobham and, after elevenses, departed in an anti-clockwise direction. Others joined in *en route* and the loose convoy paused at the southern entrance to the Dartford Tunnel, where the total was augmented by local Club members witnessing the handing-over of the Golden Jubilee Book from the South-Eastern Region to

35 *HRH the Prince of Wales discussing Vintage cars at Brands Hatch – July 1988*

the Eastern Region. Altogether, about 40 Bentleys were seen somewhere on the route and the vast majority were open Vintage Bentleys.

Many were surprised at the picturesque nature of the countryside through which this much-maligned motorway passes, and those lunching back at Cobham were enthusiastic about their enjoyment of the run.

A Royal Occasion
Our last outing in UL 7 was a truly Royal occasion. I accepted an invitation from Ed Hubbard to turn out at Brands Hatch, on 21 July 1988, where he was organizing a gathering of interesting cars, entitled 'Cars of the Century', the object being to raise funds for the Prince's Trust – the Prince being HRH The Prince of Wales. The 8-litre was selected to take part in the Grand Parade of some of the most desirable cars among the hundreds there to support the event. Prince Charles walked among the cars on the 'starting grid' and talked to the drivers. He admired the 8-litre and said he had no intention of ever parting with his Aston-Martin. Afterwards, HRH drove some spirited laps in Ed Hubbard's 4½-litre Vintage Bentley, complete with helmeted detectives in the rear seat.

And now for the 'Aggro'
Lest it be thought that the ownership and *use* of a Vintage car is an unmitigated pleasure, I will now take off my rose-tinted goggles and list, not in any particular order, some of the problems I have encountered on my 8-litre in seventeen years of ownership.

In addition to the derangements mentioned in the foregoing pages, namely:

> engine problems due to lay-up prior to acquisition;
> broken piston on M5;
> dynamo failure in South Africa; and clutch in Paris,

I have also experienced the following tribulations:

36 *Parting with a friend – Bill Woodward takes over UL 7 – July 1988*

new crankshaft (and again with new piston rods when it was decided to convert to shell bearings);

complete engine overhaul, including new three-throw drive rods, pistons, gudgeon pins, valves, guides and rockers, grinding crankshaft, reboring, remetalling bearings, and a lot more;

persistent cooling problems – overcome only after three new radiator cores (by different manufacturers) and fitting two Kenlowe fans;

new flywheel;

new dynamo casing;

crankcase cracked beyond repair, necessitating the making of new patterns and castings;

new king-pins and bushes;

rewiring throughout; and

front brake drums replaced.

What does all this mean? Well, for a start it means many weeks at a time off the road, and tens of thousands of pounds – and, of course, a much better car.

Parting with a friend

And then 'Delivery Day' – 29 July 1988 – when the 8-litre was to leave the Sedgwick household. It was a day of mixed feelings: sadness at the end of an era, alleviated by a host of happy memories and the knowledge that it was going to a good home where it would be cherished and driven both here and abroad. The drive to Hungerford, where we were to meet Bill Woodward, the new owner, was enjoyable and the Bentley had never gone better – as if to say, 'now look what you've done, getting rid of me'.

For my part, the 8-litre Bentley provided Vintage motoring at its best. Despite the troubles I experienced, the car lived up to my highest expectations and when at the wheel I felt ten feet tall. So ended nearly fifty years of Vintage

Bentley ownership . . . (A single-handed drive in the 8-litre, of 1,000 miles in one day in the UK, is described in this book in the section entitled 'Motoring for motoring's sake'.)

Post-War Bentleys – Mk VI

My Mk VI Bentley, mentioned many times in the telling of the exploits of AC 260, rendered sterling service both at home and abroad.

I had driven many miles in various Mk VIs since its introduction in September 1946, including the run across France from Le Havre to Cannes in a day – recounted later in this book – sufficient to confirm that it was an admirable means of transport. So that when, in March 1956, I judged the time had come to replace my Phantom III Rolls-Royce with a more modern and handier car, it was natural that my choice should fall upon the Mk VI Bentley. It did not take long to find 'KDN 373', which had been very well looked after by its owner, and for the first time I found myself with a modern car at my disposal.

It was delivered new in August 1952 and had done just over 50,000 miles when I acquired it.

37 *The Mk VI Bentley in March 1956, with over 50,000 miles on the clock*

The body was the Standard Steel Saloon but the engine was the 4½-litre version put into production in May 1951. This model was referred to colloquially as the 'Big Bore/Small Boot' to distinguish it from its predecessors with the 3½″ bore (4¼-litre) engine and from its successors (the R-Type) with the lengthened rear end giving an enlarged luggage boot with the lid hinged at the top.

We had several most enjoyable trips in a dozen countries, in addition to the 'nursemaid' trips to Monza, Antwerp and Montlhéry. Four particular touring holidays stand out in my mind – three in summer and one in the depths of winter.

France, Italy, Switzerland, Germany & Belgium
Our enjoyment of the first of these, in August 1957, was enhanced by the vicarious pleasure we derived from the wide-eyed interest of our daughter Carol (then 14 years old) and a school-friend, in everything and everybody, for it was

their first touring holiday in Europe. Our friends, Derek and Mary Waller accompanied us in their open Sunbeam-Talbot. Four up, with luggage stowed on a roof-rack as well as in the 'small boot', we trickled (well, for me anyway!) across France, unashamedly rubber-necking on the way. In Paris, the gigantic tricolour flag filling the Arc de Triomphe on Liberation Day was particularly moving. We went southwards via Geneva where we interviewed possible au pair girls in our room at the Hôtel du Rhône – not without a few raised eyebrows from the management who seemed to suspect a white slave deal under their very eyes.

After spending a few days at Nice we drove eastwards along the Riviera Ligure, through Genoa, and by the spectacular coastal road over the Bracco Pass to La Spezia and Viareggio. It was on arrival there that I realized my document case was missing and a phone call confirmed that it had been left in the restaurant in La Spezia where we had lunched. I rose early next morning and drove 35 miles to Spezia to retrieve the missing treasure and back again to Viareggio before the rest of the party had made it down to breakfast. The leaning Tower at Pisa was the highlight of that morning, and all of us 'did' Rome with gusto the following day – St Peter's, Colosseum, Trevi Fountain, Forum, the lot.

Then we drove along the coast road to Naples savouring to the full the warm Italian sunshine, and lunched in the open air at a restaurant overlooking the Bay of Naples. We then drove as far as possible up the slopes of Vesuvius, completing the climb to the crater's edge by chair lift. We reached our destination, the Miramare Hotel, in Positano, that evening and met up with Bill and Marion Cook in their 220 S Mercedes saloon. They had their daughter, Jacquie, with them and the three schoolgirls formed a happy, if noisy, group from then on.

We all went on a launch trip to Capri, against the better judgment of Bill Cook who didn't like the look of the weather, the sea, the craft or its crew. Bill's forebodings proved to be well founded when, on the return trip to Positano, fog came down and the engine stopped. There were no navigational aids aboard, the crew were trying to restart the engine with lighted cigarettes hanging from their lips in the resulting petrol fumes, and we knew we were drifting towards some rugged cliffs. After a period of anxiety, the fog cleared, the motor started, we were still afloat and not on fire, and reached our destination safely, Bill vowing 'Never again, etc. . . . '

We started our homeward journey after visiting the ruins at Pompei and spending a day in Florence, and chose to follow the mountain road used in the Mille Miglia over the Futa and Raticosa passes to Bologna.

An unscheduled stop was made at the top of the Raticosa Pass to replace a lost fan belt on the Mk VI. We arrived at the Grand Hotel Fasano, a modest Walkerley-recommended establishment at Cannero on Lake Maggiore, for the night. The next day Bill and I went in the Mercedes to Monza to see the practice for the Italian Grand Prix and afterwards to Johnny Lurani's nearby villa at Cernusco where we were to be house guests over-night. Johnny's house is very large and beautiful and stands in very attractive grounds. The interior is vast and the casual visitor can get lost without difficulty. The bedrooms are large, the corridors long and even the 'usual offices' are housed in rooms which could serve as living-rooms in more modest houses. Bill Cook found a 'loo' in which the meaningful appliance was situated in the far corner of a longish chamber, the door to which had no lock or bolt. Needs must when the devil drives so he ignored the vulnerability of the position in which he found himself – and I mean that, for it was not long before the Contessa entered unaware of its occupancy. With such dignity as he could muster from the throne, Bill exchanged greetings and Nelly gracefully withdrew unabashed by the encounter.

We enjoyed the Grand Prix. It was stimulating to see three Vanwalls in British Racing Green on the front row of the grid (Moss, Brooks and Lewis-Evans) with Fangio (Maserati), and very gratifying to witness Stirling's win.

The homeward trek continued up into the Alps. The Cooks left us after lunch in Andermatt to take a more direct route home and we went over the Furka and Grimsel passes to Interlaken to stay at the Krebs Hotel – the much-loved hostelry of previous holidays in the $4\frac{1}{2}$. It was whilst we were there that the Mk VI was savaged by a Swiss Army lorry which scraped its solid metal frame along the side of the Bentley which was stationary with its near-side wheels on the grass. Front and rear wings were badly dented and the knowledge that I was driving a creased car took some pleasure out of the rest of the trip.

We returned to Ostend via the Rhine Valley and spent an interesting half day at the Daimler-Benz works and museum outside Stuttgart.

Altogether a very nice holiday.

(At this juncture I should mention for the record that I had a reconditioned engine fitted in June 1958, at 85,000 miles.)

St Moritz in Winter
We decided to sample the joys of a winter holiday at St Moritz in 1958 and left home just after Christmas in the Mk VI with Carol and yet another schoolfriend. The sun shone on dry roads all the way to Switzerland, and we made the most of New Year's Eve in Zurich. It was not until the foot of the Julier Pass that we encountered snow-covered roads, and chains were recommended (or compulsory, I can't remember which) for vehicles crossing the pass. The weather was deteriorating fast and it was getting dark, so I sent my passengers on to St Moritz by one of the regular Alpine coaches whilst I waited to purchase a set of chains and have them fitted. This done, I followed and arrived not far behind.

At first I left the car outside the hotel, covered accommodation being scarce and expensive. The Mk VI looked so neglected and forlorn – snow-covered and door locks frozen – that I swallowed hard and paid a high rent for space in a heated garage. We did little motoring whilst in St Moritz, enjoying ourselves on the nursery slopes and watching others skiing, tobogganing, bob-sleighing, curling, skating, etc., taking hot chocolate in Hanselmann's, sleigh-riding and so on. Little did we suspect the nightmare journey that faced us on the way home.

When we left St Moritz it was snowing hard and the roads were snow-covered or glazed with black ice all the way to the Channel coast! I drove confidently with my newly acquired snow-chains and crossed the Julier with no trouble – until there was a loud bang. A chain had broken and was flailing round under the mudguard. It was one of the transverse chains which act as a tread and, after securing it temporarily – it needed welding – I drove slowly into the next village to find a garage. As I

entered the workshop the car stopped with a jerk and wouldn't budge. The brakes seemed to be hard on and I could see no reason for it. Then I had a brainwave. Could the chain flailing round under the car, have caught one of the lugs of the brake adjusting wheel and tightened the brakes solid? A look under the car revealed that this was in fact what had happened, so it was soon rectified. We resumed our journey, but the chains broke again on several occasions, calling for first-aid fixing at the roadside, followed by welding at the next garage. The cause of the breaking was a mystery to me. The chains were the right size, of Swiss manufacture and properly fitted. It was not until some time later that I came to the conclusion it was a mistake to fit chains at all on the Michelin X tyres which I was using on the Mk VI at the time. I imagine that the relatively unyielding tread put a strain on the chains for which they were not designed. The breakages caused cumulative delays and it was late afternoon by the time we passed through Chur. Approaching Sargans I was motoring along with care in the snow – no Monte-Carlo Rally 'special stage' dicing for me – when I saw a tractor come out of a field ahead on the left and turn to follow the road in the same direction as me. It was towing a makeshift snow-plough made of timber, rather like railway sleepers, joined to form a 'V', and an old man was perched on this device. I moved over to the left to overtake and suddenly saw that, in turning left into the road, the snow-plough had deposited a curved wall of snow about 18″ high in my path. I braked gently, took avoiding action, moving back to my own side of the road behind the agricultural equipage, but just failed to stop before touching the corner of the snow-plough – scarcely above walking pace – tipping the old boy off into the snow. Fortunately he sustained only a sprained ankle. Nevertheless, we were much delayed whilst he was carried into the farmhouse, and police were called to take particulars. He should not have been riding on the plough, which had no provision for passengers and his mate driving the tractor had thoughtlessly dropped a chicane into my path.

We ate a late dinner at the railway-station in Zurich before braving the snowstorm again to reach a motel on the outskirts. Driving into the car park through snow a foot deep, very tired and cold, we found the motel a welcoming haven in an unfriendly world.

Next morning we resumed our journey homewards. I was disgusted with the troublesome chains and discarded them at the border at Basle to be sent back to the makers for a rebuild. I had made reservations in Paris for our overnight stop and was determined to reach there despite the bad weather. The last 150 miles into the capital were covered in darkness. Heavy snow reduced visibility almost to nil and there was so much of it on the road, and so little traffic, that at times it was like driving across a ploughed field. It was a weary party that retired to bed that night, after a very trying 350-mile drive and knowing the journey to the coast the next day would be quite hazardous, the snow having given way to ice.

I was pleased to arrive home safely with my charges and I question the sense of using a car for journeys to and from a winter sports resort unless it is to be used a lot during the stay there. Even then, a comfortable jet flight to the nearest airport and a rented self-drive car could save a lot of trouble and strife, unless one is exceptionally blessed by good weather or aspires to be another Erik Carlsson.

Portugal, Spain and Morocco

That we chose the North African desert as the focal point of our 1959 holiday was not a conscious rebellion against the winter weather we had endured in Switzerland at the turn of the year, but we certainly were intent on finding warm sunshine.

It is nearly 1,400 miles from a Channel port to Gibraltar, the obvious jumping-off point for Morocco. As I wished to avoid driving out and home by more or less the same route, I decided to go by sea to Lisbon and start the motoring from there. Accordingly, we boarded the P. & O. liner 'Stratheden' at Tilbury on Tuesday, 18 August, the Mk VI having been stowed deep in the hold the previous day. The voyage to Portugal imbued us with the holiday spirit – fortunately 'the Bay' was in friendly mood – and it was in a relaxed frame of mind that we disembarked at Lisbon $2\frac{1}{2}$ days later. The sight of the Mk VI being unloaded by crane and slings, swinging high in the air, did nothing to further our sense of well-being, but all was well and we drove the short distance down the estuary to the Monte Estoril Hotel where we stayed a day or two.

We saw quite a lot during our very short say – Cascais, Sintra, the giant Atlantic rollers on Guincho beach and the wonderful museum of Royal carriages and coaches at Belém. Being inclined to collect 'mosts', I perceived that this trip would enable me to touch the *most* westerly and the *most* southerly points of Europe. The most westerly is a cape (Cabo da Roca) 30 miles west of Lisbon where we visited the lighthouse on the headland. From Lisbon we headed for Gibraltar 450 miles away, spending a pleasant evening in Seville and, the following day, visiting the Gonzalez, Byass cellars – home of 'Tio Pepe' – at Jerez de la Frontera. The southernmost point of Europe is Punta Marroqui (Moroccan Point) on Isla de las Palomas (Isle of Doves) rising in the straits, and we went as near to it as possible on the mainland at Tarifa before driving round the Bay of Algeciras to Gibraltar.

The ferry crossing to Tangier was pleasant enough and we felt a thrill of adventure as the Mk VI wheels first turned on African soil. Based at the El Minzah Hotel, we savoured .he strangeness of our first landfall in Morocco. By the time we left for Rabat the following day we were becoming accustomed to being in an Arab-speaking world, but we certainly felt very adventurous to be leaving the city for the hinterland. We knew that if we had a break-down, the language barrier would be almost impenetrable. In the villages we would have been surrounded by an inquisitive, babbling crowd – between them we would be as lonely as the bedouin whose tents we saw at intervals. We made for Rabat, 180 miles away on the Atlantic coast, and after seeing something of this capital city, turned inland to Meknes and on to Fès for the night. We found these two Moroccan towns fascinating and the native quarter unspoilt – squalid by European stand-ards, but full of interest. It was an astounding experience to stand on the high ground outside the walled city of Fès and to hear a murmuring coming up from the Medina, for it was the accumulated chatter of the inhabitants rising upon the air!

Our return to Tangier was made via Chaouen, a beautiful town of fountains and mosques on the hillside, which was a sight for sore eyes after driving 200 miles on a dusty, desert secondary road north from Meknes. We com-pleted our 600-mile-plus drive in North Africa on schedule and without incident.

Back in Spain we drove up the Mediterranean coast to spend a few days at Torremolinos, at that time a little-known place. We stayed at the newly-opened Pez Espada Hotel, then isolated on a deserted stretch of beach. I have not re-visited Torremolinos since, and I doubt if I would recognize it today. We turned inland at Malaga for Granada where we stayed at the Alhambra Hotel adjacent to the famous build-ing from which it has taken its name.

When planning this holiday I discovered that the highest road in Europe was just outside Granada and I was determined to drive up it. This mountain road in the Sierra Nevada was little known to motorists, presumably because it wasn't a pass; it led nowhere except to the top of the mountain ridge from which there was a breath-taking view over the surrounding Sierra. The road started at Pinos Genil, 3 miles

outside Granada, and climbed to a height of over 11,000 feet in a distance of about 22 miles. The upper section of the road resembled a cause-way, one car wide, built up of sharp stones chipped out of the mountain side. As we passed the Residencia Universitaria at 8,400 feet we were stopped by a monk who asked us to keep an eye open for two climbers who had left the previous day and had not yet returned. We did meet one of them higher up; he was quite all right and said his companion was following. They had made an unscheduled night stop in the mountains. I was conscious of the engine power falling off as the altitude in-creased (by no less than 25% at 8,000 feet). The road became increasingly rough and diffi-cult. I gave up, reluctantly, about half a kilo-metre from the summit, having scraped a rear wing when negotiating a tight hairpin corner between rocks, but was delighted to have made the climb. My passengers' appreciation of the wonderful scenery was tempered by the 'scari-ness' of the climb! The road has since been continued beyond the summit down the Medi-terranean side of the range, to join the road from Granada to the coast. The Col de Reste-fond (La Bonette) in France – a mere 9,193 feet – hitherto acknowledged as being the high-est pass in Europe, must yield pride of place to Spain with this 11,247 ft road. I would certainly make a return visit if I were to find myself in the area again.

From Granada I drove almost due north nearly 600 miles right across Spain, through Madrid and Bilbao to San Sebastian. We did a round of the sights in Madrid and then drove 30-odd miles out into the Guadarrama Range to visit Valle de los Caidos (Valley of the Fallen) especially to see the underground basilica of Santa Cruz. This is like a cathedral, 850 feet long, carved out of (or rather into) the solid rock of a hill, the latter surmounted by a gigantic granite cross 500 feet high and 150 feet across the arms. The whole of this was constructed as a monument to the dead of the Civil War, whose remains are buried in the valley.

The drive across France through Biarritz, Bordeaux, Le Mans – an inevitable lap or two of the 24-Hour Race circuit – Chartres and Paris was followed by a cross-channel flight from Le Touquet to Lydd. On reaching home the trip recorder registered 3,127 miles and the overall petrol consumption had been slightly more than 17 mpg.

Scandinavia

It is human nature which drives the Englishman south in search of sunshine whenever an opportunity arises to get away for a week or two from the daily round in this unpredictable climate of ours. Thus, Northern Europe – Scandinavia in particular – does not figure high on his list of possible holiday areas.

Nevertheless, in 1960 we decided to see something of the Scandinavian countries and hoped the sun would follow us. We chose August as the month most likely to be favoured with good weather and so it turned out, for we had glorious sunshine nearly all the time.

Con, Carol and I motored northwards to Newcastle-upon-Tyne during August Bank Holiday weekend to board the car-carrying boat (rudely referred to by experienced travellers as the 'Vomiting Venus') for Bergen via Stavanger. From Bergen there was really only one obvious road northwards, but it tacked backwards and forwards in order to cross or circumnavigate the deep fjords. The road was twisty and, in places, very narrow with bays to permit vehicles approaching from opposite directions to pass one another. Much of the surface comprised loose stones, and several ferries had to be taken to cross fjords. All these features added interest to this journey through magnificent scenery, but only relatively small distances could be encompassed in a day's motoring – about 80 miles was the daily average on the northward leg.

We drove eastwards from Bergen to meet the Hardangerfjord near Norheimsund and spent the night at Granvin. We had entered a mountainous land of rugged beauty and were never far from running water, waterfalls and rushing streams abounding. The sparseness of traffic was a joy and we meandered northwards through Stalheim to Gudvangen, then by a couple of ferries – one taking 3 hours and the other 10 minutes – across the Sognefjord to Balestrand, our next overnight stopping place. The next two days took us through Olden to Grotli, where we doubled back to Geiranger, after deviating to climb the then new Dalsnibba road just for the breath-taking view; that's why it was built, it led nowhere. From Geiranger we took the impressive 'Eagle Road' up the cliff-like side of the fjord and the Trollstigveien (Witches' Road) on to Andalsnes, the most northerly point on our trip. We were now 250 miles north of John o'Groats and felt pretty adventurous, until I looked at the map and found that North Cape at the 'top' of Norway was about 800 miles further north as the crow flies, and goodness knows how much further by road. The daylight hours were so long it was difficult to sleep at night and I remember reading a newspaper outdoors at about midnight.

We retraced our route to Grotli and headed eastwards into the Jotunheimen Mountains, making a pincer movement to reach Elveseter after pausing to admire one of the famous timber built stave churches at Lom. We were just about as high up in Norway as you can go by road, and the following morning went by Jeep up to a nearby glacier in very barren terrain indeed, before leaving for Oslo.

We stayed at the Royal Norwegian Automobile Club (KNA) Hotel and were shown the sights of Oslo by a keen Vintage Bentley enthusiast, Halvor Haneborg. (He managed to conceal his 3-litre from prying German eyes during the Occupation by walling-up part of his garage – and still owns the same car today!) I am not a 'museum man' myself, but I was fascinated with the display of Viking ships; being able to walk aboard Nansen's famous polar exploration

38 *Kreuger's 8-litre Bentley in the Technical Museum, Stockholm*

ship, 'Fram'; and to inspect the Kon-Tiki balsa-wood raft on which Thor Heyerdahl had drifted across the Pacific in 101 days. Possibly the most unusual experience was a walk round Frogner Park to see the Vigelund statues – well worth a visit. We left Norway regretfully, having enjoyed every minute of our stay in this delightful, unspoiled country, and beat it eastwards to Stockholm. At that time the Swedes drove on the left-hand side of the road and we had to change sides through a chicane when crossing the border. I was fascinated by the large rafts of logs being floated down by river from the forests. They were tied together and towed by one boat whilst another had hold of the rear end, more than 100 yards away, to nudge it round the bends. A compulsive scenario, this, for the amateur film-maker.

We stayed outside Stockholm at Saltsjöbaden and, frankly, found little to interest us in the city except Kreuger's 8-litre Bentley on show in the Technical Museum. From here we turned southwards along the Baltic coast to commence our circuitous journey home. The craftsmen at work in the glass factories at Kosta and Orrefors held us spellbound for a while, then we streaked across to the west coast to spend the night at Bastad before going south to cross on the ferry from Helsingborg to Helsingør (Elsinore) in Denmark. As was so often the case, all the hotels in Copenhagen were full and we had to stay outside the city.

Our guides in Copenhagen were Ditlev and Else Scheel who had made us so welcome on our first Continental motoring holiday when living in Bern. We really enjoyed our rubber-necking and must have seen everything worth seeing in and around Copenhagen during the few days we spent there; of course, it wasn't the 'porn' capital of Europe in those days. We left with some reluctance to drive to Korsør to catch the ferry to Nyborg. On the way I had a blow-out in one of my Michelin 'X's whilst travelling at 75 mph, but came to no harm and reached the boat before it sailed.

That night we reached Hamburg and stayed at the 'Vier Jahreszeiten' Hotel for a couple of nights. We went to the famous Zoo and drove along the Reeperbahn in St Pauli – though not to linger on this occasion – but the thing which Con and I will never forget occurred just as we were leaving. We were in our bedroom on an upper floor at the front of the hotel packing up the last of our belongings prior to checking out. Carol had gone downstairs to put something in the car which was parked across the road. Suddenly, we heard the screech of brakes and skidding tyres. We dashed to the window and were relieved to see Carol was safe. She had, in fact, stepped into the road momentarily forgetting that the traffic kept to the right in Germany and had caused a motorist to make an emergency stop, fortunately without physical harm to anyone, but with a fairly disturbing mental effect on all concerned.

Motoring through northern Holland, I enjoyed a fast run across the dyke enclosing the Zuider Zee; this is a level road running dead straight for about 12 miles. And so down to Rotterdam. Here we saw what I think was the first 'people only' shopping precinct, which the forward-looking Dutch had built on the ruins of their bombed city. I do not profess to understand modern art, but I must admit that the giant Zadkine statue, 'The Devastated City', conveyed vividly to me its portrayal of the city of Rotterdam having its heart torn out in May 1940 by the German bombers. We stopped overnight at Scheveningen on the Dutch coast; a fantastic firework display on the foreshore was thrown in. It was here I saw the Dutch mounted police in action. A group of youths were walking noisily and defiantly along a part of the pro-

menade which was being kept clear for passing traffic, spectators being kept on the pavements, when a mountie took one of the gang by the shoulder of his jacket and cantered off so fast that the offender's feet were scarcely touching the ground. He deposited his charge some distance away, by which time his chums had melted away!

We arrived home having done 3,715 miles in three weeks with a petrol consumption of 17.8 mpg. We have never regretted that we 'went up' instead of 'down' for our holiday that year.

In retrospect

My Mk VI Bentley proved itself to be a first-class means of transport. It was fast, safe, comfortable and a joy to drive; versatile, equally at home shopping, commuting, towing, touring; and all-in-all just about the best compromise one could wish for. I wrote at the time, 'We all have our own ideas as to which is the fastest car available; which has the best cornering and road-holding; which gives the best ride; which is the most economical; most comfortable; best value for money; easiest to drive; cosiest; best in acceleration; best braked; etc.; but no one car can possess the ultimate in all these features.

'The man who seeks the best of everything without demanding the ultimate in anything will find the mixture served up at Crewe in the shape of a $4\frac{1}{2}$-litre Standard Steel Saloon.

I would go further in the light of subsequent experience: I am firmly of the opinion that the continued success of the post-war products of the Crewe factory stems largely from the fact that the Rolls-Royce and Bentley cars have given 'the mostest of the bestest.' When I parted with the car in August 1961, a necessary step to enable me to acquire that unique Bentley, 'Olga', I had driven the Mk VI about 90,000 miles, thousands of them in a dozen Continental countries, and enjoyed every one of them – so had all my passengers.

Prototype R-Type Continental – 'Olga'

I am not keen on the practice of giving names to cars, but I bow to the tradition of calling the prototype 'R' Continental Bentley by the soubriquet *Olga*, a name derived from its registration letters long before the car came into my hands.

Encouraged – perhaps goaded would be a more appropriate word – by Walter Sleator, their distributor in Paris, Rolls-Royce took up the concept of a 'Continental' Bentley using the R-Type chassis and engine as the basis for the new car. The aim was to secure a 20% increase in maximum speed, 120 mph compared with the 100 mph of the Standard model; the two main ways of achieving this were by designing an aerodynamic body and reducing the overall weight. At that time it was considered that the best tyres available would not permit sustained speeds around 115 mph unless the kerb weight was kept down to 34 cwt.

H.J. Mulliner built a light alloy body to a form decided upon only after exhaustive wind tunnel tests, and that body is still on the car. In August 1951 the dream became the reality. Initial tests in this country gave a maximum speed of 114 mph using Dunlop Medium Distance Track tyres at 3,750 rpm. As the permitted engine speed was 4,250 rpm it was apparent that the overall axle-ratio of 2.79:1 was too high and a lower one (3.07:1) was substituted.

Then 'Olga' was sent to France for testing at Montlhéry under the supervision of Walter Sleator. Tests on the track showed that the change had in no way spoiled the car's maximum performance whilst, because the acceleration had been improved thereby, it was more quickly reached. Official timing by the Automobile Club de France gave 'Olga' an average lap speed of $118\frac{3}{4}$ mph taken over five laps, with a best lap speed of $119\frac{3}{4}$ mph. This test was conducted using Dunlop MDT tyres, inflated to 50 lbs sq in. Using India Shallow Tread Road Tyres, the maximum speed recorded was 115.5 mph.

Although very little tyre trouble was experienced during the high speed tests when using the tyres which had been designed for the purpose, a normal 6-ply tyre used under the same conditions survived for only 20 miles.

'Olga' was used by Charles Faroux as his Course Car during the 1952 Le Mans 24-Hour Race and then embarked upon a very busy life as the Works Demonstrator. It was made available to the Press for road-testing – the first Road Test report was published in the 'Autocar' on 12 September 1952 – and driven by the Sales Staff, distributors, dealers and potential customers all over Europe. At the time, the new Continental Bentley was the fastest 4-seater production saloon in the world; the best mean speed recorded by the 'Autocar' was 115.4 mph. One run, with the driver only, was timed at 120 mph. For the first time the 'Autocar' had to extend its acceleration tables to 100 mph for both third and top gears. This Road Test report concluded thus: 'This Bentley is a modern magic carpet which annihilates distance and delivers the occupants well-nigh as fresh as when they started. It is a car Britain may well be proud of, and it is sure to add new lustre to the name it bears.'

Production of the R-Type Continental continued until May 1955, but only 208 were made. Of these, the most sought after today are those similar to 'Olga', having right-hand drive, manual gearbox, and two-door H.J. Mulliner coachwork, of which 75 were delivered to UK customers. During the production run I was to drive 'Olga' on several occasions, each time enhancing my liking for the car. When no longer required as a demonstrator, 'Olga' was used as a Company car, at first at Director level and then in the hands of several senior employees. I had said to 'Doc' (F. Llewellyn Smith, then Managing Director of the Motor Car Division), that, if he ever decided to sell 'Olga', I would like first refusal. He reminded me that it was RR

39 *'Olga' reborn in June 1961 – note the rear-wheel spats in position*

policy to break up prototypes and I cringed. It was something of a surprise, therefore, when Jack Scott, the Sales Director, called me in November 1960 to say that the Company had finished with 'Olga' and was I still interested in buying it? He said it was in pretty poor shape and, if he sold it to me, he didn't want me complaining and coming back with the car, so whatever work was necessary would have to be done on delivery at my expense. I asked him to lend it to me for a week-end to enable me to make up my mind. When I drove 'Olga' that week-end I was frankly shocked at its condition – it was down on the back springs and sounded like an Underground train – which is not, perhaps, surprising as it had covered nearly 250,000 miles by then. Despite its superficial tattiness and the obvious need for mechanical attention, its underlying charm and qualities came through and I knew I was hooked. Actually, I was somewhat apprehensive that the purchase price of the car plus the cost of the

necessary reconditioning, would prove too much for me. I was biting my nails in a sweat of indecision. I felt that if I couldn't own 'Olga' myself she should go to a good home and telephoned Peter Hampton to say that if he was interested, maybe RR could be talked into letting him have the car if I turned her down. I took Peter for a ride in 'Olga', and he drove it himself in a manner and at a speed which would have done credit to an experienced driver not handicapped by the loss of use of one arm. Peter was favourably impressed and said he would give me a firm answer the next day. I returned home in torment at the thought of 'Olga' slipping through my fingers and called Peter to say 'Forget it, I have decided to take the plunge.' He said, 'Pity, I was just going to telephone you to say I would buy if it could be arranged.' It was my gain and Peter's loss – and we are still speaking to each other! For my part I have never regretted for one moment this big decision.

40 *Bentleys at a cocktail party in Antwerp on the eve of the speed trials – note the absence of mudgards and lamps*

I asked Roney Messervy (Service Director of RR) to quote for the mechanical work necessary to make the car as new and requested the same from H.J. Mulliner for the coachwork. With these quotations before me, I deducted the total from what I considered to be the (then!) market value of a similar model in 'as new' condition and offered Jack Scott the difference, which was little enough, in all conscience. I was delighted when he said 'Done', and my motoring life entered a new era. The desirable heap was delivered to Hythe Road in December 1960 and work on the mechanical side commenced. Replacement $3\frac{3}{4}$-in bore engine, gearbox and radiator matrix were fitted. The chassis and running-gear were overhauled – front suspension, propeller shaft, rear axle and half-shafts, rear springs, rear dampers, steering, electrics – brakes were relined and hose connections replaced. A new set of Dunlop RS 5 tyres was fitted and two months later 'Olga' was handed over to H.J. Mulliner at their Fulham works. Whilst at Hythe Road 'Olga' had acquired a new chassis number. The chassis number on the car when I bought it was 9 B VI, presumably an experimental number, and Roney Messervy thought it should have a number more in keep-with the series allocated to production Continentals. He chose BC 26A, i.e. one number beyond those issued to the first batch of 24 cars. Many enthusiasts have wondered how 'Olga' could be the first Continental when 24 others had 'lower' chassis numbers; now they know.

Mulliners were to restore the car to new condition. This involved repainting, re-upholstering, re-trimming, replating all chromium, new head lining, repolishing woodwork, new carpets – in fact, the lot. I made frequent calls to see 'how it was getting along' and could scarcely contain my impatience to gain possession of the reborn 'Olga'. In the event, the paintwork was sub-contracted to Hooper Motor Services and the retrimming to Wood & Pickett; both firms did a first-class job. Incidentally, I changed the colour of the body from the original darkish grey to 'Shell Grey', and had the 'orange' woodwork darkened to a rich brown. The interior of the car was fairly spartan in the interests of weight-saving, so I added a radio, a rear-window de-mister, headlight flashers, and an ashtray (!); and moved the turn indicator from the centre of the fascia to the steering column. I put the car on a weighbridge and found that the car weighed $33\frac{3}{4}$ cwt with some petrol in the tank.

I was anxious that 'Olga' should be ready in time for the Bentley Drivers Club meeting in Kensington Gardens on 1 July 1961, and the target date was achieved. It was indeed a proud Sedgwick who re-possessed 'Olga' looking like new and with a new speedometer set at 00000.

In the middle of September I took 'Olga' across the Channel for the first time – though goodness knows how many times she had been abroad in her previous life. I drove across Holland and down the Rhine Valley to Wetzlar where I had arranged to take a 4-day course in photography for Leica owners at the factory. Afterwards I drove south through Basle, over the St Bernard Pass to Turin and via the Col de Tende to Eze-sur-mer, to join, unexpectedly, Con and Carol who had flown there for a short holiday. For the life of me I cannot recall anything about the journey home, so on this occasion you will be spared a detailed itinerary and timetable.

In May 1962, I once again led a party of Bentley Drivers Club Members to take part in the Belgian Day of Records organized by the Antwerp Motor Union on the same stretch of the Antwerp-Liege motorway which we had used three years previously. This time I was driving 'Olga' which not only took over the role of maid-of-all-work, hitherto fulfilled by the Mk VI, but was to take part in the competition. Tuning for the run through the measured kilometre was limited to increasing tyre pressures and turning the wing mirrors through 90 degrees. My speed for the Flying Kilometre was 111.234 mph on the outward run, and 108.326 mph on the return, giving a mean speed of 109.760 mph. The standing kilometre time was 34.92 seconds at the first attempt and one-hundredth-of-a-second longer on the second run. (Some owners of R-Type Continentals kid themselves about the maximum speed of their cars; it is my considered view that a production car has rarely exceeded 115 mph.)

Later in the year (July) we embarked on another motoring holiday, this time taking 'Olga' into Czechoslovakia. My passengers were again Con and Carol and we were looking forward to this excursion into Eastern Europe – this was, of course, before the Russian invasion of Czechoslovakia.

After a night at Wurzburg and lunch in Nuremburg we crossed the border at Waldhaus/Rozvadov. The 'Welcome to Czechoslovakia' banners contrasted strangely with the thoroughness with which the armed guards frisked 'Olga' before we were allowed to proceed through Pilsen to Prague, 110 miles away. I found the atmosphere rather sad. The city was a mixture of beautiful old buildings – many in a state of neglect – and drab modern buildings. There was a delightful corner reminiscent of Venice; the famous astronomical clock, dating from 1460, in the old Town Hall, which we managed to reach on the hour to see the action; Wenceslas Square (the Piccadilly of Prague); fantastic illuminated books in a one-time monastery; and – not so lovely – a great monolith of Soviet leaders headed by Stalin. (This statue weighed several thousand tons and must have posed quite a problem when Moscow decreed the removal of all likenesses of Stalin. Never did hear what, if anything, happened to it.) We drove through attractive countryside crossing into Austria north-west of Vienna; I must admit to feeling a renewed sense of liberty as we left Communist soil and drove towards the capital.

It was our first visit to the Austrian capital and in addition to seeing the well-known sights – the Schönbrunn Palace, the Prater amusement park with its great wheel, the Spanish Riding

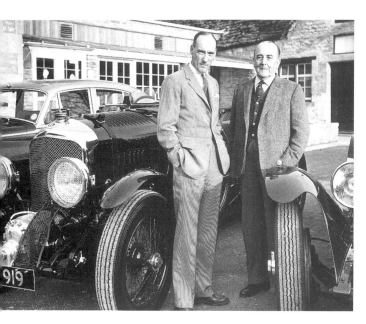

41 *The author with 'W.O.' at Chippenham during the Bentley Shell 500 – June 1969*

School – we went backstage at the Opera House, and sought out the Technical Museum to see the 'Markus', built in 1875 and claimed to be the first petrol-driven motor-car in the world – a claim strongly refuted by the historians of Daimler-Benz at Unterturkheim. The horses of the Spanish Riding School were at the stud farm at Piber near Graz and we were able to see them on the way to Venice. We stayed on the Lido and a launch trip across the lagoon proved rather costly as I dropped a ciné lens overboard.

After a few days here we removed ourselves to Cap Estel, at Eze-sur-mer. I am a restless individual, rarely staying in any one place for more than three or four days, and the Lido Venice had provided me with enough sun, sea and sand for a bit, so I flew home for a week leaving 'Olga' with Con and Carol on the Riviera. I flew to Nice a week later, collected 'Olga' and family, driving home via Geneva and Paris.

May the following year (1963) saw 'Olga' once more with the Bentleys in Belgium for the spring meeting. Unfortunately, it was no longer possible to hold this competition on the new autoroute and it was transferred to another piece of road which was not long enough to give adequate acceleration and braking distances for flying runs at maximum speed over the measured distances. Only standing start times were recorded over a kilometre and a mile. 'Olga's' time (34.33 secs) over the kilometre was three-fifths of a second quicker than the previous year. Not many of the cars reached their maximum speed by the time they crossed the finishing line at the end of the kilometre, but it seemed like it for the road was tree-lined, comparatively narrow and lined with spectators!

The following month I took 'Olga' across the Channel again, this time to Le Mans to assist in Briggs Cunningham's pit, but returned home immediately afterwards as we were not planning to have a motoring holiday in Europe that year.

I was using 'Olga' daily for travelling to and from the office, until the coming of the 70 mph limit and increasing traffic took away what little pleasure there was in this 20 miles-in-an-hour journey. 'Olga' was also used on many Bentley Drivers Club occasions. During the first $2\frac{1}{2}$ years I covered 50,000 miles and reached 100,000 miles on 22 February 1972. This later milestone in the life of 'Olga' was marked in suitable fashion. I had been invited by the Chairman and Directors of Rolls-Royce Motors to dine at the Connaught Hotel for the purpose of accepting the Company's donation to the 'W.O. Bentley Memorial Fund' and I realized a few days before this engagement that 'Olga's' mileage was 99,900+. I invited David Plastow and John Craig to be aboard when the magic figure was reached. I left the office a few miles short of the target and drove out to St John's Wood and back, and around the West End to park outside the Connaught with the distance recorder reading 99,999 miles. I was joined by the above-mentioned Members of the Board and drove off round Grosvenor Square. The faces of the three occupants broke into boyish grins of delight as the five nines gave way to the five zeroes during the third lap.

Later in the year – on 20 August 1972 to be exact – 'Olga' came of age and I conceived the idea of celebrating her 21st Birthday by inviting owners of her progeny to drive to my home and drink the health of their prototype. Daft, you may think, giving a birthday party for a car, but none of the like-minded enthusiasts who arrived in the R-Type Continentals would agree. Fourteen of these cars turned up, coming from all quarters and some quite long distances. Several owners had an opportunity of driving 'Olga' and praised her mechanical condition, handling and light steering.

42 *'Olga' waiting for a run in regularity-speed tests at Pierre Bardinon's racing circuit at Mas du Clos, near Aubusson*

43 *Joseph Cugnot's second steam car of 1770 on exhibition in the Musée des Arts et Metiers in Paris, seen during a fleeting visit*

44   *A group of enthusiasts during a visit to the Mahy Collection in Ghent. Ghislain Mahy is at the wheel of his 1906 Fondu with his son Ivan.*

From left to right are Louis Giron, Evelyn Mawer, John Hampton, Ronald ('Steady') Barker, Bill Cook, the author, and Bob Gregory

45   *'Olga's' 21st birthday party guests, August 1972*

46   *Bill Cook serves an appropriate toast on 'Olga's coming-of-age*

Germany

In May 1984 the Eastern Region of the Bentley Drivers Club arranged to join German Bentley and Rolls-Royce owners on a fairly gastronomic week's motoring based on Osnabruck, where the local organizer Stephan Titgemeyer lived and worked. I decided to join in the goings-on in 'Olga' and was delighted to find that Johnnie Green could accompany me.

We left Dover for Ostend one day after the main contingent and planned to join them at their first overnight stop at the 'Alte Mühle' at Wurselen, north of Aachen. We did not leave Ostend until 5 pm but, by conducting the R-type Continental in the manner for which she was conceived and built, we reached the German frontier near Aachen in two minutes under two hours, which meant that we had averaged 79.16 mph for the 155.7 miles.

We checked in at the hotel only to find that the others had left a few minutes earlier by coach (advisedly) for Stolberg, to dine at the Restaurant 'Schwarzenbruch', which was owned and managed by a fellow-member Peter Schmitz, and his family. Johnnie and I set off after the coach and reached our goal at the same time. Peter had gone to a lot of trouble to give a distinctly Bentley flavour to the evening, and it was a well-fed and convivial coachload of travellers that returned to the hotel with 'Olga' in its wake.

The next day the British party, now totalling ten Bentleys, drove by autobahn to the Hotel Himmelreich near Osnabruck and then to the Karmann coachbuilding works where we were joined – or vice versa – by 35 Bentleys and Rolls-Royces from all over Germany. After a tour of the factory, under the personal guidance of Herr Karmann, we proceeded to 'Gut Kuhof', the seventeenth-century country home of Wolfgang Möller, whom I had met previously in the Berlin Rally in my Edwardian Mercedes. The manor was at one time owned by King George III of England for his son Bishop Frederick of Osnabruck, and Wolfgang had been engaged in its restoration for twenty years.

That evening we dined at the 'Altes Forsthaus Beck' in Lingen. The following morning found us huddled round a log fire in the Titgemeyer's summer home – Haus Brandenburg, prior to taking part in a hill-climb in the nearby countryside, where the object was to climb, without the aid of timepieces, in as near as possible to an unspecified time set by a pilot 3-litre. It's odd how the word 'regularity' doesn't seem to have a place in the vocabulary of some Bentley drivers – thus it is not surprising that I recall Hugh Harben put up the fastest time of day and have forgotten who came nearest to the target time!

On the journeys between the various rendezvous the sight of four Speed Sixes speeding along the autobahnen ahead of 'Olga', at a sustained 90 mph, was an exhilarating one and surprised the local gentry in their BMWs and Mercedes. Unfortunately, two Brits forgot that speed limits are in force off the autobahnen and were relieved of a bundle of Deutschmarks by the local constabulary, who were then induced to give a certain Speed Six a push start on the dubious pretext of a flat battery. The city of Osnabruck is 'twinned' with Derby and on Monday, 14 May, a ceremony of dedication took place, in which a small square was named 'Derby Platz'. It was a happy coincidence that the Bentleys were in town and their attendance on this occasion was much appreciated by the assembled citizenry of both cities.

Johnnie and I did not take part, having decided to visit Amsterdam and the tulip fields before meeting up with the others just inside the Belgian border at Houthalen, where part of the great Mahy collection of cars was then housed in a new museum. At that time, many of the Mahy cars were still in the multi-storey converted circus building in Ghent, and we were privileged to see this collection on the way to the coast, conducted by the ever enthusiastic Ghislain Mahy and his son Ivan. They have a rare unrestored Bentley 'Cresta' and two other examples of the marque, one being a 3/4½-litre (Chassis No. DN1735), well-known in Club circles in the 60s and once owned by Don McKenzie and George Daniels (among others); and the other a Mk. VI (Chassis No. B388BH) with Vanden Plas coachwork.

Two happenings on this trip come to mind. As we entered the car-park at one of the several car museums visited, a beautifully turned-out Mercedes-Benz 300SL convertible drove in and parked in the centre rank where it *would* have been the cynosure of all eyes. Imagine the dismay of the owner when he was asked to move his car to the back, as Bentleys surrounded the Merc. and became the focus of attention. The other memorable occasion was in Holland. Returning to our hostel near the airport after an evening in Amsterdam I distinguished myself by running out of petrol at an intersection on the four-lane highway to Schiphol at 11.30 pm. This entailed a deal of walking and hitch-hiking until past the witching hour. Johnnie made an uncalled-for remark about it being one thing to ignore the red lights in Amsterdam, but quite another to disregard the green light on the dashboard!

The log of the journey, kept by Johnnie in his unaccustomed role of amanuensis, showed that petrol consumption for the 1,360-mile trip, much of which had been driven at between 85 and 100 mph, was 16.9 mpg.

The end of an era
With the advent of the turbocharged Mulsanne Bentley in 1982 I foresaw the way ahead for my personal motoring and, after mature consideration, I decided to dispose of 'Olga' to help me face up to the financial commitment in prospect. Well aware of the unique and historical character of the car, I wanted to be sure that it would pass to an enthusiast with a similar outlook to my own – preferably in the UK. Both these criteria were met when Victor Gauntlett reconfirmed his interest expressed a year or two earlier when an unscrupulous dealer at the Geneva Motor Show offered him 'Olga' without the slightest authority.

Thus, Con and I drove up to Town on 27 April 1985 to the Royal Automobile Club in Belgrave Square to hand over the treasured Continental Bentley to its new owner, with 122,554 miles recorded on the milometer during my 24½ years' ownership. Our sadness was tempered by the thought of the super motoring ahead in a 35-year younger sister.

(A single-handed drive in 'Olga' from the south of France to Cobham in a day is described in this book in the chapter entitled 'Motoring for motoring's sake.)

One Turbocharged Bentley after another

When the turbocharged version of the Mulsanne was announced in March 1982 it was clear that the Bentley had shed its clone existence alongside the Rolls-Royce and, after an interval of 30 years, had reassumed its rightful place amongst sports cars. Its introduction marked the first really big jump in performance since the advent of the 'R'-type Continental in 1952. In current vernacular the Mulsanne Turbo was 'something else' – a quantum leap in design. The additional power – reputedly 100 bhp – produced by the turbocharger was to provide the driver with a sports-car performance worthy of the badge and name of Bentley.

I had a taste of this new world of luxury motoring when in April 1983 I was fortunate enough to have the use of the factory 'Press' car for a weekend during which I clocked up nearly 500 miles of some of the most exhilarating driving I had hitherto experienced. The acceleration throughout the range, from a standstill to the restricted maximum of 135 mph, was outstanding and one of the main joys was the way in which one could overtake other cars – not just one, but several at a time – and continue accelerating whilst seeing them going backwards in the mirror! As with all really fast cars, such manoeuvres call for restraint, as drivers of cars approaching from the opposite direction tend to panic at the sight of two cars abreast, not

47 *Handing over 'Olga' to her new owner,*
Victor Gauntlett – April 1985

realizing that the Turbo will be back on its own side of the road long before the meeting-point.

Its outstanding performance was acknowledged by all who drove the car and evidenced by figures in the road tests of motoring papers. All praised the straight-line acceleration and speed of the car, confessing themselves astonished at the way in which such a heavy saloon (5105 lbs) – more than 1000 lbs heavier than the comparable Mercedes-Benz 500SE – outpaced the majority of cars on the road. However, they all commented that the soft suspension, inherited from the current Rolls-Royce and Bentley models, limited the degree to which the car's performance could be used on winding roads without excessive roll, which resulted in considerable discomfort on such roads, and doubts as to the car's ability to follow the intended course with safety. This shortcoming was acknowledged at Crewe, and, as a result of the ensuing development work, the front and rear end roll stiffness was increased by 100 per cent and 60 per cent respectively, a Panhard rod being incorporated at the rear. These and other modifications first appeared at the Geneva Motor Show in March 1985, the improved model being designated the 'Turbo R' – the 'R' said to stand for 'road-holding'.

Le Mans – en passant

June 1984 marked the sixtieth anniversary of the first Bentley win at Le Mans, and Rolls-Royce Motors – or should I say Bentley Motors (?) – took the opportunity to subsidize a pilgrimage of Bentleys to Le Mans, giving prominence to the

Mulsanne Turbo. No less than seven of these models were in evidence at the circuit, two of them in an official capacity as Course cars. I was to be a guest of the company for the weekend, but time did not permit me to travel by road with the cavalcade – or rather motorcade – so I flew to Paris and continued the journey to Le Mans by train!

The company put on a comprehensive exhibition of pictures and memorabilia relating to the Bentley days at Le Mans, and Peter Ward (then Managing Director of the Marketing Division of Rolls-Royce Motors and now Chairman of the company) presented to the Club a specially-commissioned painting by Michael Turner of a Bentley Mulsanne Turbo passing Les Hunaudieres on the eponymous straight. (This painting is reproduced on the back of the dust jacket of this book.)

The Mulsanne Turbos were in great demand for demonstration runs, and it was said that ordinary, law-abiding Frenchmen on a nearby autoroute were astonished to be overtaken by a Bentley doing over 200 kph – with a load of high-ranking gendarmerie as passengers!

I did not have to use public transport on the return journey, being entrusted to take one of the Mulsanne Turbos back to London. Altogether a very pleasant interlude – with a pit-view of the 24-hour race thrown in for good measure.

With retirement from an active business life in prospect I set my sights on owning a Turbo Bentley some day, but realized that I would achieve this only by disposing of a car or two, and even then rising only to a used example. Fortune smiled on me, and before I had taken any irrevocable step towards achieving my objective, the Turbo R was announced and, by selling my well-known 'R' type Continental, 'Olga', and my late Silver Shadow II, I was able to effect a virtually level swap of hardware on a two-for-one basis, and took delivery of a brand-new Turbo R from Jack Barclay's showroom in Berkeley Square on 1 August 1985. Truly a red letter (or label) day in my life! I committed myself to taking this car without having driven one before, confident that the 'handling package' would transform the Mulsanne Turbo into my ultimate dream car – and so it proved.

On taking delivery I was surprised to find that I was exhorted not to exceed 70 mph – as if I would – for the first 750 miles, not for the sake of the engine, which had been run-in on the bench, but for the tyres. Perhaps not a great hardship when familiarizing oneself with a new car – but every time one fits a new set of tyres??!! (Perhaps this applied only to Pirellis; the request was not made in relation to my next Turbo, which was fitted with Avons.)

Continental foray

Having completed this compulsory crawl, Con and I left home for a keenly-anticipated tour on the Continent. Leaving Cobham at 9 am (BST), we took the familiar autoroutes from Calais to the south of France and reached what we have found to be a convenient and very pleasant stopping-place if one is taking two days to cross France – the Hostellerie de la Poste at Avallon. We arrived there at 6.30 pm (French time) with 412.2 miles recorded, of which 317.8 were in France. We left Avallon the next morning at 10 o'clock, in pouring rain which persisted for 150 miles, and reached our destination – Cap Estel at Eze-sur-mer – at 6 pm, having added a further 460.6 miles to the trip and making the door-to-door distance 872.8 miles. Checking the odometer against kilometre markers showed that the instrument was over-recording by less than half-a-mile over a distance of 200 kms (124.27 miles). Petrol consumption was 12.42 mpg.

One morning during our stay I found that an attempt had been made during the night to break into the luggage boot of the Turbo R. As the car was in the hotel's private car-park it should have been obvious to any hopeful thief that the boot would be empty, so the culprit(s) may have been aiming to tunnel through the boot and back seat to reach the radio. Who knows? Anyway he/she/

they weren't successful as the jemmy (or whatever) had been used at the wrong level to lift the lid and, unfortunately for all concerned, served only to damage paintwork and trimming.

The return journey was a relatively leisurely meander through the tunnel at the top of the Col de Tende into Italy – still with its dripping roof – to Ascona, just in Switzerland, where we spent the night at the excellent Castello del Sole; then over the Nufenen Pass to our old friend, Krebs Hotel at Interlaken; and northwards through Germany, Luxembourg and Belgium. This itinerary totalled 1347.8 miles and by the time we arrived home I had driven 2248.6 miles, averaging 12.22 mpg. Two-and-a-half litres of Castrol GTX had been used. The astonishing acceleration and high-speed cruising I had experienced on the Mulsanne Turbo were there for the asking, but the added joy of being able to drive with absolute confidence 20 mph faster through curves and S-bends was immense. (Incidentally, my daughter, who has never been able to travel in a post-war Crewe product – with the possible exception of 'Olga' – without feeling sick, professed herself completely unaffected in this way in the Turbo R.)

I have only two criticisms of the car – the relatively limited amount of luggage space and the excessive wind noise in the higher speed ranges. Four people would be hard put to it to accommodate adequate luggage for a couple of weeks away from home. There were three of us; the boot was full and one bag rode on the vacant seat. The depth of the boot from front to back – such a boon in the models preceding the Silver Spirit/Mulsanne range – has been reduced to accommodate the petrol tank amidships and thus to conform with the law in many countries.

As to wind noise – I am afraid Turbo R owners will have to lump it until a new body shape is produced, as it seems that any material improvement on the 'barn door' now being pushed through the air is beyond any coachbuilder's 'tweaks'! It will be interesting to see how the new Continental R fares in this respect.

Buxton and around

With its fondness for anniversaries, it was inconceivable that the Bentley Drivers Club should let pass its fiftieth birthday without a number of celebratory happenings. The week bracketing the end of June and the beginning of July 1986 was designated Golden Jubilee Week, and provided drivers with many opportunities to show, drive and extol their Bentleys. It started with the annual Concours in Kensington Gardens on the Saturday, followed the next day by joining the Brooklands Society's Reunion at the famous track where the club started life in 1936. Some 70 members and relatives travelling from overseas in their luxury coach stopped off on the way at Cobham for introductory refreshments to the week's goings-on.

The motoring backbone of the week comprised 'Snowball Runs' to Buxton in Derbyshire, i.e. suggested routes from various places terminating in Buxton, which members joined at convenient points *en route*, snowballing into a final descent upon the Palace Hotel on the second day. I decided to take part in the Turbo R, and lent my 8-litre to Hugh Young, who was visiting from Canada, with a proviso that I could commandeer it at will. My motoring memories of this Buxton weekend are, firstly, making rapid tours of the surrounding moorland with full complements of passengers anxious to experience the potentialities of the Turbo R, which model was not yet available outside the UK. Secondly, a parking ticket slapped on my windscreen at midnight outside the Pavilion, where I had left the car when I had finished acting as a taxi for several loads of ladies in evening dress who had not relished the prospect of a walk (or a ride in an open Bentley) from hotel to ballroom. Several non-motoring activities were included in the programme – Inter-regional swimming contests, old-time music-hall, etc., but there was plenty to occupy the drivers too – a *concours d'elegance* and driving tests at Chatsworth, a scatter rally and a scenic run, and regularity runs at Oulton Park. By the time I reached home the

Turbo R had done 630 miles – I did not enquire too closely into the mileage covered by the 8-litre!

France and Switzerland again

With just over 10,000 miles on the car we set off again for the south of France in September 1986 following the direct autoroutes, but, in deference to my travelling companions, breaking the journey overnight at the Hostellerie de la Poste in Avallon. The return run was made by the Route Napoléon to Grenoble and, after an overnight stop at the Ombremont Hotel at Le Bourget-du-Lac, we joined a party of Bentley owners, resident in Switzerland, for lunch at the Vieux Manoir au Lac at Meyriez-Murten. Then we drove to Brussels for the express purpose of visiting the Mahy's newly-opened automobile museum. Many will remember this great collection of cars just after World War Two when it was housed in the converted circus building in Ghent. It is now displayed in an impressive museum-type building and has been augmented by the collection of the late Charlie De Pauw. It comprises 400 vehicles, mostly on the ground floor, but many more on the spacious balcony which affords an impressive view of the assembled machinery below. This is now known as 'Autoworld' and the curator is Ivan Mahy, whose father, Ghislain, amassed the collection and devoted his life to the authentic restoration of the cars.

The round trip totalled 2,218 miles and the Turbo R consumed 145.6 gallons of petrol at the rate of one gallon every 12.87 miles. The following month – October saw us crossing the Channel again, this time bound for Luxembourg.

Luxembourg

Luxembourg – 'brake hard on crossing the frontier or you will be out of the country on the other side' – so say the cynics. Ask any of the three score enthusiasts (and their passengers) who drove their interesting British cars there and back in a weekend and they will tell you what an attractive country it is – especially when the autumn colours enhance the thickly-wooded slopes. The reason for their trip to the Duchy was an invitation from the British Ambassador extended to the members of several UK motor clubs to participate in a 'Britain in Luxembourg' promotion. Roger Moran, then an enthusiastic Morgan owner (and now a Bentley owner) resident in Brussels, acceded to a request to organize the gathering and, with the help of the following clubs: Aston-Martin Owners Club; Bentley Drivers Club; Jaguar Drivers Club; Morgan Sports-Car Club; Rolls-Royce Enthusiasts Club and the Vintage Sports-Car Club; mustered as fine a selection of products of the British motor-car industry as one could hope to see on such an occasion. They ranged from a 1925 Rolls-Royce Phantom I to the latest Bentley Turbo R (mine), later to be joined by a new Jaguar.

Con and I joined the convoy of over 60 cars sailing from Ramsgate on 'Sally' to Dunkerque, on a Friday morning at the end of October 1986, to commence a 250-mile sprint to Luxembourg in time for a cocktail party to mark the inauguration of the 'Britain in Luxembourg' exhibition by HRH the Duke of Kent, and in the presence of HRH Crown Prince Henri of Luxembourg.

Despite the short time available after our arrival at the Inter-Continental Hotel, the ladies changed into dresses appropriate to a royal occasion, and the drivers complied with the request to drive their cars to the Novotel where the function was to take place. The occasion was a great disappointment – not the fault of Roger Moran, but of our hosts, who had made no provision for the parking of the cars, supposedly an important British element in this affair, and then neglected to collect invitations or check the names of guests – for there was no receiving line. Instead of the expected ambassadorial cocktail party, one found oneself squeezing through a crowd of Luxembourgers in a trade fair and lucky to find a refill for the glass proffered at the door. The lights failed and had not been restored when we left some time later – and the royal 'minders' must have been having kittens.

Back at the otherwise excellent Inter-Continental Hotel the two restaurants were unable to cope with the numbers wanting dinner and there was much to-ing and fro-ing in taxis between downtown restaurants and the hotel.

The next day called for participation in a cavalcade – motorcade, surely – through the city, but the embassy would accept only seven cars, leaving the remaining 60 or so drivers back at the hotel to amuse themselves as best they might. Poor recognition for the 800–1,000 miles round trip driven voluntarily to show the flag. Admittedly, no more than the few selected cars could have been accommodated in the small section of the busy market-place allocated for the purpose, but then we followed a military band to a nearby square which could easily have contained *all* the cars and, if publicized, would have attracted hundreds of interested citizens.

However, from then on Roger was free from diplomatic restraints and everything went extremely well. In the afternoon, the whole contingent motored along the flooded Moselle valley to a wine-tasting by courtesy of the Wormeldange Wine Co-operative, followed by an excellent lunch. The evening was enlivened by dinner and dancing as guests of the hotel. Brian Tustain, of the AMOC, speaking on behalf of the clubs, thanked our hosts and all concerned for the part they played in making the weekend a success, especially Roger Moran who, in the face of considerable difficulties, had achieved a possibly unique gathering of six marque clubs.

Despite the creaks in the organization, everyone voted the weekend an enjoyable social and motoring occasion, during which existing friendships were complemented by new cross-marque relationships. For the record – the Turbo R clocked up 811 miles consuming petrol at the rate of a gallon every $12\frac{3}{4}$ miles and it took $2\frac{1}{4}$ litres of Castrol GTX to bring the oil level up to 'MAX' on arriving home.

These Continental journeys served to endorse my high opinion of the car. My motoring friends must by now have tired of my repetitive eulogies, though I must say that I have not noticed any of them refusing an opportunity to ride with me. One long-standing friend – a discerning motorist if ever there was one – who had an enviable collection of cars (mostly high-performance ones of German and Italian origin) had never been tempted to buy a post-war Crewe product. He had a Silver Ghost, but contentedly stared through a three-pointed star when on his everyday outings. On acquiring a Turbo R I thought to myself that this car must elicit a positive response from my 'anti-Roller' friend and I took him briskly through the roads and lanes of Sussex. He *was* tremendously impressed and wrote to me afterwards that, if it had not been for a medical setback, he would have bought one the next day! Such a response from this quarter was, I think, the supreme accolade for the Turbo R.

Switzerland and on

In June 1988 the Bentley Drivers Club organized a tour to Switzerland. Con and I decided to join on the outward run in the Turbo R and peel off at Lausanne to continue our holiday on the Riviera. This event attracted over 30 Bentleys, of which one-third were from outside the UK, and a coach was to follow the tour for the benefit of those unable to field a PMC (proper motor car). We started a day after the main body, crossed from Dover to Calais and turned north-eastwards on unfamiliar roads towards Huizen, near Amsterdam, 200 miles away. The whole party was entertained that evening by Paul and Josine Veenhuijzen in their beautiful house and garden. (No wonder it was commandeered by the Gestapo during the Occupation, for most of the Bentleys were lost on more than one occasion between the hotel and the house – and they had maps!)

On the way to Maastricht the next day we were scheduled to lunch at a place called Thorn on the Belgian border. This, too, proved elusive and we found lunch laid on at the restaurant next door to the one prescribed in the navigational instructions! I distinguished myself in the car-park at the Golden Tulip Hotel in Maastricht when, moving the Turbo R to facilitate the manœuvres of another visitor, I scraped the driver's door on an unseen concrete flower pot. I was pleased to find that a rally plaque placed carefully over the damage proved a complete disguise and saved embarrassing questions and wisecracks from then on.

From Maastricht one was free to take a route of one's choice to the Novotel in Saarbrücken some 300 miles away. We elected to go into Aachen to meet an old friend for 'elevenses' and then to follow the Rhine Valley to Bingen. Others visited the Nurburgring in the Eifel Mountains and put in a lap or two on this historic circuit. Next day, on the way to the Mövenpick Hotel at a place called Egerkingen, south of Basle, some went via Molsheim to see the one-time Bugatti works and other memorabilia in the town. The following day called for a short drive to Berne, and the ever-obliging coach driver volunteered to go back to Mulhouse for those who wished to visit the ex-Schlumpf Museum before heading for the capital city. We lunched next day at Murtens, on the way to Berne, where we stayed at the excellent Hotel Bellevue Palace, which I had last visited in the days when the Swiss Grand Prix was run through the wooded Bremgarten circuit. The gala dinner and dance there in the evening, following a reception given by Rolls-Royce Motors International, was the highlight of the tour's three days in Switzerland.

Our enjoyment of this tour was enhanced by the fact that our daughter Carol, and her husband Roger, were taking part in their first Continental run in their $3\frac{1}{2}$-litre Bentley, which had emerged from a rebuild, spread over twenty years, to win its class at Kensington Gardens. We had seen something of each other on the road, but travelled separately most of the time, joining up in the evenings to compare experiences. Proceeding leisurely through the Alsatian country-side we entered the town of Marckolsheim and

were pleased to see the $3\frac{1}{2}$-litre ahead, stopped in the main street. Our joy was short-lived when we found that, when making a U-turn after stopping to buy cheese rolls, there had been a sudden scraping of metal on metal and Roger knew that he had suffered a serious derangement in the back axle. We transferred Roger and Carol and their luggage into the Turbo R and pushed the disabled Bentley into a nearby garage for safe-keeping until transportation home could be arranged.

The next day the now car-less Salters regretfully took a train to Zurich to fly home, having to abandon the tour and the rest of their planned holiday.

We continued on the rally route to Lausanne and, after spending the night at the Mövenpick Hotel on the lakeside at Ouchy, took our leave of the others who were turning northwards for home. We went through the Great St Bernard tunnel, round Turin and over the Col de Tende to Eze, where the trip recorder showed that we had covered 1,472 miles since leaving Cobham. Our return journey via the Autoroutes 8, 7, 6, 1 and 26 provided the effortless, comfortable, fast motoring which is the hallmark of the Turbo R. The mileage on mainland Europe totalled 2,436 and the fuel consumption averaged 13.19 mpg – 14.28 on the leisurely outward leg; only 10 mpg during 94 miles in and around Nice; and 13.61 on the faster homeward run.

Millbrook

On 1 October 1988 I was invited to Millbrook by Rolls-Royce Motor Cars to try out their current models. Millbrook – the proving ground constructed by General Motors for Vauxhall/Bedford, but now operated by a separate company under the Lotus umbrella – covers 700 acres of Bedfordshire countryside. It includes a variety of terrain and surfaces laid out to provide a Hill Route and a City Course; and, of special interest on this day, a level Mile Straight and a High Speed Circuit. The latter is a circular, banked track, five lanes wide, having a length of 2.7966 miles, which permits continuous running at the maximum speed of most of today's production cars. Among the cars available to guests the star attraction was the Turbo R. The engines of these cars never stopped, as disembarking drivers were eagerly replaced by others keen to experience the performance of this model. We were encouraged to drive on the various circuits and the Mile Straight, but not on the High Speed Circuit where prudence dictated that cars be driven only by the manufacturer's test drivers.

I was driven round at the top of the banking for several laps at a sustained speed of 150 mph by Derek Rowland, who had not long before put up a record there, covering 140.91 miles in one hour. I found this experience both educational and exhilarating. As the neutral 'hands off' speed rating of this part of the track is 100 mph, circulating at 150 mph calls for experience and unwavering concentration. (That's why we weren't allowed at the wheel.)

All change
By this time my Turbo R was three years old and had covered 26,000 miles. A number of important changes had been made in the specification of the model during that time, including Bosch fuel injection (in place of the Solex carburettor) and the Bosch anti-locking braking system. Additionally, changes to the engine structure involved substantially stiffening the engine/gearbox interface to improve driveline smoothness at high speed, and introducing a cross-bolted crankcase to further reduce noise on acceleration. The Bosch 'Motronic' digital engine management system replaced the KE2 Jetronic system and an inter-cooler was added between the turbocharger and the inlet manifold. These changes allowed the engine to run on 95-octane unleaded fuel and for catalysts to be fitted on cars exported to countries where these are required by law. The engine management system is self-adjusting to recognize the fuel rating and no formal adjustments are necessary.

My Turbo R was super, but it is only natural

that my thoughts should turn to ways and means of updating this desirable mode of transport. For some time I had been considering disposing of my well-known 8-litre Bentley (UL 7) after 17 years of ownership and taking this step was the only possible way of contemplating the purchase of the latest Turbo R: the die was cast. The 8-litre passed into the ownership of Bill Woodward, than whom there could be no more appreciative and caring custodian for the next years of its existence.

Just before parting with my first Turbo R I experienced a not-always appreciated disadvantage of anti-locking braking systems. I was travelling up the M1 amongst heavy, fast-moving traffic in all three lanes. Perceiving some unorthodox behaviour of the traffic ahead I braked and came to a stop behind the car in front of me (which had also come to rest) only to be shunted in the rear by the following car, whose driver was unable to stop in time – and he in turn was then given a nudge by the car following him. Until such time as all cars have ABS, it is wise for drivers so privileged to brake so that they come to stop at the last possible moment, rather than as soon as possible, only to watch the inevitably unstoppable vehicle behind growing larger in the rear-view mirror until the moment of impact.

The Continent on Turbo R Number 2
I took delivery of my second Turbo R in October 1988 and in the following June set off again for the Continent. (Non-European readers may not realize that, although part of Europe, we insular Brits refer to mainland Europe as 'the Continent'.) This trip was virtually a re-run of the 1985 outward journey to Eze-sur-mer and the return through Ascona to Interlaken. Thereafter we crossed into France to Basle following the autoroute (A35) to its end at Ste Croix-en-Plaine, south of Colmar, and then drove on into the congested centre of Strasbourg for lunch. On leaving the city we eschewed the access to the A4 and cut off a corner via the N4 to join the autoroute near Saverne, staying on this for 76

48 *Our latest transportation (the second Turbo R) at Cap Estel – June 1989*

miles until we reached the intersection with A31 north of Metz, which we then took to reach our night-stop at Thionville, 12 miles to the north.

The next morning we high-tailed it for Calais 300 miles away. Leaving Thionville at 9.43 am we rejoined the A4 19 minutes later and, following this autoroute to Reims and then A26 all the way, we reached the docks at Calais at 2.45 pm, having stopped for 1 hour 17 minutes for lunch and petrol near St Quentin. The distance from the hotel to the ferry was 301.8 miles, which had taken 3¾ hours driving time, i.e. an average speed of 80.5 mph. The petrol consumption for the round trip of 2128 miles was 13.7 mpg.

February 1990 saw another speedy journey – this time to Paris to visit the annual Classic car show 'Retromobile' – averaging a mite over the limit from Calais to Le Bourget.

In August 1990, with another journey to the south of France on the agenda, I decided to try a different route. Having driven from Paris to Calais earlier in the year by way of the 'old' main road (N1 as it was), and finding it relatively traffic-free and a pleasant alternative to the autoroutes A26 and A1, I chose that route for the first leg of our journey.

I planned to keep to the west of Paris, Lyon and the Rhône Valley instead of taking the usual route on the eastern side. I elected to spend the first night at the Novotel at La Source just south of Orléans – 271 miles and 5 hours 10 minutes driving time from Calais. This route involved some tricky navigating round Paris after leaving the N1 at L'Isle d'Adam on to the N184, skirting Pontoise and then following signs to St Germain-en-Laye and Versailles, crossing the A11 to N191, and going on to the N10 round Rambouillet to join the autoroute (A10) at Allainville for Orléans.

Resuming our journey towards the Camargue the next morning, we took the A71, which was by then opened for 304 kms (190 miles), as far as Clermont-Ferrand, and gave us some excellent motoring. (If time pressed we could have continued from Clermont-Ferrand by autoroute A72 to St Etienne and the A47, to join the familiar A7 near Vienne.) We chose to leave on the N9 to Issoire and thereafter drive through the hilly country via St Flour, Mende, Alés and Nîmes to our overnight destination at Castillon-du-Gard, 25 miles short of Arles. The reason for this choice was a long-cherished wish to see the nearby Pont-du-Gard – the famous Roman aqueduct constructed on three tiers of arches – and we were not disappointed. The motorist may drive across the bridge on a road built into and alongside the top of the lower tier of arches – the intrepid pedestrian may cross on the unprotected top!

The next day, in torrential rain, we opted to take secondary roads through the Camargue in the – alas, forlorn – hope of seeing some of the horses associated with this part of France, to join the A55 near Martigues leading to the A7 at Aix-en-Province and so to Eze. This was an itinerary which made a pleasant change and when the autoroute from Clermont-Ferrand is completed to Montélimar will afford an alternative quick way to the Midi.

Having made the outward trip by a route to the west of the main drag I decided to return on the opposite side. This meant following the Route Napoléon (N85) from Nice to Grenoble, then travelling by the A480 and A41 past Chambéry and Annecy, leaving the autoroute at the exit for Cruseilles (7 kms beyond the Annecy Nord exit) and through the outskirts of Geneva into France again to Divonne-les-Bains, 12 miles to the north. Here the beautifully situated Château de Divonne ranks as a gourmet stopover and is very conveniently located for departure over the Col de la Faucille on the N5 for Dijon. From there we took the autoroute (A31) as far as Chaumont and were disappointed to find – contrary to our advance information – that the onward A26 to Troyes had not been opened. When this section is in use – and the further length to Reims – it will be possible to drive all the way from Calais to Dijon by autoroute without going anywhere near Paris. We spent the second night at the Royal Champagne at Champillon near Epernay and took the opportunity to visit the caves of Mercier to see the biggest barrel in the world, which has a capacity of 200,000 bottles of champagne!

This tour totalled 2066.6 miles and consumed 150.39 gallons of various brands of Super Unleaded 98 octane petrol at an equivalent UK price of £2.64p per gallon. At 13.74 mpg this means 19 pence – or to my generation nearly four shillings – per mile for petrol alone. What is it they say – 'No pleasure comes without pain'? A significant improvement over my first Turbo R was that of oil consumption, which was virtually nil.

Describing one's fast journeys in these days of speed limits in most countries presents some difficulties to the writer. My view has always been that speed of itself does not cause accidents, but it should be indulged in only when certain preconditions are satisfied. These are: the right road and traffic conditions; the right driver; the right car; and the right weather. If all these factors apply then, at the right time, driving fast is not the lethal, murderous activity that some would have us believe. Motorway traffic in the UK, in reasonable conditions, moves along in the mid-eighties – miles per hour, that is. No greater danger arises when a suitable car is driven a lot faster than that by a competent driver, but let there be no misunderstanding; I hold no brief for the idiot driver speeding at the wrong time, and any relaxation or abolition of speed limits should, in my opinion, be countered by increased

policing and penalties for bad driving. Having expressed that view, no one will be under the delusion that I have never exceeded 70 mph in this country, or the corresponding speed limits abroad – especially in my Turbo R, whose natural gait is such that 'dropping back to the ton' becomes commonplace. Specifically, I have driven in excess of that figure for considerable distances on the Continent – would 165 miles in 90 minutes cause you to suspend belief? – but never in circumstances where other road users have been inconvenienced, much less endangered. Since I acquired my present Turbo R further modifications have been made, the chief of which, from the driver's point of view, must be the automatic ride control. This achieves the best of both worlds – a more comfortable ride under normal driving, but Turbo R handling characteristics when required. Three damper settings are available ('comfort', 'normal' and 'firm') and these are selected, entirely automatically, in as little as 1/100th of a second by a micro-processor responding to vertical, lateral, and longitudinal accelerometers, and braking and steering inputs. I guess it sees the bumps and holes before the driver!

Nought to ten feet

The story behind an unusual statistic has emerged from the US Government Agency which puts cars through the Type Approval tests. This is that the Bentley Turbo R is the quickest car they have ever tested – from 0 to 10 feet. Yes, 10 feet from a standing start! What this means, of course, is that the tremendous torque of the $6\frac{3}{4}$-litre turbocharged engine is actually put on to the road by virtue of the weight of the car and the width of the tyres. Quite something to be able to beat *anything* from the lights!

49 *Arriving at Castillon-du-Gard. Ground clearance $6\frac{1}{2}$in. – wall clearance about the same! – August 1990*

For the record – my Avon 255/65 VR15 Turbospeed CR 27 R/5 tubeless tyres have given excellent service. They do not lose pressure and still have 3 mm of tread after 15,000 miles. Good job too, as the 'retail list' price is £411.90 *each*!

The future?

The media have kept alive the persistent rumour and guesswork about the 'next' Bentley: what it would be like and when it would appear. The company stole a march on everybody by introducing the new Continental R Bentley at the Geneva Motor Show in March 1991 – a whole year before even the best-informed were expecting it.

History has repeated itself after a lapse of 40 years since the advent of the R-type Continental, in that it is a two-door saloon, the body being a steel pressing, whereas the H.J. Mulliner 'fastback' saloon was hand-made of aluminium alloy. It is also to be built in limited numbers – 280 in the first year of production – and deliveries are not likely to commence before the third quarter of 1991.

The engine and chassis specifications are basically the same as the current Turbo R with the exception of the transmission. The 3-speed gearbox has been superseded by a 4-speed box in which third is direct drive and fourth acts as an overdrive. With a lower rear axle ratio and one-inch diameter larger wheels, the overall ratio in overdrive is only fractionally higher than that in third (i.e. top) of the Turbo R.

The price foreseen when the Continental R reaches the market is about £160,000 – a lot of money even in a Rolls-Royce context.

For my part, although I enjoyed so many miles at the wheel of 'Olga', I am not enamoured with two-door coachwork except in cars intended to carry only two persons. One gets all the comfort and amenities of the more expensive (inevitably) two-door models without their disadvantages when owning a standard four-door saloon. Why risk being dragged out of the car when opening one of the very wide doors in a high wind? No woman has the strength to close the passenger door from the inside when the car is parked on a cambered road – all right, I know the driver should be gallant and do it for her from the outside – he may have to because the door is so wide that it scrapes the pavement when the car is leaning only slightly towards the kerb. In two-door cars driver and passenger have to be contortionists to find and fix the seat-belts; and rear-seat passengers to get in and out, and that is after his fellow-travellers in the front seats have dismounted to permit such ingress or egress. And not everyone has a garage that is as wide as it is long to avoid having to climb out through the sunshine roof!

The two-door format is said to be essential if the body-designer (stylist?) is to achieve a pleasing roof-line. One wonders if any of those responsible have ever looked at the roof-line when the hood of a convertible is (ostensibly) stowed! Most of them even today – and this applies to the products of Crewe – have an ugly foot high lump behind the seat.

Personally, with the UK price in 1991 having increased by 62.2 per cent over the basic price of the Turbo R of £68,831 when introduced six years ago, I cannot realistically foresee any prospect of further updating my transportation.

The reader will have gathered that the Turbo R *is* my ultimate dream car – Rolls-Royce comfort with Ferrari performance – what more could one ask?

And I count myself privileged indeed to have owned one at the same time as my 8-litre Bentley, for they made a magnificent pair and gave me the best of Vintage and modern motoring over a number of years.

Metric musings

I am opposed to many of our national customs and standards being 'harmonized' out of existence by the EEC into some unfamiliar common denominator with a dozen other countries, but my opposition does not extend to the adoption of kilometres as a measure of distance – especially on our roads. Its use is, of course, well-established in many countries – even continents – outside the Common Market and probably the majority of UK drivers have had experience of the kilometre on the 'Continent'.

I am concerned, however, that the anti-motoring lobby would regard the change as an opportunity to seek to vary the speed limits by rounding-off downwards. As 30 mph equates to 48.28 kph there would be a cry for 45 kph; similarly for 70 mph (112.65 kph) to become 110 kph.

Thinking motorists would opt for an upwards approximation, but I would go further and suggest that all existing speed limits expressed in mph should be doubled in terms of kph. This would mean that the present 30 mph limit would become 60 kph (i.e. 37.28 mph) and the 70 mph one 140 kph (86.99 mph), thus bringing the present legal 'fiction' into the realm of reality.

If legislation were then introduced authorizing the numbers on existing speed-limit signs to be doubled *mentally* to indicate the revised limit in kph, pending the erection of new signs, it would enable the thousands of signs to be replaced over a period of time instead of overnight, with a resulting large saving in cost.

I suppose we could cling to our present method of expressing petrol consumption in terms of distance to quantity, which would mean kilometres per litre, but the litre is too small a unit for comparison in common usage. The metric method of expressing consumption in terms of litres per 100 kilometres makes more sense, but would take some getting used to. (Incidentally, to convert mpg (Imperial) to litres per 100 km, divide the mpg into 282.5.)

My other cars

The 'Merc' in my life

Acquisition

By a stroke of good fortune an ambition of many years was realized when I acquired my Mercedes at the end of 1960. I was lunching with Lord Montagu at Beaulieu on the occasion of a Bentley Drivers Club gathering and was introduced to a fellow guest from South Africa, Count Luccio Labia, and learnt that two De Dietrich cars referred to by 'Peterborough' in the 'Daily Telegraph' a few days earlier were owned by his mother.

These two cars of 1903 and 1905 had been put into a furniture depository, together with other family possessions, by Luccio's grandfather, Sir Joseph Robinson, when he returned to his native South Africa before World War I, and had remained untouched ever since. Luccio's mother, Princess Labia, had taken the family's fabulous collection of pictures out of store and Luccio, already the proud owner of more than one Vintage car in South Africa, was set on restoring the cars and using them. He was, however, returning to his home in South Africa and wanted the restoration done here. Ronald ('Steady') Barker and I undertook the unenviable task of arranging and supervising the restorations. There were many pitfalls along this road but when finished, both cars were in 'as new' condition. The 1905 car went to Cape Town and was enjoyed by Luccio for many years; the 1903 one was lent to the Montagu Museum and has been driven by the owner on several Brighton runs since.

What has all this to do with the Merc? Well, on one of his visits to England Luccio mentioned that there was another car belonging to the family in a house near Brighton. My eyes lit up at news of a big Edwardian, and when the car was brought up to the depository in London 'Steady' and I, with Maurice Smith, then Editor of the 'Autocar', went to look at the Mercedes. It was extremely dusty, and a bit battered. The aluminium steering wheel was smashed and the wooden rim lay in pieces on the floor. The windscreen was broken and the tyres were flat and iron-hard. We could see that it was substantially all there and would make a wonderful car if restored properly. Luccio decided that he did not want to take on another restoration job and offered the car to 'Steady' and me jointly for a nominal price. 'Steady' was planning the restoration of a Napier and reluctantly opted out. I couldn't believe my luck when I found myself the owner of a 1910 Mercedes with large closed bodywork. It was a dream come true.

I went to work enthusiastically to learn all I could about the car and to plan its restoration. I had neither the knowledge nor the facilities to undertake the job myself, and count myself fortunate that Louis Giron agreed to deal with the mechanical side; Leslie Willis, who had been trying for years to retire from coachbuilding to farm quietly in Kent, was persuaded to do just one more job for me.

Whilst waiting for Louis to start work I wrote to Dr Schildberger, then Curator of the Daimler-Benz Museum at Stuttgart, giving the Serial number of the car and asking if he could identify the model and establish the date of manufacture from his records. He replied that the Mercedes was a type 28/50 PS and that it had been delivered to their agents in Düsseldorf on the 20 December 1910.

The specification of the car soon emerged from inspection and contemporary literature. Known as the 45/50 hp model in this country, it had a four-cylinder engine with a bore of 120 mm and stroke of 160 mm giving a capacity of 7,241 cc, the T-head cylinders being cast in pairs. The carburettor, of Mercedes manufacture, was fed from a pressurized tank at the rear. Before starting the engine one worked vigorously at a hand pump, air pressure thereafter being maintained by an exhaust-driven pump. The Bosch Dual Ignition comprised a trembler coil (used only for starting) and a magneto. Usually the engine would start from cold on the switch once the cylinders had been primed and the engine

50 *Twins – the 'tulip' back coachwork is by J.A. Lawton – a 1911 Silver Ghost Rolls-Royce in front of the author's 1910 Mercedes*

turned over a few compressions. I did this by exerting all my weight on the starting handle through my foot. Although not strong enough to swing the engine on full compression, I could do so without undue strain on half compression. This is arranged by pulling a handle conveniently located under the radiator, which lift the exhaust valves.

Very unusual is the scroll-type clutch, which comprises a spring coiled around a drum, within a cylinder lubricated at will by the driver. When the clutch pedal is depressed, the spring is compressed and the resulting increase in diameter brings the spring away from the outer surface of the drum, thus disconnecting the engine from the gear-box. This works very well indeed, but after changing gear one must allow

the clutch time to become fully engaged before pressing the accelerator again, otherwise there is juddering and slip. The only disadvantage of this type of clutch is that the engine cannot be started by towing the car in gear and engaging the clutch in the usual way; the coil then tends to unwind and will not transmit the drive from road wheels to engine.

A contemporary catalogue gives the range of engine revolutions as 300 to 1,250 per minute.

The gate-change gear-box has four speeds, and this car must be one of the first Mercedes to have a propellor shaft drive instead of the sprockets and chains that were used at least up to the 1908 models. There is an arrangement for water-cooling the drum of the transmission foot-brake, but this was disconnected when the car came out of storage and has not been re-connected. The handbrake works internal expanding cast iron shoes (later relined with Ferodo) in the rear wheel drums. All wheels were fitted with 935×135 beaded edge tyres, although the catalogue refers to 915×105 for the front wheels.

The body is an elegant open-drive limousine by J.A. Lawton & Co. and is notable for the double-curved back – sometimes called the 'tulip' back. I know of only one other similar body, on a 1911 Silver Ghost, owned for many years by Fred Watson and built by the same firm. The Merc. is 7 ft 6 ins high and weighs 1 ton $19\frac{1}{4}$ cwt. The price of the Chassis was 16,500 Marks ex Works (about £825) which is some £160 less than the Rolls-Royce Silver Ghost of the period.

Restoration

The Mercedes bore the Registration No. 'XB 6193' on a crumpled number plate and an earlier number 'P 8462' painted on the radiator honeycomb, barely discernible. It was the latter number which Surrey Council agreed to revive for the car, despite all their records of that time having been destroyed. (On several occasions after that when the sunlight fell on the radiator from a certain angle, I was convinced that the

51 *The 1910 Mercedes arriving at Weybridge after being off the road for forty years*

fading number was actually 'P 6462' but did nothing further about it.)

On the 4 March 1961, Adam Bros. of Kingston winched the car on to a low-loader and transported it to a garage at the back of the Oatlands Park Hotel, Weybridge, where Louis set to work, the doors of his own workshop nearby not being high enough to admit it.

Our first attack was on the tyres, which had to be removed from the rims with a hacksaw. It proved impossible to obtain 935 × 135 covers; the 880 × 120 cover fits the same rim and I decided to use this size on the front wheels. The informed consensus suggested that these tyres would be too narrow in section for the rear wheels and that it would be better to use 895 × 135, which were still in the Dunlop range. To implement this decision the two rear wheels had to be reduced in diameter, and the work was entrusted to Thomas Tingley, Limited of 92, Brandon Street, Walworth, London, S.E.17, one of the few wheelwrights still around who

would undertake this sort of job. Once the new dimensions were calculated it was a simple matter to cut a piece out of the detachable rims, re-roll them to the new circle, and then to weld the ends together.

The wheels themselves were quite another matter. They were wooden-spoked and the iron rim had one side bent up at right angles and the other side down. Thus, they could not be rolled to a new contour when cut and shortened, and they had to be cut into two semi-circles and reshaped to a template before being welded into a circle again. New felloes were made and fitted to the shortened spokes. The detachable rims were originally secured to the wheels by eight bolts and wedges. One of these disappeared when the rims were cut down, and to respace the remaining bolts, with or without the insertion of another one, was really out of the question. So the rear wheels then had seven securing bolts, two of them more widely-spaced than the rest; this arrangement gave no trouble whatsoever.

I could not afford to have the chassis and engine stripped down to the last nut and bolt and then rebuilt from the ground up. The compromise I decided upon was to make sure that the mechanical side was superficially clean and working safely and efficiently, and to give the coachwork the full treatment inside and out.

Louis Giron, with characteristic thoroughness and painstaking care, began the long task of examining and restoring to full working order every mechanical part of the car without, if possible, dismantling the engine. This had seized solid, but yielded to a soaking in Redex and after a few days could be turned freely by hand. We were pleased to find that the radiator was neither blocked nor leaking. Work proceeded slowly but surely. Every oil pipe was cleaned out and its function ascertained; petrol and air lines and the petrol tank cleaned and tested, and so on. The magneto was sent away to be overhauled and re-magnetized, but the Bosch coil presented more difficulty. I could find no one who would re-wind it and wrote to Stuttgart in despair. Imagine my surprise when Dr Schildberger wrote to say that Bosch were sending me a replacement, but pointed out that '. . . they could not say in advance how long a product that was manufactured about fifty years ago will continue to work satisfactorily.' They also sent a wiring diagram and made no charge. The coil was fitted, and was still working perfectly when I sold the car.

The radiator cap was missing, so a new one was manufactured from brass and 'Woodite', based on photographs of Bill Cook's 1908 Mercedes radiator cap and an impression in dental wax of the internal thread of the radiator filler. I must digress here to refer to the radiator badge. This was in the form of a circular medallion bearing the name 'Daimler Motoren Gesellschaft' round the periphery and 'Mercedes' across the centre. Dr Schildberger could not understand why the car did not bear the three-pointed star which came into use in 1909, and

we did not discover the reason until a knowledgeable member of the Mercedes-Benz Club said to me, 'I see your car is an English delivery.' He then explained that he knew this by the circular radiator badge, which was fitted to all Mercedes delivered in this country at that time, because the Star Motor Company objected to the use of the three-pointed star. My informant went on to say that if I prised off the badge I would find the three-pointed star underneath. Not wishing to do any damage to satisfy my curiosity, I removed the radiator cap, and peered hopefully into the radiator. Sure enough, the star was embossed on the radiator just where the medallion covered it. I spent quite a time after this examining files and letters at the Patent Office and, although finding nothing to show that anyone had objected to the use of the three-pointed star on cars in England, I feel sure that the covering up of the manufacturer's trade mark must have resulted from something of the sort.

Then one day Louis said to me 'I am going to start her up tomorrow morning.' And he did – just like that. The exhaust manifold was off and the noise of the engine, running on its 40-year-old plugs, was music to our ears.

Soon after – on Remembrance Day 1961 to be exact – the car was driven for the first time, a trouble-free run of 50 miles from Weybridge to Leslie Willis' farm near Gravesend. The body had not been touched, except for repairing the steering wheel and replacing the broken plate glass windscreen with laminated glass. The car looked very shabby indeed, but its performance belied its appearance. It was to spend the winter at Leslie's for coachwork restoration.

The old finish was removed to the bare metal and coat after coat of paint was applied, the final one being varnished three or four times. The colour used for most of the body was ruby with the upper part black, and yellow lining added where appropriate.

The cloth upholstery and head linings in the rear compartment were stripped out and redone in similar material. Blinds, cords, window straps, etc. were all renewed as near to the original as possible; the silk tassels and buttons were made by an old lady of eighty. A new carpet was made for the back, and white ribbed rubber matting found for the front floor. Interior fittings were re-nickelled, the windows replaced with toughened glass, and the front seats recovered in black leather. This work went on through the winter and each visit to see the progress being made heightened the anticipation of the day when the Merc. would take the road again, as good as new.

Meantime, I conducted a search for lamps and a horn, for none of these were with the car when it was brought out of its resting place. Louis Holland found for me a beautiful pair of 'Rushmore' Searchlights and 'King of the Road' side and tail lamps. The headlamps could have been connected up to the acetylene cylinder in the polished wooden box on the running-board, and the oil lamps made to work. As I had no plans for after-dark driving in the Merc. I decided not to use the old lamps for lighting, but merely for appearance. The car had a small battery to operate the coil and Louis ran hidden wires to almost invisible sockets at the foot of the bulkhead and to the bottom of the body at the rear. If I am inadvertently caught out on the road after dark, I put four rubber diver's helmet lamps, two white and two red, on the side and tail lamp brackets, plug them in and I had legal get-you-home lighting.

'Steady' Barker let me have one of a pair of flat trumpet horns which had come with his Napier. I spent a long time trying to locate a suitable speaking tube and mouthpiece to connect to the brass earpiece behind the driver's head. I eventually found a firm which supplied tubing and fittings for ambulances. Their colour range was limited, but Leslie removed the woven outer covering and recovered it with the material used for the upholstery, and he even found an authentic mouthpiece with a tiny bulb-horn to attract the driver's attention.

At last, on 8 April 1962, I went down to Meopham to collect the finished car. It looked magnificent and was a credit to Leslie. It was a proud cortège that accompanied the Merc. back to Cobham.

Realization
All old cars interest me from an historical point of view, but I would not want to own a veteran car which had no other merit than its technical or historical interest. I had always wanted a big Edwardian which would be powerful enough and reliable enough to take its place as a means of transport in modern traffic conditions. And now I was the proud owner of such a car.

The Merc. always stood ready for the road at any time and I used it as the spirit moved. I would drive it anywhere I would drive a modern car; it would take longer and manoeuvring would be more difficult, but everything else would be taken in its stride. Strangely enough, I found it less frustrating driving the Merc. in quite heavy traffic on the open road than modern cars, for the reason that the Merc. ran right along with the traffic, which always seemed to be travelling between 40 and 50 mph, and the repeated desire to overtake did not arise. The only real hazard arose from the lack of front wheel brakes. One left a greater space, between oneself and the car in front, than would normally be the case and all went well until some selfish driver overtook and crowded in front, reducing by a half the braking distance.

After several shakedown trips I decided to enter some Concours d'Elégance – and I mean just that – competitions in which the elegance of the car was to be judged. If the rules called for the occupants to wear contemporary costume, so much the better. I admired Veteran and Vintage car owners who were able to maintain (or have someone else maintain) their cars in immaculate condition outside, inside, underneath and everywhere else, but this was not for me. It was my practice to maintain and present the Merc. in a bodily clean condition, with the engine only

52 *The Mercedes in a Concours d'Elégance at Crystal Palace, with Con, Carol and Amanda – three generations – and the author in Edwardian costume*

53 *The engine of the 1910 Mercedes, superficially clean and working safely and efficiently*

superficially clean – but, most importantly, in perfect working order.

As to the wearing of costume, I strongly disagreed with the policy of the Veteran Car Club of Great Britain which discouraged 'dressing-up'. I think that one of the gratifying things about owning a veteran car is the obvious pleasure it gives to other motorists and passers-by. If the fear is that costume will manifest the onlookers' enjoyment in the laughter of ridicule, then I have seen more evidence of this on the Brighton Run at some of the all-weather kit worn by some participants which might be more appropriate if they were skin diving or inspecting sewers. By all means keep dry, but don't decry those who go to the trouble to find or make authentic period costume. In my view it is just as meritorious to seek contemporary apparel as it is to seek contemporary accessories. It has also struck me that some of the veteran motorists who decry the wearing of costume are *still* wearing the costume they were wearing in those days anyway, without apparently being aware of it!

I am fortunate in having a wife who enjoys dressing-up, and was quite prepared to don a period chauffeur's uniform to match, when the occasion arose. Our first competition for an elegant combination of car and lady was on the occasion of the Silver Jubilee of the British Automobile Racing Club at Goodwood in July 1962. I entered the 'Day at the Races' class with my daughter, and was placed second, and in 'Motoring in Grandfather's Day' with Con as passenger. The latter combination won this class, also the Prix d'Honneur for the best turn-out of the day.

It had been in my mind from the moment I acquired the Merc. that the best way to fulfil my particular enjoyment of veteran car ownership would be to drive the car back to its birthplace in Stuttgart. And so in May 1963 I took the Merc. to Germany, accompanied by Con, Louis and Barbara Giron and three other friends, with two other cars. Louis took the car via the Dover/

Ostend ferry to meet us after the Speed Trials in Antwerp. The next morning we set off about 9 am and drove via Liège, Aachen, Cologne and Bonn to Linz-am-Rhein. The Merc. had covered 180 miles in the day as a matter of course, and on the following day we drove the remaining 215 miles to Stuttgart, the Merc. cruising happily enough at 50 mph for mile after mile.

It was our misfortune to visit Daimler-Benz AG during their only strike for fifty years and this made the promised tour of the Works impractical. We were, however, welcomed by Dr Schildberger, Prince von Urach and Artur Keser who were delighted that we had made the pilgrimage and admired the Merc. very much indeed. There is no example of this model in the museum and the Merc. was garaged for the night in the museum in a place of honour.

We drove on the test track – eyes straying to a prototype '600' undergoing development – and many photographs were taken.

On the next day, Thursday, we covered 200 miles to Luxembourg. We had only one spot of bother, when the fuel-pump ceased functioning in the centre of Saarbrücken in the evening rush-hour. Some dirt had lodged in the valve and was eventually removed by squirting petrol on it and jiggling it up and down. This was one of the very few troubles which stopped me on the road occasionally – we called it doing a 'Saarbrücken' – and the same cure was always effective. It happened as I was leaving the last Time Control in a Rally the following year and led to some spirited motoring along the Guildford Bypass to reach the Final Control dead on time.

The journey to Ostend on the Friday (205 miles) was notable for very wet weather. The Merc. bowled along regardless and on the Autoroute between Brussels and Ostend covered 49 miles in the hour.

We arrived home safely on Saturday evening, having covered a most enjoyable 1,100 miles in a week. Apart from routine lubrication and adjustment of brakes, the car required no atten-

tion, but Louis did one or two things as a result of experience gained on the Continental journey. These included the dynamic balancing of the flywheel in situ by the addition of weights, and the fitting of a pressure release valve in the radiator overflow to prevent an excessive quantity of water being expelled unnecessarily by the powerful water pump.

Berlin bound

When I learnt that the Allgemeiner Schnauferl*-Club was to hold its 11th Deutsche Schnauferl-Rallye in West Berlin I seized the opportunity to combine a visit to a city on my 'must-be-seen-sometime' list with another sortie with my 1910 Mercedes into the land of its origin.

And so, after giving the Mercedes a thorough checking-over and the cleaning of a lifetime, we left Dover for Ostend on a Belgian ferry during the seamen's strike on Monday, 6 June 1966. I was accompanied by Con, niece Anthea, and Louis Giron, and took my R-Type Con-

tinental Bentley along as a tender car. Disembarking at 4 pm we made for Antwerp where we were to spend the night.

The distance to Berlin was divided into three daily stages of approximately 170 miles each. These stages were dictated partly by the need to cover the autobahn across East Germany from Helmstedt to West Berlin more or less non-stop, and partly by the wïsh to confine our motoring to daylight hours. I knew from experience that the Mercedes could be relied upon to cover between 35 and 40 miles in an hour and thus planned on five to six hours' driving each day on the outward journey. Louis and I took turns driving the Merc. and the Bentley, rarely doing less than 50 miles at a stretch.

Not long after leaving Antwerp, Louis, driving the Merc. around the 50 mph mark· felt the engine getting tight and stopped before it had time to seize up. The engine was tight when turned by hand, but after removing the compression taps and injecting a quantity of oil

* From the verb 'schnaufen': to breathe hard; to snort.

55 *Paul-Heinz Rohll's 1925 Mercedes once owned by Richard Tauber*

into each cylinder, it ran freely and we moved off cautiously into nearby Aachen, giving liberal supplementary squirts of oil into the engine by means of the hand-pump on the dashboard. The engine was now misfiring and this was attributed to the magneto not functioning properly. During lunch the engine cooled sufficiently to enable an investigation to be made. The magneto presented no problem to Louis who whipped it off and removed the carbon dust which was causing arcing. The tightening-up of the engine, however, caused us some concern.

We soon saw that No. 3 cylinder was the culprit by the newly-applied paint on the lower uncooled part of the block becoming discoloured with the excessive heat. The engine is lubricated by a mechanical pump which feeds oil to the bearings and cylinder walls. The two rear cylinders are served by a common supply and it was apparent that somehow or other the internal feed to No. 3 cylinder must have become obstructed. Gloom descended on the party, figuratively speaking, as we worked for a couple of hours in blazing sunshine in a not-so-back street amid a keenly interested and pressing crowd of Aachen citizenry. Would we have to abandon the trip and return home or should we go on for a bit and see what happened? Louis decided that the starved cylinder might receive sufficient lubrication if the manual supply of oil to the crankcase gallery was operated at frequent intervals; this would use a lot of oil, as the other three cylinders would be receiving more than they needed in order to ensure that No. 3 was sufficiently lubricated.

We decided to go on and left Aachen at 5 pm bound for Solingen, near Düsseldorf, 70 miles away. The magneto was now working properly and when we regained the autobahn we resumed motoring on the basis of not much exceeding 40 mph and giving three shots of oil on the hand-pump every mile, with additional shots when going up hills. The engine ran freely and, although we were aware of a non-standard

56 *Spectators on the Kurfurstendam lining the route of the parade which concluded the Deutsche Schnauferl-Rallye in Berlin*

56 *Spectators on the Kurfurstendam lining the route of the parade which concluded the Deutsche Schnauferl-Rallye in Berlin*

knock at low revs and a weak compression in one cylinder, there was no lack of power at our cruising speed. Our confidence in the Merc. returned as the miles went by and we were to complete the round trip to Berlin and back without any aggravation of the trouble.

We reached our night stop – the delightful Burg Hohenscheid Hotel near Solingen – well before dark despite a further delay when the Merc. ran out of petrol after 162.7 miles. The tank had been filled, that morning, in Antwerp, but I had over-estimated the distance which it could cover on a tankful and paid for my optimism by having to drive 17 miles up and down the autobahn in the Bentley to fetch 10 litres of petrol from a filling-station barely more than a mile away! Topping up at the next garage took another 78 litres, so I then knew that my tank held 20 gallons.

We were now well into Germany, and the passage of the Mercedes attracted a great deal of attention from passing motorists and lorry drivers. Our arms grew tired from acknowledging waves of appreciation, and we were amazed at the amount of motoring done by overtaking drivers whilst they were looking backwards at us. On one occasion a fast-moving car travelling towards us on the other carriage-way ran smartly into the back of a truck for no apparent reason, and it was not for some time that the thought occurred to us that the driver might have been looking at the Merc., instead of where he was going.

Veteran and Vintage cars were a rare sight on the roads of Germany, there being no exemptions for old cars from the ever-changing legal requirements as to direction indicators, etc. In the matter of being able to use our Veteran and Vintage cars without let or hindrance on the roads of Britain we are more fortunate than our fellow enthusiasts on the Continent, who find it difficult to drive their cars except on special occasions and often (seemingly) under police supervision. From the time that we entered the Common Market vigilance has been exercized by all concerned to see that the owners of old vehicles in the UK are not 'harmonized' off the road.

The next day we settled down to a steady progress at the rate of one kilometre in one minute ($37\frac{1}{2}$ mph) and put 170 uneventful miles of autobahn motoring behind us, arriving at the comfortable Parkhotel Motel at Hanover in good time for dinner. We made an early start next morning on the last leg of our journey as we did not know what delay might be encountered at the East German border and we wanted to report at Rally HQ in Berlin in mid-afternoon. On arrival at the Helmstedt Control we found many other Veteran, Vintage and Classic cars on their way to Berlin. The tedious form-filling and queueing at one desk after another, to obtain visas and make currency declarations, occupied an hour. Going through the Iron Curtain by road was always a sobering experience and one's enjoyment was damped by the implication of armed guards in watch-towers and barbed-wire fences patrolled by dogs. I could not conceal a smile when I observed the East German officials carrying out their mandatory search of the boots and bonnets of the cars on trailers; even the owners themselves were hard put to it on some occasions to find any luggage compartment on their cars capable of holding concealed contraband. The rear seat cushions of the Mercedes came in for a severe pummelling before the last barrier was raised to permit us to embark on the 100-mile stretch of road through East Germany to West Berlin. Our expectations of finding somewhere to eat were not fulfilled and, as foreigners were not allowed to leave the autobahn, we arrived very hungry at the West Berlin border at 3.15 pm. Formalities here took only 35 minutes and we arrived at the end of the Avus just before 4 o'clock, where we were greeted at the Rally HQ by Wolfgang Möller, Secretary of the Rally. The Merc. had travelled 654 miles and we had enjoyed hot, sunny weather all the way. We checked in at the nearby new hotel Europäischer Hof, which had been taken over for the Rally, and then set about cleaning the car before rushing off to a civic reception at the Kongress-halle.

The cars competing in the Rally were housed in a colossal exhibition hall; it must have been 60 ft high and about the size of a football field. The 143 entries were divided into six classes: pre-1900; 1901–1908; 1909–1918; 1919–1925; 1926–1930; and 1931–1940. There were 41 Veteran and Edwardian cars; 82 Vintage cars; and 20 Post-Vintage Thoroughbreds. The vast majority of the entries (91) were from Germany; the largest foreign entry (13) came from Holland, closely followed by Czechoslovakia with 12. There were seven entries from Great Britain besides myself. The cars themselves were a mixed bag. Many of them were of makes and models rarely seen on this side of the Channel. Their condition varied from the immaculate to the indifferent and their appearance from elegant to hideous. On the whole, however, they were a credit to their owners, and certain cars stand out in my memory – for example, the Brescia Bugatti of Fritz Hintermuller from Switzerland; the ex-Richard Tauber 1925 Mercedes of Paul-Heinz Rohll, President of the Berlin Section of the ASC; and the 1893 Benz of Kurt Krannich.

I turned my attention to the Rally Regulations, which Charles Meisl had helped me to translate from the German before I left home. When I told friends in Berlin that some points were obscure, I was told not to worry as they were obscure to the Germans too. Anyway, the route and speeds had been altered and after an hour or so with Wolfgang Möller I had a pretty good idea of what was expected. On this occasion the organizers were faced with the job of planning a 60-mile route within the confines of their beleaguered city. Understandably, the police did not want route-finding and regularity tests in the city centre, and a good deal of ingenuity was needed to work out a route in the suburbs which scarcely ever left pleasant wood-land and lakeside scenery.

During this run there were three short Regularity sections, two of them of unknown length, which had to be traversed at the very low average speed of 20 kph – a second-gear pace for the Merc. and many other cars! An arbitrary penalty of 60 marks on all cars fitted with speedometers seemed less fair than the practice adopted in England of covering up speedometers and thus placing all competitors on the same footing. As luck would have it, my speedometer chose the middle of the morning to cease functioning altogether and I suffered the double disadvantage of having no instrument and collecting the penalty points as well.

Enthusiastic crowds greeted the cars on their return to the Exhibition Hall, more like the finish of Pekin to Paris than a jaunt in the woods. In the evening the entrants and their passengers – seemingly hundreds of them – were taken on a 'beer and bangers' trip in a large pleasure boat on the Wannsee. This lasted until nearly midnight and, to one standing on the upper deck in the gathering dusk, the lusty German drinking songs emanating from the portholes below contrasted strangely with the unlit armed East German police boats patrolling menacingly beyond a line of buoys marking the edge of freedom.

The next morning, Saturday, was devoted to a complicated driving test devised to reveal the dexterity of the driver and the manoeuvrability of the car. It necessitated starting the engine – those fortunate enough to have a self-starter were allowed to use it – driving a slalom course through pylons into a garage and stopping within 20 cm of the end wall; reversing similarly into another garage; driving forward up quite a steep ramp, stopping and restarting without running back; reversing off the ramp and driving forwards to stop with the front wheel opposite to the driver's side on a white rectangle painted on the ground. There was the usual mixture of extremely skilful and completely clueless per-

formances, but, generally speaking, the drivers did wonders with vehicles often totally unsuited to the exercise. For my part, the accolade went to Kurt Krannick driving the 1893 Benz, whose performance throughout the Rally commanded the admiration of all.

This is no place for a political dissertation, but one cannot write of a visit to Berlin without some reference to the situation there. Having driven the length of the umbilical cord through East Germany one experienced a sense of relief on perceiving the familiar trappings of the Western World on reaching West Berlin. The knowledge that an excursion in any direction would lead one into the barbed wire before long, although always present in the subconscious mind, did not inhibit our enjoyment of the Rally – and did not appear to permeate the minds of the Berliners themselves. Nevertheless, to stand looking over 'The Wall', or through the wire, was an experience which administered a mental shock quite beyond anything gained from the written word or the television screen. I found it difficult to credit that such a division could exist in an adult world, but any tendency to ridicule the situation in one's mind was instantly suppressed by the thought that a false step in the wrong direction would invite a lethal fusillade. I certainly left Berlin with a better realization and fuller understanding of the position in which the Berliners found themselves at that time.

Saturday evening saw the Prize-giving Dinner in the Kongressehalle, and the fierce thunderstorm raging outside provided a Wagnerian background to the speeches of visiting dignitaries from the Veteran Car Clubs of other countries. In the absence of any such personage from the UK, I was prevailed upon by the British competitors to say a word of thanks to the organizers.

I have never seen a more lavish array of prizes at any motoring 'do', and it looked as if everyone was to receive something. In the event, the allocation of awards seemed quixotic, to say the least. My seventh place out of 15 in the class did not merit – and did not get – an award, but Major Collings confessed his surprise at receiving a prize for his 26th place in an admittedly very large class. Garrett seemed as surprised as anyone else when he collected two jolly good items for having been the first person to enter the Rally and for having a German-born wife: A very nice gesture was the presentation to 'England' of an engraved silver tray. (It seems that Veteran Car rallies were not known in Germany until the early '50s when a member of the ASC returned from a visit to England and started the series of Schnauferl Rallies, of which this year's was the 11th.) The oldest member of the ASC – both in age (80) and in membership (50 years) – Richard Lüders, gave this award in recognition of the tremendous amount of enjoyment which Veteran car enthusiasts in Germany had derived from what was, as far as they were concerned, an idea from England. I accepted this silver tray and handed it to the President of the VCC of GB on my return.

The Rally concluded on the Sunday morning with a parade of all the competing cars through the centre of Berlin. As far as we were concerned, this turned out to be the highlight of the Rally. The sun shone and the crowds lined the route in 'Brighton' fashion. I have not seen more enthusiastic spectators at a Veteran event, and the keen interest displayed had to be seen to be believed.

When the parade arrived back at the TV Tower we reluctantly bade farewell to friends old and new, and turned the Merc. westwards along the old Avus track towards home. We cleared the tiresome frontier formalities at 12.45 pm and retraced our path to Hanover. Next day we continued along the autobahn, but made a southerly detour near Köln to spend the night at the Burg Ockenfels Hotel overlooking the Rhine at Linz.

The following day we left Linz-am-Rhein at 8.15 am for Ostend planning to keep a 6 o'clock appointment in Ghent to see Ghislain Mahy's private collection of cars. We were, in fact, 10 minutes late after covering 216.4 miles, surely a tribute to the reliability of the Mercedes.

We found it difficult to drag ourselves away from the fabulous collection of several hundred cars, but we wanted to reach our destination before dark and did so, arriving at Ostend just before nine after a day's journey of 255 miles. We had left Berlin at noon on Sunday and completed the 658 miles to the Belgian coast by Tuesday evening without any trouble whatsoever.

The following day when passing through Sevenoaks, only 30 miles from home, we had a puncture – the first one during my ownership of the Merc. – and changed the tyre and rim, counting ourselves fortunate that we should encounter such little tyre trouble after hearing the dire tales of others. An examination of notes made during the trip reveals that the total mileage covered during the 10 days was 1,535 and the overall petrol consumption was 8.36 mpg (Phew!!).

Edinburgh to London in daylight
In 1968 the advance publicity for the Veteran Car Club London-Edinburgh Rally threw out the challenge of 400 miles in four days as being designed to sort the men from the boys. From the point of view of an Edwardian owner this seemed to me to be rather overstating the case, and I lightheartedly added to my 'declaration of intent to enter' a postscript in the words 'Why not sort out the giants from the men by organizing the return trip in one day instead of four?' I should have known better! The Competitions Committee took up my suggestion and I found myself lumbered with it, but not that much organizing was required.

Dawn breaks very early in Edinburgh in midsummer – lighting-up time ended at 4.16 am on the day in question – so it was decided that intending participants could start at any time of their own choice between 5 am and 6 am. To qualify for a certificate it was necessary to arrive at the Royal Automobile Club in London before lighting-up time at 9.31 pm. The choice of route was entirely free; two, but not more, persons could drive, and all persons travelling in the car were to act as observers on behalf of the Club to see that the car was not towed – except the minimum distance to reach a garage to effect repairs. (In the event, none of the cars was towed at all.) In every other respect the run was to be regarded as a normal pleasure drive for those who enjoy Veteran or Edwardian motoring in the grand manner.

Five members presented their cars and their Road Books to 'volunteer' Starting Official Brian Mawer, waiting in the grey dawn in the coal yard behind the ice rink, where the cars had spent the night. They were, in addition to myself – R. Lewis (1907 Napier), G.E. Dorrington (1913 Renault), L.B. White (1913 Rover), and S.A. Smith (1914 Vauxhall). All except the Napier left Edinburgh impatiently on the dot of 5 am of a dry Sabbath, while Lewis left a quarter-of-an-hour later.

Accompanied by Louis Giron who shared the driving, I opted to follow A1 as far as the Doncaster Bypass, then to turn off on to the recently opened M18 motorway connecting with M1 at Rotherham. This route measured 405 miles and was the longest of the various alternatives. It was, however, relatively level and included some 240 miles of dual carriageway. The first two hours saw $77\frac{1}{2}$ miles behind us on dry roads, but when I then handed over to Louis the heavens opened. For the next 50 miles conditions were appalling. There was continuous, heavy, driving rain; several miles of flooded road which rendered the brakes useless for a spell; some fog, and all this laced with a cold east wind blowing off the sea. We passed quickly into Newcastle ($3\frac{1}{4}$ hours/118 miles) and out again. The rain ceased and the car was going like a train until the outskirts of Durham when the engine just stopped without any warning. There was air pressure in the petrol tank, but the carburettor was dry. Householders appeared in their doorways and proffered tea and help – it was

barely 8.30 am. A few strokes on a foot-pump applied at the carburettor end of the fuel line cleared whatever unaccountable foreign matter had caused the obstruction. Nothing of the kind had occurred since the tank was thoroughly cleaned when the car was reconditioned seven years previously, and there was no recurrence afterwards. This stop, and replenishment of the tank at a nearby garage, occupied 42 minutes and my voiced hopes of reaching London in well under 12 hours dwindled.

We pressed on, aiming to breakfast at Scotch Corner, which we reached at 10.02 am, only to be told that breakfasts finished at 10 am. On to the motel at Leeming, 12 miles further, where we found the restaurant closed until lunchtime.

The Merc. was cruising consistently at 50 mph and five hours later we were 218 miles nearer London, having averaged 43.6 mph, including two stops for petrol. Our average speed for this 218 miles, excluding stops, was 45.9 mph – this without exceeding 50 mph. At 3.50 pm we reached the London end of M1 and 34 minutes later drew up outside the RAC in Pall Mall, where we found that the Prince Henry Vauxhall had clocked in 39 minutes earlier. (If only we hadn't had that 42-minute stop for the petrol stoppage . . .!) Our running time from Edinburgh to London (405 miles) was exactly 10 hours, an average speed of $40\frac{1}{2}$ mph. The total time, including stops amounting to 84 minutes, was 11 hours 24 minutes, which meant a door-to-door average of $35\frac{1}{2}$ mph.

I was delighted with the magnificent demonstration of reliable performance given by the Mercedes, and the credit for this goes to Louis Giron who was entirely responsible for overhauling and maintaining the mechanical side of the car. It was a great joy driving the Mercedes for mile after mile at a steady 50 and, even at this modest speed by modern standards, it was surprising how many cars we overtook on the motorways. Not quite so pleasing was the petrol consumption – 9 mpg! I know the car weighed over 39 cwt, but a penny a furlong in

57 *The author and Louis Giron outside the RAC in Pall Mall after the run from Edinburgh*

those days – phew!

S.A. Smith, driving N.A. Ridley's ex-Pomeroy Prince Henry Vauxhall, had followed A1 all the way from Edinburgh to London and drove the entire distance himself. The car had no hood and the occupants were well soaked in the border country. Mrs Smith had to dig into her luggage for a skirt to replace her slacks before being allowed past the august portals of the RAC to take tea as a guest of Brian Dinsley, who had given up his Sunday afternoon and evening to verify the arrival times of the 'Edwardians'.

R. Lewis drove his 60 Napier the whole way himself and was unaccompanied – a creditable performance. He left Edinburgh at 5.15 am and checked in at the RAC at 7.33 pm – a very good solo effort.

G.E. Dorrington also turned in a solo performance in his 1913 Renault, but had a passenger to help him cope with a blow-out on M1,

50 miles from London. He followed the same route as the Mercedes and with a top cruising speed of about 40 mph achieved a door-to-door average of 27.3 mph.

L.B. White, in his 1913 Rover, also drove all of the way. He came up with the Napier at Swiss Cottage only to lose it in the traffic. As the Rover approached the RAC the Napier appeared out of a side turning, both cars arriving together at 7.33 pm. White had completed the 375 miles in 14 hours 33 minutes, thus averaging 25.8 mph.

Some may think that this venture might be called 'And Five Were Foolish', but it must surely be admitted that the Run served as a demonstration of the high standard of maintenance of these old cars and that, when it is demanded of them, they can put up a performance which would not disgrace a modern car. Perhaps it just shows that they really don't build them like that any more.

58 *Philip Mann and John Rowley in the former's 1914 Grand Prix Mercedes*

Mercedes 70th anniversary run – 1971

Always on the look-out for an excuse to undertake a long trip in the Merc., I accepted with alacrity an invitation from Erik Johnson, Marketing Manager of Mercedes-Benz (Great Britain) Ltd, to participate in a run to Stuttgart to mark the 70th Anniversary of the name 'Mercedes' and, co-incidentally, the 85th Anniversary of the birth of the first cars of Gottlieb Daimler and Karl Benz.

So it was that Louis Giron and I found ourselves on the quay at Harwich on Friday, April 23, waiting in pouring rain to embark on the 'Prins Oberon' with 15 other cars. The wet and cold weather, coming after nearly a week of warm sunny days, was most disappointing and set the pattern for the following five days. It had not been possible to persuade the owners of some of the best Mercedes in the country to join the run, and owners of other makes, mostly associated in some way with Daimler or Benz, were invited to make up a worthwhile contin-gent. There were, in fact (in addition to my 45/50), only three Veteran Mercedes taking part: Tom Lightfoot's 1902 Mercedes Simplex, Charles Howard's ex-Malartre 1913 37/95 tourer and – joining us on Sunday evening at Köln – Philip Mann's beautifully restored 1914 Grand Prix car. Other 'associated' cars were Ted Woolley's 1897 Daimler Phoenix, the tube ignition of which fascinated crowds wherever it was taken off its trailer to be driven in parades and processions; George Dorrington's Benz-engined 1900 English Mechanic; Tom Lightfoot's 1901 7 hp Daimler-engined Panhard, entered by Philip Sumner (these latter two cars were trailered on the road sections); Cecil Bendall's Prinz Heinrich Austro-Daimler driven by John Mitchell; and the two British-built Daimlers of Murcott (a 1908/9 22 hp open tourer once owned by King Edward VII) and Acock (1910 15 hp two-seater). Anachronistic accompanists were the 540K Mercedes-Benz of Charles Howard, a good-looking but out-of-character Freestone &

Webb semi-razor-edge saloon, and the 1937 Roadster of John Barley, Chairman-elect of the Mercedes-Benz Club. The total of 16 starters was made up of Bryan Firth's 1909 12 hp Adler; Cecil Bendall's 1911 Rolls-Royce Silver Ghost, known as 'Stripes' from its unusual paint treatment; the 1914 Hupmobile of near-octeganarian Tommy Johnson; and 'AA 1', the well-known 1904 Renault Park Phaeton of the Automobile Association, driven by George Thompson and David Tuckfield.

The Run commenced with a 'send-off' reception in the Council Chamber at Harwich and it was not long before all the cars were safely aboard, Brian Robins (Editor, Motoring Programmes, Television Outside Broadcasts) and his 'Wheelbase' team joined us, as did Clement Freud representing the 'Daily Telegraph' Magazine.

The overnight crossing to Bremerhaven lasted 16 hours and proved to be a very satisfactory way of making a landfall in Germany. We were met on the quayside at Bremerhaven by a contingent of personnel and vehicles sent from Stuttgart by Daimler-Benz AG to accompany us on the 1,100-mile round trip to Ostend. No words of praise can exaggerate the tremendous contribution which this party made to the well-being and peace of mind of all (well, nearly all) participants. The Stuttgart party comprised three young executives, Helmut Holstein, Klaus Sekol and Ranold Mjornell, each driving a red 350 SL Mercedes-Benz – the new model to be unveiled in showrooms all over Germany that very week-end; Mr Kern, engineer and mechanic responsible for the exhibits in the famous D.B. Museum at Unterturkheim driving a 280 SE 3.5 saloon with a boot full of every imaginable tool, material and piece of equipment which might be needed during the run (including an oxy-acetylene welding outfit); a low-loader breakdown vehicle of the ADAC to convey disabled cars to the next stop; and a petrol tanker from ARAL. At every stopping-place participating cars – and those pulling trailers –

were tanked-up free of charge by the ever-willing tanker driver. (As my Mercedes did only 8/9 mpg it was a great joy to be 'towing' a tanker full of free petrol.)

Thus protected and provided for, the convoy of vehicles set off for lunch at Syke, near Breman. The drivers of the three 350 SLs were keeping in touch with each other by radio telephone. They did not always manage to keep us on the right route, but what they lacked in experience of organizing runs of this nature they made up for by a dedicated concern for the safety and comfort of all; they did not rest until their flock was safely corralled at each stopping place.

The Austro-Daimler was the one casualty and, after a ride on the low-loader, was abandoned by its crew, the sleeve in No. 4 cylinder having come loose. That night saw us in the unlikely stopping-place of Bielefeld and it was still raining on Sunday morning when we left for lunch in Düsseldorf. The cars arrived in a very travel-stained condition but attracted an enthusiastic and appreciative crowd. It was here that the Run (and Düsseldorf) were enlivened by the arrival by air of 'Denny' – one of the 'Young Generation' dancers – wearing hot pants beneath an ankle-length fur-trimmed coat.

After lunch, I made a personal pilgrimage to 63/65 Graf Adolf Strasse which, although now a Ford showroom, had been the premises of the General Agency for Daimler-Motoren-Gesellschaft for Rhineland and Westphalia to which my car was delivered when new in 1910. With Clement Freud busy writing in encapsulated seclusion in the back of my car and 'Denny' in the front, we made a police-escorted tour of the city and then set off for the night stop at Köln.

Next, the AA Renault broke a bolt on its universal joint and was administered to by Mr Kern, who fabricated a new one in the nearest Mercedes-Benz branch. (Incidentally, all the Mercedes-Benz branches on or near the route had been alerted to stand by in case any help or facilities were required to keep the cars running.)

59 *Clement Freud at the wheel of Charles Howard's ex-Malartre 1913 37/95 Mercedes*

60 *Louis Giron willingly acts as doorman for photographers attracted by Denny of the 'Young Generation' dancers*

Philip Mann and John Rowley, in the former's 1914 Grand Prix winner, joined us at the recently opened Esso Motel at Köln, having been at the Vintage Sports Car Club Meeting at Silverstone the previous day. They had driven from Rotterdam in five hours and this historic car made a welcome addition to the convoy. Fitted with mudguards to comply with the law and a rudimentary luggage rack, it motored at 70–80 mph and was indeed an impressive sight. It sounded great, too, and was usually last to leave the starting point and first to arrive at the end of each section.

On Monday, the route took us up the Rhine Valley to Bingen for lunch and on to Heidelberg for the night.

At Mehlem, about 10 miles south of Bonn, we came upon Bryan Firth's Adler at the roadside; a cheerful enquiry as to whether everything was OK died on our lips as we perceived that the car had been severely damaged. It transpired that whilst his attention was momentarily distracted by acknowledging a 'straight-on' signal from a travelling marshal the traffic lights had changed to red and he was unable to avoid running into the back end of a suddenly very stationary truck. Bryan was able to steer to the right, thus avoiding damaging the radiator, chassis or engine, but the side of the body demolished itself against the heavy metal corner of the truck. The front wing crumpled; the windscreen pillar was swept away taking with it part of the dashboard; the main door pillar was fractured and the roof bent up; the windscreen and division shattered and the roof cracked. By great good fortune, daughter Henrietta who was sitting in the front seat was uninjured and her mother in the back sustained only slight cuts. At first glance the poor little Adler looked to be ready

61 *Outside 63/65 Graf Adolf Strasse in Düsseldorf where the Mercedes was delivered to the (then) general agency of Daimler-Motor Gesellschaft in December 1910*

for shipment home for extensive rebuilding. In the event, Louis Giron produced copper wire and ingenuity and tied the car together, and buoyed up by the thought of the ever-present low-loader, Bryan elected to continue the Run, disposing of his passengers in sundry vehicles. Fully exposed to the elements, he drove his car safely to Stuttgart and the experts there, working under Mr Kern, proceeded to strengthen the body structurally with angle-iron, fabricate a new windscreen and generally screw the car together in a most commendable fashion for the journey home.

During the morning another incident involved George Dorrington who had braked to such effect on one occasion that his 1900 English Mechanic leapt out of its wheel slots in the trailer and crashed into the back of the towing

62 *Bryan Firth's Adler after colliding with the rear of a truck*

LD 2250

63 *An accident with the 1900 English Mechanic caused by hard braking – the moral: 'Never mind how safe it looks, tie it down!'*
64 *The emergency repair to the split detachable rim near Luxembourg*

Renault 12 Estate car, whose occupants were shocked to be run into by themselves. A dented rear panel and a broken window were sustained by the Renault but the Veteran received only a slightly bent track rod. (Moral: never mind how safe it looks – tie it down.)

After dinner we were taken out by the Regional Chief of the Schnauferl Club to the 'Red Ox' – an ancient students' pub in Heidelberg. Here, led by John Mitchell in lusty renderings of traditional English songs, we vied with singing German students. Philip Mann, who had said on arrival at Köln that he was 'only here for the beer', was put to the test when confronted by a glass boot containing 2.5 litres – over 4 pints – but he passed with flying colours, not only consuming the entire contents but also mastering the technique of emptying the 'toe' without suffering a drenching.

The next day, Tuesday, culminated in our arrival in Stuttgart where we were greeted by Daimler-Benz and civic officials in the Killes-berg Park. After lunch, during which our cars were washed by personnel thoughtfully provided by DB, we went through a lengthy driving test inside another part of the building. Unfortunately, the door through which the cars were driven into the building was not high enough to admit my car (7 ft 6 in high), nor Cecil Bendall's Rolls-Royce and one or two other cars. Meantime, judges had been inspecting the cars for quality and turn-out. It says much for the enthusiasm and skill of Bryan Firth that, despite his unfortunate accident, his Adler won the Concours and was placed second in the Driving Tests behind Tom Lightfoot.

Leaving the cars locked up for the night at Killesberg we made a rapid sightseeing tour of the city by coach and checked into our hotels before walking over to the Graf Zeppelin Hotel for the reception and banquet to be given by Daimler-Benz. Awards and mementoes were presented; speeches of welcome, appreciation and thanks were made. The Renault was again in trouble and the untiring Mr Emil Kern was busy in the Museum workshop making new bushes for the front universal joint on the propshaft.

Both Adler and Renault were ready for the road next morning when we presented ourselves and our cars at the factory at Unterturkheim. We spent some time in the museum and in the afternoon we made a tour of a small part of the huge plant at Sindelfingen and were able to appreciate something of the investment, planning, organization and techniques which go into the production of Mercedes-Benz cars. The convoy then left for Karlsruhe, where the night was spent at the Schwarzwald Hotel.

Friday dawned bright and sunny and was to be the first day without any rain. Cecil Bendall suffered the first of a series of punctures in 'Stripes' before arriving at the lunch stop at Saarbrücken, while a flat tyre on the Renault was dealt with in the car park amid an interested audience. There followed an uneventful run through attractive scenery to the Luxembourg border. Whilst waiting for the stragglers, I was chatting with John Rowley when he noticed by chance a slight bulge on the inside of one of my front tyres. Further examination revealed that the detachable rim had split circumferentially for a distance of about eight inches. We drove slowly into Luxembourg and, when caught up by 'the support team', had the rim and tyre bandaged with wide adhesive tape by Mr Kern. We crawled into the city and, after a brief appearance in the Market Square for publicity purposes, drove to the local Mercedes-Benz branch, where Louis and Mr Kern had the rim off, welded up and refitted in a very short time – and so to dinner and to bed, in anticipation of a 5.30 am call for the pre-lunch run of 150 miles to Brussels.

It became evident that the organization had creaked a bit when we came down at 6 am to find that no arrangements had been made for breakfast to be served at this early hour. It was a bright sunny morning, so we took a taxi to the Mercedes-Benz garage to collect our cars and left philosophically planning to stop en route for breakfast. Louis and I drove 40 miles before breakfasting – incidentally the only meal we paid for during the entire eight-day trip, all the others (with wines), our hotel accommodation, and sea crossings, being provided by the organizers in return for the modest entry fee of £20 per person.

The 150 miles to Brussels passed swiftly under our wheels and midday saw us competing with residents and tourists for parking spaces in the Grande Place. We were sorry to see Howard's 'Ninety' Mercedes, which had gone so well, arrive on the low-loader, having stretched a chain to the point where driving at any speed produced the most alarming noises as the chain jumped the sprockets. After lunch in a nearby hotel, we proceeded to Ghent amid the Friday evening Bruxellois speeding coastwards along the autoroute. That enthusiastic collector, Ghislain Mahy and his son, Ivan, joined us at dinner and afterwards, despite the late hour, invited those interested to see some of his collection of nearly 600 cars. It was 1 am before the party returned to the hotel, still marvelling at this Aladdin's cave. Saturday morning – the last day. Farewells all round in anticipation of haste and confusion at the Ostend docks.

And so our Run came to an end. As we sailed, our three shepherds/nurses walked back to their 350 SLs to drive back to Stuttgart freed from their charges, as did Mr Kern and the low-loader driver.

We had enjoyed ourselves immensely. Our reception in Germany had been warm-hearted, not only at the official receptions, radio interviews, TV parades and processions, but from fellow-motorists all along the route.

As I put my faithful Mercedes back in the garage, ticking over as sweetly as she did when we started out nine days and 1,300 miles earlier, I could not help trying to think of an excuse for proposing a repeat performance in the not-too-distant future.

500 miles in a day

Most of the important rallies of the Veteran Car Club include a competition based on the distance travelled to the Rally. Entrants may select a single turning point between their home, or other starting place, and the Rally venue and may start their journey up to two days before Reporting Time at the Arrival Control. The award goes to the car which covers the greatest mileage measured in straight lines on a map.

In 1970 I declared Newcastle-upon-Tyne as my turning point on the way to Crystal Palace and, with co-driver Louis Giron, left Cobham on Saturday morning. We drove to Newcastle, asked an astonished AA scout in the Market Place to sign a statement that we had passed that way that day, and drove back to the Selby Fork Motel for the night. We resumed our journey early next morning in driving rain and checked in at the Crystal Palace a few minutes before 11 am to win the Distance Award by a considerable margin.

I have a liking for round numbers – being an accountant may have something to do with this idiosyncracy – and the idea of doing 500 miles in a day in the Mercedes appealed to me. Past performances indicated that, with reasonable luck, such a distance could be achieved in daylight if a substantial part of the trip were to be undertaken on motorways.

When the Regulations for the 1972 London Rally arrived I perceived an opportunity to fulfil this ambition and called Louis Giron to ask if he felt like another marathon run in the Mercedes. He said, 'Yes, when?' I told him the plot and declared my turning point to be Gretna Green.

We left my home at Cobham, Surrey, at 3 pm on Friday, 4 August, with 180 miles to go to reach our night-stop at the Saxon Cross Motel on the M6 near Sandbach. The location of the night stop had been chosen so as to leave a 500 mile journey for the Saturday, on to Gretna Green and back to Cobham, where we planned to spend the night before a leisurely trundle across the suburbs to Crystal Palace the following morning to check in by 11 am.

The drive to Sandbach was uneventful – Kingston/Chiswick/North Circular Road/M1 and M6 – and we arrived there at 8.30 pm. It had been a wet journey and already the August Bank Holiday traffic had commenced streaming northwards. The speedometer cable broke after 65.2 miles and subsequent mileage and speed calculations had to be done by 'dead reckoning'. Before turning in, we went to a nearby garage to replenish the petrol and oil tanks, the former being filled appropriately enough from an old-fashioned hand-operated pump, though the brand name on the surmounting globe was unknown to us – 'Globe', in fact.

An early start was necessary to cover the self-imposed distance in daylight, and after a 4.30 am call we turned on to M6 again at first light (5.20 am) for the 155 mile journey to the end of M6 beyond Carlisle and on to Gretna Green. We were astonished at the volume of traffic so early in the morning as holiday-makers made for the Lakes and Scotland – difficult to believe that so many caravans existed in the country.

I was driving and not hurrying on the cold engine. When I did try to bring it up to its usual brisk pace I met with little response and found it necessary to change down to third, and even second, on gradients which I would have expected to scale in top. We did not know the topography and thought that the grades might be steeper than they appeared, but soon stopped kidding ourselves and accepted the fact that the car lacked power. It was perhaps natural (but, as will be seen, entirely unjustifiable) that we put the blame on the strange fuel taken on the previous evening, and we resolved to perk up the mixture with some higher octane at our planned breakfast stop.

We topped up the tank at the West Burton Service Area and gave up the idea of breakfast when we saw the length of the queue in the cafeteria (at 7.40 am!). Confession is good for the soul, they say, and here comes a sizeable contribution to the well-being of mine: when I went to swing the engine on restarting I saw that the compression lever was already pulled out and, may the ghosts of Stuttgart forgive me, realized that I had driven 85 miles on half-compression averaging $38\frac{1}{2}$ mph! (Apologies to the purveyor of petrol who might otherwise have remained unabsolved for life.)

We were soon on the road again in full song and with apparently unharmed exhaust valves, rejoicing in the regained vigour of the Merc. as we approached Shap Fell. A quick look into the cafeteria at Tebay revealed continued congestion at the counter, so we opted to continue to Gretna for breakfast. We arrived there at 9.30 am and got the AA Inspector on duty to verify the fact on my Rally number-plate, then we looked for breakfast. No luck at the Lovers' Leap Motel, but a very friendly reception at the Gretna Hall Hotel where sizzling bacon and eggs was prepared for us.

At 10.25 am I pulled out of the Hotel car park and now joined the Scots rushing southwards with boats and caravans. The traffic was heavy all the way to London, but presented no problems for us Edwardian motorists ambling along at 50 – mostly in the slow lane but overtaking quite a lot of cars for all that. We now had ahead of us the whole length of M6 from Junction 44 to Junction 1, and then M1 to London, the distance from Gretna Green to Cobham being 335 miles. We took on 14 gallons of petrol at Killington and at 2.08 pm passed the Saxon Cross Motel at Sandbach, from whence we had started nearly 9 hours previously, by then having covered 311 miles. We knew that we had 182 miles to go and I reckoned that, if we took the same driving time as on the outward trip the previous day, our ETA at Cobham would be exactly 7 pm.

The Mercedes was going beautifully and most of the time we were covering 48 miles in the hour. We shared the driving and progressed steadily towards London, and completed 400 miles just after joining M1. At 5.20 pm; after

12 hours on the road, 443 miles had been covered.

We arrived home at 7.10 pm, quite unfatigued with the Mercedes running as well as when we had started out 674 miles earlier. The day's run was 493 miles taking 13 hours 50 minutes = 35.6 mph. Deducting stops for petrol, oil and food totalling 1 hour 57 minutes, the driving time of 7 minutes under 12 hours showed an average speed of $41\frac{1}{2}$ mph.

I see from my notes that the whole length of M6 and then M1, a total distance of 304 miles, took 7 hours 34 minutes (40.2 mph) and, deducting stops totalling 37 minutes, the running average speed was 43.7 mph.

Petrol consumption was as expected – between 8 and 9 mpg – 75 gallons having been burned – and not a single Green Shield Stamp collected!

This performance was a great tribute to the designers and engineers who built the car more than 60 years previously, and to the incomparable Louis Giron who kept it in first-class condition. Apart from the broken speedometer cable, no harm befell the Mercedes – until Sunday morning when I drove out of my drive and caught an unclosed rear door on my own garden wall. This bent the handle and spindle, calling for some quick work by Louis so that the door could be opened and shut at Crystal Palace – an important matter this, as it was on the side from which Con would have to alight in the Fashion Competition after the Driving Tests.

As a postscript, I must record that during this journey of over 600 miles on motorways on the busiest week-end of the year, we saw only one accident – and that not serious – and were not held up by any congestion. The standard of driving was high despite the many holidaymakers with packed and (over)loaded cars. I estimate we saw about 50 cars in trouble with tyres or overheating and three broken windscreens. This long run on our motorways served to confirm my view that they were among the best in the world.

In August 1972 the Mercedes appeared in an episode of the then current television series 'The Duchess of Duke Street' and in October 1975 participated in the Society of Motor Manufacturers & Traders Cavalcade, from Hyde Park to Earls Court, in connexion with the Diamond Jubilee Motor Show – on both occasions chauffeured by Louis Giron in my absence abroad. It was always ready to go and I used the Mercedes in Veteran Car Club rallies and for much driving for sheer pleasure on social occasions.

End of Edwardian motoring
Early in 1977, when my rented lofty garage accommodation ceased to be available and Louis Giron was no longer able to maintain the car, I decided to sell my much loved Edwardian motorcar after 15 years' ownership. It was bought in April 1977 by Ing. Werner Lutzky, an Austrian glass-maker who had a collection of cars – mostly Mercedes – in his Schloss at Kremsmünster near Linz. He sent a van and trailer all the way to London to collect the car and, as I watched it leave, I could not help regretting that circumstances prevented me from delivering it personally to the new owner under its own power. Con and I called in at the Schloss when passing through Austria in September 1978 and were pleased to find 'our' Merc. occupying a place of honour in the museum and bearing signs of having taken part in a recent rally.

65 *The Mercedes about to set off for its new home in Austria – April 1977*

66 *The would-be off-the-street parker's dilemma!*
67 *The Mercedes has functioned at many weddings – here the passengers are bridesmaids*

68 *The Phantom III Rolls-Royce acquired in December 1952*

68 *The Phantom III Rolls-Royce acquired in December 1952*

Rolls-Royce Phantom III

Motoring in the grand manner

To own a P III is a unique experience for in truth one has a town carriage with a performance which until recent years would not have disgraced a sports car. I remember L.C. McKenzie saying to me about the P III: 'It has a maximum speed of 94 mph and a cruising speed of 93.' Certainly this great car is a stirring sight at speed, the only noise coming from the tyres and the exhaust gases fighting to reach the atmosphere. Many a time I have accelerated away from traffic lights overhauling 'boy racers' in sports cars, their faces betraying amazement as several yards of seemingly house-high automobile whooshed past.

I acquired my P III from Harold Radford just before Christmas 1952, with nearly 60,000 miles on the clock. It was a 1937 BU series chassis with solid tappets, not the earlier hydraulically-operated type, and the body was a semi-razor-edge Touring Limousine with division built by H.J. Mulliner. It had louvred bonnet sides, instead of the more usual three door vents, and was painted black. Beauty is very much a matter of personal taste and I consider this particular coachwork the most elegant to be seen on a closed Phantom III, perhaps because it looks right from every angle. From an owner-driver's point of view, the absence of a division would have been preferable, but the limited fore-and-aft adjustment of the front seats was sufficient for my longish legs and the division was scarcely visible from outside the car.

In the P III I found I could average 50 mph point-to-point almost anywhere in England; not much, perhaps, by today's standards, but quite creditable in those days before motorways. I took it to France once or twice – to Le Mans and Reims where I was timing Briggs Cunningham's cars in the long-distance races. At Reims I gave 'Bira' a lift to the circuit on Grand Prix day, and

69 *The Phantom III on the Mulsanne Straight at Le Mans, June 1954*

70 *A king among cars – the Phantom III in the car park at the Reims Circuit*
71 *On the way back to New York from the Classic Car Meet at Morristown, Pennsylvania, accompanied by another Phantom III*

he was quite perturbed because the petrol warning light was on and he thought I might run out of gas on the way. I reassured him and dropped him at his pit; and, although it was not funny at the time, we have laughed together since, because it was he, Bira, who ran out of fuel – in the race!

I drove the Rolls up to Town and back each day, an expensive pastime at 10 mpg. (Come to think of it, this is the sort of consumption I have been enjoying (!) in different cars on my lawful business these many years.) I did not regard the commuter grand prix in and out of London as a pleasure. In my case, it was marginally less inconvenient and time-consuming than the alternative car-train-taxi transport available to me. It was, of course, educational and, providing one curbed the competitive spirit and excercised restraint when provoked by aggressive and unmannerly drivers, commuter driving in the Metropolis does keep one's driving up to scratch. I doubt if there exists a more demanding 'univer-

sity of the road' than 200 miles a week mixing it in the cut-and-thrust of commuter driving. No quarter is given – and none asked. Every driver knows what he is doing and what others are doing. Lane discipline is good and everyone is intent on getting along. There are black sheep and I could write a book on the 'back-doubles' and the degrees of gamesmanship permissible – and frowned upon.

But I digress. . . .

When I was using the P III daily in London during the weeks preceding the Coronation period I benefited from the regal aspect of my carriage, for there were many crowned heads and heads of state in Town. The appearance on the scene of a large Rolls-Royce, which might be carrying who-knows-who, was spotted by bobbies who jumped to speed one's transit at the next intersection.

In March 1955 at 78,241 miles, I had a new back axle fitted with a higher ratio (3.9 to 1) than the standard 4.25 to 1. Less than a dozen

of these ratios, which gave 80 mph at 3,400 rpm, were fitted under the aegis of Roney Messervy in P IIIs belonging to enthusiastic owners. My speedometer was recalibrated and on one or two occasions in France I reached a sustained 100 mph. In August that year the P III was laid up whilst I was personally out of circulation with maintenance problems of my own. Not long after putting the car on the road again I was faced with the prospect of an engine overhaul, estimated to cost £1,250, and decided to change to more modern transport – the Mk VI already described. I had experienced nearly 30,000 miles of memorable motoring in the grand manner.

There was no difficulty in finding an owner for the P III who would do the necessary and thereafter provide a good home. Briggs Cunningham had often admired the car and had asked for first refusal if and when I decided to sell. He bought it in March 1956 and had it completely restored to new condition before adding it to his collection in the States. Whilst undergoing the mechanical overhaul at Hythe Road a new exhaust system, specially designed to absorb less horsepower and yet to achieve the same degree of silencing, was fitted. Mulliners removed the division and built additional strength into the door pillars and roof to make it into a real owner-driver car. That Briggs acquired the P III was my good fortune, because I could drive it whenever I visited his home. The first time I stayed with him (then in Connecticut) after the reborn Rolls had been delivered coincided with the Annual Concours d'Elegance of the Classic Car Club of America in Morristown, Pennsylvania, and I borrowed my beloved old car to take part. On arrival at the venue I was surprised to see more than one enthusiast prostrate himself on the pavement almost before my wheels stopped turning. I'd heard of the dedication of RR fans in the States, but this was ridiculous. It transpired that these enthusiasts had heard of my intended arrival in Briggs' new P III and they wanted to examine the new exhaust system! The Rolls was not judged to be the best one there, but it did take second place. This gives some idea of the high standard of perfection demanded, and attained, by our Transatlantic cousins. The PIII had an honoured place in Briggs Cunningham's museum until he sold the collection to Miles Collier at the end of 1986.

250 GT Ferrari

Motoring in a new dimension

Surely it is the ambition of every true motorist to be the proud possessor some day of a thoroughbred from Maranello. I was no exception, but like so many others saw little prospect of having the wherewithal to realize my ambition. The price of a new Ferrari was quite beyond my means and I realized that the purchase of a used one was indeed a dicey business. Little did I think that I would ever have a Ferrari – and a unique one at that – but so it came to pass.

I have already mentioned Gerry Crozier, that motoring enthusiast par excellence. He had owned more cars in his time than anyone I knew. He was always changing them and he, too, aspired to owning a Ferrari. One Sunday he telephoned to see if we would be at home if he came over, his normal practice when he had acquired a new car, and I was not surprised when the blue nose of a Ferrari turned into the drive, Gerry at the wheel with an 'at last' expression on his face.

It was a 250 GT Berlinetta, recently imported from a private owner in Italy, and Gerry said it was thought to be the car which had won the 1961 Tourist Trophy Race at Goodwood. The colour was certainly 'Rob Walker' blue. He really enjoyed this car, but died not long afterwards and it was bought by Neil Corner.

I asked Neil, without any real expectation of being in a position to afford it, to let me know should he decide to sell it at any time. This he did in April 1967 and I fell, deciding to convert a holding of BP shares into the Ferrari. In a letter to Neil I wrote: 'I cannot tell you how

72 *The 250 GT SWB Lightweight Ferrari.* *(The figure in the designation of Ferrari models, with a few exceptions, indicates the capacity* *of one cylinder, thus 250 cc multiplied by twelve cylinders gives a total of 3,000 cc)*

excited I am at the prospect of owning this car. Its purchase is a deliberate Act of Folly and, instead of acknowledging that I am buying a car beyond my means, I am kidding myself that I am making a temporary investment in it, with a view to taking the dividend in pleasure instead of depreciated taxed currency!'

Driving a Ferrari for the first time introduced me to a new dimension in motoring. The instant performance at one's command and the sense of total stability and controllability at high speed has to be experienced to be believed. The turbine-like torque of the V-12 3-litre engine was exhilarating. One didn't overtake other cars, one squirted past. The vivid acceleration had to be used with restraint, lest other road users unaware of the capability of the Ferrari took avoiding action in anticipation of a collision which was never even a possibility. My Ferrari was not temperamental, as everyone assumes a Ferrari to be. It would poddle along slowly in traffic without boiling, oiling up or stalling; and

would accelerate afterwards to high speed without any fluffing. And this was not an ordinary road-going Ferrari, it was a sports-racing car.

No sooner had the Ferrari arrived home than I began to delve into its history, which neither of its previous owners had done. I wrote to the factory – and Ronnie Hoare very kindly gave me access to his files at Maranello Concessionaires – which established that my car (Chassis No. 2119GT) had indeed won the Tourist Trophy, but in 1960, not 1961.

The car had been ordered from the Works by Maranello Concessionaires for Rob Walker on 13 July 1960, specifying right-hand drive; light alloy body; 600×16 Borrani wheels; engine to full competition specification, limited slip differential; 7/32 rear axle ratio; and painted Midnight Blue to sample provided. The letter concluded: 'The car will be collected from Modena on 10 August. This date is vital as the car is to be driven by Stirling Moss in the Tourist Trophy Race on Saturday, 20 August.'

73 *Stirling Moss winning the Tourist Trophy at Goodwood in 1960*

The car arrived in England in time for practice, and Stirling won the TT – 108 laps of Goodwood – at an average speed of 85.58 mph, his fastest lap being 89.44 mph. He won the Redex Trophy at Brands Hatch the following week at 80.35 mph, setting a new GT lap record at 82.09 mph. In December 1960 Stirling drove the car to victory in the 'Tourist Trophy' in Nassau, and then the Ferrari passed into the ownership of Équipe Endeavour.

Michael Parkes led from start to finish in the 12 lap Lombank Race for GT cars at Snetterton on 25 March 1961 winning at 89.51 mph – sharing the fastest lap at 91.18 mph with Graham Whitehead in another Ferrari. At the Goodwood Easter Monday Meeting Parkes won the 10 lap Fordwater Trophy Race at 83.22 mph, beating Innes Ireland (Aston Martin DB4 GT) and Stirling, who was 3rd, in an Aston Martin Zagato, and again achieving fastest lap (85.37 mph). At Oulton Park, Jack Sears drove it into 4th place, with E-type Jaguars making their debut and taking 1st and 3rd places. Michael Parkes spun-off twice in the BRSCC Norbury Trophy Race at Crystal Palace in May, and retired with a suspect rear wheel, but not before making fastest lap jointly with Roy Salvadori in an E-type at 77.70 mph – a new record for GT cars over 1,000 cc. The Ferrari's last appearance on a racing circuit was at Brands Hatch on 3 June, 1961 when Parkes won the 10-lap Peco Trophy Race at 82.30 mph, beating Salvadori and Graham Hill in E-types and again making fastest lap (83.39 mph).

The car then went back to Modena and in reply to an enquiry from Maranello Concessionaires in July 1961 the factory telegraphed 'EX MOSS BERLINETTA ALREADY SOLD REGARDS FERRARI.' And so the car went into limbo. I was delighted with the fruits of my researches and to learn what an excellent racing history lay behind my car. It is surprising how few Ferraris with racing histories are still extant, and I doubt whether any other can claim six first places.

Neil had repainted the car Ferrari Red, which pleased me. Perhaps, when I had it repainted again I should have gone back to the blue of its racing days, but Italian Racing Red looks right to me on a competition Ferrari. As a matter of interest, I put the car on a weighbridge to find that it turned the scale at 22 cwt with oil and water, but no petrol. I much enjoyed my initiation into Ferrari motoring that summer, driving off to distant places on the slightest pretext. The petrol consumption was a steady 17 mpg and the 25 gallon tank thus provided over 400 miles of motoring without the need to refuel. The only disadvantage of using this car was its very small ground clearance, about 3" under the silencers. One had to be careful emerging from driveways with centre gate-stops; crossing gullies; surmounting bumps and ridges; negotiating rutted roads, etc. The scarred bottom of the sump told its own story, and it wasn't an idle whim that caused the exhaust system to be suspended on flexible hangers – with some spare ones in the tool-kit!

Clearly, the full potential of a Ferrari cannot be enjoyed in this country and I was determined to let her have her head on the Autostrade of her native land. Accordingly, I decided to combine a few days in the South of France with a visit to Monza for the Italian Grand Prix; a 'pilgrimage' to the Ferrari's birthplace and a thrash down the Autostrada del Sole just for the hell of it.

Con and I left home on 6 September 1967 with rather less luggage than usual. The already small boot was further reduced by the large petrol tank, but we made up partly for this by inserting two medium-sized suitcases behind the seats.

The Ferrari exhaust was smoking more than I liked. 'They' tell me that Ferraris always smoke, but I reckoned my car was burning more oil than it was designed to do.

We crossed on the 'Lord Warden' from Dover to Boulogne, made for Arras and joined the A1 Autoroute for Paris. At last, I could give the Ferrari her head and I had my first taste of

74 *On the starting grid (94) at Goodwood in the Fordwater Trophy Race in April 1961, won by Stirling Moss*

high speed motoring in this car. We stayed the night at Les Pléiades, at Barbizon and next morning resumed our journey south in beautiful, sunny weather. Miles and miles at over 100 mph. The race breeding of the Ferrari manifested itself in the ease with which it cruised at 120, 130 – with occasional bursts at 140 mph. Its roadholding and instant response to throttle, brakes and steering gave one confidence and a feeling of safety which, I think, puts Ferrari motoring into a different dimension.

We made more leisurely progress after leaving the Autoroute before Aix-en-Provence, and arrived at Eze-sur-mer in time for dinner. Con opted for a quiet stay at Cap Estel instead of flashing pointlessly up and down Autostrada and sampling the doubtful amenities of Monza on Grand Prix day, but our motor-minded niece, Anthea, jumped at the opportunity of flying down to Nice and accompanying me in the Ferrari on the planned 1,600-mile round trip. We left next morning for Turin to visit the

Pinin Farina works. On the outskirts (or rather 'inskirts') of Turin I summoned a taxi to lead me to the obscure location of the famous coachworks, a ploy which saved much time and frustration. It was interesting to see Farina bodies being made by mass production methods. The body on my Ferrari was a Farina design but had been built by Scaglietti in Modena. Our destination was Como, where we spent a couple of nights to attend the Italian Grand Prix. Early next morning we went to Johnny Lurani's home on the way to Monza. Louis Chiron, who was staying at Cernusco, certainly appreciated the Ferrari, and when I came to a stop in the car park at Monza the car attracted – dare I say it? – more attention than the very latest creations from the Italian drawing-boards.

The next day, Grand Prix day, was bright and sunny. Jim Clark had been fastest in practice and we were delighted to be invited by Colin Chapman to be in the Lotus pit during the race. The start of the Grand Prix was a shambles.

75 *The Ferrari in good company: on the left, Heathcote-Drury's 1959 250 GT Berlinetta, and on the right, the 250 GT of the late Adrian Conan Doyle (note the unusual front end treatment)*
76 *The Ferrari on the Mulsanne Straight at the Hippodrome in company with Bill Cook's DB 6 Aston Martin during an exploratory visit to Le Mans*

The idea was that the cars would form up on a 'dummy' grid and, on a signal, move forward about 100 yards on to the proper grid to await the Starting Flag. In fact, most of the 18 starters 'mistook' (!) the first signal for the starting signal and streaked off with no regard to the proper grid; by the time the astonished Starter dropped his flag most of the field were braking for the first corner.

Jim Clark led the race, but on lap 13 came in with a flat tyre, punctured by a nail. When he went back into the race he was 1 lap and 20 seconds behind the leading car and set about catching him. Graham Hill in the other Lotus had to retire with a blown-up engine when leading the race after 55 laps. Jim was driving like the master he was, overtaking one car after another, and seven laps from the end regained the lead. The leading cars – Clark, Surtees and Brabham – went into the last lap, two seconds bracketing all these cars. We were preparing to celebrate another victory for Jim,

but it was not to be, for he slowed down with fuel starvation and was passed by both Brabham and Surtees on the last corner, the former winning by one-fifth of a second! It was cruel luck for Jim Clark who had, I think, driven the race of his life. In effect, he had given all the other drivers a lap and 20 seconds start and overtaken them all in 48 laps. And as if to rub salt into the wounds of disappointment, it was found that the tank still contained 3 gallons of fuel, the trouble being something to do with the anti-surge material. After a brief visit to the BP Cocktail Party we pushed off to spend the night at the AGIP Motel outside Milan at the start of the Autostrada del Sole.

Next morning was The Day as far as I was concerned. Driving over 500 miles, the whole length of the Autostrada del Sole and back again, just for sheer enjoyment. It was, as I expected it to be, a most enjoyable day's motoring at fast cruising speeds on that delightful road of straight level stretches and sweeping bends through the mountains, over viaducts into cuttings, round the perimeter of towns and cities. In fact, a perfect testing-ground for the manufacturers of super sports cars located near Modena and Milan.

We left the Motel at 9.15 am; had 'elevenses' at Florence Sud; lunched at the toll-gate north of Rome; circumnavigated Rome on the Raccordo Anulare and continued on the Autostrada (A2 from Rome) reaching the toll gate at Naples at 4 pm (480 miles). The Autostrada south then became A3 and (at that time) terminated 5 kilometres before Salerno, where we turned off for Positano. Our day's motoring – the length of A1-A2-A3, 512½ miles – had taken 7 h 17 m including stops, a point-to-point average of 70.3 mph. Deducting the two stops totalling exactly an hour showed a driving average speed of 81.4 mph. Looking back, I think it should have been a good deal quicker, considering that I crossed France twice in the Rolls-Royce Corniche rather more quickly in 1973. It is true that we were slowed by single-lane working for road works near Piacenza, and again between Bologna Nord and Bologna Sud, but there were no more than the usual delays such as crawling uphill behind slow-moving vehicles in the over-taking lane.

The highest figure touched on the speedometer was 146 mph at 7,000 rpm; this I reckon is truly 140/141 mph. Timings over measured kilometres indicated that the instrument was exaggerating by 5 mph throughout the range. I was using Pirelli VR covers – (400 × 175) at 32 lbs psi – which give 793 road revolutions per mile with the 9/34 rear axle ratio equating to 20 mph per 1,000 rpm (i.e. 7,000 rpm = 140 mph).

Next morning we left Positano as a heavy thunderstorm turned itself off, retracing our path northwards at a more leisurely pace. We made a lightning tour of Pompei and then climbed to the top of Vesuvius. Unfortunately, I was directed up a road I did not recognize and, far from being the smooth surfaced road

I had taken on a previous visit, it was a very rough road with a surface of lava rocks, 5 miles long. The journey up and down was more suited to a Land Rover than a Ferrari with 3″ ground clearance. The undertray and exhausts were scraping along every time a large lump or ridge of the volcano appeared in the road.

We resumed our journey and lunched at Caserta on the Autostrada. We ran in company with a new Maserati for many miles at 120+ mph, first one leading and then the other. Speed on this road is limited only by the capability of the car; 100 mph seems to be dawdling on some stretches and when getting along at 120 it is no uncommon thing to be passed by a Ferrari on 'Prova' plates as if one is standing still.

Our destination was Modena and as we pulled up at the Real-Fini Hotel, having driven 451.6 miles that day, we saw another 250 GT Berlinetta parked outside. It had an unusual pointed nose and belonged to Adrian Conan Doyle.

Early next morning we crossed the road to the Ferrari Service Department and saw more Ferraris gathered together than we had ever seen before in one place. We were taken to nearby Maranello and shown round the factory where Ferraris were taking shape in an atmosphere of clinical cleanliness. What impressed me most was seeing crankshafts for the V-12 engines being machined out of solid steel billets. Back at the Service Dept I swallowed hard and asked them to examine my engine and give me an opinion as to its condition. The chief technician attached an instrument to make a crankcase compression test, revved the engine straight up to 7,000 rpm and laconically said that it needed a complete overhaul! It was a bitter pill, but I was not really surprised as the oil consumption was by then phenomenal, no less than 7¾ gallons having been added since leaving home – 2,265 miles = 290 mpg.

Somewhat chastened I left Modena, but with no doubt in my mind about the car's continued ability to perform as hitherto, for it was going very well and the oil pressure was being maintained. It was clear, however, that some serious thought would have to be given to the need for a major job on the engine. The smoking exhaust was worse and it wasn't funny being overtaken by a cloud of blue smoke every time I came to a standstill! We had a very wet journey up the Autostrada to Milan and then on A7 to Genoa. The drive along the coast was particularly trying, what with heavy rain and heavy traffic, and we did not reach Eze until 10.50 pm, after stopping for a meal in San Remo.

We spent a few days at Cap Estel, during which I distinguished myself by falling backwards off an 8-foot wall trying to photograph a dolly bird sunbathing on the rocks below; a mishap which necessitated a taxi ride to the hospital in Monte-Carlo to stitch up a lacerated elbow, but which might have been much worse as I missed by inches an ugly tree stump before measuring my length on the ground. Anthea took a 'plane back to London and Con and I left for home in the Ferrari arriving the following day with the car still going like a bomb after the 3,494-mile trip, despite the gloomy verdict of Modena.

Considered in the home environment, it was clear that the engine overhaul could be postponed no longer. I wrote to Modena and received a quotation which compared favourably with the cost of having the work done here, even allowing for the cost of delivering the car to Italy and collecting it later, and for the Customs Duty of 25.2% payable on the bill. Since it also included a bench-test of the engine after rebuilding – a facility not available here – I decided to have the job done at Modena, together with some additional work of various sorts. I cannot pretend that the prospect of driving the Ferrari out to Italy and back was not a factor in reaching this decision.

For business reasons it was convenient for me to drive the Ferrari to Modena in January 1968, not the best month for a trans-European journey. On this occasion I was accompanied by my nephew Andrew, Anthea's brother, and I was more than pleased to have his aid and company in the adverse conditions we encountered. When we left home Europe was in the grip of ice and snow. It was quite an achievement to reach Dover where we spent the night. Cross-channel services were disorganized and when we arrived at Lydd the following morning, it looked more like Alaska than Kent. The airfield was icy and snow-covered and Le Touquet was also giving a realistic imitation of Greenland. It was 2.30 pm before we started off in the direction of Paris on ice and compacted snow. It took us five hours to reach Orly, and we ate a meal in the airport before continuing into the night at 8.50 pm for Avallon, where we stopped at the Hôtel du Chapeau Rouge at 11.15 pm.

We continued next morning in rain with the temperature at freezing point. We made good progress for the first 52 miles, then the roads became really icy. Lorries were crawling and so were we. In the hilly country near Chagny we came to a stop behind a queue of stationary traffic. To add to our difficulties my battery had become quite flat and the hand-brake would not hold the car. As we pushed the car to the brow of a hill it slid on the black ice to the opposite side of the road. Lorries were jack-knifed across the road and it was three-quarters of an hour before gritting enabled the traffic to move along. In the interval the battery recovered sufficiently to kick the engine into life. On towards Lyon; signposts had been knocked down and a number of trucks and cars were ditched, some overturned. We left the N6 at Tournus, turning east on N75 towards Geneva. Only half the width of the road was usable, the other half being occupied for mile after mile by telegraph posts and wires laid flat by the weight of snow. Lumps of ice dropped off the trees, some falling on the car roof with startling bangs. We stopped at Cuisery for lunch and were pleased to observe some vehicles coming through with Italian plates and assumed that the road to Geneva was passable, for no news was available because of the wires being down. At 2.20 pm we started again, drove through Bourg-en-Bresse and after Pont d'Ain came upon a roadside notice – 'CHAINES OBLIGATOIRE.' I had none, so proceeded with care on my naked Pirelli HS tyres without any dreaded sideslips! It was not until 7.30 pm that we pulled up outside the Hôtel du Rhône after negotiating the snow-covered streets of Geneva.

The next morning, a telephone call to the Touring Club of Switzerland enquiring about road conditions resulted in advice not to go to Italy at all that day; even the valley road to the Simplon train tunnel was under snow. Andrew was game and I decided to have a go rather than sit around waiting for who-knows-what. The ailing battery had been recharged during the night, and an inspection plate in the under-tray, which had been doubled back on frozen snow ridges and was acting as a sprag on the road when reversing, was hacked off. We left Geneva in good spirits, for the sky was blue and the sun was shining brightly. We headed for the Mont Blanc Tunnel and made satisfactory, if slow, progress enjoying to the full the wintry mountain scenery. I felt rather adventurous driving the Ferrari in these conditions, but it was a sobering thought that the driver of the huge petrol tanker and trailer in front of me was merely doing his ordinary day's work. It took us 2 hours 20 minutes to reach the entrance to the Tunnel, which I was seeing for the first time. It is a truly magnificent engineering achievement running straight through the mountains for over 11 kms at an altitude of 1,300 metres. I couldn't help remembering that a friend – who had better be nameless in this context – had reached over 100 mph in one traffic-free passage in his Lamborghini, the lights and bells installed in the tunnel to monitor the speed of vehicles 'doing their nut' at this unwonted intrusion. To digress even further, I know another Lamborghini owner resident in Hong Kong who exercised the privilege of part-proprietor of the Cross-Harbour Tunnel to drive his Miura through prior to the opening at a speed never before or since (nor ever again to be) equalled in the Colony! Is there an underground World Speed Record?

As we emerged on the southern slope and parked for refreshment, the Ferrari attracted interested enthusiasts as it always did, wherever it stopped in the land of its birth. The sun was shining brightly and the snow and ice on the road were melting. It was great to reach the plains below and to turn up the taps on the Autostrada near Aosta, getting along quickly again on relatively dry roads. We reached the Milan AGIP motel at teatime and thankfully discarded our fur-lined coats and snow boots. The Ferrari was filthy – I have never seen it dirtier. After a snack we sped down the Autostrada del Sole to Modena arriving at the Real-Fini at 6.20 pm, pleased that we had disregarded the advice of the TCS on this occasion, having completed 937 miles of Monte-Carlo Rally type motoring without mishap.

The Ferrari was handed over to the Service Department having covered 2,760 miles since she was !ast there for the drastic diagnosis leading to her present visit. Andrew and I returned home by train and plane looking down upon the snow-covered terrain which had done its best to hinder us. I wouldn't choose mid-winter again for such a trip.

Peter Newens, another Ferrari owner, jumped at the opportunity to see the factory at Maranello and to ride back in my reborn car. We flew to Milan on 14 March and took a train to Modena. I collected the car and was told not to exceed 4,000 rpm (75/80 mph in top gear) for, I think, 1,000 kilometres, so we had a leisurely trip home via Geneva, where we looked in at the Motor Show and joined an enjoyable dinner party with visiting Brits. The Ferrari was running very sweetly and quietly. I felt somewhat naked without the familiar smoke-train, but it was a joy to know that the engine had been stripped down and rebuilt with new parts as

77 *Neil Corner approaching the pits at Le Mans in the 50th Anniversary Race for historic cars, June 1973*

necessary.

We arrived at Lydd on a Sunday evening, and there was no Customs staff on duty able to deal with assessing the duty payable on the cost of repairs which I declared. I paid a deposit of £180 and completed several forms. In the following weeks there followed a good deal of correspondence with the Customs people and I still feel aggrieved. They threw the book at me. Before leaving England to collect the car I had paid the bill for the work done on the car – about $1\frac{1}{4}$ million lire at an exchange rate of about $1,504\frac{1}{4}$ lire to the £ – but I arrived back in England with the car during a week-end when sterling was losing value and the authorities converted the cost in Italian currency at the estimated rate of 1,486 ruling on the day of re-importation, thus charging me on £10 which I had never paid. I asked them to deduct from the bill the cost of certain running repairs which had been done at the same time as the engine overhaul; the cost of petrol used in bench-

testing the engine; and oil and anti-freeze put in after the rebuild. They refused and added insult to injury by adding a notional figure of £25 for getting the car to Italy and back! I have always been meticulous about declaring everything at Customs – and still am – but I am inclined to feel a bit 'Bolshie' when I think how I was treated on this occasion. Sure – the Customs could quote chapter and verse in support of their contentions and I could not refute them, but I certainly felt it was a case for an agreed settlement rather than the extortion of every penny which could be squeezed according to the letter of the law.

The rejuvenated Ferrari gave me much pleasure. I took it across the Channel again in the Spring of 1969 to make arrangements for the visit to Le Mans of the Bentley Drivers Club to celebrate the 50th Anniversary of the marque, and enjoyed a few blinds up and down the Mulsanne Straight in company with Bill Cook in his DB 6 Aston Martin.

In December 1972 Anthony Bamford expressed renewed interest in acquiring my Ferrari. He drove it once round Hyde Park and gave me my asking price of £4,500. I sold the Ferrari because I was finding it more difficult and, therefore, more costly to maintain in the manner to which it was entitled to become accustomed. I had enjoyed to the full six years and 15,000 miles of motoring in this new dimension.

Anthony at once repainted the Ferrari in 'Rob Walker' Blue and I was delighted when he entered it in the 50th Anniversary Race for Historic Cars at Le Mans in June 1973, to be driven by Neil Corner. It gave me quite a kick to see it circulating on the famous circuit at racing speed. The race was for cars up to 1959, but with the quixotic facility one has come to expect from the French, the Ferrari of 1960 was allowed to compete in the 45-minute race with a penalty of 2 minutes. The result was that Neil was placed second to Willie Green in a 'D' type Jaguar at an average speed fractionally over 100 mph.

It's a strange world – I replaced the Ferrari, fortuitously, with a V-12 Daimler, and I enjoyed just about the same performance, but with four passengers and luggage, air-conditioning and radio. That's what 12 years' progress in automobile engineering can do for us.

Thank you, Commendatore, for a great experience.

In September 1990 a similar model of Ferrari was sold at auction for £1.3m. Mine is now enjoying a new life with Paul Vestey.

'Detroit Iron'

There would always be room for a luxury American car in my 'stable' as long as circumstances permitted – an assertion which may seem to come oddly from one so keen on Edwardian cars, Vintage sports-cars and high-performance thoroughbred cars, but I know what I like when it comes to comfortable, safe and speedy transportation.

Come to think of it, the first car I ever drove (sitting on my school-cap before the days of driving tests) was an American one – my father's 1925 Chrysler '65' with an open touring body. It was quite an unusual car to see in England and I enjoyed being at the wheel.

The second American car in my life has been the subject of much badinage between Con and me, for it belonged to her father and the point at issue is whether it was Con or the Chrysler Imperial which inspired our first tryst! Anyway, it was a great car and would accelerate from standstill to 60 mph in 10 seconds, a performance, if I remember rightly, beaten only in pre-war Road Tests by the Railton which took a fraction of a second less.

My next experience of an American car was in 1950 when Briggs Cunningham lent me his latest Cadillac, which was being used over here by Donald Healey. It was a revolution in transportation to me and I found its performance quite staggering. It was the first time I had driven a car with Hydramatic Drive and, as a result, came to the conclusion that two-pedal motoring would eventually oust the 'stick shift' for the average motorist buying a large or medium-sized car. I drove the Cadillac about 700 miles and could scarcely believe that all this could be had for the equivalent of £1,000 in the States.

Although I subsequently drove borrowed and rented cars for short distances during visits to the States, my first real taste of modern American automobile engineering came in March 1966, when I assisted my Chairman to ferry his new 1966 Lincoln Continental 4-door Sedan to Greece. We flew to Rotterdam and first set eyes on the car when the agent brought it round to the Hilton on the evening before our departure. I read the Owner's Manual, familiarized myself with the controls, filled up with petrol and put the car in the garage keenly anticipating the drive southwards on the morrow.

We cruised on the autobahn at 75/80 mph to Basle – a distance of 516 miles. A check against kilometre stones over a distance of 164 kms showed that the odometer was under-recording by 6.7%. Timing the Lincoln for 4

78 *The 1925 Chrysler '65' which belonged to the author's father*

79 *Briggs Cunningham's 1950 Cadillac at Eastbourne*

80 *1966 Lincoln Continental on the way to Naples. The car was registered in New York where front number plates are not required*

kms at a steady indicated speed of 90 mph later during the journey established that the speedometer was 6.9% slow at that speed, the true speed being 96.2 mph.

The next day was a pleasant Alpine drive of 356½ miles through the St Gotthard Tunnel to Milan and the following day took us the length of the Autostrada del Sole to Naples, 489 miles, where I left the Lincoln to fly back to London. The petrol consumption over more than 1,000 miles had been 12.45 mpg.

I really liked that Lincoln and as I bade 'Bon Voyage' to its owner, who was driving on to Athens, I said, 'If ever you decide to sell this car, please give me first refusal. I probably won't be able to afford it, but I'd like the opportunity to own it.'

Little did I think that the Lincoln would become mine in August 1969, 3½ years later. I collected it in Monte-Carlo with only 11,000 miles on the clock. It was unblemished, but one of the four silencers was leaking as a result of condensation. I had this temporarily repaired for the journey home and arranged for a replacement to be ordered for fitting on my return to England. The temporary repair failed, and so did another one, with the result that for most of the journey home the Lincoln sounded like a dragster! Acceleration in built-up areas called for delicate foot-work to avoid offending the ears of gendarmerie; and the blast of exhausts somewhat marred our otherwise dignified arrival at the Château de Saran of Moët et Chandon near Epernay for an overnight stay.

Although one reads a lot about driving British, European, and Japanese cars in the British motoring press, little is written about American cars. This is understandable as only a relatively small, if growing, number of them are in use in this country. Unfortunately, there is a good deal of uninformed prejudice against them, even among experienced motorists who should know better than to condemn them without trial. The way I see it is this: it stands to reason that wealthy citizens of the United States,

surely the most technologically advanced nation in the world, may be expected to demand a means of personal transport produced to the highest standards. That these standards are not those set by British motorists is not grounds for dismissing all American cars out of hand – often with derisory references to such things as gargantuan proportions, wallowing suspension, acres of chromium-plate, no brakes, etc., etc. The 'automobile' does not take the same place in the American home as the 'car' occupies in the Englishman's family. It is a utilitarian article – in the same sense as a refrigerator or a dishwasher – in that it has a job to do, and it is called upon to do it as efficiently and unobtrusively as possible. In the case of a car, the owner has perforce to be in constant attendance when it is in use, so additional criteria are that he should be made as comfortable as possible and called upon for as little effort and thought as is necessary to ensure its proper control. All this must be set against the background of conditions in the States, particularly the availability of cheap petrol, the vast system of motorways, countrywide strictly enforced speed limits, a love of things big, and space to indulge it. Accordingly, the present generation of top quality American cars, represented by Lincoln of Ford and Cadillac of General Motors (and, I imagine, the Chrysler Imperial), meet the requirements admirably. Beauty is in the eye of the beholder and I do not quarrel with those who find American cars in general vulgarly ornate, but I considered the Lincoln Continental to be elegant in its simplicity of line and freedom from embellishment.

During the 2½ years I owned the Lincoln I covered 23,531 miles, of which about 5,000 miles were on the Continent. (One of these European trips is described later in this book.) The remainder included 200 miles weekly, commuting from home in Surrey to office near Park Lane. I would be the last to suggest that such a large car (18 ft 5 in long and 6 ft 7¾ in wide) was designed with busy London streets

81 *The Continental boot is large by any standard, as Con and Anthea demonstrate*

82 *1974 Lincoln Continental Mark IV*

in mind, but it says a lot for the ease of control that neither the size nor the left-hand drive caused me any bother at all. The automatic transmission, power steering and power brakes called rather for the conveyance of wishes to the mechanism by a finger and a toe than any orthodox driving effort. Sitting on the near-side, one tended to drive closer to the kerb than with a right-hand drive car, and this compensated partly for the extra width. Visibility of the road ahead was sometimes enhanced when sitting on the extreme left and rarely was one inconvenienced by having to follow closely a slow-moving van.

My Lincoln Continental, which left the factory in August 1965, incorporated several features that had still to appear in the best European cars. The parking brake was applied by foot and could then be forgotten, being automatically released when the selector lever was put into 'Drive' or 'Reverse' to move off again. Not only did the car have air-conditioning, but the heating and cooling systems were integrated and controlled thermostatically, the driver merely having to 'dial' the temperature which he wanted inside the car. Heated or cooled air was blown into the car as necessary to maintain the temperature at the selected level, and the atmosphere was dehumidified continuously. There was a vacuum-operated central locking system for the doors, controlled from the driving seat as were the controls for the electrically operated six-way front seat, the windows and the aerial. The car was strongly built and unfailing in its reliability, but had an appetite for silencers, of which there were four.

During the time I owned the Lincoln I became used to raised eyebrows, incredulous stares, gibes and worse, from my motoring friends on seeing me in the Continental. They could not reconcile my liking and ownership of Edwardian, Vintage and Sports cars with actually choosing an American 'barouche'. They did not know what they were missing – many of them didn't want to know! For my part, I derive differing pleasure from driving different types of cars, and count myself more fortunate than most in having had a Lincoln Continental at my disposal. (A drive from the south of France to Cobham in a day is described in this book in the chapter entitled 'Motoring for motoring's sake'.)

I had no plans to change the Lincoln, but a unique opportunity came my way in March 1972 to acquire a 1971 Cadillac Fleetwood Brougham at a sensible price. It was one of the other makes of car which Rolls-Royce Motors buy from time to time for evaluation. They had completed their examination, in the course of 6,346 miles, of the best that their transatlantic competitors could produce. I took this opportunity to up-date and widen my experience of American cars, selling the Lincoln to an American business associate and becoming a Caddy-commuter.

The Cadillac had many of the 'luxury' features of the Lincoln, including automatic temperature control. The variable-ratio power steering was better; there was slightly less lean on corners; the luggage space was considerably less; the aerial built into the windscreen was an improvement; but I never liked the shape of the body. On balance it was an enjoyable means of transport and in it I made my one and only trip from home to the south of France in a day.

Con had preceded me by air to Eze. I left Cobham alone at 6 am on Monday, 25 September 1972 and arrived on the quay at Dover exactly 2 hours later (95.9 miles). It was 10.55 am when I pulled away from the Customs shed at Boulogne and I passed the Casino in Nice at 10.25 pm. The total elapsed time of $11\frac{1}{2}$ hours for the 759 miles equated to a point-to-point average speed of 66.0 mph. My stops en route added up to 1 hour 10 minutes and the net driving time of 10 hours 20 minutes from Boulogne to Nice gave a running average speed of 73.5 mph. The total distance driven that day was 855 miles, accomplished in the air-conditioned, fatigue-free comfort characteristic of the

83 *1974 Lincoln Continental Mark IV at Moët et Chandon's Chateau de Sarans near Epernay*
84 *The Mark IV parked alongside a four-door sedan at Beaulieu*

best American cars. The overall petrol consumption was 11.2 mpg. Incidentally, during the journey I checked the odometer and speedometer with the aid of kilometre markers and stop-watch. The former was under-recording the mileage by 2% and the speedometer was $6\frac{1}{2}\%$ slow.

After a few days we left for Aubusson (collecting Peter and Jane Newens at Clermont Ferrand airport on the way) for the Ferrari and Bentley competition week-end at Pierre Bardinon's Mas du Clos circuit. The high street in Aubusson is very narrow and it is almost impossible to park outside the Hôtel de France, even to unload baggage. Con said, 'Wherever are you going to park this great car?' 'Outside the pub', I replied, hoping my serendipity in this regard would not let me down. As I drove down the road I could see cars parked nose-to-tail all the way past the hotel. It didn't look too promising, but just as I reached the hotel a car started to pull out from the kerb and, believe it or not, it was a Cadillac Fleetwood – the first I had seen since leaving London – and I swept into the vacated space amid cries of astonishment from my passengers, conscious that if it had been any smaller car I couldn't have got in!

Whilst enjoying the Cadillac, I was trying to decide which of the four 'top' American cars – the Cadillac Fleetwood or Eldorado, or Lincoln Continental or Mk IV – I would like to have when the time came to sell the Cadillac. I drove an 8.2 litre front wheel drive Cadillac Eldorado in California; another (a convertible) in Belgium and a third one for a week-end in England. I found little difference between the front- and rear-wheel drive in the kind of driving I was able to do, and I rejected the concept of a convertible in England. It would be used in the down position on relatively few days in the year, the temperature-controlled air-conditioning being preferable on really hot days, and the top soon became shabby in the raised position; the cover was difficult to fix in the lowered position and the top took up a large part of the lug-

gage space when stowed. My preference inclined towards the Lincoln rather than the Cadillacs and I preferred the four-door Lincoln Continental sedan to the more expensive two-door Mk IV Continental. In the case of the latter model, I have never quite accepted the RR-inspired radiator shell and I dislike the vestigial hump in the boot-lid which no longer houses the spare wheel. I gather it is retained as a status symbol for US owners, but in my opinion it detracts from the otherwise acceptable lines of the car.

The Cadillac did give place to a Lincoln – but to a Mk IV, not a four-door Continental saloon! It came about in this way: ideas of buying a suitable used Continental in the US, during one of my visits and importing it came to nought by reason of the Common Market regulations – extremely important but not widely known relating to cars manufactured after 1 January 1972. I fear there are owners of such cars inadvertently using them here, unaware that the absence of an 'E' plate could invalidate their insurance cover in the case of an accident, while the resale value of their cars could be little more than the scrap price.

Accepting that the road to the purchase of a new or recent model in the States was closed, I turned my attention to the possibility of finding one here in the UK. When several months had passed without the smell of a four-door Continental I was tempted to look at a 1974 Mk IV Lincoln which Steve Ouvaroff – he owns the American Car Centre in Kingston-upon-Thames – was selling for a customer. It had several important features. First and foremost it was 'E'-plated, having been imported by Ford for their stand at the Motor Show at Earls Court in October 1973. Furthermore, it had done under 2,000 miles, was in immaculate condition, and was very reasonably priced. A short drive convinced me that the opportunity was one not to be missed, and so, the Mark IV superseded the Cadillac.

The first thousand miles were driven whilst

the 50 mph speed limit imposed temporarily in the interests of conserving petrol was in force. I used this car for commuting from home to the office. It is difficult to counter allegations of anti-social behaviour, using such a large car to convey a single occupant 20 miles each way instead of using such public transport as is available. So be it; until the law decrees otherwise I shall continue to use such cars as I can afford, preferring to enrich oil sheikhs, rather than tobacco and liquor barons. I have heard others who have been criticized for using large thirsty cars, but have not yet been at the receiving end of abusive remarks concerning the assumed high petrol consumption of the Lincoln which looks very large indeed. (Actually, the Double-Six Daimler is just about as thirsty, but is regarded as 'just a Jag' by the uninformed public and passes more or less unnoticed.)

Con and I planned to spend a week in the South of France in September 1974 and decided to take the new Lincoln. The small luggage boot posed no problem for us – until we invited two friends to join us for the journey home! Only by exercising great ingenuity in loading the boot and having one large suitcase on the rear seat between the passengers were we able to manage. Except for the difficulty of ingress and egress for rear seat passengers – a characteristic of two-door saloons, but made more difficult in this case by the totally unsuitable seat belt anchorages fitted to comply with British law – the Lincoln proved itself an excellent means of transport. Our route included motorways, main and secondary roads, mountain passes Grimsel and Nufenen; and pottering round Italian lakes and along the Côte d'Azur. At all times we travelled in supreme, air-conditioned, armchair comfort and more than once my passengers were enjoying a post-prandial snooze whilst cruising along at 100 mph. Petrol consumption for the 1,000-mile outward journey was 12.7 mpg, varying from 13.4 mpg on flattish main roads to 11.4 mpg over the mountains. Two additional passengers and luggage doubtless

accounted for the drop to 11 mpg on the homeward run. The Lincoln consumed 180.8 gallons of petrol (Super in France, 4-star here) during the round trip of 2,120 miles, i.e. 11.7 mpg.

I saw only one other Lincoln Mark IV during the fortnight, but was intrigued by the coincidence when I found the only empty parking space at the Metropole in Beaulieu next to a 4-door Lincoln Continental saloon. I was able to compare the two cars side by side and to discuss their relative merits and demerits with the Belgian owner. Strangely enough, I preferred his model (four doors and larger boot) and he preferred mine, chiefly for its looks. If it hadn't been for the potential resultant Customs complications and expense, we might have made a level swap, for both cars were 1974 models, the same colour and had covered almost exactly the same mileage.

My car attracted a good deal of interest wherever it was parked. Several locals in Switzerland and France recognized it as being identical to the one used by the detective, Cannon, in the television series. Many people, including fellow countrymen, peered at the car to find out what make it was, staring at the radiator, wheels and rear-end without success. The name 'Lincoln' does not appear externally, only 'Mark IV' and 'Continental'. I would not be surprised if some holiday-makers returning to the UK brought back tales of having seen a new experimental or prototype Rolls-Royce being tested on the Continent!

Whilst the first edition of this book was going through the processes of the publishing business I seized an unlooked-for opportunity, despite earlier misgivings, to acquire a Cadillac Eldorado. My eye caught an advertisement in the 'Autocar' in October 1974 describing an Eldo offered for sale: as new, under 1,000 miles, nine months old, and at a figure not much over half list-price. As it was to be seen only 10 miles from my home I succumbed to the temptation to see and try. One look and a short drive round the houses, and I was hooked. Once again General Motors super-

85 *Change-over day: the incoming Cadillac Eldorado (left), beside the outgoing Mark IV Lincoln*

seded Ford in the Sedgwick garage.

The petrol economy speed limits imposed as a result of the Suez crisis were in force at the time and it was Easter 1976 before I took the Eldorado across the Channel. The 12,500 miles covered by then had been in somewhat restricted conditions, mostly in commuting to and from the West End of London. The weekend trip to Paris demonstrated the customary American approach to quiet and expeditious, straight-line cruising in temperature-controlled comfort. The petrol consumption during the 704-mile journey worked out at 10.96 mpg.

Did I like the car? Yes. Its six inches longer wheelbase and shorter overall length compared with the Mark IV Lincoln gave it an improved appearance. Everything was, of course, automatic and worked faultlessly – except the never-used electric sunroof which jammed open when operated late one night to enable Australian friends in

the back seat to see the floodlit dome of St Paul's! The automatic air-conditioning and temperature control was superb. The Cruise Control was consistently accurate and the many other aids to effortless driving and comfortable travel worked well. The quietness of the engine ranked with the best.

It was not long before I perceived the advantage of front wheel drive. One experienced a sensation of being pulled round bends instead of being pushed straight on as with the models having conventional drive. The resulting flat floor was a bonus making for comfort and mobility within the car.

Disadvantages? Yes – there were some, mostly arising because of the two-door coachwork. There was insufficient headroom for comfort in the rear seats for passengers of normal stature; the doors were large and heavy to close, and visibility for rear passengers was somewhat limited. For such a large car the luggage space was ridiculously small and it was difficult to accommodate quite modest suitcases because of the intrusion of the huge spare wheel.

Nevertheless, this two-year old Cadillac had several features which I was surprised not to find on the new Camargue, such as; pedal parking-brake, self-releasing when the selector level was moved to 'D' or 'R'; back of front seat released electrically when door was opened; fibre optic tell-tales for rear lights, brake lights and turn-indicators; remotely controlled mirrors on *both* sides; lighting (variable intensity) on passenger's vanity mirror; antenna rising automatically when radio was switched on.

Anticipating the delivery of my second Double-Six Daimler I sold the Eldorado in July 1976. I had driven it 15,850 miles and this brought to a conclusion a period of seven years' continuous ownership of top-of-the-range American Automobiles.

Having experienced the two- and four-door versions of both Cadillac and Lincoln, I adhere to my selection of the Lincoln Continental four-door sedan as the Best Buy – for me anyway.

Daimler Double-Sixes

The high regard in which I hold these cars is evidenced by the fact that I chose to have three of them in succession, over a period of nearly 12 years, for mostly business purposes which included about 10,000 miles annually in and around London.

The periods of ownership and mileages of these cars were as follows:

Registration no.	Period of ownership	Mileage
LVK 710 L	Jan. 1973 – Aug. 1976	16,544
NPM 296 R	Aug. 1976 – Feb. 1980	49,806
GPF 616 V	Feb. 1980 – Sept. 1984	44,269
		110,619

They gave smooth, fast, quiet and effortless motoring equal to any and superior to most other makes, although some of the electrical and mechanical failures and breakdowns experienced over the years nearly drove me up the wall at the time. Most of these related to components and accessories, but the origin of the trouble was not uppermost in one's mind when, having been speeding along secure in a cocoon of comfort with a sense of well-being (inevitably on a dark wet night), something went bang – or didn't – and the car came to ignominious stop and was transformed into a useless lump of hardware. Usually, I was not too far from home to telephone Con to come and fetch me, please, and to call Coombs of Guildford to pick up the car as soon as possible. The cause of the trouble would be quickly diagnosed and remedied and I was fortunate in having another car available while the Daimler was off the road. Very annoying, but it is surprising how quickly these bad experiences fade into insignificance when one is motoring happily again. Nevertheless, I could well understand why Jaguars were getting a reputation for unreliability in the United States and elsewhere overseas where there was no service facility just 'down the road' and a simple breakdown often meant the car being out of use for weeks at a time.

The most interesting drive I had in the first of these cars was to the south of France and is fully described later in this book in the chapter entitled 'Motoring for motoring's sake'.

When my second Daimler was delivered to me in August 1976 with 716 miles on the clock, I soon covered another 560 miles and sent it in for its first service preparatory to another Continental trip. Lest it be thought that Jaguar (and Daimler) owners often moaned about faults in new cars without being specific, I set out below the notes I made during the ten days before the service:

1. Wheels with Jaguar insignia instead of Daimler.
2. Steering wheel not central, i.e. spokes not horizontal when wheels are straight ahead.
3. Pulls to the left especially when braking.
4. Aerial should be electrically operated.
5. Cigarette burn on right rear seat near centre arm.
6. Excessive wind noise, but no draught, from front of front left passenger door.

and in the ten days after the service:

Day 1 Air conditioning not working.
2 Faulty fuse replaced. Clock stopped – will not restart. Electrically-operated aerial will not rise.
3 Replacement fuses remedied clock and aerial faults. Wind noise at front of front passenger door has not diminished.
4 Into bodyshop to remedy wind noise. Diagnosed as ill-fitting door. Collected. Wind noise remedied.

I know I am particular, but I take the view that a new car should be delivered in perfect condition and I make sure that all defects and shortcomings are remedied as they become evident and certainly before the expiry date of the guarantee.

So, with 1,482 miles from new we set off for France. I drove the first 500 miles with a self-imposed limit of 3,500 rpm (i.e. 85 mph), increasing it by 500 rpm every 500 miles. I made checks on the accuracy of the mileage recorder over distances of 50 and 100 miles against the kilometre markers on the road and established that it was over-recording by less than 0.1 per cent. Similarly, using a stop-watch at steady speeds of 60 mph and 70 mph, over 3 kms and 5 kms respectively, the speedometer proved to be accurate.

Checking the rev-counter against the speedometer I recorded the following figures:

Rev-counter	Speedometer	MPH per 1000 rpm
3000	72	24
3300	80	24.2
3500	85	24.3
4000	97	24.25
5000	122	24.4
5400	134	24.8
5700	140/2	24.8

and I see I made a footnote to this table:
Harry Mundy says 1000 rpm = 24.7 mph, therefore speedometer is accurate, but one will not reach maximum permissible rpm (6500) in top gear.

We returned home via Turin, the Mont Blanc tunnel, Berne, and the Rhine Valley, the round trip mileage being 2,218. Petrol consumption was 15.07 mpg for the 770 miles from Cobham to St. Tropez and 13.65 mpg for the coastal meandering and the run home. I commented in my notes that the price of petrol in France was equal to £1 per gallon followed by an exclamation mark. (Oh, happy days!)

In May 1977 I made a trip to Gleneagles via Sunderland to visit an oil rig off Aberdeen, returning by Windermere. This journey showed 14.1 mpg for the 1,130 miles.

Then, in September 1978, we were off again to the Continent, this time going by Fère-en-Tardenois (Hostellerie du Château) and Stras-

bourg to Rouffach (Château d'Isenbourg) where we stopped overnight with a view to visiting the Schlumpf collection of cars in Mulhouse the following morning. The collection was revealed to the public gaze on 7 March 1977 by the workers in the family textile mill next door – an event which has been likened to the opening of Tutankhamun's tomb. It was in the hands of the workers – indeed it was called the Musée des Travailleurs – who clearly resented the fact that the Schlumpf brothers had lavished money on their museum and cars to the detriment of their business. The cars were covered in dust, and interspersed with placards referring to what the Schlumpfs had done 'on the backs of the workers'. It is now the National Automobile Museum of France and the collection of hundreds of cars has been too well publicized to warrant detailed description here. I can never understand why anyone should amass such a collection of cars – reputedly never driven – containing so many duplicates, triplicates, even multiplicates, or whatever the word is.

We went on through Basle and Zurich into Austria at Feldkirch and, after a night-stop in Innsbruck (Maria Theresia Hotel), drove on to Salzburg to be well placed for a visit next day to Kremsmünster near Linz. This diversion was made especially to see 'my' 1910 Mercedes in its new home – the Schloss Kremsegg where Herr Ing. Werner Lutzky, then President of the East Austria Veteran Motor Club, kept his collection of Mercedes and other cars. (Well worth a deviation, but intending visitors would be well-advised to telephone in advance – [0]7583 247.)

We retraced our route on the autobahn, round Salzburg, crossing a narrow neck of Germany after queuing for half-an-hour at the Customs. Leaving the autobahn at Bad Reichenhall to cut off a corner we rejoined it at Wattens, just east of Innsbruck, continuing south over the Brenner Pass. The night was passed in Bolzano (Park Laurens Hotel) where we fortuitously met some English motoring journalists refreshing themselves in the market-place on the way home from the Italian Grand Prix. They encouraged me to pursue an idea I had in mind to cross the Stelvio Pass – one of the few famous Alpine passes I had not yet crossed – so we left Bolzano by the road to Merano and enjoyed the climb and descent of this pass, with its 48 hairpin bends on the way up and about the same down on the other side. From Bolzano to the top of the pass was 66 miles and took two and a half hours.

We followed the obvious route via Tirano to the tip of Lake Como, along its eastern shore to Lecco, round Milan and then southwards on the A7, A26 and A10 to our customary destination – Le Cap Estel at Eze-Bord-de-Mer.

We returned home by the direct route across France, breaking the journey at Condrieu, 7 miles south of Vienne on the right bank of the Rhône. One of my stops for petrol was at Aire de Sézérin on the south side of Lyon and it proved to be an educational one. I knew I was very low in fuel and told the attendant to fill both tanks, which he did, but when I went to pay I noted that the quantity of petrol shown on the pump was greater than the combined capacity of both tanks! I protested and called the *patron*. I demonstrated to him the discrepancy by reference to the specification in the instruction book and paid only for the amount of petrol I estimated to have taken. The crook serving me had clearly not zeroed the pump after the previous customer whose money he had presumably pocketed, planning to recoup it from the next (unsuspecting) customer. It was his bad luck that it was me! (Whilst on the subject of crooks – on one occasion I sent one of the office drivers to the company's nearby garage in a side-street in Mayfair to bring the Daimler round and was surprised to receive an agitated telephone call from him saying that the car wasn't there and was another person using it? No. He had inexcusably left the garage, leaving the doors open with the Daimler poised at the threshold ready to go. It went all right – it had been stolen! I recovered it next day, the police having taken it in after chasing it near St John's Wood where it had been

in a minor shunt sustaining front end cosmetic damage.)

Well, that Continental holiday added 2,768 to the car's mileage and accounted for 215.69 gallons of petrol being burnt at the rate of a gallon every 12.83 miles.

In September 1983 we went again to Eze, this time in my third Daimler Double-Six (a Series III) via Metz, Burgenstock and Portofino, thus lengthening the journey to 1,100 miles. We decided to see something of the Camargue on the return trip and stopped a night at the Hotel Jules César in Arles. This hotel is on the main street and has a very small in-and-out drive with a not-very-easy access. When I arrived I was unable to enter the drive because of a badly-parked (French registered) car obstructing the entrance. I went to the reception desk and asked that the owner be contacted and requested to move his car, but the answer came back that he had refused. As a result our luggage was unloaded in the street and the car had to be left there all night. I really wanted to inconvenience the owner of that car as much as he had incommoded me, but rejected the ideal of deflating tyres as too public an action and doubtless unlawful. Then I had an idea during breakfast. I put a paper napkin in the palm of my hand, slapped a spoonful of marmalade on it and – you've guessed – as I walked to my car past the offending vehicle I took a comprehensive grip of the door handle on the driver's side, and then disposed of the napkin! (I would have liked to have seen the resulting encounter!)

Before leaving Arles on the homeward journey I filled up with petrol and topped up the oil. After 183 miles we lunched at the Porte de Lyon; again refuelled and I noticed nothing untoward about the car. However, when I next stopped for petrol after 233 miles at Nemours I saw smoke coming from under the bonnet. When I opened the bonnet, it was not a pretty sight. There was oil everywhere – and I mean everywhere. I then saw the oil-filler cap resting on top of the engine and realized that I had not made sure it was properly replaced when I topped up in Arles that morning. The engine had been throwing out oil all day. There was no oil on the dipstick and it took six litres to bring it up to the maximum level. There had been no loss of oil pressure – I am an inveterate instrument watcher – but I feared the worst. It was a sobering experience, and after proceeding gingerly for a while I was relieved to find that no harm had been done. This trip covered a distance of 2,238 miles and the overall petrol consumption showed a slight improvement over the two previous models at 14.38 mpg.

And that concluded my experience of Daimler Double-Sixes which I considered to be the best value for money in the world at that time – bar none.

A solo 'non-stop' drive across France in the first of these Daimlers is described in the chapter entitled 'Motoring for motoring's sake'.

Rolls-Royce Silver Shadows

In March 1980 I acquired a 1971 Rolls-Royce Silver Shadow with 29,656 miles on the clock. It was a car I had known since new and in which I had driven several thousands of miles – some of which are referred to later in the chapter entitled 'Borrowed Plumes'. It was a standard steel saloon in very good condition and had been chauffeur-maintained and serviced by Rolls-Royce at Hythe Road.

I did not take this car abroad until the following year, 1981. Then, after a weekend trip with friends to Paris in March – made the more pleasant by finding Jackie Stewart overnighting in the same hotel, La Résidence du Bois (now sadly closed) – we left home for the south of France early in September. Our first night was spent in the Hilton near Orly, to facilitate an easy start next morning for Marseilles where we stayed at Le Petit Nice on the Corniche du Président J.F. Kennedy. This delightful establishment is a two-star Michelin restaurant with some accommodation, overlooking the island and fortress of Château d'If (made famous by Alexandre Dumas in his novel *The Man in the Iron Mask*). The bedrooms have names of appropriate historical importance – Con took pleasure when ordering her breakfast by saying 'Ici Marie Antoinette'!

We returned through the Grand St Bernard tunnel, staying in Montreux, then via Chaumont to Epernay where we were guests of Moët & Chandon at the Château de Saran. Altogether 2,179 miles of very pleasant motoring – oh, yes! – and at 12.21 mpg.

The Silver Shadow I, as it has been called since the introduction of the Silver Shadow II, gave me four years and 12,578 miles of happy motoring and I really had no thought of changing it until one day in February 1984 when passing Axtell's garage in Wormley, Surrey, I stopped to look at a T2 Bentley for sale on the forecourt and fell for a Silver Shadow II alongside. It was three-and-a-half years old and had done 20,085 miles. So the Silver Shadow I was replaced by the Silver Shadow II, but not for long; not because I did not like it – indeed it was a significant improvement on its predecessor – but because the Bentley Turbo R joined the stable on 1 August. And ever since, my loyalty to the products of Crewe rests firmly in the round-chested versions.

86 *Change-over day for the Silver Shadows – I on the left, II on the right – February 1984*

Borrowed plumes King for a day, or two, or more

R-Type Continental Bentley

In the post-war years it has been my good fortune to be lent motor cars by other people; sometimes the manufacturers, sometimes trusting owners. I seize every opportunity to drive good cars, preferably large and fast, and am blessed with a total lack of the apprehension which deters many experienced motorists from enjoying borrowed plumes. Many's the time I have got into a strange car and driven off in London's West End rush-hour traffic on a wet and dark Friday night. This is not a boast, merely my good luck. Nor does it imply a lack of concern; quite the opposite, in fact, for I drive as if it were my own car and no one can ask for more than that.

One of the most enjoyable borrowings took place twenty years ago, when I had the use of one of Briggs Cunningham's R-Type Continental Bentleys for a holiday on the Continent.

Few motoring enthusiasts, except the small circle of journalists whose professional activities included the testing of cars, had yet driven the Continental Bentley. I was elated when, early in 1953, in the course of correspondence on the subject of Le Mans arrangements, Briggs Cunningham suggested I 'deliver' his new left-hand drive Continental to him at Le Mans and, after the race, borrow his 'old' one for a touring holiday. 'Old' in this case meant eleven months and 11,000 miles.

I collected the brand-new Continental at the Conduit Street showrooms of Bentley Motors and was pleased to find that my recollections of the fine qualities of this car had not been gilded by the passage of time. Two changes had been made which affected the external appearance of the car. The first was the fitting of more substantial steel bumpers designed to cope with transatlantic driving habits, in place of the original ones of light alloy. The second one was the outcome of public opinion and concerned the radiator cap. The prototype and the earlier

87 *Wishful thinking – Le Mans line-up 1953. From Left to right: Briggs Cunningham's 1953 Continental Bentley, Bill Spear's Continental,* *Walter Sleator's Continental, and Briggs' 1952 model. (Only Sleator's car has Bently wings on a dummy radiator cap.)*

production models had had no filler cap, dummy or real, but it was not long before a flat (dummy) filler cap surmounted by a small 'B' became a standard fitment. Both Briggs Cunningham's cars had the early type of radiator shell with no filler cap. Briggs had specified that the steering column gear-change lever customary on left-hand drive cars was to be replaced by a central gate change. This gear-change mechanism proved itself to be as positive and pleasant in use as its more usual right-hand counterpart. Briggs shared my view that the absence of rear-wheel spats improved the car's appearance. (Partly for this reason, and partly because of expensive-to-remedy corrosion at the anchorage points, I discarded 'Olga's' spats.)

The journey to Le Mans was uneventful but exhilarating. No one will claim that the Continental Bentley can accommodate comfortably more than four adults, but we managed to squeeze five grown men into the car and an incredible amount of luggage into the boot. This heavy load naturally detracted a little from the phenomenal performance of the car, but on several occasions the speedometer needle remained well over the 100 mph mark. Leaving Le Touquet at 4.22 pm, we reached Le Mans at 9 o'clock, where we checked in at the headquarters of the Cunningham team of which we were to form part. I was pleased to hand over my precious charge to its owner and very interested to find that the car was now one of three Continental Bentleys on the strength. During the vast amount of pre-race work which was going on I managed to collect Briggs and Bill Spear with their Continentals, and Walter Sleator, the Paris representative of Bentleys, with another of these cars, and to marshal them in front of the pits as if ready to start in the race. How dearly I wished that this was the shape of things to come.

After a very full week-end dominated by the great race, we left Mulsanne Corner in Briggs' 'old' Continental, on Monday at 11 am, having made a final lap of the course, with Guéthary – just south of Biarritz – as our destination. Con and I were accompanied by Bob Gregory (with whom I had done the week-end trip to Monte-Carlo and back in his 1904 Darracq three years previously) and his wife, Marjorie. Advantage had been taken of the considerable amount of room in the luggage boot by selecting the most suitable cases and adhering to a pre-arranged stowage plan. Our route went by Tours, Poitiers and Bordeaux; this road – N10 – was new to me, but I had been told that it was fast and straight. And so it proved, especially after Bordeaux, when I covered 70 miles in an hour – quite a respectable performance in 1953. It demonstrated the effortless high speed cruising capability of the car, and perhaps the most important aspect of it all was that the passengers' comfort (and peace of mind) remained undisturbed at speeds over 100 mph.

We reached our hotel, the Eskualduna, at Guéthary some $8\frac{1}{2}$ hours after leaving Le Mans, $384\frac{1}{2}$ miles away. The 18-gallon tank was filled to the brim as we left Le Mans and I could hardly believe the apparently optimistic figures resulting from mental calculations made during the day on the basis of instrument readings. I decided to satisfy myself beyond all possible doubt on the consumption figures by emptying the tank as nearly as possible.

The distaff side of my crew clearly expressed its views as to the undesirability of running out of petrol far from a pump and I was eventually prevailed upon to stop in Bayonne. We had covered 374 miles without running out of petrol and put in 83.45 litres (18.36 gallons) to replace the quantity used (I know that this is more than the capacity of the tank, but the filling tube holds a considerable quantity), and thus my computations were confirmed; the Continental was covering more than 20 miles to the gallon; on this day the figure was actually 20.37.

In the course of the evening, we drove into Biarritz and I said to my passengers: 'There will be lots of Rolls-Royces and Bentleys around, but I'll bet there won't be any Continentals.' At the next cross-roads we came face-to-face with another Continental, and didn't see another Rolls or Bentley all evening!

Our plan was to leave the Côte Basque the next morning and to drive the length of the Pyrénées, thence to Barcelona. Accordingly we set off and went through St Jean-de-Luz to St Jean-Pied-de-Port – a picturesque village clustered round an ancient fortified prominence which, when one looks down upon the house tops from above, looks as if a sackful of building blocks has been emptied into a heap. We made a detour to visit Pau. It was raining heavily, but this did not deter us from doing a couple of laps of the Grand Prix course before continuing our journey back into the mountains. The higher we went the worse the weather became. When we eventually reached the Hôtel Col d'Aubisque at the top of the pass, visibility was down to about 20 yards or so and remains of the winter snow added to the gloomy scene. Our depression was soon dispelled by the warmth of the welcome given to us by the patron and his wife, who were surprised to see us arrive in such weather in spite of a long-standing reservation.

Weather conditions had not improved by the next morning. The plot for that day was to follow the Route des Pyrénées and spend the night some 250 miles away at the Grand Hotel at the summit of the Col de Puymorens, but the clouds were so low as to obscure the scenery and to take the pleasure out of driving. We went into Lourdes and had a look round that remarkable religious city; thence to Barbazan where we finally made up our minds that the Pyrénées were not for us that year. We decided to turn southwards into Spain in search of sunshine, and sent a telegram of regret to the hotel on the Puymorens.

A study of the map revealed that the nearest frontier crossing was on a comparatively minor road near Luchon between Fos and Lés. We tanked up with Supercarburant at St Béat, the last village in France, and crossed the border on

the road, if so it can be called, to Lérida. The formalities at the frontier caused no trouble. Although individual tyre numbers had to be declared in the Carnet de Passage, no one checked them, but an hour passed before we had cashed travellers' cheques and started off in the rain. I was told that of the two possible roads, one climbed the Puerta de la Bonaigua (6,798 ft) and the other went through a tunnel, but was very narrow. I chose the former and we were soon climbing steeply on a narrow, unsurfaced road which would have brought a flush even to the cheeks of rally organizers who describe execrable tracks as being 'of a non-chassis-breaking nature'. We were soon in the clouds, which mercifully obscured the precipitous drop from my passengers' eyes. I found it advantageous to lower the tyre pressures to secure maximum adhesion and steering on the narrow, muddy road, and blessed the good lock of the Continental on the hairpin bends. The mud was splashing everywhere and it was not finally cleaned out of the engine compartment until its return to England. We continued through occasional poverty-stricken villages and eventually reached Lérida half an hour before midnight, feeling hungry and tired. In spite of the lateness of the hour, the staff at the Hotel Nacional set about cooking a meal.

On driving the car out of the garage the following morning I found the side of the body caked with mud, in some places half-an-inch thick, which gave it the appearance of being finished in two colours. The sun was shining as we left Lérida for Barcelona, 100 miles to the east. This road, a section of the main route from Barcelona to Madrid, was a curious mixture of comparatively smooth finish and occasional stretches of badly broken surface. More surprising and dangerous was the existence of an occasional pot-hole of anything up to 6 inches deep in an otherwise good stretch of road. After a deviation to drive up to the Monastery at Monserrat, from which we had an unrivalled view across the plain to the foothills of the

88 *The Continental at Lerida, the mud giving
the appearance of a two-tone finish*
89 *Crossing the bed of the Rio Tordera near
Blanes on the Costa Brava*

Pyrénées, we reached Barcelona for lunch.
The car was washed during lunch at the extremely low charge of 25 pesetas (23p), and I
was surprised to find that one night's garage
cost the same amount. We visited friends who
themselves were keen motorists, although their
activities were more than somewhat limited
by the 250% import duty levied on foreign –
and therefore all – cars. One of my friends was
very keen on motor-racing and read all the
English motoring journals. He was very interested in the Bentley – which would have cost a
Spaniard about £17,500 – and I took him for a
ride on the Peña Rhin circuit, during which we
did 90 mph along the Avenida Generalissimo
Franco.

The next morning Bob and I drove out to the
Pegaso factory and presented our 'credentials'.
We were ushered into the board room to meet
several directors of ENASA and the chief
designer, Señor Ricart. Imagine our surprise
when we found Harold Radford, Pegaso con-
cessionaire in the UK, in solemn conclave.
The main activity of the factory was the production of impressive heavy commercial vehicles,
but it was, of course, the Pegaso sports car
section which interested us. We saw about 20
chassis and bodies in course of manufacture
and were able to examine the partly dismantled
car which Jover had crashed at Le Mans.
Those Pegasos were undoubtedly fine cars, but
necessarily appealed to a very limited and
specialized market.

It was early afternoon when we filled up with
'Plomo', the best, but not so good, petrol available in Spain, and left Barcelona driving northwards along the coast road towards the Costa
Brava. This we approached with mixed feelings.
I had flown over the coast and had no doubt
that the scenic beauty would live up to descriptions we had heard, but the reports of road surfaces given to us by motoring friends made me
wonder just what we were in for. One of them
had described the surface in some places as
being made of loose rocks as big as footballs.

The road from Barcelona to Blanes, where the Costa Brava really started, was moderately good, but thereafter one left the main road to Gerona and took a secondary road following the coast. Very soon we came to a broken bridge across a wide dried-up river where the wheel marks of traffic led down to the river bed itself, with patches of treacly mud in places – to regain the road on the far bank. The road between here and Tossa was narrow and there was no wall on the 'drop' side, but the surface was reasonably good.

There was very little traffic on the roads in Spain and I could not help feeling a bit of a pioneer at times, especially in the sparsely populated areas, but my ego received a severe jolt upon entering a tiny place like Tossa only to find the streets blocked by cars bearing GB plates. (They had, of course, arrived from the north and not by our circuitous route.)

From Tossa we drove along the coast road, stopping frequently to admire the coastline, and on the recommendation of our Barcelona friends dined at the hotel at the point near San Sebastián marked on the map as Ermita y Faro (Hermitage and Lighthouse). The hotel was actually the old hermitage and was situated on a high promontory from which one had views of breath-taking beauty along the coast in both directions. From Palafrugell we cut across country to Figueras to avoid the longer road through Gerona. The route we chose was shorter but the surface was so bad that we had to keep our speed down to little more than walking pace for several hours. This section was covered in the dark, and was so bad as to defy description. Across the frontier, the roads of France seemed like a billiard table. It was a weary group of motorists which entered the Grand Hôtel at Perpignan at midnight and sought their beds without delay.

The following morning we sped along the road to Marseille where we arrived for a late lunch. We were due at Eze-sur-Mer, between Nice and Monte-Carlo, that evening and left Marseille in the late afternoon to follow the winding coastal road all the way. I was very pleased to find that our road out of Marseille took us past the block of flats on stilts built by Corbusier as I had often seen photographs of this remarkable architecture. We pottered along the coast, lingered a while in St Tropez and celebrated a wedding anniversary of the Gregorys' dining at the Tour de l'Esquillon at Miramar, another restaurant situated on a promontory with wonderful views along the coast. Before continuing our journey, we had to disconnect and remove a fog lamp, the bracket of which had fractured as a result of the pounding received on the Spanish roads. We discovered subsequently that the bracket supporting the other fog lamp had similarly broken and we had two new ones made and fitted. The breaking of these lamp brackets – not of Bentley manufacture incidentally – was the only trouble we experienced throughout the holiday.

We spent three happy days at Eze and one day I took Bob to Nice to see a fine collection of old cars that I had discovered in a breaker's yard the previous year. Here were about twenty veteran cars, some of them genuine nineteenth-century vehicles. Most of them were runners and had an annual outing during the Cannes Carnival. There were Darracqs, De Dions, Peugeots, Panhards and an Audibert-et-Lavirotte. The latter car had two wheels on the steering column, one above the other. The top one was used for steering in the orthodox manner and the bottom one to change gears, a quarter-turn representing each ratio. Truly a collector's piece.

We commenced our journey home by climbing up to La Turbie, thereby making the most of the last glimpses of the Mediterranean, and then following part of the Monte-Carlo Rally Regularity-speed Test course over the Col de Braus to Sospel. We crossed the frontier into Italy by the tunnel at the top of the Col de Tende and sped along fast straight roads to Turin for lunch. Leaving Turin we turned westward and drove over the Mont Cenis pass to Lanslebourg where we headed for the Col de l'Iseran, the summit of which is 9,088 ft above sea level. A flurry of snow at the top of the pass turned into thunder and heavy rain as we descended on the northern side. This rain persisted all the way to Geneva and marred what would otherwise have been a very pleasant run.

On arrival in Geneva, we went straight to the Hôtel du Rhône only to find every room taken. After trying half a dozen hotels, some of which were full and some of which were too expensive, we eventually found accommodation at the Angleterre on the lake. Next morning we left for Paris, taking the usual road through Morez, Poligny, Dijon, Sens and Fontainebleau.

In Paris, we shunned the expensive show places and left the following afternoon for Le Touquet to take a 'plane at 8.15 pm for Lympne. We stopped for half an hour at a pâtisserie in Beauvais for tea and reached the airport three hours after leaving Paris. Having a little time to spare, we drove into Le Touquet itself to do some last-minute shopping and caused some eyebrows to be raised when the Marchal Fulgor horns came on of their own accord and stayed on just as we passed a 'Zone de Silence' notice. The time-honoured panacea of a sharp bang with the hand remedied this fault for the time being.

Customs formalities were almost completed at Lympne when suddenly I was told that I would not be allowed to drive Briggs' car away as it was owned by a non-resident and could not, therefore, be imported on touring documents unless accompanied by the owner personally. I was dumbfounded and expressed my annoyance at length and in no uncertain terms to everyone within earshot. I pointed out that I expected some difficulty when entering a country like Spain with an American-owned British car on French 'TT' plates while travelling on a British passport and speaking no Spanish, but to be prevented from bringing the car into my own country, where I was known and could

provide any guarantees or undertakings required was enough to drive anybody 'nuts'. Chapter and verse of the appropriate regulations (Notice No. 115 A) were produced and, sure enough, anybody resident in this country is prohibited from driving a car imported on touring documents by a non-resident owner. These regulations were, of course, designed to prevent the illegal use in this country of cars which had not borne Purchase Tax, but one would have expected there to be provision for exceptional cases. The Continental was impounded until it could be collected by a Bentley Motors driver. It was particularly irksome for me as I planned to take the Bentley over to France again the following week-end to assist the Cunningham team at Reims and then to bring it back to the Works for routine maintenance. The inconvenience of having to unload everything from the car and to finish the journey home (90 miles) by taxi can be imagined.

The Continental had carried us 2,576 miles in safety and comfort and had averaged 20.09 mpg over that distance. The remarkably economical petrol consumption was, of course, the result of lightness, good streamlining and a high axle ratio and showed just what could be done. (Petrol cost the equivalent of 29p, 23p and $22\frac{1}{2}$p per gallon in France, Spain and Switzerland respectively!

I found that as far as petrol was concerned the conditions of the previous year had been reversed. The Continental pinked on the best petrol obtainable in France, Spain and Switzerland, but not on the premium grade fuels which had become available in this country; of course, petrol here was still cheaper than almost anywhere else, in spite of the penal tax element included in the price. Another thought: I could have wished bottom gear synchro-mesh, as the change-down from 2nd to 1st, used on steep, tight hairpins, was by no means easy to make silently.

The cost of hotels and meals on this trip in June 1953 form an interesting basis for compari-on with today's prices:

Hotels

Guéthary (Hôtel Eskualduna)
Demi-pension, with bath	1,800 francs per person including service, etc.	£1.83

Col d'Aubisque (Hôtel d'Aubisque)
Room, no bath, no running hot water ..	500 francs (for two)	51p
Dinner	500 francs each	51p
Service	10 per cent	

Lérida (Hotel Nacional)

Double room with bath, two single rooms,
no bath	115 pesetas (for four)	£1.06
Supper	35 pesetas each	32p
Service	15 per cent	

Barcelona (Hotel Condado)
Room with bath	145 pesetas (for two)	£1.33
Lunch	45 pesetas each	41p
Service	15 per cent	

Perpignan (Grand Hôtel)
Room, no bath	900 francs (for two)	92p
Service	15 per cent	

Eze-sur-Mer (Le Bananeraie)
Demi-pension with bath	1,900 francs per person including service, etc.	£1.93
Demi-pension, no bath	1,700 francs per person including service, etc.	£1.73

Geneva (Hôtel d'Angleterre)
Room, no bath	42 Swiss francs (for two)	£3.44
Service	15 per cent	

Paris (Hôtel Brighton)
Room with bath (no restaurant)	3,000 francs (for two) including service, etc.	£3.05

Restaurants

Barbazan
Chez Bergé	800 francs plus 15 per cent	81p

Paris
Le Madrigal	800 francs plus 15 per cent	81p

Miramar de l'Esterel
   Le Tour de l'Esquillon   ..   ..   ..   950 francs   97p
                                            plus 15 per cent

Poligny
   Restaurant de Genève   ..   ..   ..   750 francs   76p
                                            plus 12 per cent

The rates of exchange at the time were as follows:

	To the £
French francs	983
Spanish pesetas	102
Swiss francs	12.2

Jaguar XK 120
In July 1954 I had the opportunity of 'delivering' a drophead XK120 to the South of France for a friend, so Con and I, with 10-year-old Carol on a foam rubber cushion between us, commenced our summer holiday in this manner. I decided to go from Le Touquet to Nice by the shortest, not the quickest, route and many quite experienced continental motorists were surprised to learn that this took one into Switzerland, then into Italy and back into France. The detailed itinerary was as follows:

Route	Intermediate Places	Roads	Kms		Miles	
Le Touquet	Montreuil, St Pol	N318, N39				
Arras	Cambrai, St Quentin,	N39, N44b				
	Laon	N44	97		60	
Reims	Chalons-sur-Marne,					
	Vitry-le-Francois, St	N44, N4				
	Dizier	N67	169	266	105	165
Chaumont		N19, N67	180	446	112	277
Langres	Gray, Besançon	N67, No. 85	35	481	22	299
Lausanne		No. 9	226	707	140	439
Montreux	Martigny, Col du Gd	No. 9, No.				
	St Bernard, Aosta,	114, No. 27				
	Ivrea	No. 26				
		Autostrada	25	732	16	455
Turin	Cuneo, Col de Tende,	No. 20				
	Sospel	N204	243	975	151	606
Nice			216	1191	134	740

It will be seen that the journey could conveniently be broken by overnight stops at Reims and Montreux, making three stages of 165, 290 and 285 miles, respectively, and it was in those stages that we decided to do the trip.

We left Le Touquet at 7 o'clock in the evening – after a six-hour wait at Ferryfield due to bad weather – and pressed on, arriving at Reims 3 hours 35 minutes later. The next two stages were covered in more leisurely fashion. We left the Hôtel Welcome at Reims at 9.50 am after two laps of the Grand Prix circuit and lunched three hours later in Langres. We stopped 20 minutes for tea in Pontarlier (233 miles), spent a quarter-hour at the Swiss frontier and arrived at our destination, Montreux, exactly nine hours after leaving Reims. The Jaguar, which had provided the cosy comfort of a closed car on the wet drive from the coast to Reims on the previous evening, proved its versatility by giving us a wonderful day of open-car motoring.

We left Montreux at 9.20 am in glorious sunshine for the most interesting part of our trip, and arrived at the summit of the Great St Bernard Pass soon after 11 am after a tedious climb behind slow-moving traffic. (This was 10 years before the road tunnel was constructed and the 8,114 ft high road over the top had not long been free from snow.) An hour later we moved off through the Customs into Italy having visited the kennels of the famous St Bernard dogs at the Hospice. We lunched at Aosta having done only 77 miles since leaving Montreux, and set off again passing through Ivrea and entering the Autostrada at 3.45 pm. The eight miles of Autostrada soon passed beneath the wheels of the Jaguar, which sped joyfully along at 100-plus in contrast to the mountaineering so recently finished. We passed through Turin, stopped for tea and petrol, and crossed the frontier back into France through the dripping tunnel at the top of the Col de Tende at 6.45 pm with 235 miles behind us. The remaining 50 miles of winding roads over mountainous country, the latter stages well known to Monte-Carlo Rally competitors, was covered in $1\frac{3}{4}$ hours. The journey of 285 miles from Montreux to Nice took us just over 11 hours and we enjoyed every minute of it.

This route to the Riviera may still be followed (with some changed road numbers) and may be shortened, if so desired, by using the Grand St Bernard Tunnel and/or the autostrada from Aosta to Turin.

300SL Mercedes-Benz

I am still not quite sure how it came about that Mercedes-Benz (Great Britain) Ltd came to entrust me with the Works demonstrator, but I was agog with anticipation from the moment my name was entered in the diary of the 'Silver Lady' until I stepped off a bus in Camberwell New Road one Friday afternoon in March 1955, and approached the new Service Department with fingers crossed lest some VIP's requirements had deprived me of 'PLB 23' for the ensuing 72 hours. The car was awaiting my arrival and, after satisfying the management that I had acceptable insurance cover, I listened to some well-chosen words of advice and instruction from 'Mac' and drove back to the West End conscious that the car was the cynosure of all eyes. I became used to the car being stared at and was not surprised when one interested driver in an adjacent line of traffic in Hyde Park motored gently into the car in front before his attention was drawn away from the Merc.; my fair passenger said: 'Aren't men funny. He was looking at the car – not me!'

On reaching my office I was pleased to find my Chairman's Continental Bentley parked nearby and seized the opportunity to photograph the two cars side by side. Two fine cars, each designed with a different purpose in mind, which achieved perfection in their respective fields; the magnificent outcome of engineering skills not so long ago applied towards mutual destruction. What an excellent pair of cars for the man with £11,321 to spend – in January 1991 equivalent to £133,000.

At six o'clock the next morning Gerry Crozier, erstwhile owner of a 38/250 SSK model of the same breed, and I left my home to see the start of the AA Veteran Run to Hastings. The roads were lightly covered with sleet and melting snow. At Kidbrooke the 300SL contrasted strangely with the venerable cars carrying Guardsmen to the coast, and Bill Cook's 1908 Mercedes was singled out to render photographic evidence of the results of nearly a half-century of progress.

Thereafter, every opportunity was taken to keep the passenger seat of PLB 23 occupied by a series of discriminating motorists keen to have first-hand experience of the car. There were about a dozen of these chaps who owned, between them such cars as 57SC Bugatti, 2.9 supercharged Alfa-Romeo, C-type Jaguar, and DB2 Aston Martin; their standards of judgment were, therefore, very high. They were prepared to be impressed by the Merc, albeit some were doubtful if it would live up to its reputation and a few were prejudiced by its country of origin. Having ridden in the car, they confessed themselves, without exception, astonished at the performance and praised its many qualities, finding little to criticize. One or two went off with that glazed look in their eyes which augured an unusual interview with their bank managers. Bill Cook placed an order for one within a few days.

Few will deny the beauty of the line of the 300SL. Its unorthodox appearance was characteristic of everything about the car – done that way for a purpose. Those supple and inquisitive enough to look underneath were met with the sight of an all-enveloping undertray which completed the streamlining of the whole car. The method of entry into the car was by the well-known 'gull's wing' doors. These enabled one to step over the high sill without bending double or banging one's head and, contrary to popular belief, the fair sex could get in and out gracefully – though the practising period was not without interest! My own two yards of skin and bone (me, not my wife) shot in and out of the driving seat dozens of times without taking advantage of the folding steering-wheel. Once in the seat it was apparent that the instruments were where they should be – it was a bit of a shaker to see that the speedometer registered up to 180 mph, not kph – and the controls were very well placed.

So much for the static – now for the dynamic. The first thing I noticed was that the indirect gears were noisy. It was a husky noise which was music to the ears of one brought up on vintage sports-cars, but might well have proved unacceptable to some drivers. Then – the acceleration. It was meteoric and consistent from tick-over to 6,000 rpm in all gears. The speedometer needle flashed round the dial and it was quite usual to reach 'the ton' in third before changing into top. Without the slightest exaggeration 100 mph soon became common-place. Cruising speed along traffic-free roads was limited only by visibility and the frequency of hazards. Quite long stretches were covered between 110 and 115 and the two-mile-a-minute mark was instantly attainable by further slight depression of the throttle pedal. Such was the steadiness of the car, the instant response to the finger-light steering and outstanding retardation afforded by the brakes, that highspeed motoring of this order engendered, in driver and passenger alike, a feeling of safety and control which would be difficult to surpass. In top gear the Merc. was as quiet as anyone could wish, but the 240 hairy horses in the engine compartment let out a throaty roar when the revs reached the 4,000 mark.

In the course of our wanderings in the southern counties we called on Peter Hampton to find him fixing reflectors to the cars in his collection. After the inevitable demonstration run in the 300SL we pushed his 1903 Mercedes out of the motor-house – 'garage' does not seem an apt description – for another photograph of ancient and modern products from the same factory.

The next morning I opened an eye at 7.15

and realized that it was a case of now or never if I was to do any really fast motoring, so I hurried unshaven to the Merc. which stood outside covered with an icy film. I pulled out the petrol-injection equivalent of the choke and the engine started at once. I waited a few minutes while the de-icing fan cleared the windscreen and then motored slowly round the houses to warm up the engine before heading for Guildford and the Hog's Back. It was a sunny morning and the road was dry. Conditions permitted a rapid run towards Farnham with the needle between 100 and 125 mph most of the way. As the road became less open I turned round and commenced the return journey, this time accelerating rapidly until I perceived the needle at 135 mph before I decided that I was using up the available road awful fast and lifted my foot. At this speed the Merc. was rock steady and controlled with consummate ease. Incidentally, this car had the lowest of the then available axle ratios (3.64 to 1) and would poddle along quite happily and quietly in top down to 22 mph.

On reaching home I washed the car and then spent precious time shaving and breakfasting before going out again, this time with Dennis May, dug out of Sunday morning domesticity, on my right. This was the first of several more runs that day, each with a different passenger, and it became standard practice to do 100 mph in third and more on top on each occasion. What a car!

The week-end drew to an unwelcome close and 8.30 on Monday morning saw PLB 23 headed towards Town occupied by two bowler-hatted types apparently oblivious to the novelty of doing 'the ton' a couple of times on the way to the office. I drove into the Mercedes-Benz works as 580 miles came up on the trip-recorder and handed over the car, safe and sound, to the owners. The car had then covered a total mileage of over 13,000, was quite rattle-free and had that well buttoned-up feeling of a new thoroughbred car. I had made not a single adjustment and

the engine had never missed a beat.

In retrospect, the Mercedes provided me with an unforgettable motoring experience. I found no vices in the car, but I should make it quite clear at this stage that my treatment of the car was somewhat different from that meted out by some motoring journalists and others who, self-confessedly, go out of their way to make a motor car misbehave. I drove the car as if it was my own: as fast as road conditions and commonsense permitted. I did not attempt to take bends and corners at a higher speed than experience had taught me to be safe; to me it seems a pointless pastime to drive a car faster and faster round a corner until it breaks away and then to say: 'It's all right until it breaks away and then you've had it' – ignoring the fact that the break-away occurred at a speed far higher than any sane driver would use unless racing. Likewise, I did not overdo it on wet roads and soon found exactly how hard I could step on it when accelerating without wheelspin making the tail wag. No doubt some purpose is served by the gallant chaps who, in the course of a road test, deliberately put a car out of control to see how it responds to corrective treatment, for this way lies the ultimate basis for comparing the road-holding qualities of different cars in similar circumstances – but such goings on are not for me.

A week-end with the Mercedes served to underline two things. Firstly, the complete failure up to that time of our road system to keep pace with the progress made by the automobile industry. Secondly, no matter how skilled and careful is the driver of a fast car or how well-fitted for high-speed motoring the car, the personal safety of the driver and passengers is dependent to a very great extent on the common-sense and skill of other road users. Ordinary concepts of motoring must be discarded when driving cars with the potential performance of the 300SL, and even more so in the case of much faster cars which have come on to the market since its introduction in 1954.

Gaps and opportunities for overtaking, which just do not exist for the ordinary driver, occur all the time. It is more than ever necessary to exercise discretion in using the potential of the car so that others are not frightened or embarrassed, and it must be remembered that others do not always appreciate the speed of fast-travelling cars.

Truly, the 300SL 'Gull-wing' is now recognized the world over as a 'Classic' – and deservedly so.

Rolls-Royce Silver Shadows & 'T' Series Bentley

The 'Silver Shadow', – and the 'T' series Bentley, became familiar sights on our roads; not surprising really, for 33,000 were produced between 1965 and October 1980, when they were superseded by the 'Silver Spirit' and 'Mulsanne'. It was, however, a great privilege when, in August 1966, I was able to borrow the Works Demonstrator Bentley for a week-end.

When lending me this car ('1900 TU') Jack Scott, Sales Director of Rolls-Royce, wrote '. . . this is one of the very first semi-prototypes and the production cars have certain modifications and improvements, but with the shortage at the moment it is impossible to let you have one of the very latest. I hope you will bear this in mind . . .' The car was indeed the first of the new Bentleys and had done over 21,000 miles.

During the week-end I covered nearly 500 miles of most enjoyable motoring and this afforded me a taste of honey – as Tommy Wisdom described a similar drive in 'Autosport' – and generated an appetite for more.

Each time a new model has emerged from the Crewe factory it has been my good fortune to have one on loan for a week-end. On each occasion the car has stirred in me admiration, and I have felt that it would be difficult to improve on it, yet each successive model has, in the nature of things, been an improvement on its predecessor. But not since I first drove 'Olga' in 1952 had I thought that the new Bentley was so far in advance of the model it superseded as the 'T' Series.

For my part, the new Bentley gave me the fastest, safest, smoothest, most comfortable, effortless and untiring driving I had ever experienced. What more could one ask of a car? The individual characteristics which go to make up a car's performance can be found in some measure in every car. Different makes and models are notable for particular qualities and these features play a part in the choice of a car. If 140 mph cruising instead of 100+ is sought, then a Ferrari might be chosen; for enormous luggage capacity American cars cannot be beaten; habitual shoppers in congested areas would opt for a Peugeot or one of the lookalikes and the seeker after superb cornering might go for a Lotus. These examples demonstrate that excellence in one direction is invariably achieved only at the expense of one or more of the others. It just isn't possible to incorporate the ultimate in all the qualities in a single car, but, in my judgment, the new Bentley incorporated 'the mostest of the bestest'. A compromise, if you like, but in the best sense of the word, and one which yielded nothing to the very high standard in all aspects which a person paying over £6,000(!) was entitled to expect.

At the risk of raising a laugh, I must report that most of the time the loudest noise in the car was the ticking of the clock – but this is absolutely true. There was some noise from the suspension occasionally, mostly at very slow speeds, and the engine was quite audible at – I was going to say speeds over 80, but I had better say – 70 mph. The fresh air inlets were very good and enabled the car to be driven with windows closed even in quite hot weather, so that the wind noise level was exceptionally low.

From the appearance point of view, whether or not the car appealed to one was entirely a matter of personal taste. I know that many Rolls-Royce and Bentley owners of long-standing expressed themselves disappointed with the lines of the new car. I think many of them were surprised that the designers, having paid heed to the criticism that the S-Types were old-fashioned in appearance, produced a car which looked like a car of the present – and not a car of the future. ('It looks like a Peugeot 403 or a Merc., etc.')

I accepted the design of the body for what it was: a car of the 1960s. I liked it and I think that the S-Types really did look dated beside the new car. The more I saw of the car, the more I considered it to be better-looking than any of its contemporaries. The model had not yet been road-tested by the weekly motoring papers and I had no opportunity of comparing notes with anyone else who had driven the car any distance. My impression was that it was a great car by any standards.

Never had I returned a borrowed car so reluctantly to Lillie Hall, even though the faithful 'Olga' was standing by for the completion of my journey to the office. (Oh, yes! The petrol consumption for the whole week-end was 14.6 mpg, which was slightly less than the average claimed by the manufacturers.)

I have driven numerous 'Silver Shadows' since and recall a drive across France in December 1971. The car was a standard 'Silver Shadow' with under 1,600 miles on the clock. I left my office in the West End of London at 12.30 pm and pulled up at the Ferry Terminal in Dover exactly two hours later. It was half-past four when the Hovercraft beached at Boulogne and it was cold, foggy and nearly dark. It took two hours to reach the toll-gate at the Arras entrance to the autoroute (79 miles) and freezing fog was a nuisance the rest of the evening. I stopped to eat at Le Bourget Airport and then drove on, round Paris on the Boulevard Péri-phérique, and down the A6 to spend the night at the Novotel at Evry.

When I resumed my journey at 8 o'clock the next morning it was still dark and the freezing fog persisted all the way to Valence. I had covered 300 miles by noon at an average speed of 75 mph. I am not quite sure why I found it

safe to drive at speeds between 50 and 80 mph in these foggy conditions on the French auto-routes, when I would have been driving at little more than half the speed on our own motor-ways. It was not that I was brave, or fool-hardy; nor unheeding of the dangers of multiple crashes. I think it was largely because of the much lighter traffic encountered, which meant that such vehicles as were on the road travelled steadily along in different lanes. Heavies kept to the nearside lane; private cars to the middle and outer lanes. There was, therefore, no danger of running into the rear of a stationary truck and the likelihood of the sparsely-spaced cars running into one another was virtually non-existent. Even if one were to come upon a slow-moving or stationary car there would have been an empty lane to steer into to avoid a shunt. On reflection, maybe it wasn't so foggy, after all, but it certainly was freezing – the aerial trailed a fringe of ice! Anyway, the driving demanded unremitting concentration of a high order and the heated comfort of the Shadow certainly helped to reduce the fatigue.

I lunched at Montélimar and was pleased to see the last of the fog. I missed the turn-off for Nice at Salon and decided to stay on A6 to Marseille and then to take A52 and N 560 to N7 east of Aix-en-Provence. (I reached the end of A6 at Marseille at 2.40 pm with the day's mileage at 460 – 6 hours 40 minutes, including a 5 minute stop for petrol.) It was a mistake to go this way. In order to reach A52 from A6 it was necessary to drive through the streets of Marseille for 4 miles, taking 10 minutes, which seemed like hours. The autoroute eastwards was very short – 11 miles – and the N560 (and D1) was hilly and tortuous. I rejoined A7 near Trouves. At 5 pm I pulled into the Shell Station on the Promenade des Anglais at Nice – the journey of 576 had taken just 9 hours (including stops totalling 37 minutes) = 64 mph.

Checks against kilometre posts showed the speedometer to be $2\frac{1}{2}\%$ fast at 100 mph and the distance recorder to exaggerate by $1\frac{1}{2}\%$. Overall

90 *The 1965 '600' Mercedes alongside the
1910 '45/50' at Cobham Park 1966*

petrol consumption from Boulogne to Nice
(807 miles) was 13.7 mpg.

I could not have wished for a better car for
this trip, 500 miles of which had been in miserable conditions, and the experience served to
confirm my high regard for the car.

This car belonged to my company Chairman
and, ever alert for opportunities to drive interesting cars – the further the better – I was pleased
when he accepted my offer to drive his car to
Monte Carlo where he was planning to join his
yacht. He was to go by air, and I would fly back
after delivering the car. Similar opportunities
arose again in February 1977 and February 1978
with the same car and over the same journey.

Both trips were uneventful and provided the
customary cosy, expeditious runs, frequently in
nasty wintry conditions. The first of these
accounted for 820 miles at a petrol consumption
of 13.08 mpg, and the second was 934 miles (but I
have no record of the petrol used). I bought this
car in March 1980 with 29,656 recorded miles – of
which I had driven a substantial proportion
myself – and have recounted subsequent trips in
the chapter entitled 'My Other Cars'.

In the 1970s, when I was acting in the capacity
of RAC Steward on the Veteran Car Run to
Brighton and at Club Race Meetings, Rolls-
Royce lent me one their current demonstrators. I
see from my diaries that I had the use of a T2

Bentley and a Rolls-Royce Carmargue, each on three occasions, and a Silver Spirit. The distances I drove on these cars was in the 200 to 300-mile range and do not merit individual mention. There was a noticeable improvement from year to year, and always a hope that the Bentley would one day come into its own – but it was not until the turbocharged version of the Mulsanne was announced at the Geneva Motor Show in March 1982 that a new era for the winged 'B' was heralded.

Not a motoring marathon, I know, but a pleasant family occasion occurred when Con's aunt attained the age of 100 in July 1978. I borrowed a Phantom VI from Rolls-Royce, donned a chauffeur's cap, collected her at the home in Berkshire where she was living at the time, and brought her to Cobham for a celebratory lunch. The drive in this car – the same as the Queen's, I told her – added greatly to the enjoyment of all concerned.

In October 1977 I was privileged to borrow the Rolls-Royce Company's T2 demonstration car to coincide with the annual Western Region Weekend of the Bentley Drivers Club, centred on Barnstaple. It was the same car in which Steve Stone had chauffered Margaret Bentley on the '77 Run.

As with all Bentleys manufactured since the 'T' series was introduced in October 1965, the specification was identical to that of the Rolls-Royce Silver Shadow. Only the radiator shell, cap and wing badge, and the appearance of the name 'Bentley' on the hub caps – but not alas on the cam-cover or instruments – distinguished it from its square-rigged stable-mate. How we all looked forward to the day when a Bentley sports car, as different from the standard RR cars as was the R-type Continental in 1952, would emerge from Pym's Lane (Little did we know what was in the pipeline for us in the shape of turbocharged Bentleys.)

The T2 was not a new model, but was quite a different animal from its 12-year-old progenitor, having been modified and redesigned over the years, in several major aspects and in hundreds of minor details. The two most significant changes from a driving point of view were the rack-and-pinion steering and the automatic air-conditioning.

As far as the steering was concerned, I was immediately aware of a quick response to movement of the steering-wheel, not a feature of earlier cars, and when driving – not dawdling – along the twisty roads of North Devon experienced a quicker degree of control which, with reduced roll, inspired greater confidence with cornering. (Looked at now from the driving seat of a Turbo R Bentley, it still left a lot to be desired in this department, and has since induced the production and fitting of suspension packages which many owners have found to their taste.)

Automatic air-conditioning – ah well, now! I had long been a devotee of air-conditioning and automatic temperature control and had criticized Rolls-Royce for lagging a decade behind the Americans in this field. I was very pleased when

91 *100-year-old aunt 'queening it' for a day with a Phantom VI Rolls-Royce*

the Camargue was unveiled in March 1975, to find that the hitherto complex controls of the air-conditioning system had given way to a dial-your-temperature installation – but I was puzzled to find that the boffins at Crewe had tried to outdo their transatlantic cousins by providing for the selection of two temperatures at the same time for interior temperature – one 'upper' and the other 'lower'. My misgivings that this concept was mistaken and involved over-engineering, were confirmed by my experience of driving Camargues, Corniches and T2s so fitted. I could not see how it was possible to maintain two different temperatures in the top and bottom halves of the passenger compartment without using what amounted to an interior 'tonneau-cover' from front to back. I found that the most comfortable conditions were obtained by setting both upper and lower selectors to the same temperature and have never gone along with the 'fried feet and frigid face' brigade. Having said that, the system generally worked extremely well, and still does in my current Turbo R. The equable temperature maintained in the car makes for fatigue-free driving and, I think, takes the 'aggro' out of motoring for those unfortunate enough to suffer from car-sickness.

The drive to Barnstaple via the M4 and M5 brought us into Devonshire in an indecently short space of time and adequately demonstrated the effortless and unfatiguing transportation provided by the products of Crewe.

The circular tour planned for our enjoyment the following day embraced most types of road, and the North Devon coastal area demanded the unflagging attention of those at the wheel. With power assistance to steering and gear-changing I felt embarrassingly advantaged over Vintage Bentley drivers changing down into first on the hairpin bends climbing 1 in 4 gradients.

I returned home to Surrey via the A303 and M3 (to Bagshot) and was surprised to find that the journey back took ten minutes less than the (admittedly 25 miles longer) outward trip which included 141 miles of motorway.

Altogether, my weekend with the T2 accounted for 560 miles of very varied motoring, including motorways, country roads and lanes, suburban and Home Counties driving, and commuting journeys in and out of London's West End. The overall petrol consumption was 14 mpg with the automatic air-conditioning system in operation all the time.

(A single-handed drive across France and back in a day in a Rolls-Royce Corniche is described in this book in the chapter entitled 'Motoring for motoring's sake'.)

Mercedes '600'

Within a week or two of driving the 'T' Series Bentley for the first time, I was lent a '600' Mercedes for the week-end and drove this remarkable motor car for 300 miles. It was not the stretched version, just the standard saloon about 19′ long! This car was so responsive to the controls that its immense size very quickly ceased to be a factor. The suspension was superb – especially the way in which the car could be swept through a series of fast left and right-hand bends without the front end varying perceptibly from the level. I found the changing of gears very smooth. The hydraulic operation of seats, windows and boot lid I thought quite perfect. The most astonishing feature to my mind was the very small turning circle – the same as a Morris 1100 I had at the time. The front seats were very comfortable, but I thought the rear seat surprisingly below the standard of the car, too hard, bench-like and without any lateral supports.

I reckoned the '600' would appeal to many discriminating drivers in this country if only the body were not so (difficult to find the right word) aggressive (?), Germanic (?), heavy-looking? Doubtless designed with Heads of State in mind and bought by some, the '600' found much favour with 'pop stars' – I wonder why?

Mercedes 280 SE

Would I like to take delivery of a new car at

the factory and drive it to Athens? Would I?? I cancelled the Stuttgart-Athens leg of an air ticket taking me to the Far East on a business trip and took Con with me for the ride from Germany to Greece. We took a taxi from Stuttgart Airport to the Daimler-Benz factory at Sindelfingen 20 kms away arriving there in time for lunch on Friday, 9 March 1973. We were impressed, but not really surprised, to find how well D-B were geared to deal with customers collecting their new cars. Luggage whisked away by porters as if arriving at a large hotel; comfortable lounge and restaurant; efficient paper-work and expert instruction on the use and operation of the car.

The particular Mercedes I was to take over had been completed some weeks previously and had to be brought from a nearby storage warehouse. This took some time and it was 4.32 pm before we drove out of the factory gates with a full tank and a recommendation not to exceed 120 kph for the first 1,000 kms. The owner had specified one of the most sensible 'extras' I have ever heard of, described in the export price list as 'Break-in 300 km (including first service) 325 DM.' A Works driver had driven the new Merc. for a couple of hundred miles and any faults found had been rectified and necessary adjustments made.

From the start I realized that this Mercedes was a first-class automobile. (Undistinguished-looking, I thought, but functionally designed with the accent on practicality and safety.) Cruising on the autobahn at not more than 75 mph, we arrived at the Schweizerhof in Lucerne having done 225 miles in $4\frac{1}{4}$ hours.

I planned to reach Rome, 520 miles away, the following evening and left the hotel at 8.05 am to catch a train at about 9.30 am from Göschenen through the St Gotthard Tunnel. Lunch at the Melegnano Tollgate at the start of the Autostrada del Sole south of Milan took an hour. The drive down the A1 at the running-in speed of 75 mph – which I strictly observed – was a contrast to my previous blind down this

road in the Ferrari, but pleasant enough. We left the autostrada on the outskirts of Rome at 6.30 pm, and it was not until two hours later that I pulled up outside the Hassler Hotel! All sense of direction leaves me as I enter the Italian capital and, by the time I was within striking distance of our destination, the system of one-way streets and the Saturday evening congestion nearly drove me round the bend – not always the right one, at that.

We were due to report in Brindisi at 3 pm the next day to catch the boat to Patras, so we made another early start, again leaving the hotel at 8.05 am. With more than 1,000 kms on the clock I was now able to increase our cruising speed and reckoned that if I put up my limit by 20 kph every 100 kms, I would be able to drive at maximum speed on the last stretch of autostrada before Bari. And so it turned out. I covered 10 kms at a sustained 200 kph before we stopped for lunch at the AGIP Motel at 12.30 pm.

We boarded the 'Mediterranean Sea' and sailed at 5 pm. No small car-ferry this ship, but a converted ocean-going liner – quite an odd sensation driving down ramps from one deck to another. We very much enjoyed the voyage and disembarked in Patras in warm sunshine the next morning. I completed (as I thought) the necessary formalities to regularize the importation of the Mercedes into Greece and drove the 135 miles to Athens, and 15 miles beyond to the Astir Palace Hotel at Vouliagmeni.

The petrol consumption increased with the speed. From Basle to Milan (235 miles) it was 21 mpg; from Milan to Rome ($353\frac{1}{2}$ miles) it was 20 mpg; and from Rome to Korinth (443 miles) 18 mpg. (The distance recorder was accurate against kilometre posts.)

Our short stay at Vouliagmeni was interrupted when I discovered that I had mistakenly 'entered' the car with the Customs as a temporary tourist. This necessitated a 300-mile round trip to Patras with a Greek-speaking companion and a tiresome afternoon traipsing from office to office collecting rubber stamps and signatures until everything was at last in order. Before we went our separate ways by air – Con to Benghazi to visit daughter Carol, son-in-law Roger, and their two children currently resident in Libya, and I to Bangkok – I put the car in store to await the arrival of the owner. I really enjoyed driving that car; everything about it was right and it performed impeccably. Not a thing had gone wrong; not a squeak or rattle had developed in the 1,200-mile trip. This is a tribute to the inspection at Sindelfingen and, I like to think, to that initial 300 km break-in by the manufacturer.

Jowett Javelins in Monte-Carlo Rallies

Although not exactly lent to me, I feel justified in regarding my participation in the Monte-Carlo Rallies of 1950 and 1952 in other people's cars as falling within the description of 'borrowed plumes'.

I considered myself honoured to be asked by the Jowett company to be the third man in one of the three Works Javelins entered in the 1950 Rally and eagerly seized the opportunity to compete in this great event.

The Monte-Carlo Rally had been revived the previous year after a 10-year gap bracketing World War II, and was passing through a transitional phase when amateur owner-drivers could still take part with a good chance of doing well, manufacturers had not yet really got into the act with professional drivers, expensive pre-rally reconnaisance and immense support teams. Some manufacturers, realizing the publicity value of success in International Rallies, were assisting private owners with the preparations of their cars and others were participating with works-prepared cars, but with one or two possible exceptions their drivers took part on an 'expenses only' basis.

I travelled by train to Bradford in early January to meet those responsible for entering and preparing the cars and the other team drivers. 'My' car was in charge of Horace Grimley, a

member of the factory staff, the other co-driver being Reg Phillips, a well-known trials driver. One of the other Javelins was manned by seasoned competitor John Eason Gibson, and Reggie Minchin who was responsible for supervising the operations of the Metropolitan Police Motor Driving School at Hendon. The third Jowett in the team was that of Tommy Wise and Mike Wilson.

In the event, that year's Rally turned out to be one of the hardest since the series started in 1911. Out of 283 starters, 101 failed to reach Monte-Carlo at all. Of those that arrived in the Principality, 62 were outside the time limit and only 5 cars completed the course without losing any marks for lateness. The reason for this thinning out of the ranks was, of course, the weather.

We started from Glasgow at tea time on 22 January in company with 64 others, facing 2,000 miles of night and day motoring to the Côte d'Azur to be covered at 31 mph plus – including all stops. Patches of ice on high ground in Scotland and the North of England presented no difficulties and it was a cheerful boat load of competitors which left Folkestone the following morning for Boulogne. In Northern France, Luxembourg and Holland the roads were dry – fortunately so as the temperature had been below freezing all the way from Glasgow. We felt it couldn't last and at Controls we heard rumours of snow in Central France. Sure enough by the time we reached Nevers snow was falling, slowly and relentlessly, as if it was in no hurry and would go on for ever.

By the time we passed through Lyon the snow was lying 6″ deep and still falling. Such were the delays incurred by competitors that only six of the Glasgow starters checked in here on time.

I can't remember how late we were, but the maximum lateness allowance of 3 hours at the finish was being whittled away. Between Valence and Digne conditions remained the same, but seemed somewhat less daunting in daylight.

92 *The Jowett Javelin team, from left to right, John Eason Gibson, Reggie Minchin, Horace Grimley, Reg Phillips, the author, (?), Tommy Wise and Mike Wilson*

93 *Bob Nelson-Harris and the author in a Jowett Javelin arriving at the Liège control during the 1952 Monte-Carlo Rally*

The Jowett Javelin flew along, Horace Grimley handling it in masterly fashion. The speed at which he went up and down the slippery mountain roads was really something. Reg Phillips, no doubt accustomed in trials to his car pointing only vaguely in the direction of travel, drove with commendable speed. Frankly, I was pretty scared at times and I fear that my co-drivers must have been irked by the pace which I deemed to be my fastest in the icy conditions when entrusted with the wheel.

Despite the most valiant efforts – especially on the part of Horace – we fell further and further behind our scheduled time. We arrived in a rainy Monte-Carlo without mishap and were placed 96th. Tommy Wise and Mike Wilson finished 44th. The Eason Gibson car had gone off the road in an uncontrollable slide when cruising at about 50 mph where the average motorist without the competitive urge would be driving at 10 mph. Later the windscreen wipers ceased working in most trying conditions, all of which resulted in his Javelin reaching the Finish Control one minute after it had closed!

The Rally was won by the Frenchmen Becquart and Secret in a 1939 3½-litre 'Paris-Nice' Hotchkiss, followed by Gatsonides' Humber Snipe and three Simcas. (It says a lot for the quality of the Hotchkiss car, for this make had won the Rally six times in the 1930s.)

The Rally had proved to be a severe endurance test for crews and, as a contemporary motoring journalist put it: '. . . a searching eliminator of inefficient cars.' The Jowetts gave us a fast, safe and comfortable journey and we were impressed by their performance. It was a very tired and worn crew which left the Javelin in the parc fermé and made for the hotel.

When I telephoned Con before falling into bed for a long sleep, to tell her of our safe arrival, she told me that a friend of ours had been 'successfully delivered of a son.' Next morning I sent the joyful mother a telegram which tells its own story; it read: 'Congratulations, I nearly had a baby, too.'

Two years later a private owner of a Jowett Javelin, Bob Nelson-Harris, invited me to join him as co-driver in the 1952 Monte. This time there would be only two drivers. Again we chose Glasgow as our starting point and this year, too, turned out to be one of the most gruelling 'Montes' on record. It will live in our minds as Sydney Allard's year, for he won the Rally in a car of his own construction – a Type P Allard Saloon – being the first Englishman to do so since Donald Healey won in 1931.

The weather and road conditions presented no problems this side of the Channel and all was going well on the other side until we approached Bourges where it was snowing hard. The road from Le Puy down through the Rhône Valley to Valence was very bad. The N7 was narrowed by deep snow, and cars were involved in crashes and ditchings; many were fitting chains; others pushing in the hope that wheels would eventually secure a grip on icy gradients. Only 17 cars were on time at Valence. Sydney Allard, with co-drivers Guy Warburton and Tom Lush, was among them, but not so Mrs Allard and her two sisters, driving in a similar car. They had skidded off the road in the Rhône Valley and hit a kilometre stone. Sydney's Rally Number was fifteen higher than his wife's which meant that the ladies left each Time Control a quarter-of-an-hour ahead of Sydney. Going like the clappers on the black ice, Sydney recognized his spouse's car stationary on the snow-covered verge. He slowed down, wound down his window and yelled, 'You all right?' Back came the wifely reply, 'No.' Quick as a flash: 'Pity,' retorted Sydney, winding up the window and accelerating away without actually coming to a stop. Of such determination and dedication to the task in hand are Rally winners made!

The atrocious conditions persisted in the mountains to the East of the Rhône. One stretch of road was a shambles. Crews were taking hours to get out of ditches; others were stuck on hills and many were baulked by fellow competitors unable to get going. Ken Wharton's Ford went straight on at a corner, through a gap in a wall and dropped into a ravine, landing on top of a crashed Citroën, which was itself on top of another car.

And then it happened to us. Bob was driving at a commendable speed on the frozen snow when the car side-slipped into an invisible snow-filled ditch on a left-hand hairpin bend and bumped into a wall. It was beyond our human strength and other aids to get the Javelin back on to the road, so I trudged through the night in knee-deep snow to rouse a farmer, who un-protestingly (and suitably rewarded) brought a pair of oxen to the scene. The beasts were hooked up to the car and, on the command of their master, leaned forward and loped through the deep snow recovering the Jowett with no more effort than drawing a cork out of a bottle. Throughout the rescue operation competing cars were speeding past in the dark, our presence adding to the hazards of the slippery road, and our own situation being more than somewhat dangerous. Inspection revealed that the front suspension and steering had been bent and further motoring at competitive speeds was out of the question. We drove slowly to the next town, being at pains not to impede more fortunate competitors and, after effecting repairs, continued our journey to arrive in Monte-Carlo too late to rank as a finisher.

It was disappointing not to be among the finishers, but no disgrace, for more than half the 328 starters met the same fate, and only 15 reached Monte-Carlo without penalty.

The highest placed 50 cars on the road section were required to compete a couple of days later in a Regularity Test at 50 mph round a 50-mile mountain circuit inland from Monte-Carlo. Either the route or the speed – I forget which – was changed and I spent the 'rest' day before the Test reworking all Sydney's pace

notes. The British contingent was overjoyed when he drove the Allard into the Palace square to receive the winner's laurels from Prince Rainier.

An incident on the non-competitive run home stays in my memory. About 150 miles south of Paris we took pity on a lonely figure thumbing a lift on a deserted stretch of road in very heavy rain. We sat him between us on the bench-type front seat, the rear compartment being 'loaded to the gunwhales', and at once regretted it, for we were enveloped in an aroma of garlic which persisted and increased all the way to Paris. I detest the smell of garlic and my discomfiture in the coude à coude accommodation of the Javelin can scarcely be imagined.

My Monte-Carlo Rally experiences in the Jowett Javelins gave me a healthy respect for these great little cars. They were easy to drive, willing performers and the road-holding qualities had to be experienced to be believed. What a pity that production ceased two years later.

Franglais

In the early 1950's the English translations issued by the Automobile Club de l'Ouest relating to the organization of the Le Mans 24-Hour Race left much to be desired, as witness the following privilege car park windscreen sticker –

Cette carte de garage n'est valable que si elle est entièrement collée sur le pare-brise.

Elle ne peut être vendue sous peine de retrait immédiat et de poursuites judici-aires.

For to be valid in the garage, this cart-board ought to be entirely glued on the windscreen. It cannot be sold under punishment of immediate shrinking and judicial pursuits.

Motoring for motoring's sake

For me motoring is an end in itself. In no way is this more clearly demonstrated than by the pleasure I derive from driving a good car a long distance, preferably alone, and with as few stops as possible.

As I have often said to incredulous friends, if someone were to offer me an expenses-paid choice of either a return air ticket to Rome with first-class accommodation there for a week, or a good car to drive there, twice round the Colosseum and straight back, I would not hesitate to choose the latter. I have been fortunate in being able to indulge myself in this regard in a variety of cars, but the first really long non-stop journey I did – in 1949 – was in the capacity of a navigator/timekeeper – not as a driver at all – and, incidentally, it was my first experience of Veteran car motoring.

Veteran venture

The hero of this tale of adventure was a 1904 Darracq belonging to my friend, Bob Gregory. It was known as the 'Flying Fifteen' and had a 3-litre 4-cylinder engine, and carried a body consisting of two armchair bucket seats and a locker-cum-dickey behind.

The Idea
Most motorists at some time or other, when doing a long journey on main roads at a fairly high speed, have been surprised to find that they are overtaking heavy lorries which they have already passed earlier in the day. On such occasions it is quickly realized that one has stopped for a meal or for some other reason, whereas the lorry has just pressed on. It is very often the case that the commercial vehicle travelling at an average speed of 20–25 mph and rarely, if ever, exceeding 40 mph covers long distances in the same time as a car which has nullified its bursts of high speed by frequent stops en route.

It was this realization that led Bob Gregory to liken his Darracq to a commercial vehicle in this respect. He thought that the Darracq driven consistently with a minimum number of stops of the shortest possible duration would cover great distances in a comparatively short time. His theory was put to the test when he started from Land's End to the Veteran Car Club's Eastern Rally at Norwich early in 1949. On this occasion the Darracq covered 405 miles in 16 hours, averaging 25 mph, including stops, with a running average speed of 32.7 mph.

The Land's End run having been accomplished, it followed that John o' Groats should be the next extremity to receive attention. Bob declared this remote spot to be his starting-point for the VCC of Great Britain Northern Rally at Southport, and took the opportunity to make a non-stop run beforehand from Brighton to John o'Groats.

The Preparation
In preparation for the long run Bob decarbonized the engine and gave the Darracq a thorough going-over.

Safety considerations on a run of this nature suggested that something more than the ordinary oil and acetylene lighting should be provided. One electric headlamp, two side lights and a tail light were, therefore, fitted and a fully charged 12-volt 75 amp hour accumulator was slung alongside the prop-shaft. An additional 10-gallon petrol tank of contemporary design was fitted at the rear of the chassis, thus giving a total fuel-carrying capacity of 20 gallons. The relatively low position of this tank necessitated the use of pressure feed. An ordinary foot-pump was fitted on the floorboards – in a position only too convenient for the passenger's right foot.

In accordance with the traditional way of things, Bob completed the reassembly of the car only a few hours before the planned time of departure from Brighton, 70 miles away. After a rapid two mile test run, during which no trouble was experienced, the car was loaded and left for the South Coast.

Brighton to John o'Groats was a distance of 760 miles and to accomplish the journey in 24 hours entailed an average speed of 31.67 mph, including stops, no mean demand to make upon a 45-year-old motorcar. The selected route was the main road from Brighton to London and thence the Great North Road to Scotch Corner; westwards to Carlisle, then via Lanark, Stirling, Perth, Inverness and Bonar Bridge.

We decided not to aim at maintaining a steady average speed throughout, but to vary the planned average according to the terrain being crossed. Three separate hours, the first including Beattock Summit, the second Killiecrankie and Drumochter and the third Berriedale, were plotted at 25 mph each. The greater part of the run through England was planned at 33 mph. Most of Scotland was planned at 32 mph. Optimists that we were, the above hourly mileages were to include stops for petrol, food and other essentials. In other words, we would have to improve upon our self-imposed schedule in order to stop at all! Theoretically we would be forced to stop only once for refuelling but, as will be seen, it did not work out like that.

For the run from John o'Groats to Southport we planned to retrace our route as far as Penrith and then to proceed via Lancaster and Preston, a total distance of 522 miles, which we hoped to cover in little over 17 hours, including stops.

The Journey North

We arrived in Brighton about 10 pm on 13 November 1949, and were made welcome at the Brighton and Hove Motor Club. As midnight struck we left the Palace Pier for points north.

A drizzle commenced and lasted nearly all the way to London. We made good time and arrived at Hyde Park Corner 1 min early at 1.34 am, where the driver's long-suffering wife waited to pass us two Thermos flasks of tea, two ditto of soup and two biscuit tins full of good things to eat. Ten minutes later we left with 9 mins to catch up. We did not stop again until four hours had passed, and the petrol tanks were switched over. We next stopped at 8 am to replenish the radiator (which had mysteriously started boiling) from a steam-roller crew at the roadside. We had covered 270 miles in the first 8 hours (one-third of our allotted span) and stops included in that time totalled 22 mins. We were, in fact, 7 mins ahead of schedule in spite of the stops.

We could not know that the radiator was to be a constant source of trouble and delay for many miles. It was made up from horizontal tubes, and the apertures for the passage of water were very small. Some scale had come loose, which was sufficient to prevent adequate circulation, and boiling resulted.

We pressed on, and in half an hour found a level-crossing at Leeming Bar closed in our path, so we pulled into a conveniently situated petrol station, topped up both tanks, and took on oil and water.

We took the opportunity of eating a sandwich or two and drinking a cup of tea. In fact, we established a drill which was followed throughout. When we stopped for petrol, the driver attended to the replenishment of the car, what time I dispensed soup or tea from flasks and produced food from our store. When we moved off both of us were still munching sandwiches. While driving we found chocolate a very satisfactory food and consumed many weeks' ration in as many hours.

The radiator soon boiled again and we stopped at a garage, whipped off the bottom hose and ran water from the mains in at the bottom of the radiator allowing it to flood out of the filler. This seemed to clear the stoppage, at least temporarily, and on we went. This procedure was repeated a number of times in the course of the next 70 miles, and on each occasion took about 15 mins. One mile south of the Border the nuts of the prop-shaft were tightened and the radiator drill was carried out. We had aimed to reach the Border (367 miles) in 11 hours, but had actually taken 12 hours 36 mins.

After another 20 miles the radiator drill was repeated, as it proved, for the last time.

We then covered over 100 miles without any boiling and stopped only twice (once to change over petrol tanks and once to replace a plug lead) before reaching Perth (504 miles) at 17 hours 13 mins. We spent 25 mins here taking on petrol and generally preparing for the night section. We left Perth two hours late, but still full of optimism now that the radiator seemed to be behaving.

Less than 20 miles after Perth the pot-joint cover – improvised to keep out dirt – became excessively noisy and it took over half an hour to remove it. At Aviemore (588 miles) 20 hours 42 mins had passed and we were 2 hours 17 mins late. It was now dark and it was clear that we could not cover the remaining 150 miles within the desired 24 hours. We had been 'in the saddle' for a long time and succumbed to the temptation of hot soup and tea, the only occasion on this run on which we stopped specially for sustenance.

Over the Top

After half an hour we went on for another 50 miles when tiredness necessitated a 5-min stop for 40 winks just outside Maryburgh. Then on to Dingwall where we (that is, I) made the only navigational error on the trip; I missed the right-hand fork for Tain, and we reached Strathpeffer before realizing we were on the wrong road. We returned to Dingwall (in silence, but without having words!) and left by the correct road.

Midnight found us at Evanton, 648 miles from our starting point – and we stopped to celebrate the failure of our plan; the hooter, a hand klaxon, was given a wind, this being the only time it was used during the run. We were 112 miles short of our destination, but our stops had accounted for 4 hours 37 mins, of which two hours were directly attributable to the radiator trouble.

We were both admittedly tired by this time

and the weather had deteriorated to rain and wind. It was on this stretch over the Struie that the only incident of the trip occurred. We were descending a steep hill and negotiating a real hairpin at slow speed with brakes hard on and the wheels on full lock. The Darracq decided that it was just a bit too much and gracefully turned right about and stopped in the middle of the road facing the wrong way.

Fatigue, filthy weather and wet roads considerably reduced our speed. Our object now was just to reach John o'Groats. This we did as dawn was breaking at seven minutes to six. (The 17 miles from Wick seemed like 70!) We had taken 29 hours 53 mins to cover the 760 miles, an overall average of slightly over 25 mph. Actual running time was 24 hours 21 mins, which is a running average of 31.2 mph, and during the first 12 consecutive hours' running time we had averaged over 35 mph, covering 424 miles.

We knocked up the proprietor of the John o'Groats House Hotel who had just retired, having waited up for us all night. From the moment we arrived to the minute we left Alastair MacKenzie and family went out of their way to be helpful and took a great interest in our doings. Our dripping clothes were dried and we fell into bed and were asleep at once.

We were up at noon, having had five hours sleep, and after lunch set to work on the car. Bob removed the prop-shaft and Alistair MacKenzie took me into Wick, where a keen garage mechanic set about making new pins and bushes at 4.15 pm. At 10.30 pm we set off to return to John o'Groats, complete with the new bits and the mechanic, who realized that he might never see another 45-year-old car and was intent not to miss this opportunity. During our absence Bob had removed the radiator and turned it upside down, flushed it thoroughly with a hose and refitted it.

It was 1 am before the prop-shaft was back and, as we planned a 6 am start for Southport, we went to bed without a trial run.

The Journey South

Our arrival and stay at John o'Groats had co-incided with the worst spell of weather they had experienced for many a day, but this day dawned bright and sunny.

The Darracq started first pull up, and having loaded our replenished Thermos flasks and food containers we pointed the radiator south-wards. We started at 6.45 am, and it says a lot for the interest and enthusiasm of the pro-prietor and guests of the John o'Groats House Hotel that they all turned out in their night attire to bid us 'Bon Voyage'.

We were pleased to be motoring along the east coast of Scotland in brilliant sunshine after the miserable trip in the opposite direction. After 82 miles, covered in 2 hrs 34 mins, we stopped to examine and oil the repaired uni-versal joints, and drove on again for more than 100 miles before stopping for petrol and food, the latter for the first time at the civilized hour of 1 pm!

We then covered the longest non-stop dis-tance of the whole trip, 191 miles in 5 hrs 50 mins, and this stop was necessitated because we could not get at the drum of oil without getting out of the car. Oddly enough, this stop, too, coincided with the normal mealtime of 7 pm, and we partook of refreshment with some relish. The border was crossed before dusk, the 407 miles being covered in 13 hrs 33 mins, in-cluding stops totalling exactly one hour – an overall average of 30 mph and a running average of 32.43 mph.

In Carlisle we refuelled and had a snack, setting off in darkness after 20 mins on the last lap of 105 miles to Southport – a piffling dis-tance to us at the time. This we accomplished without stop, and the Darracq made light work of the well-known Shap Pass, needing second gear for 100 yds only, the rest being done in top gear. The weather deteriorated rapidly in Lancashire and we entered Southport in a howling gale and driving rain soon after mid-night. Reading a street plan in very trying cir-

cumstances and groping for the Palace Hotel, we were hailed by two chaps who appeared from nowhere in dripping raincoats. They proved to be keen types of the local Press, who had waited up to get a story from the intrepid motorists from John o' Groats.

We stopped outside the Palace Hotel (closely followed by another newshound in a taxi) after 17 hrs 48 mins, 37 mins behind our opti-mistic schedule. Our four stops – many would shudder at so few in nearly 18 hours' modern luxury motoring – had taken up 1 hr 25 mins. Our overall average for the 522 miles was just under 30 mph, and we had maintained a running average speed of nearly 32. The run had been absolutely trouble-free by any stand-ard, and the car had responded to every demand made upon it. It was after 1 am on Saturday by the time our belongings had been unloaded and the Darracq garaged, and as we had slept only nine hours since early Tuesday morning we were asleep as soon as our heads touched the pillows.

Next morning – not so early by recent stand-ards – we were polishing up the Darracq's brassware in time for the midday parade. On the way to the Rally Point we had to divert to the local goods station to get a ticket from the weighbridge: 1 ton 1 cwt. In the afternoon the Darracq took part in the Speed Trials and covered a standing quarter-mile in 32.3 secs, winning its class. It was also a member of the winning Relay Race team.

Next day we left Southport for Slough, in-tending to keep a lunch date in Stoke on the way. The journey was uneventful and the dis-tance of 225 miles was covered in a running time of 7 hrs 19 mins – 30 mph; rather slower this section, as I was permitted to drive three-quarters of the way.

So ended 1,600 miles of motoring in five days, and the bonnet had not been opened since leaving John o'Groats, now some 770 miles behind!

Retrospect

Bob and I derive much pleasure from recalling the reception given to the équipe throughout the journey, and the many incidents which come to mind will always be happy memories.

North of the Clyde most people had apparently never seen a veteran car at all. A flute player in Perth dropped his instrument from his mouth in the middle of a note, such was his astonishment. Another amusing incident was the arrival of the Darracq in the square of a Midlands town inadvertently at the head of a Battle of Britain procession, band and all, to the surprise of the waiting dignitaries.

With rare exceptions, the police and long-distance transport drivers were very co-operative and very interested in the Darracq. The look on the faces of the habitués leaving a Highland hostelry at closing time as the Darracq passed had to be seen to be believed. The Darracq was streaking through the village and must have been a truly ghostly sight with the driver protecting his face from the driving rain with a handkerchief worn highwayman fashion.

The Darracq had all the appeal of a Veteran combined with a performance not unworthy of a modern car of the time. We found that we could pass loaded motor coaches uphill, but that they could just 'do' us downhill. We passed a bus load of dockers returning home to Glasgow much to the delight of the occupants, but apparently the driver was a bit narked. The bus was definitely 'Vintage', and eventually came bucketing past at about 55 mph and really looked quite frightening. Few cars passed us, and we passed countless family cars, much to the astonishment of the drivers, most of whom hadn't been looking in their mirrors.

Several drivers of fastish cars raised their hats to us as they passed, and numberless drivers nearly ran out of road looking at the strange sight of a 45-year-old car getting along at no mean lick. Even Chris Jennings, the Editor of 'The Motor', who passed us in a 1950

Minx, found it difficult to believe his eyes and took a wrong turning in consequence!

Driving the Darracq called for no great skill, but the steering was very (repeat very) heavy. There must have been something wrong with the geometry as, although there was no difficulty on straight roads or curves, the turning of a corner or negotiating a hairpin called for herculean strength with which, fortunately, the owner was blessed.

Whilst not claiming to have done anything outstanding, it was a source of satisfaction to have completed a tour at which many would have boggled given a current model, and at a speed which would not have disgraced such a car. We had proved the 'press-on' theory and at no time exceeded 45 mph.

Mediterranean Weekend

John o'Groats having been visited in 'The Darracq', our thoughts turned across the water for a possible future foray, but the costliness of a Continental venture both in time and money deterred us from pursuing this idea. Imagine, therefore, the delight with which we received a suggestion from Auto-cheques early in 1950 that we should make a rapid trip to the South of France and back to publicize the cross-channel car-ferry operated by Silver City Airways and the hotel facilities provided by the former company.

The engine of the Darracq had not been touched since the John o'Groats run and it was decided to decarbonize it. A visit was made to Dunlops to fit a new set of tyres and tubes (815×105); what a blessing it is to veteran car enthusiasts that this concern continues to manufacture obsolete sizes. The improvised foot-pump hitherto used to pressure feed the fuel was replaced by a large capacity hand-pump, and Gallays made a replica of the original midships tank which had become work-hardened and was splitting.

Third Party insurance was effected for a modest premium and much work was put into

94 *The Darracq boarding the Bristol Freighter at Lympne*
95 *A routine refuelling stop for the Darracq*

the compilation of a road-book and a time-table based on an overall average of 45 kph. At the last minute it was decided by the sponsors that an A 70 Austin should accompany us and, although we saw little of this car for hours at a stretch due to the more normal feeding habits of its occupants it always turned up in a most friendly fashion.

We left the West End of London at 9.45 am on Friday, April 14 with the A 70, and a television cameraman in a Vanguard. A police motor-cyclist accompanied us to the outskirts of the Metropolis and we reached Lympne (66 miles) in 2 hours 22 minutes.

After a Press lunch the cars were loaded on to Bristol Freighters, the Darracq looking a little incongruous against this modern background. Twenty-five minutes later the Darracq was being filled with 'super-carburant' at Le Touquet by Shell, who went to a deal of trouble to provide refuelling facilities at prearranged points along the route, and at 4.30 pm we left for Nice.

We planned to stop only for the needs of the car and to feed while on the move or during refuelling stops. To contemplate thus crossing the 750 miles of France and passing by such gastronomic haunts as the Hôtel de la Poste at Saulieu and the Compagnons de Jehu near Mâcon will seem to many people to border on sacrilege if not insanity. Fortunately Bob Gregory and I found little difficulty in subordinating human demands to the job in hand and a gallon of hot soup in Thermos flasks, some sandwiches and a couple of pounds of chocolate sufficed to keep us going for a day or two.

Abbeville (149.5 kms) was reached in 3 hours, but soon afterwards we had to stop to replace a punctured inner tube, a task which took 56 minutes. This was the only tyre trouble experienced. We reached Paris after 5½ hours on the road, including the stop, and called at the main French Austin Agency. This stop occupied 45 minutes and we proceeded down the Champs Elysées at 10.45 pm for Essonnes which was to be our first 'pit stop'. Fuel and oil tanks were

96 *The Darracq on the Promenade des Anglais, Nice*
97 *The author's turn to crank the Darracq*

replenished and we sped into the night. Our single white headlight caused approaching indigenous drivers to direct upon us a veritable Christmas tree of jaundiced gloom, but only one so far forgot himself as to drive across the road straight at us. Several stops were made during the night to change drivers and to grease the squeaking prop-shaft universal joint, and 12 hours after leaving Le Touquet found us at Avallon (458 kms).

Tanks were topped up at Villefranche-sur-Saône and Lyon was entered at 1 pm on Saturday. Another refuelling stop at Montélimar and at 4.30 pm, 24 hours after the start, we were 25 kms short of Aix-en-Provence. We passed through Fréjus at 7.30 pm, took the less hilly coastal road through St. Raphaël to Cannes and pulled up in the drive of the Continental Hôtel at Nice at 9.30 pm, exactly 29 hours after leaving Le Touquet, having maintained an average speed of 41.47 kph (25.8 mph) over the total distance of 1,202.7 kms (748 miles). Stops on the road had totalled 5 hours 20 minutes and the running time of 23 hours 40 minutes showed an average speed of 50.8 kph (31.6 mph). The greatest distance covered in any one hour was 60 kms (37½ miles).

Into Italy

The next day, having serviced the Darracq, we decided to skip lunch and drive along the coast into Italy to see the San Remo Grand Prix. Little did we know that the winner, a virtually unknown South American, was to become a future World Champion and his name a household word – Fangio! On our return into France, we were talked into starting the return trip from Monte-Carlo instead of Nice and accordingly left the car there overnight.

Early on Monday morning we returned to Monte-Carlo, collected the Darracq and, followed by greetings and good wishes from M. Anthony Noghes and his colleagues on the

Monte-Carlo Rally Organizing Committee, we were officially(!) started on the homeward run at 10.30 am.

On reaching Cannes we decided to go 'over the top' to Fréjus. The Darracq climbed gallantly although the radiator boiled for a short time. After 3 hours 20 minutes on the road the steering-column gear lever broke (came 'orf in me 'and, guv'nor!) and things looked somewhat difficult. However a 'Mole' wrench from the tool-kit was locked on to the remaining stub and, despite the loss of locating notches, we drove home changing gears with the wrench which remained in position throughout. We refuelled at Montélimar at 7 pm and again at Villefranche-sur-Saône after just 12 hours on the road (548 kms).

The night was cold. Driving rain set in at Saulieu and continued for the remaining 15 hours of the trip. It was most unpleasant and even caused us to erect the hood – an unprecedented proceeding.

At 8.30 am on Tuesday (22 hours after leaving Monte-Carlo) we reached Essonnes and refuelled, having covered the 960 kms at an average speed of 44 kph ($27\frac{1}{2}$ mph) including all stops. After a welcome cup of tea we proceeded into Paris and crossed the Place de la Concorde 23 hours 23 minutes after leaving Monte-Carlo.

Exercising Discretion

The Darracq was going like a bomb and we were surprised to hear the first signs of expensive noises in the engine about 80 miles from Le Touquet. Despite our disappointment we decided that it would be foolish to risk the possible breakage of irreplaceable parts for the sake of completing the last hop under its own power. Reluctantly, a tow-rope was attached and the journey that followed was the least pleasant part of the whole outing. The water (etc!) thrown up into our faces by the back wheels of the towing A 70, added to the 'stair-rod' rain, was very trying. (It was gratifying to find when the engine was dismantled on its arrival home

98 *The Darracq being started from Monte-Carlo for home by the Automobile Club de Monaco*
99 *Bob Gregory out and under the Darracq*

that the noise was caused by nothing more serious than a sheared water-pump drive.) The petrol consumption over the whole trip was 25/26 mpg.

It is difficult to do justice in words to the effect of the Darracq's passage upon French and Italian villagers and motorists of all nations. Everywhere we left behind a trail of shaken characters whose initial incredulity was frozen into astonishment at the sight of the receding 'GB' plate.

We had a wonderful time and one thing is certain: we carved up another notch in the annals of the 'mad dog the Englishman' and caused merriment among thousands of Frenchmen during five days of real motoring.

Doing it the Hard Way – the Easy Way

Two years were to elapse before I had another opportunity to dash across France again and this time my conveyance could hardly be more of a contrast to the stark reality of the Darracq.

An opportunity arose to 'deliver' a Mk VI Bentley to the South of France and I did not hesitate to seize the chance of achieving yet one more of my ambitions to drive solo and virtually non-stop from the English Channel to the Mediterranean.

The car was a 1951 Standard Steel Saloon with the $4\frac{1}{2}$-litre engine and at 9,500 miles the original tyres showed no appreciable signs of wear.

I left the West End of London after a day at the office on Friday, 7 April 1952 with luggage equivalent to two adult passengers, stopped off at home for a meal, packed an overnight bag and drove to Southampton in heavy rain. I filled the petrol tank 'right up the spout' just outside the dock gates and waited to see the car safely loaded in the forward hold of the ss 'Normannia' making its second trip. The accommodation was well-appointed and very comfortable by the standards of the time, and its stabilizers were a welcome feature.

It was 8.30 am when I left the Customs Shed at Le Havre and pointed the bonnet to the South. The roads were wet enough to be slippery, but it was not raining, and these conditions existed for the first 100 miles.

Distances quoted in this report are based on the car's odometer, which recorded 707 miles on arrival at Cannes. The distances over the same route as given by the Guide Michelin, the RAC, and the AA are 706, 713 and $715\frac{1}{2}$ miles respectively. It may be assumed, therefore, that the instrument reading is near enough for all practical purposes.

The accompanying table shows exactly how I progressed upon my way. I drove more or less as fast as road conditions permitted, but rarely exceeded 80 mph. I was interested to see whether or not an average speed of 50 mph could be maintained without overdoing it. It was one thing to cover 50 miles in an hour or even 100 miles in two hours, both of which I had done on several occasions in England, but quite a different thing covering ground at such a pace for hour after hour. It is surprising what a great effect a hold-up of short duration can have upon one's average speed.

A Speed Trap

I was stopped twice by police who examined the car – for contraband or Communists or something – and sent me on my way without question. When I was signalled to a stop for the third time I was beginning to find the procedure monotonous, but soon perceived that this was a stop of a different sort for the car following me was waved on to continue its journey. A policeman, one of three, then informed me that I had averaged 68 kph through the last village. I did not dispute it, deeming apology and promised observance of the 60 kph limit in future to be the politic course but I wondered how, if indeed at all, one could refute such an allegation. It seemed that I had been timed through a 'village' and my time and description had been radioed to a wireless car

parked at the roadside some distance farther on.

The first refuelling stop was at Avallon with 271 miles covered in 5 hours 20 minutes. It took 75.4 litres of fuel to replace that used since Southampton, indicating a consumption of 17.05 mpg. I drank a Coca-Cola, purchased two ham rolls and was on my way in ten minutes, resolved not to stop again until the flashing fuel indicator demanded attention. After the ham rolls, I reached into the dashboard pocket to make a start upon my supply of chocolate to discover only an empty paper bag – all the chocolate had been stolen on the boat.

The Need for Speed

Valence was reached 10 hours after leaving Le Havre, which meant that I had done $485\frac{1}{2}$ miles in that time including the single 10-minute stop. It was dusk and I decided to combine replenishments of car and self. I entered the Hôtel de l'Europe and addressed the manager whom I had met previously in less happy circumstances when in – or rather out of – the Monte-Carlo Rally. I said that I realized that wining and dining in France was a pastime, an art, a means of passing an evening and altogether a leisurely occupation, but please could he whip up a quick omelette for me and call an hotel in Cannes to reserve a room while I went to fill up with petrol. He really did appreciate that hurry was the order of the day (the first time that I had ever succeeded in getting this point across in France) and when I returned from putting in 55 litres of fuel and 2 quarts of oil (taken out from England) the repast was ready and the reservation made. I went off again into the dark in exactly half-an-hour. The petrol consumption for the $204\frac{1}{2}$ miles from Avallon to Valence worked out at 16.90 mpg.

The darkness and the tortuous nature of the road towards the end of the journey reduced the average speed. However, no further stop was made until I pulled up at the Carlton in Cannes 20 minutes after midnight. Seven hundred and seven miles had passed beneath the Bentley

wheels in 10 minutes under 16 hours, with but two short stops totalling 40 minutes.

The Bentley was whisked away to be washed, and it is characteristic of this car that it was apparently in exactly the same state of mechanical efficiency as at the beginning of the trip; no rattles, squeaks, vibrations or other unpleasantnesses had developed on the way. I was tired – or rather sleepy – but not fatigued or worn out. The journey had been comfortable and I had not consciously changed my driving position to combat fatigue or cramp. Replenishment of the petrol tank next day showed that the consumption for the last section of the journey had been 17.54 mpg. The overall petrol consumption for the journey of over 700 miles reasonably rapid motoring had been 17.3 mpg.

Quicker by Road

Inevitably my mind went back to the days of 'beating the Blue Train'. The fastest train across France occupied 17 hours 39 minutes in its journey from Calais to Cannes, over $1\frac{3}{4}$ hours more than my time from Le Havre.

The journey served to confirm my opinion of the Bentley Mk VI. It was (and still is) an ideal method of getting from A to B in speed, safety and comfort and the greater the distance between A and B the more apparent and appreciated those qualities became.

Progress Tabulated

	Hrs	Mins	Hrs	Mins	Miles		Miles in the Hour	Running Average Speed
Le Havre (8.30 am) ..	0	0						
			—	30	21			42
			1	—	49	28	49	49
Rouen	1	10			55			
(Delay for obstruction = 5 mins)								
			1	30	67	18	46	45
			2	—	91	24	42	45½
	2	10			100			
			2	30	117	26	50	46.8
Versailles	2	45			130			
Just before Les Belles			3	—	139	22	48	46.6
Epines			3	30	165	26	48	47.1
Fontainebleau	3	40						
			4	—	194	29	55	48.5
(Champigny – police radio speed trap)			4	30	224½	30½	59½	49.9
			5	—	254	29½	60	50.8
Avallon	5	20			271			
(Stopped 10 mins for 75.4 litres of Super at 64.96 frs per litre = 4,900 frs, and ham rolls)								
Restarted	5	30	5	30	271	17	46½	49.3
Saulieu	6	—	6	—	295½	24½	41½	49.25
			6	30	322	26½	51	49.5
Chalons	7	—	7	—	346	24	50½	49.4
			7	30	373	27	51	49.7
Macon	7	40			381			
			8	—	399	26	53	49.9
Lyon			8	30	422	23	49	49.6
(Lot of traffic)								
Vienne	9	—	9	—	441	19	42	49.0
			9	30	466	25	44	49.0
Valence	10	—	10	—	485½	19½	44½	48.5
(Stopped ½ hour (6.30 pm to 7.00 pm) for meal and 55 litres of ANTAR Super at 63.80 frs per litre = 3,511 frs. Put in ½ gall Castrol XL.)								
Restarted	10	30	10	30	485½	—	19½	46.2
(Dark – driving with lights)								
			11	—	503	17½	17½	
			11	30	525½	22½	40	45.7
Orange	12	00	12	—	546	20½	43	45.5
Avignon	12	25	12	25	562			
			12	30	567	21	40½	45.4
			13	—	587	20	41	45.2

	Hrs Mins	Hrs Mins	Miles		Miles in the Hour	Running Average Speed
Aix-en-Provence.. ..	13 30	13 30	611	24	44	45.2
		14 —	632	21	45	45.1
		14 30	655	23	44	45.2
		15 —	678	23	46	45.2
Fréjus	15 10	15 10	684½			
		15 30	695	17	40	44.8
Cannes 12.20 am ..	15 50	15 50	707			44.7

EXCLUDING STOPS – 15 hrs 10 mins. 707 miles = 46.6 mph.
PETROL – 271 + 2 miles =   75.4 litres = 16.6 galls = 17.05 mpg.
        204½   miles =   55.0 litres = 12.1 galls = 16.90 mpg.
        251½   miles =   63.7 litres = 14.0 galls = 17.54 mpg.
        737 + 2 miles = 194.1 litres = 42.7 galls = 17.31 mpg.

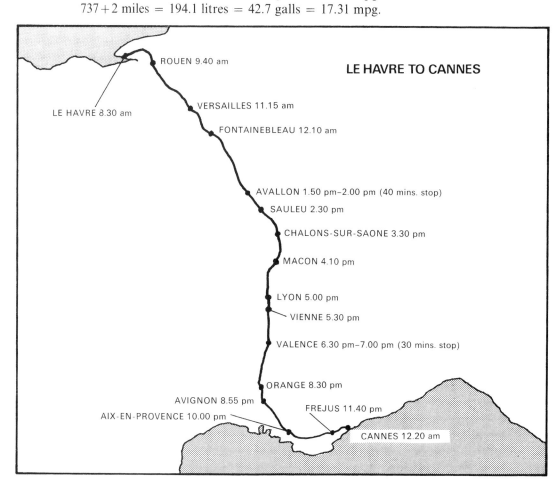

1 *The route from Le Havre to Cannes in a*
Mk VI Bentley

Paris to London

Although not a long-distance run I feel it is worth mentioning a trip I did the following year in the same Mk VI from Paris to London.

I left Paris on a Saturday after an early breakfast passing the Arc de Triomphe at 7.30 am, crossed the Channel by the Le Touquet–Lympne Air Ferry and reached my home at Cobham, Surrey at 1.05 pm for lunch.

Total elapsed time was 5 hours 35 minutes occupied as follows:

Paris to Le Touquet (137.9 miles)	2 hours 43 minutes
At Le Touquet	22 ,,
In the air	20 ,,
At Lympne	25 ,,
Lympne to Cobham (77 miles)	1 hour 45 ,,
	5 hours 35 minutes

The distance from Lympne to Cobham was 10 miles more than the direct road to London and progress across country was necessarily impeded by Saturday morning shopping traffic in Godstone, Redhill, Reigate, Dorking and other towns en route. The total driving time was 4 hours 28 minutes, but I consider that only the overall door-to-door times are of any practical importance.

'Mini' Motoring

The only occasion when I have driven any length of journey on the Continent in a baby car was in October, 1962 when I brought a 'cooking' Mini Minor home from Monte-Carlo. This car was 'bog standard' and had covered less than 3,000 miles. This was before the days of the Autoroute du Sud and I saw it as something of a challenge to drive from Monte-Carlo to Paris in a day in a Mini.

I left Monte-Carlo at 6 am with a full tank and over 600 miles ahead of me. I resolved to stop only when it became necessary to replenish the tank, matching my needs for sustenance to those of the car, and (estimating the range at something over 200 miles) hoped that two pauses would suffice.

I passed Nice Airport at 6.30 am and at the end of the first hour had done 43 miles. I had the unique experience hereabouts of driving a car which could not reach the speed limit! It was on a curvy, uphill stretch of an excellent new road skirting the Estorel Mountains which had a limit of 100 kph and the Mini flat out was progressing materially below this speed. The next hour encompassed 49 miles; the following two another 90, the average being $45\frac{1}{2}$ mph. I stopped 2 kms south of Montélimar at 10.45 am for petrol and breakfast. It took 23.9 litres (5.16 gallons) to fill the tank, showing the consumption to have been 42.44 mpg and confirming that only one more stop would be necessary before Paris. I resumed my journey after 23 minutes and did not stop again until La Rochepot (between Chalon-sur-Saône and Saulieu), 196 miles and 4 hours 10 minutes later. The tank took $19\frac{1}{2}$ litres (4.29 gallons) and I took food and drink. Just before Auxerre 500 miles came up and 11 hours 47 minutes (including the two stops totalling exactly one hour) had passed since leaving Monaco.

By 7 pm it was dark and raining. Twelve hours at the wheel had covered a distance of 566 miles – an average speed of 47.2 mph. The remaining 48 miles to the Place Vendôme took 1 hour 10 minutes. The trip of 614 miles had taken 14 hours 10 minutes (including 1 hour of stops), the door-to-door average speed being 43.33 mph. The driving average was 46.62 mph and the overall petrol consumption 44.3 mpg.

I was surprised to find that I was not exhausted and stiff. It says a lot for this car that after a meal I was still sufficiently unfatigued to pay a visit to the Motor Show before retiring to bed.

The average speed seems slow in the context of the continuous Autoroutes now in existence between Calais and the Côte d'Azur, and the same journey could doubtless be covered in a similar car today in 3 or 4 hours less. In those days, the route via N7 to Fontainebleau, N5 to Sens, N6 to Lyons and N7 to Nice was 593 miles (955 kms) and one heard light-hearted claims to have 'done it in 10 hours flat, old boy.' The subject of average speeds will always be a bone of contention, but I feel sure that very, very few such claims would have stood up to close investigation. I do not contend that it was impossible to do the journey from Paris to Nice or vice-versa at a 'start-to-stop' average speed of 60 mph, but it must not be thought that a fast car and a good driver, both capable of sustained high-speed, non-stop motoring, were all that was necessary. Six hundred miles is a long stretch of road and I never did the trip without encountering one or more phenomena which caused unavoidable delays. Road repairs somewhere or other were almost certain to necessitate a lengthy deviation over minor roads; a mishap or police check may have brought traffic to a standstill; level-crossings could be confoundedly pro-railway (and why did one always come up behind a crawling camion on entering a 'No overtaking' zone?); these and other more unusual obstacles – markets, fairs, army manoeuvres, road-blocks manned by dissatisfied taxpayers, etc. – combined to make an unhampered run an outside chance.

In my view the completion of the journey from Paris to Nice or vice versa in less than 12 hours in those days, providing that safe driving was the keynote throughout, not only reflected great credit on car and driver, but meant that Dame Fortune had been sitting on the radiator cap.

A Day in the Life of 'Olga'

When crossing France, I usually made an overnight stop in Paris in each direction and the longest stretch in a day was the 600 miles or so between the capital and Nice; not a stupendous day's driving, but a different proposition in those pre-autoroute days.

It was not until September, 1970 that I drove all the way home from the Riviera in a single day, single-handed – and then it was unplanned. The car was my well-known R-Type Continental Bentley in which I had done 92,000 miles since having the car rebuilt 10 years previously and which was then in its twentieth year. After a few days in the sun at Cap Estel I was to drive home, leaving Con to follow by air a week later. I left Eze-sur-Mer – between Nice and Monte-Carlo – at 6 am on a Friday, aiming to spend the night in Paris and to complete the journey to my home in Surrey the following day.

In the event I made such good progress that I reached the Porte d'Italie, Paris, at 3.54 pm having made only two stops for petrol and sustenance totalling 50 minutes, and covered the 589.7 miles from Eze in a running time of 9 hours 4 minutes (65.04 mph). From Nice – 9 miles fewer – the driving time was 8 hours 49 minutes (65.86 mph). It was so early in the day that it seemed unnecessary to stop over in Paris and I had been calculating that I should be able to reach a Channel port in daylight. Would it, I pipe-dreamed, be possible to reach home that night?

With these thoughts in mind I turned on to the Périphérique and drove round Paris in about a quarter of an hour. I missed the exit for N1 and left the ring road at the Port Clignancourt. After a slow few miles on the suburban end of N14, I regained N1 for Beauvais.

As I sped northwards I was considering the possible courses open to me. I knew that N1 was closed for repairs for a considerable distance entailing a diversion between Montreuil and Boulogne, so I decided to go to the airport at Le Touquet to see if by any chance there was a space on a 'plane to Lydd. I stopped at the airport building at 6.43 pm having added an additional 143.9 miles to my drive since Paris without any further stop, thus covering 732.9 miles in a running time of 11 hours 53 minutes – an average speed of 61.67 mph. The average speed from Nice to Le Touquet (including stops) was 56.19 mph (723.9 miles in 12 hours 43 minutes).

The last plane for Lydd had left two hours previously; I learnt that the hovercraft was not operating from Boulogne due to bad weather in the Channel, but that a boat was due to leave Boulogne at 7.45 pm. A brief 10 minutes after pulling into Le Touquet Airport, I was on the move again to Boulogne, the RAC having telephoned ahead to secure a place on the boat and to notify my late arrival. I reached the boat at 7.25 pm with 752.3 miles on the 'clock'. My three stops had totalled exactly 1 hour, so I had been at the wheel for 12 hours 25 minutes. From Nice to Boulogne – 743.3 miles in 12 hours 10 minutes running time – produced a 61.08 mph average.

The ship was the 'Vortigern' and, although almost the last car on board, I secured a cabin, had a welcome meal and reported my whereabouts by radio-telephone to an astonished Con in Eze. I left Dover at 9.45 pm in the dark and rain for the horrible cross-country journey to Cobham in Surrey, arriving home five minutes before midnight with 847.3 miles now recorded.

I was delighted to have done something which had not previously entered my head as a possibility: driven from the South of France to my home in a day. It had taken 5 minutes under 18 hours. As they say in athletics, this was a 'personal best' for me, the longest distance I had driven in a day.

I do not claim any records, but what does impress me is that my magnificent Bentley was performing as when new, and how well those responsible for her conception knew the requirements for long-distance touring. Only two petrol refills were necessary to cross France – just over 300 miles on a tankful – and I was not fatigued after 14½ hours at the wheel. 'Olga' had required no attention other than filling with petrol during the journey and was running as sweetly at the end of the trip as when she had left home 10 days and 2,000 miles earlier.

The road included at that time some excellent stretches of autoroute (no speed limit); some good main roads (110 kph speed limit) and considerable distances on narrow roads where passing was prohibited or difficult – notably between Fréjus and Aix-en-Provence and between Mâcon and Pouilly-en-Auxois. I cruised between 90 mph and 105 mph on the autoroutes with occasional bursts of 110 – many miles at 100 mph (3,650 rpm) – and in 1 hour covered 91½ miles. About one-third of the journey in France was on wet roads and I experienced some delays at the scenes of seven major accidents and one caravan well ablaze on the roadside.

Incidentally, I was able to check the accuracy of my distance recorder over long distances by reference to the kilometre stones and determined that it was under-recording by 1 per cent. (Corrected figures are quoted in this report.)

Petrol consumption for the journey was 17.34 mpg. During the whole round trip of 2,196¾ miles, including messing about on the Riviera, some 123.88 gallons of petrol were used (4-star here – 'Super' in France) giving a figure of 17.73 mpg for the 3¾ in bore (4,887 cc) engine, compared with 19.4 mpg when road-tested by Autocar in September 1952 with the 3⅝ in bore (4,566 cc) engine.

No wonder these R-Type Continentals have become collectors' pieces – but not, I hope I have demonstrated, museum pieces.

Across France American Style

A year later, in similar circumstances, I was again driving home from the South of France, but this time in a 'Continental' of a different kind – my 1966 Lincoln.

I left Eze-sur-Mer (9 miles beyond Nice) at 6 am and reached Cobham at 10.35 pm; i.e. 1 hour 20 minutes sooner than in 'Olga' the previous year and, if the Hovercraft had not been late leaving Boulogne, I could have been home by 10 pm. Yes, the journey in the Lincoln

100 *1966 Lincoln Continental at Cap Estel in August 1969*

was quicker than that in the Bentley Continental and even less tiring. Not surprising though, when one considers that nearly 80 miles of additional autoroute were open and that the Bentley was 13 years older than the Lincoln and had a manual gear-box and steering. I was not conscious of driving either one quicker than the other; certainly I would drive 'Olga' more quickly on twisty roads and on wet surfaces, but on the autoroutes which comprised most of the route I drove each car at the speed which seemed to be its natural cruising speed. The Lincoln Continental settled down beautifully at about 90 on the speedometer, which read about 7 per cent slow. Apart from the short stretch of autoroute from Nice to Fréjus (32 miles), the road to Sénas, about 20 miles south of Avignon, was undulating, curvy and narrow, divided for long stretches by a solid white line with a resulting lack of opportunities to overtake the slow-moving vehicles which abounded in this area. I reached the autoroute (A6) at Sénas

at 8.40 am after covering the 143.8 miles in exactly the same time as in 'Olga' the previous year and settled down to fast cruising to Lyon nearly 160 miles away with the object of crossing that city before its inhabitants burst upon the streets for the noon dash home to lunch. One disadvantage of the Lincoln was its thirst for petrol, an average consumption of a gallon every 11 miles – which increased to 10 mpg on motorways – necessitating refuelling stops at intervals of 180/200 miles. The first such stop was at Montélimar (205.5 miles) for breakfast. (Checks of the distance-recorder against kilometre markers over long distances established that the instrument under-recorded by $6\frac{1}{2}$ per cent – corrected mileages are given throughout this report.) The tunnel in Lyon was reached at 10.55 am (300.3 miles) – 33 minutes sooner than in the Bentley – and another stop for petrol was made at Beaune at 12.03 pm (388.2 miles). This was on the stretch of autoroute opened early that year – a distance of 74 miles from Mâcon to Pouilly-en-Auxois – replacing a twisty, hilly 77-mile section of N6. This section took 1 hour 22 minutes in the Bentley and I estimate that it took half an hour less in the Lincoln on A6. We (I had my motoring enthusiast niece, Anthea, as a passenger as far as Paris) left 35 minutes later and in each of the next three consecutive half-hours covered 44.7 miles, 47.9 miles and 48.9 miles respectively, i.e. 96.8 miles in the last hour.

The Péage at the end of the toll-paying section of the autoroute at Fleury (Fontainebleau) was reached by 2.20 pm (3.25 pm in 'Olga) and soon afterwards I left the autoroute to drive to Orly Airport over some 8 miles of miserably congested suburban roads. After negotiating the seemingly endless feeder roads and spirals inside the airport – some of them at least twice – I disgorged Anthea and her luggage, filled up with petrol and set off again at 3.00 pm. On towards Paris and on to the Boulevard Périphérique, which I left at Porte de la Chapelle at 3.32 pm, with 589.7 miles behind me, having decided to take the autoroute (A1) as far as Arras. The 101.5 miles to the exit for Arras took 1 hour 13 minutes and the remaining 79.1 miles to Boulogne via St Pol and Montreuil another $1\frac{1}{2}$ hours, bringing me into the Hoverport at exactly 6.15 pm. The total distance from Eze, including the detour into Orly, was 770.3 miles which had been covered in 12 hours 15 minutes. I pulled into the Hoverport exactly 12 hours after driving along the Promenade des Anglais in Nice, stops on the road having totalled 1 hour 15 minutes. The overall average speed (including stops) was 62.8 mph and the distance 770.3 miles had been completed in driving time of exactly 11 hours – i.e. at an average speed of 70 mph.

Comparing this with the run in 'Olga' – the distance was greater by 18 miles, mostly by reason of travelling from Paris by autoroute instead of RN1, and the point-to-point time taken was 1 hour 10 minutes less. (I see from my notes that I passed Montrueil at 5.48 pm,

only 33 minutes earlier than in the Bentley, having lost time deviating into Orly, but did not then deviate into Le Touquet as I had done in the Bentley). I had caught the 7.45 pm boat for Dover with only 20 minutes to spare when driving the Bentley and I was hoping to leave on the 6.30 pm Hovercraft on this occasion. I did, but it left late and I spent 55 minutes waiting about with no opportunity to eat. No food was served on the Hovercraft, so part of the time saved compared with a boat crossing had to be spent in Dover taking sustenance. I left Dover, after topping up the tank, at 8.20 pm and savoured the delights (I don't think!) of motoring again in England for $2\frac{1}{4}$ hours in the dark to arrive home in Cobham, 94.2 miles away, at 10.35. So I had been at the wheel for $13\frac{1}{4}$ hours during which time I had covered 864.5 miles at an average speed (including this speed limit restricted country of ours) of $65\frac{1}{2}$ mph. Apart from slipping accessory-drive belts squeaking on acceleration, the Lincoln was running as sweetly as ever and I really was not tired. Some American friends of mine commenting on my trip in 'Olga' have said that they could not understand what was remarkable about driving over 800 miles in a day – until they had experienced road and traffic conditions in Europe! Journeys of greater distances are not uncommon in the States, but they take place entirely on motorways with no need to stop except to replenish car and drivers. Admittedly, the American motorways are subject to speed limits, but the limit (? plus 5) tends to be the average, so it is simple arithmetic to determine in advance the likely duration of a journey. A 900-mile trip at 60 mph would take 15 hours; at 70 mph just under 13 hours.

1,000 Miles in a Day

Motivation

Who in his right mind would want to drive 1,000 miles in a day – and in England, too? Well, me for a start, for this was no ill-considered jaunt, but a planned effort to achieve a self-imposed task.

Why? Well – for fun really. The 1,000 miles in a day target had been sculling around in the back of my mind for some time. Having twice driven from the South of France to my home in Surrey in a single day, a distance of some 860 miles, I had on each occasion wished that I had farther to go to bring the day's mileage up to the magic (for me) figure of 1,000.

Inspiration

It was not until the opening of several stretches of motorway at the end of 1971 that it occurred to me it might be possible to drive that distance in a day in this country. The prospect of being able to do it without the expenditure of time and money involved in crossing the Channel was pleasing indeed.

Preparation

When? What route? How long would it take? Which car? Also, who should I invite to accompany me?

The answer to the first question was easy. It made sense to undertake the journey in midsummer to have the advantage of long hours of daylight and to choose a day in the middle of the week to avoid week-end traffic. As I could not expect the weather to be fine all over England in a single day I decided to go on a predetermined date irrespective of the weather and forecasts. The day fixed was Tuesday, 20 June 1972 when lighting-up time terminated at 4.13 am and began again at 9.51 pm.

After many permutations on the motorway system, aimed at covering as much of as many different motorways as possible with a minimum of doubling back, I settled on a route starting near London Airport so as to eliminate slow suburban driving from home to a motorway.

The route selected on was as follows:

M4   London Airport to Chiswick Flyover
A406   (North Circular Road) to Brent Cross

and A41 to Fiveways Corner
M1   to end at Junction 43 (near Leeds)
M1   back to Junction 32 and M18 to edge of Doncaster
A1(M), A1 and A194(M)   to end near Newcastle-upon-Tyne
A194(M), A1(M) and A1   back to Scotch Corner
A66   to Penrith
M6   to end at Junction 44 (near Carlisle)
M6   back to Junction 30 (near Preston)
M61 and M62   to end at Junction 23 (near Huddersfield)
M62 and M61 back to Junction 30 and northwards to Junction 31 to join
M6   to Junction 8 (near Birmingham)
M5   to Junction 15 (near Severn Bridge)
M4   to end at Junction 28 (near Newport, Mon)
M4   to London Airport.

Of this route only the following sections would not be on motorways:

		Miles	
Chiswick Flyover to M1	$10\frac{1}{2}$	Urban dual carriageway
A1 between Doncaster Scotch Corner	$68\frac{1}{4}$	Dual carriageway
A66 Scotch Corner to Penrith	49	Narrow, hilly single carriageway
	$127\frac{3}{4}$	

The remaining 870-odd miles would be on seven different motorways and two 'A' roads built to motorway standards, i.e. dual carriageways with no intersections.

I assumed an average speed of 60 mph except between Chiswick Flyover and M1 (40 mph) and Scotch Corner to Penrith (49 miles in the hour). This indicated a driving time of 17 hours 10 minutes and, allowing for three stops of half-an-hour each, the time on the road looked like being about $18\frac{1}{2}$ hours. With a 4 am start this meant a finishing time of about 10.30 pm – virtually all in daylight.

Which car? I could have used my Cadillac, which had by then replaced the Lincoln – if ever a car was designed for motorway driving this was – and enjoyed air-conditioning, stereo and effortless motoring, but, as the 70 mph limit would have to be observed, it was obvious that the proposed journey was well within the capacity of my Vintage Bentley which I had cruised at 85 mph for long distances in France. The idea of doing the trip in a 40-year-old car had a special appeal for me and how nice it would be to be driving all of a midsummer day in an open car. Little did I know what a flaming (awful) June was in store for us. Having decided to use the 8-litre I proceeded to make sure that it was in every way fitted for the journey. The car needed little attention. A new exhaust system was fitted, rear flashers installed and a dynamo cut-out switch inserted to avoid over-charging the battery. The new silencer was so effective that I then appreciated the volume of engine noise caused by a worn crankshaft damper. A new one was fitted which trans-formed the car. A new set of Dunlop Fort 6.50/7.00 × 19 in tyres was fitted, petrol tank filled to the brim (just over 30 gallons) and the car was ready for the road.

So far, so good. Now, who had the qualifica-tions to fill the passenger seat and – what was equally important – would accept an invitation to accompany me? My criteria required some-one who could endure 18 hours as a passenger in an open car with me; who could gear the demands of nature – both input and output – to match the refuelling stops dictated by the size of the petrol tank and the petrol consumption; who could keep an intelligent log of the journey; who could apply himself to any mechanical adjustments or work which might prove neces-sary; and who could take over the driving if I should tire before completing the distance. It goes without saying that he would have to be an enthusiastic Vintage motorist and that the prospect of each other's company would have to be a mutually pleasing one. A telephone call

to Graham Woodrow Hill in Esher, whom I knew met most of my desiderata, revealed that longish intervals between stops for food and drink would not be a cause for concern and, to my delight, that he would like to join me on the run.

Realization

And so the 8-litre quietly burbled out of the hotel car park in the early dawn light carrying two figures enveloped in fur-lined coats and waterproof clothing which was to be worn throughout the day. The sky was clear, the roads dry and almost devoid of traffic. The time was 4 am and breakfast nearly a tankful of petrol away.

What a pleasure to drive on an empty M4 and North Circular Road. Alongside a solitary Scammell at traffic lights the driver shouted, 'Best car in the world – had a 3-litre once.' By the time we reached M1 (33 minutes) the engine and transmission had warmed through – water temperature was steady at 68 deg C and the oil pressure settled down at 57 psi at 2,500 rpm – 70 mph in top gear.

The sun was rising to our right and we soon ran into ground mist which characterizes this section of motorway. It gave rise to no problems in view of the almost complete absence of other vehicles, but one had a sense of potential danger – especially seeing fields full of thick mist spilling over on to the road. However, it was not long before we had finished with the fog, switched off wipers and lights, and settled down to enjoy a beautiful day.

I decided to drive consistently at 70 mph and can honestly say that, although the needle tended to stray up a point or two, the speed never exceeded 75 mph at any time during the 1,000 miles. It was not necessary to keep an eye constantly on the speedometer as a marked increase in the whine from the straight-cut rear axle was audible as soon as the speed exceeded 70.

We reached our first turning point at the end

of M1 near Leeds at 7.04 am – 26 minutes ahead of schedule – having done 201.5 miles. We had already checked the trip recorder with the distance posts on the road and found it to be accurate over a 34-mile stretch. The sun was shining and after back-tracking on M1 and taking M18 we pulled up at the Selby Fork Motel for fuel and breakfast at 8.02 am, with 266.1 miles on the clock after just over four hours. It took 25.9 gallons to refill the tank to the brim, confirming the expected petrol consumption of about 10 mpg, and three quarts of oil in the sump. (It holds five gallons!) Thirty-one minutes later we were on the road again and encountering more traffic – especially 'heavies'. At 9.07 am three hundred miles came up making the average speed just under 60 mph including the breakfast stop. The end of A194(M) was reached at 9.59 am (357.6 miles) still more than half-an-hour ahead of schedule and we retraced our path to Scotch Corner. The hour I had allowed for the cross-country section from Scotch Corner proved to be more than enough and we joined the M6 at Penrith at 11.40 am with 446 miles behind us, encouraged to note that the rest of the journey would be on motorways. A smattering of rain reminded us that the forecasters had predicted wet weather on the west side of the country.

The end of M6, north of Carlisle and our furthest point from home, was reached at exactly noon – 468.8 miles in eight hours (58.6 mph including the stop at Selby). We turned southwards for the run along M6; then it started raining. The half-way distance (500 miles) was reached at 12.28 pm. The weather over Shap was appalling and we searched hopefully ahead for a break in the clouds. It was still pouring when we made our second stop at the Anderton Service Area after turning off M6 to go the length of the M61 and M62 motorways over the Pennines to Huddersfield and back. We had now covered 572.6 miles and took on 30.3 gallons of petrol – must have been close that time as I thought it was a 30-gallon tank – and a gallon of oil. Lighter by £11.35 (it seemed a lot at the time!) we went into the cafeteria to eat whilst it rained and rained. We must have lingered there, for 47 minutes elapsed before setting off into the soaking hinterland. Even in the rain we enjoyed driving on this motorway. It is a triumph of engineering and provides a constantly changing vista of moors, mills, towns and countryside, skillfully weaving up hill and down dale between large centres of population. As we approached the end of M62 the wiper blade – slow and inefficient even when working properly – gradually reduced its swept arc and finally stopped. We took the opportunity to enjoy a moment of shelter in the underpass at our turn-round point to dig out a spanner and tighten the wiper arm on its spindle. This cured its ills and was the only occasion on which we did anything to the car throughout the run. This welcome five-minute stop brought the total time of stops up to 83 minutes, but when we turned southwards again on M6 at 655½ miles we were still well ahead of schedule.

Just before 4 pm we had covered two-thirds of the 1,000 miles. Traffic and weather entailed slowing down to about 65 mph, and after two hours of rain we cheered up when it eased off and stopped as 700 miles came up on the 'clock' at 4.22 pm. Three-quarter distance (750 miles) was passed at 5.09 pm. I was able to drive consistently at 70 and averaged very nearly this figure.

The Severn Bridge towers hove into sight as we pulled into the Aust Service Area at 6.25 pm for our third replenishment stop (840.3 miles). Fifteen minutes later we left having taken on 26.4 gallons of fuel and another gallon of oil and drove over the Severn Bridge in a gale of drizzle. Traffic was confined to one lane, the bridge not having been passed as strong enough to carry more traffic, except at week-ends when presumably there are fewer heavies, and proceeded at about 25 mph. We had a wet run to the end of M4 beyond Newport and back again to the Bridge. It was nice to know that we were now really on the home stretch. The cross-wind on the bridge was unbelievably strong and took off my cherished cap. As I turned between the cones into the unused lane to stop and retrieve it, Graham said 'It'll cost you a fiver if you stop.' It didn't need a computer to tell me that it would be cheaper to buy a new cap and I turned smartly back into the traffic stream and continued with a very numb skull until I could stop to find my spare headgear.

I now focussed my mind on the telephone call I had undertaken to make between 7.30 and 8, to the BBC television studio in Birmingham to record a progress report in conversation with Cliff Michelmore for inclusion in the 'Wheelbase' programme to go out later in the evening. We decided to stop at the service area at Leigh Delamere and pulled into the car park at 7.48 pm able to report a trouble-free, uneventful run to that point of 908.1 miles. This interlude occupied 28 minutes bringing the total time of our stops to two hours nine minutes. We had no need of petrol, decided to postpone eating and set off on the last 90 miles or so along M4. The rain had stopped and the road was dry. As we approached London Airport we had to do a bit of calculating so as to complete the 1,000 miles as near to our starting-point as possible. In the event it necessitated continuing along M4 to Junction 3, doubling back to Junction 5, then turning on to A4 eastwards again. The trip recorder turned up all the noughts again on the Colnbrook By-pass at 8.34, and we came to a stop in the hotel car park three minutes later having covered 1,000½ miles since we left there 17 hours 37 minutes earlier in the day. I then drove home to Cobham and put the Bentley in the garage running as sweetly at the end of 1,016.2 miles as it was at the beginning. Great cars these 8-litres.

The start to finish average speed worked out at 56.9 mph – but for the assignation with 'Wheelbase' it would have been 58½ – and the driving time was 15 hours 25 minutes, i.e. an average speed for the 1,000 miles of 64.8 mph.

I filled the tank right up the spout again the next day and established that 99.6 gallons had been consumed in 1,016¼ miles giving an overall consumption of 10.2 mpg. Oh yes, the oil fill-ups totalled 3¾ gallons – more lost than burnt. Rather a lot, but oil was relatively cheap and I don't believe in pulling down for overhaul an engine which is running well. (I used Duckham's oil, but couldn't understand why it cost 42p per quart in a service station and only 26p in Woolworths!)

Evaluation
As for myself, I did not feel tired out. I could have continued driving quite happily and, in my judgment, I was driving as well as in the morning – Graham said 'Better' and I didn't quite know how to take this. I really do rather lose patience with organizations and individuals who pontificate about how long people should drive at a stretch, or in a day. It is quite impossible – and therefore a waste of time – to generalize on this subject. Every driver is different in his physiological and psychological make-up, and the importance of such variables as comfort, weather conditions, type of road, the designed performance of the car and the margin within which it is being driven, and the condition of car, cannot be exaggerated. (As for sitting in a simulator for four hours with an optical contraption strapped on one's head – a procedure used by a research organization – the very thought of it makes me tired!)

The seats in the Bentley are very comfortable and I can remember consciously changing my position on only one occasion. Doubtless the ease with which the Bentley ran along at 70 mph – so well within its compass – contributed to the lack of tiredness. This relaxed speed, plus the absence of the need for gear-changing and slow-speed steering, greatly reduced the fatigue factor. It is true that the run demonstrates that it is possible to observe the 70 mph speed limit and to cover long distances in a relatively short time, but this should not be interpreted as an endorsement of the validity of a 70 mph limit on motorways. If there had been no speed limit I would have driven 15–20 mph faster for most of the time. The higher speed would have been more demanding, but the journey would have taken less time. The safe speed limit in any particular circumstances can be determined only by reference to the skill and experience of the driver and the designed performance and condition of the car. Many cars overtook the Bentley during the day. Most of them were probably not exceeding 80–85 mph, but we saw no cases of bad driving in these circumstances. Most journeys on motorways are not long-distance ones and it seems to me that there should be no speed limit on motorways at all. I would, of course, support the meting out of severe treatment for careless, selfish and dangerous driving – and for unfit vehicles.

The most remarkable thing about the drive was that it was uneventful. We were not held up by road-works; we saw no accidents; we saw no interesting cars; we had no 'moments'; we made no wrong turns; the car performed impeccably; neither of us experienced any fatigue or ill-effects – both Graham and I were at work in our respective offices the next morning at the usual times.

The drive confirmed my view that our motorways will stand comparison with any on the Continent. From a driving point of view the three-lane motorways are excellent and have been made much safer since the heavies have been stopped from using the outer lane. On the two-lane motorways in any country one lorry slowly overhauling another can soon cause a queue of impatient motorists – a most undesirable state of affairs, so please let us not build any more of these. A welcome addition to our motorways would be rest or picnic areas, similar to those on the Continent, with simple toilet facilities.

Motorway design and landscaping have come a long way since the southern part of M1 was built. The best of them are, in my view, now an enhancement to the landscape rather than an eyesore. Surfaces vary and even new stretches are sometimes more uneven than the best main roads. The sign-posting is good on the whole and, providing he knows where he wants to go, the spaghetti junctions need hold no terrors for the inexperienced motorist – one flows along one's own particular road barely conscious of the enveloping cat's cradle of concrete.

Appreciation

Another memorable drive added to my personal experience. It would be ungracious of me not to acknowledge the part played by others in this venture, so my thanks to W.O. for conceiving and building these wonderful cars; to Fred Hofmann and Basil Mountfort for keeping my personal example in good trim; to Dunlop for making tyres in small numbers to keep Veteran and Vintage car owners on the road – no measurable wear on mine at the end of the run; and to my navigator/timekeeper/companion, Graham Woodrow Hill, for his patient, uncomplaining participation.

– and Commiseration!

The reactions of friends (and others!) on hearing of the run varied from congratulations from like-minded enthusiasts to the more common – 'You must be mad' and 'Rather you than me.' Others said – 'Sedgwick doing his Thing' – 'All that beautiful money wasted on petrol' – 'When does your case come up?' – and so on.

*   *   *

This drive received fairly wide publicity and no one has yet come forward to answer the question I posed at the time; has anyone else driven 1,000 miles in a day in England in any car?

Across France and Back in a Day

On returning home from the South of France in my (then) Lincoln Continental in September, 1971 having driven 864 miles in the day, my

101 *The Rolls-Royce Corniche at the Aire de Service de Nemours*

feeling of self-satisfaction was quickly deflated when I opened the current issue of Autocar and read the following statement in the Road Test of the Ferrari Daytona – 'Across Europe it would undoubtedly prove the fastest touring car that traffic conditions would allow, easily coping with a trip from the Channel to the South of France and back in a day'.

This struck me as an assertion worthy of demonstration and I resolved to see what could be done about it if an opportunity arose. Realization proved less easy than I had hoped, none of my Daytona-owning friends appearing to be in need of a co-driver to put hundreds of miles on the clock with the object of finishing up where they had started, so the idea went into the memory bank.

I had since driven my open 8-litre Bentley 1,000 miles in a day in England in a total time of 17 hours 37 minutes and I perceived that the same length of time at the wheel of a fast, modern, closed car – on roads free from speed limits – would encompass a considerably greater distance. It followed that I could drive all the way across France and back in a day myself

given a suitable car. On further consideration I came to the conclusion that such a journey would be more meaningful if accomplished in a full-size saloon instead of an out-and-out sports-car. Thus it was that I asked a mildly surprised John Craig – Marketing Director of Rolls-Royce Motors – if I could borrow a Corniche for the trip. I was even more surprised when he said 'Yes', and I proceeded to make plans.

Preparation

I was faced with the usual questions – When? Who with? What route? The answer to the first question was easy. It made sense to undertake the drive when the daylight hours were longest, but before the holiday rush, and to choose a day in the middle of the week to avoid week-end congestion. I decided upon Tuesday, 22 May (1973) and tackled the next question – who should I invite to accompany me? The occupant of the passenger seat had to be prepared to take three days' leave; to match his bodily needs to the mandatory stops for petrol; to keep a detailed record of time and distance throughout the trip and be prepared to be driven uncomplainingly at high speed in my sole company for 18 hours or so. I was fortunate in recruiting a Canadian friend, Hugh Young, to this (mobile) office which, in the event, he fulfilled untiringly and meticulously. What is more, he enjoyed every minute of it.

The choice of route to be followed gave me food for thought. Obviously the maximum use was to be made of autoroutes and this presupposed using A1 to Paris, A6 to Lyon and A7 beyond. Hitherto I had joined the A1 at Arras having driven from Calais, Boulogne or Le Touquet, but this was a tedious drive of about 70 miles passing through many villages and several towns which took anything between $1\frac{1}{4}$ and $1\frac{3}{4}$ hours according to conditions. I was pleased, therefore, to discover that a new stretch of autoroute had been completed from Dunkerque to Lille which entailed only a short distance through the outskirts of the latter city to reach the start of A1. I decided to use this new route feeling sure that the additional mileage would be more than justified from a time-saving point-of-view – and so it proved. I selected Marseille as the turn-round point, for this met the fundamental aim of crossing France from Channel to Mediterranean, and set about building up a target timetable.

From a study of maps, AA and RAC routes and my own records of previous journeys, I computed the mileage from Dunkerque to Marseille to be 657.6. The target timetable, i.e. a yardstick of possible progress – against which to assess the actual, which I devised was as follows:

Urban areas –	Miles	Hrs	Mins
Lille	2.5		4
Paris			
(Boulevard	8.5		12
Périphérique)			
Lyon	3.0		5
Vienne	5.6		8
	19.6	–	29

Autoroute – 638 miles			
at 90 mph	638.0	7	6
	657.6	7	35

Stops for petrol (and refreshment) 2×20 minutes			40
		8	15

Allowing for a 45-minute meal break in Marseille, and the same time for the return journey, the total time (including stops totalling 2 hours 5 minutes) added up to $17\frac{1}{4}$ hours, thus a 4.30 am start indicated a return to the starting-point by 9.45 pm – just about the duration of daylight at the time of year.

Realization

Another happy coincidence was the opening of 'La Motellerie' at Armbouts-Cappel on the outskirts of Dunkerque just off the 'Voie Express' (dual carriageway road) which becomes the autoroute A25 after 8 miles. So we crossed from Folkestone to Calais on the 5 pm ferry 'Hengist', drove to Dunkerque, filled the petrol tank to the brim, and turned in early at 'La Motellerie' after requesting a 4 am call. The astonished night-porter couldn't believe his ears when I said that we were going to Marseille for lunch.

We left the motel at 4.20 am and drove back into Dunkerque to the roundabout at Petite Synthe, 3 miles west of the ferry terminal, where the 'expressway' leaves the coastal road N40. I stopped there to take a photograph of the Corniche against the dawn sky before we set off at 4.31 am. The cloudless sky augured a fine day and the sun was soon shining brightly. As the engine warmed up I increased my cruising speed, mindful that the 45 miles to Lille should be covered in half an hour, and was surprised to find that 4,000 rpm corresponded with an indicated speed of 110 mph. Knowing that the true speed at 4,500 rpm was 118 mph I assumed that the rev counter was correct and that the speedometer exaggerated. I speeded up to find that 4,200 rpm equated to 120 mph on the speedometer and, at 4,500 rpm (which marked the start of a yellow segment covering the next 500 rpm before changing to red at 5,000 rpm), the needle was going 'off the clock' at 130 mph. Thus it was evident that an indicated 130 mph corresponded to a true ground speed of 118 mph – an error of approximately +10%. I knew, therefore, that so long as the instrument reading did not indicate more than 130 I would not be stressing the engine in any way. (Actually, my mandate from Rolls-Royce Motors was '. . . there should be no need to place any restrictions on the maximum speed for sustained cruising other than those dictated by road and traffic conditions.')

Just before reaching Lille we overtook our first car – it was a light grey 3½-litre Bentley saloon pursuing its gentlemanly progress, presumably having crossed on the night ferry. (We didn't see another UK-registered car for another 400 miles and only five all the way across France). Odometer readings, only 0.2 per cent out, were taken as accurate. The distance to the toll-gate at Arras was 75 miles and we passed through 51 minutes after leaving Dunkerque – only two minutes later than planned – thus endorsing the choice of route. The traffic was light and the trip recorder registered 139.7 miles at the end of 1½ hours.

We reached the end of the toll section at Survilliers (159.2 miles) at 6.13 am, having averaged 98 mph from Lille. The large number of cars approaching Paris at this early hour surprised us, and traffic was running in all lanes on the Boulevard Périphérique. It was, however, maintaining a speed of 55 mph so that the drive round to the Porte d'Italie took only a minute longer than I had allowed. We sped off down A6 mentally calculating where we should replenish the tank and take our first sustenance of the day. Rolls-Royce Motors had indicated that I

could expect to do not less than 11 mpg. This meant a range of about 250 miles – hence my plan to make five stops for petrol. We stopped at the Aire de Service Principale de Nemours at 7.14 am and put in 94.6 litres (20.81 gallons) of Super to replace that used in covering the 233.5 miles to this point plus 5.7 miles prior to leaving the Channel coast. This showed a consumption of 11.49 mpg at an average speed of 86 mph.

We partook of a 'continental' breakfast at a stand-up counter and the wheels were turning again after only 23 minutes. The next stage would take us to Lyon and we could not have had better conditions for the journey – dry road, sunshine, moderate traffic not too frequently obstructing the overtaking lane and only short stretches of single-working due to road works. I was cruising with the speedometer needle rarely dropping below 120 – a true speed of about 110 mph – and was conscious of the readiness of the car to exceed this gait without effort – but more of this later.

The first hour after breakfast saw another 96.4 miles behind us and then we were overtaken for the first time – by a 280CE Mercedes – as my speedometer showed 130, i.e. 118 mph. We repassed it 10 minutes later at the same speed and did not see it again. At 9.31 am, five hours after leaving Dunkerque, I had driven 418.7 miles (=83.74 mph) and 23 minutes later, i.e. after five hours driving time, 455.6 miles, which made the average driving speed 91.12 mph. We reached the toll-gate at Villefranche at 09.52½ (dead accurate, this Young fellow) and five minutes later at Les Chères (458.5 miles) I put in nearly 22 gallons. We decided not to eat – it was not yet 10 o'clock in the morning – and the stop took only 7 minutes. We reached the entrance to the Tunnel de Fourvière at Lyon at 10.12 am (469.3 miles). This tunnel has eliminated the slow, twisty, downhill run through the 'agglomeration' to the river bank and takes all the strife out of crossing Lyon. Five minutes after entering the tunnel we had resumed high-speed cruising on A7.

It always surprised me how rarely one was held up in Vienne where the main road ran between the town and the River Rhône and narrowed to a single lane over a temporary flyover at the main intersection. We were on top of this flyover at 10.28 am (489.3 miles) and passed through the Péage at Reventin four minutes ahead of our target timetable, fuelling stops having occupied only 30 minutes against a budget of 40. The 137½ miles of autoroute to the Péage at Salon Nord, including 8.2 miles of single lane working, took exactly 1½ hours (=91.67 mph).

We arrived at the large roundabout encircling the triumphal arch which marks the end of A7 at Marseille at 12.29 pm and pulled up at the Cathedral on the Quai de la Joliette at 12.31 pm, exactly eight hours after leaving Dunkerque and a quarter of an hour ahead of our target time. The point-to-point average speed for the 666.3 miles had been 83.29 mph and, deducting the two stops aggregating 30 minutes, the driving time of 7¼ hours (5 minutes less than planned) represented a driving average speed of 88.84 mph.

Instead of stopping in Marseille for lunch as programmed we decided to wait until we reached a 'Jacques Borel' restaurant which we had noted 26 miles out on the autoroute. So, after a stay of four minutes in the South of France to photograph the Corniche against the background of Cathedral and docks, I turned the car and headed back to our starting-point. The mistral was blowing strongly, but the weather was still fine and sunny.

We stopped for lunch and petrol as planned. Two litres of oil went into the engine as a safety measure for none had been added for nearly 900 miles. The press-button oil-level indicator was not designed to give a correct reading at the speeds I had been doing, when most of the oil is doing its job elsewhere than in the sump, and the engine hadn't had a chance to cool sufficiently to obtain a valid reading on the dipstick. We were lucky to be on the move again after

49 minutes. This meant that our stops now added up to within a minute of my original target timetable. As Hugh put it, we rejoined the autoroute as our ghost went past.

Just after 3 pm with over 800 miles behind me I sensed what I described as a lowering in my threshold of awareness. This is not really sleepiness, but I become conscious of blinking and of taking fractionally longer to refocus my vision when transferring the eyes from road to instruments. After five minutes 'zizz' in an appropriately named 'Aire de Repos' I was completely refreshed and resumed this most enjoyable drive. (Inured by this time to making calculations from recorded data my indefatigable Clerk of the Course wrote in the log; 40 winks in 5 minutes = 8 winks per minute!)

The traffic was lighter in this direction and the Corniche purred happily along in the manner of the fast, well-mannered touring car that it is, as is evidenced by the fact that the distance of 196.4 miles between the toll-gate at Villefranche and the Courtenay/Sens Junction was covered at an average speed of 99 mph. I see from the log that I averaged 100.17 mph over the last 117.7 miles of this stretch.

At 5.23 pm we had clocked up 1,000 miles which had entailed 11 hours 18 minutes driving at an average speed of 88.5 mph. Just after 6 o'clock we were overtaken by our second car – a Citroën SM going like the clappers – and the weather deteriorated rapidly. Clouds gathered, lightning danced round the horizon and by the time we passed the exit for Courtenay and Sens it was raining very hard indeed. There was a brief respite at Fontainebleau and then a torrential downpour commenced which was to continue unabated for more than an hour and a half. The traffic was heavy approaching Paris and was reduced to a crawl and stationary jams by shunts and breakdowns. The Périphérique was congested and it took 23 minutes to drive from the A6 to the A1. At Le Bourget the thunderstorm continued, it was as dark as night though only 7.35 pm, and the torrential rain

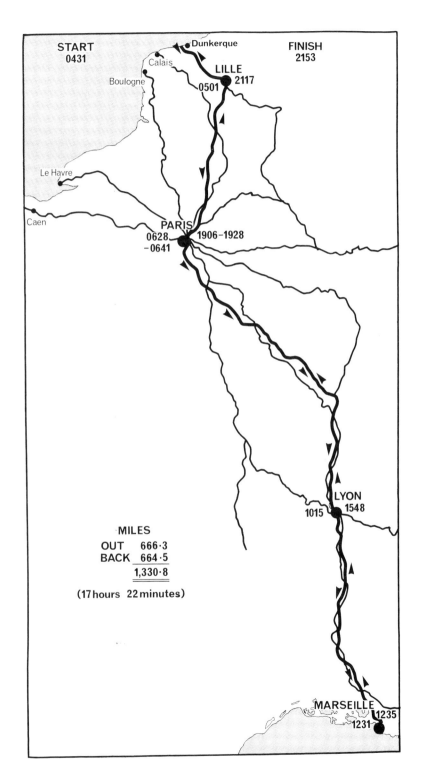

2 *The route from Dunkerque to Marseilles and back July 1973*

was bouncing high off the road. We took advantage of a covered petrol station to refuel for the last time.

The weather cleared before Lille and we found the rather tricky route round the town using the partly-constructed Boulevard Périphérique whereon happened the only 'untidy moment' of the whole trip when I found myself faced by an unlit barrier marking the end of the completed surface and an unsignposted deviation to the other carriageway. I stopped without touching anything and the biggest surprise was the cloud of self-raised dust which overtook the car after it had come to rest on the unmade surface! It is not difficult to imagine the thoughts that went through our minds at this happening so near to our goal. As we joined the A25 auto-route west of Lille for the final run-in Hugh told me that according to our target timetable we were due in Dunkerque, 40.4 miles away, in a quarter of an hour! The road was dry and traffic-free and we made it in 23 minutes, thus producing a sprint finish to our 1,330 mile run at 105.5 mph. We stopped at the Petite Synthe roundabout at 9.53 pm, eight minutes later than our target arrival, shook hands and drove back to the motel for supper and to honour our reservations.

The return trip had taken longer than the outward run, which had been made in as favourable conditions as one could ever hope to get. The following is a summary of the journey:
Dunkerque–Marseille (666.3 miles)

Total Time
    8 hours   = 83.29 mph
Driving Time
    7 hours 30 minutes   = 88.84 mph
Marseilles–Dunkerque (664.5 miles)
Total Time
    9 hours 18 minutes   = 71.45 mph
Driving Time
    8 hours 14 minutes   = 80.74 mph
Round Trip from Dunkerque to Marseille and back to Dunkerque (1,330.8 miles)
Total Time

    17 hours 22 minutes   = 76.57 mph
Driving Time
    15 hours 44 minutes   = 84.54 mph

I reckon that, on the basis of the above-reported progress, and remembering that $25\frac{1}{2}$ miles were driven on single lanes where speeds were often restricted by heavy trucks to 40 mph or less, I must have driven more than 1,000 miles at speeds in excess of 100 mph. The overall petrol consumption was 11.35 mpg. It was rather better on the run south (11.95 mpg) than on the way back (10.83 mpg) – presumably because progress was more free-flowing necessitating fewer bursts of acceleration. (Incidentally, the SP Radial 205 HR 15 Dunlop tyres were inflated to 34 psi rear and 30 psi front compared with the recommended all-round pressure of 28 psi for normal running).

The following breakdown of the times taken to drive the various stages on the outward journey will serve as a basis for those interested enough to compare their own progress on the way to the Côte d'Azur without going to the unlikely destination of Marseille:

Miles		Hrs	Mins
178.0	Dunkerque to Paris (Porte de la Chapelle)	1	57
9.3	On the Boulevard Périphérique		13
282.0	Paris (Porte d'Italie) to Lyon (Tunnel de Fourvière)	3	1
20.0	Lyon (Tunnel de Fourvière to Vienne (top of flyover)		16
153.9	Vienne (top of flyover) to where the auto-route to Aix-en-Provence and Nice forks off 8 miles south of Salon	1	42
643.2		7	9

Evaluation

That neither of us was really tired at the end of this long run says a lot for the Corniche. We wore the seat belts all the time and, although we expected to be uncomfortable because of the relatively low top anchorage point (dictated by the construction of the two-door body) necessitating the strap coming up from behind the shoulder, we were not, in fact, inconvenienced. It is true to say, however, that the belts were more comfortable when not wearing a jacket.

Once placed in the right position the seats were so good as to call for no further adjustment and neither of us found it necessary to change our postures; nor were our joints stiff on getting out of the car. Two other factors played a tremendous part in making such a long journey unfatiguing: the air-conditioning and, because this enabled one to drive with all the windows closed, the insulation from outside noise.

The Speed Control device is not designed to function at speeds over 90 mph, so it was not much use on this drive. I did use it once, however, when we were confined to a single lane by road works, to check the speedometer reading at 100 kph against a timed kilometre – this distance took 38 seconds which is a speed of 94.74 kph indicating that the instrument was over-reading by about $5\frac{1}{2}$ per cent at this speed. (It should be said that it is almost impossible to time accurately from a moving vehicle – especially at high speed – even using a split-second chronograph. At around 100 mph an error of only one-fifth of a second in reading the time between one kilometre marker and the next makes a difference of more than $1\frac{1}{2}$ mph).

The Corniche performed impeccably. The fact that this particular example was built prior to the introduction of the major changes to the front suspension made little difference in this type of motoring. Only one fault manifested itself – in addition to the annoyingly optimistic speedometer – and that was the interior mirror being loose on its stalk. The right size Allen key would have fixed it in a moment but it was aggravating having to reposition it at frequent intervals. When I handed the car

back with 33,882 miles on the clock it was as smooth and quiet as when delivered to me.

Altogether I considered that the Corniche proved itself to be a very, very good fast touring car. Not quite fast enough, mind you, and I made an open plea to those at Crewe to offer a higher axle ratio as an option for those who habitually drove on the Continent. I felt that the car had reserves of power and that the resulting slight falling-off in acceleration, if any, would be a small price to pay for an available top speed nearer to 140 mph and a cruising capability in the region of 125–130. (If not an option on the Rolls-Royce version, I suggested that it should be standard equipment on the Bentley!) Such a modification would have met the oft-heard criticism that the top-end performance of the Corniche did not match up to the standards set by certain other manufacturers of very good, but less costly cars.

To those who cringed at the price of the Corniche – and I was one – and who, having read this were inclined to say . . . 'So it should,' my reply would have been 'Well, it did, didn't it?' Of course, no-one in his right mind would wish to drive across France and back in a day, but it showed that a four-figure mileage on the Continent in daylight was well within the capability of this car. A few more miles of autoroute, and destinations way down in Italy (normally thought of as being at least two days away) could well have been reached between an early breakfast and dinner, especially with two drivers.

Justification
I offer none. I undertook the drive solely for the pleasure I would derive from it ('one man's meat . . .'). I was not disappointed. It cost a good deal of money and didn't last very long, but I can't think of anything which would have been more rewarding to me in terms of sheer enjoyment and I don't anticipate ever again using nearly £60 worth of petrol (119 gallons) and paying out over £12 in tolls in a day. Little did I know what the future held!

Thank you RR for a lovely day and thanks to H.J.T.Y. for bearing with me.

Rumination

It is interesting (to me, anyway) to note that the 1,330 miles took 15 minutes fewer than the 1,000 miles in the Vintage Bentley in England. Just to think of it – the average speed across France and back, including all stops, was nearly 10 per cent above the maximum speed allowed in this country.

My average speed for the round trip (76.57 mph) was slightly higher than that of the winning Speed Six Bentley of Woolf Barnato at Le Mans in 1930 (75.88 mph). I realize that the Bentley's average was maintained for 24 hours, but there were two drivers! There has been some progress in automobile and road engineering in the intervening years.

Was this the longest U-turn in history?

Marseille Revisited

Early in 1973 I acquired a new Double-Six Daimler (fancy Jag. – you know!) and it will come as no surprise that in the course of a holiday trip to the Cote d'Azur I took the opportunity of making a comparative 'outward only' drive in this car. It had covered 6,000 miles and certain teething troubles had been overcome.

Accordingly, after a 4 am wake-up call at the Dunkerque Motellerie on the first Friday in September, I found myself once again at the Petite Synthe roundabout making a 4.30 am start for Marseille. I was not out to beat the RR time, but to drive in a similar manner, i.e. as fast as weather, road and traffic conditions permitted and at a sustained speed at which the car settled down happily. I expected to be able to cruise somewhat faster than previously, but fully realized that (say) 10 mph on the cruising speed would not increase the average speed by the same increment.

First the good news:

In the event, the total point-to-point time from Dunkerque to Marseille, including stops, was 6 minutes less than that taken by the Corniche. Stops for petrol and sustenance totalled 35 minutes – 5 minutes more than the Rolls-Royce as the result of the need for an additional refuelling stop – making the driving time 11 minutes less than the Corniche.

The elapsed times and average speeds were as follows:

	Daimler Double-Six	Rolls-Royce Corniche
Total Time	7 hrs 54 mins	8 hrs 00 mins
Stops	35 mins	30 mins
Driving Time	7 hrs 19 mins	7 hrs 30 mins
Mileage (corrected)	665.5	666.3
Average Speed – Overall (including stops)	84.3 mph	83.3 mph
Driving	90.95 mph	88.8 mph
Petrol Consumption	10.45 mpg	11.95 mpg

The bare figures do not tell the whole story. I started at the same time of day (4.30 am), this time alone, but whereas it was just getting light in May when I did the journey in the Corniche, on this occasion it was dark and there were patches of fog which brought my speed down to 20/30 mph more than once before reaching Lille. The first glimmer of dawn appeared as I passed through the Arras Toll, running 10 minutes behind RR's schedule! I turned on to the Boulevard Périphérique at Paris at 6.34 am, the darkness and the fog contributing materially to the 7 minutes lateness compared with the Corniche. I circumnavigated the City to the start of A6 in 11 minutes – 5 minutes less than previously – and thus turned south again only 2 minutes down.

The likely petrol consumption was an unknown factor and prudence called for replenishment at a 'Petrol only' service area before reaching, 7 minutes later, the planned breakfast stop at Nemours. Leaving the latter at 7.39 am

102 *The Daimler Double-Six at the Cathedral at Marseille*

with 233.1 miles completed, the Daimler was now running 3 minutes behind the Corniche's timetable. The weather was perfect and, although the traffic was noticeably heavier than in May, one could not have wished for better conditions. It was at this point that I really began to move and covered the next 164.8 miles in $1\frac{1}{2}$ hours – an average speed of 109.9 mph. I would have liked to have completed 2 hours non-stop, but the beast was getting thirsty again and I had to stop to refuel after only 1 hour 43 minutes, albeit having driven 186.8 miles in that time (108.8 mph). I took on 101.1 litres ($22\frac{1}{4}$ galls) of Super which is rather more than the manufacturers give as the combined capacity of the two tanks – so I must have cut it fine. Expressed as a gallon every 5 minutes at 50p per gallon it sounded horrific, but conventionally interpreted as 8.8 mpg, I considered it satisfactory at this speed. (The overall consumption for the journey to Nice was $10\frac{1}{2}$ mpg and just over 11 mpg for the 2,100 mile round trip.) The mileage completed during the 2 hours after breakfast, including the 6 minute stop for petrol, was 205.

I entered the Tunnel de Fourvière at Lyon 5 hours 31 minutes after leaving Dunkerque, the Corniche's 'ghost' now trailing by 10 minutes. By the time I crossed the 'fly-over' at Vienne I had lost $2\frac{1}{2}$ minutes, but from here on gradually improved on the Rolls, being $15\frac{1}{2}$ minutes to the good at the Sénas Toll. Mental calculations now confirmed that I could not reach Marseille without another stop for petrol and this clipped 7 minutes off my time advantage. I lost another $2\frac{1}{2}$ minutes in traffic before pulling up at the Cathedral on the dockside at Marseille at 12.24 pm, thus having completed the journey in 6 minutes less than the Corniche and, after deducting stops aggregating 35 minutes, had been on the move 11 minutes less; i.e. a driving average speed for the $665\frac{1}{2}$ miles of 90.95 mph.

The sustained high-speed cruising capability of the car was further evidenced by the time of 4 hours 44 minutes (excluding stops) taken for the 455.5 miles from the Porte d'Italie to the point on A7 where the A8 forks off for Aix and Nice, which, of course, included negotiating Lyon and Vienne, i.e. an average speed of 96.24 mph.

As for the car, it behaved impeccably. A check on the odometer over a distance of 100 kilometres showed it to be over-recording by 1.9% and stop-watch tests by a passenger on a previous run in France indicated that the speedometer was exaggerating by 4%. The needle remained between 120 and 130 most of the time with occasional stretches at an indicated 130 and 140, usually when a BMW, Citroën SM, Mercedes or Porsche was in the vicinity – note, the order is alphabetical. The silky smoothness characteristic of this car was somewhat marred above 100 mph by slight vibration. It felt like out-of-balance wheels, but I had had them balanced statically and dynamically before leaving home. Incidentally, tyre pressures were 6 psi above normal.

I found the Daimler no less comfortable than the Corniche, but the air-conditioning was not man enough for the job and, although absorbed in the general noise level experienced in any car at high speed, it was much too noisy when operating fully. It must be remembered that I drove only one way in the Daimler and, although I cannot therefore say how I would have felt if I had driven straight back to Dunkerque, I would have undertaken the double journey in the Double-Six without hesitation had the circumstances arisen. The efficiency of the Rolls-Royce air-conditioning system made driving in the hot weather more pleasant than in the Daimler. I was pleased to learn that the 1974 Jaguars and Daimlers were to have automatic temperature control. An excellent feature this and one which had been available on quality American cars for years, but which RR had delayed introducing . . . 'until the system has been developed and proved to their customary high standards of performance, reliabilty and silence'. It was to be hoped that this 'leap-frogging' of Crewe by Coventry would be accompanied by increased refrigeration capability, for it would be no improvement to be automatically too warm instead of manually not cool enough!

– And now the bad news:

My enchantment with the Daimler plunged below zero when, a week later, returning home almost as quickly, the engine stalled (an irritation which I had been living with since just before leaving England) in the toll-gate on the autoroute near Fontainebleau and the starter refused to work! I was pushed clear of the slot and there I stood between ten streams of returning holiday traffic not knowing exactly what the trouble was or what to do about it. (I think I received a few metaphorical 'Harvey Smiths' from drivers who had reluctantly yielded the overtaking lane to the speeding Daimler during the previous hour or so!) I suspected a stuck Bendix, (now I know it hasn't got one!), but the bonnetful of machinery and the low ground clearance did not make for easy examination of such things and eventually I succumbed to the ignominy of a suspended rearward tow (to which owners of immobile automatic-transmission cars are committed) to the Jaguar agents, Île de France Automobiles in Fontainebleau 16 miles away. It was 7 o'clock on a Saturday evening, but managerial and technical staff were available to assist me and in no time at all the trouble was diagnosed as a flat battery due to the alternator having ceased to work. The appropriate warning light indicated this fault, but I find it difficult to believe that it was illuminated whilst I was driving the car as my eyes were flashing to the instrument panel every minute or so though not, apparently, to the voltmeter which would have warned me of the dying battery. We proceeded to Paris for the week-end to await further investigation on the Monday morning. By noon on that day I learnt that the trouble was a good deal less serious than I feared, the alternator drive-belt having worn itself to the thickness of a boot-lace and finally ceased to function. There were not many 12-cylinder Jaguars in France and I give full marks to this garage for finding a replacement belt and completing the fitting – a tedious job involving the removal of the other drive belts – to enable us to resume our homeward journey the same day.

And the Conclusion:

Had I completed this account before commencing my return journey – i.e. before experiencing the alternator belt trouble – then it would have concluded with virtually unqualified praise for the car. I still hold this view (when the car is in motion under its own power), but a delay of two days and the consequent expense of taxis, hotels, meals, etc., must detract at least temporarily from any car's appeal in the eyes of the most patient owner – even when the breakdown is caused by something comparatively trivial.

However, it is surprising how quickly breakdowns and inconveniences of this sort fade in significance in one's memory when one likes a particular car and, if one accepts that such a failure could have occurred on any make of car, then I feel that the already-drafted paragraph is still valid.

The drive served to confirm my opinion that the 12-cylinder Daimler/Jaguar was the best value for money in the world and that both the Rolls-Royce and Daimler cars do great credit to the British Motor Industry.

*   *   *

Re-read at the end of 1990, these pages have a nostalgic ring, for speed limits imposed in France (and most other countries) in the interest of petrol conservation seem unlikely to be lifted in a hurry – if at all.

How fortunate I am to have been able to do these fast runs before the Third World took the fun out of motoring – except, of course, for Veteran and (many) Vintage car owners who have not been much worried by speed limits anyway.

United States – Coast to Coast

The 'Cannonball Run' was an illegal race across America, from the Atlantic to the Pacific, held every two or three years to commemorate the remarkable single-handed drive from New York to Los Angeles by Erwin G. (Cannonball) Baker in 1933, in a supercharged Graham. He covered the distance of over 2,800 miles in $53\frac{1}{2}$ hours at an average speed of over 52 mph. and it has long been an ambition of mine to do such a run. The record for the run from Darien, Connecticut to Redondo Beach, California is held by Heinz and Yarborough, driving a 1978 Jaguar XJS in the 1979 'Cannonball Baker Sea to Shining Sea Memorial Dash'. Their time was 32 hours 51 minutes making an average speed of about 87 mph. My aspirations were rather more modest!

Having flown across the United States many times, I realized that the only way to gain an appreciation of its vastness was to drive from coast to coast. However, my urge to do this was diminished by the imposition of a country-wide speed limit of 55 mph in 1973 as a fuel-saving measure of doubtful (I think) validity. In the subsequent years, some states would have liked to have raised or abolished this limit, but were constrained from doing so by legislation which would have deprived them of Federal funds for road projects should they fail to maintain the country-wide 55 mph limit. The extra time needed to drive the 3,000 miles at such a restricted speed proved a significant deterrent to the fulfilment of my wish. Suffice it to say, however, that with the passage of time, the 55 mph limit was regarded by the majority of US motorists as unrealistic and was honoured more in the breach than in the observance, for traffic rolled along, sometimes four lanes abreast, at 65, 70 or more mph, and in the vast open spaces even juggernauts cruised at 80 mph+ on the empty twin-track highways.

Any idea I had of driving from east to west across America was also frustrated by my inability to secure the use of a car at a modest outlay, until the introduction of the Avis 'Discover America Best' scheme afforded an opportunity to pick up a car of one's choice at any Avis key city and to leave it at any other, at a fixed daily rate of hire of $35, with no mileage charge and no drop-off charge. This, coinciding with an invitation to attend the race meeting being held in California at Laguna Seca as a tribute to Briggs Cunn-ingham, provided too good an opportunity to miss.

So it was that I bought an open-jaw PanAm ticket from London to New York returning direct from Los Angeles, and sought a congenial companion prepared to accompany me, but not to drive unless I was overcome with fatigue; who would keep a detailed log of times, distances and petrol consumption; and who would subordinate his bodily needs to those of the car. Such an enthusiastic – some would say equally crazy – volunteer was found in Don Weber, who flew up from Texas to join me under the prescribed conditions.

I had devoted a good deal of thought and study to planning a route and timetable beforehand and compiled a route book on the basis of four overnight stops between New York and San Francisco following Interstate 80 all the way. On arrival at John F. Kennedy Airport on a Sunday afternoon in August 1981, I caught the Avis shuttle bus and collected the low-mileage Olds-mobile Cutlass four-door saloon which was to be my magic carpet for the next ten days. This car was a 'Standard Plus' model in Avis Group 'E' and had a V6 engine of 3,785 cc with a catalogue maximum speed of 99 mph, not that one could ever check it as the speedometer read up to only 85 mph, at which point the needle came up against a stop.

The plan was to start off at about dawn each day and drive for a couple of hours or so before stopping for breakfast, then making stops for lunch and tea as the spirit moved or the stomach demanded. Accordingly, we rose at 5.30 am on the Monday morning and 35 minutes later left our hotel in upper Manhattan, driving up the Henry Hudson Parkway as Don positioned and connected up his magic anti-radar box which was to save many a highway patrolman a lot of writing during the ensuing four days. It was a clear, sunny morning as we turned westwards over the George Washington Bridge, musing that the next such construction we should see would be the Golden Gate Bridge in San Francisco, 3,000 miles away.

Our destination that day was a Best Western motel at Lansing, south of Chicago, 800 miles away, 171 miles of which was covered before we stopped for breakfast just before 9 o'clock. As a precautionary measure we topped up the petrol tank at every meal stop, but the car was so economical that it had a cruising range of about 400 miles. Don took the opportunity of checking the odometer with the roadside mile markers and found it to be accurate within 0.3 per cent over 50 miles – this was confirmed subsequently over a distance of 210 miles. This speaks well for General Motors and will give comfort to Avis customers renting on a mileage basis! Notices on the roadside in Pennsylvania proclaimed a scale of fines for exceeding the 55 mph speed limit ranging from $45 for 60 mph, to $75 for 75 mph. It was apparent that drivers with the benefit of radar detection devices and/or CB radios were travelling a good bit faster than the majority not so equipped, and I was puzzled at first as to why two or three cars were 'tail-gating' me, slowing when I did and accelerating with me, until I realised they were using me as a mobile protective screen from the 'smokies'. My average driving speed (excluding stops) for the 400 miles to the Ohio state line was 65 mph and it was evident that an overall average speed in the region of the speed limit was being maintained. The section of Interstate 80 which passed through Ohio and Indiana was a toll road, but the 400 miles or so was cheap compared with similar roads in Europe, costing only $6. We stopped 20 miles west of Toledo, two minutes late on our target time of 4.30 pm, with exactly 600 miles behind us, to take refreshment with an equally eccentric friend who, regretting his inability to be with us, had driven down from Detroit with his wife to speed us on our way. It was not long before we crossed from the Eastern Time zone into Central Time and put our watches back one hour. Driving westwards across the continent instead of flying minimizes the effect of the three-hour time difference – we slept in a different time zone each night and thus gained an hour each day – or so it seemed. We reached our planned night-stop before dark having driven for three minutes under 12 hours and completed 794 miles – just over a quarter of our journey.

Tuesday, the second day, saw us on the move at 6.27 am in continuing beautiful weather. Although an inveterate mirror-watcher I did not become aware of a following Highway Patrol car until he was right on my tail and I pulled over to let him pass at something over 80 mph. His presence had not registered on our magic box, but he must have been hell-bent on more important matters than speeders, for that was the last we saw of him. I see that Don made a note in the log at 9 am – 'no breakfast yet but ate two apples'. We did stop a few minutes later with 185 miles under the wheels. By 10 am we had completed 1,000 miles since leaving New York, having averaged (dare I say it?) 59.1 mph including meal and petrol stops. At midday we passed a semi-trailer overturned at the side of the road and it is noteworthy that this was the only accident we saw on the whole trip.

We were now passing through the corn belt – the so-called 'bread basket' of America – and the stock farms of Iowa. By 4.37 pm we had done 600 miles since dawn and decided that our scheduled night-stop at North Platte was not far enough along the route, so we popped into a Best Western motel to cancel our reservations and rebook rooms at Big Springs, some 70 miles further on. My confidence in Don's electronic device became my undoing before we reached our destination. Just as I had remarked that the last three hours had seen more than 200 miles covered, a policeman standing by the roadside

waved me to a stop with a orange flag. He said I had been timed at 75 mph by an aeroplane! The airborne officer was timing cars over a measured distance – $\frac{1}{4}$ mile, I think – marked on the road surface and radioed a description of the transgressing vehicle to the waiting police car a few miles ahead. This dented my ego a bit and he said that as an out-of-state resident I could elect to pay a $40 fine (plus $8 costs) on the spot. In these circumstances the police officer was not allowed to accept money and it was customary for the offender to follow the patrol car to a post office so that he could witness the cheque being put into a mail-box. This could have involved a long detour in the wide open spaces, so we were pleased to be informed by the trooper that his was the only county in Nebraska accepting payment of fines by Visa credit cards on an experimental basis. Fortunately Don produced his Visa card and we were on the move again in 22 minutes after taking a posed photograph of the lawman handing me my ticket.

The day's mileage totalled 823.1 and over dinner, during which I declined to sample 'mountain oysters' and thus put paid to any possibility of assuming a cowboy image, our thoughts turned to completing the cross-country trip in four days instead of five. The third day took us through the cattle-raising terrain of Wyoming with place-names enshrined in cowboy films – Cheyenne, Laramie, etc. About midday there was a little rain, giving us the only six miles of wet roads throughout the whole run. We were really getting along. The Cutlass was behaving impeccably – extremely comfortable, unfatiguing, with excellent air-conditioning – and we decided to press on beyond our scheduled overnight stop at Salt Lake City to Wendover on the Utah/Nevada border. In the mid-afternoon we saw the first signpost to San Francisco – 791 miles. As we left Salt Lake City for the run across the lake – including a 40-mile dead-level, dead-straight section – we decided to make our only sightseeing deviation from Interstate 80 to drive out on to the salt flats which have been the scene of so many world speed record runs. The most impressive feature is one's inability to judge distance – one approaches hills which seem a mile or two away, only to find them looking exactly the same after driving for another quarter-of-an-hour at around 80 mph. Here the road markers for the flying speed cops were in the form of airplane silhouettes painted in white on the hard shoulder at the start and finish of the measured distance. Needless to say it was advisable to spot the first airplane symbol and to take appropriate action. Incidentally we found the speedometer to be accurate when timed at a steady 80 mph over a measured mile.

The state line bisects the village of Wendover – which was the base camp of Campbell, Cobb, Eyston and so many more – and I lost a dollar or two in one-arm bandits during a post-prandial stroll into Nevada.

We resumed our journey at 6.11 am on Thursday, the fourth and last day, with our sights on the Pacific coast. I found the mountainous desert country of Nevada the most interesting scenery we had encountered, perhaps because it is unlike anything found in Europe. We breakfasted in Elko and stopped for lunch in Reno, knowing that another 219 miles would bring us into San Francisco. At 4.01 pm we caught sight of the Golden Gate Bridge in the misty distance, and crossed the Oakland Bay Bridge into the famous city 35 minutes later. Not unnaturally we shared a glow of satisfaction at having completed our self-imposed task – NY to SF (2,959.4 miles) in four days driving from dawn to dusk. Actually, by the clock it was less than $3\frac{1}{2}$ days from 6.05 am Monday to 4.36 pm Thursday. The start to finish average speed, excluding only night-stops, was 56.56 mph and I had been at the wheel for 43 hours 20 minutes, during which more than a mile a minute had been left behind.

We drove on another 120 miles to arrive at Briggs Cunningham's temporary home at Pebble Beach on the Monterey peninsula, to the utter surprise of our fellow-guests who thought us to be bedding down for the night in Reno.

Altogether a most enjoyable and rewarding drive for me and apparently for the long-suffering Don, an enthusiastic long-distance motorist himself, who had not been allowed a turn at the wheel.

During the following six days I covered another 750 miles pottering about and driving down the Pacific coast to San Diego, finally returning the car to Mr Avis at Los Angeles airport before flying home. I had driven that Oldsmobile 3,861 miles and it had averaged $22\frac{1}{2}$ mpg (i.e. American gallon, which means 27 miles to the Imperial gallon) with the air-conditioning in operation the whole time, and had used virtually no oil. A quart was added after 3,239 miles, but the dipstick showed an acceptable level even before replenishment. Incidentally, this car cost less than $7,000, with automatic transmission and power steering.

What was the cost of the trip? Well, disregarding food and lodging, ten days' motoring totalling nearly 4,000 miles had cost $451 in rental (including collision damage waiver premium and local taxes) and the 162 gallons consumed cost $237, i.e. an average of $1.46 per US gallon equivalent to $97\frac{1}{2}$p per Imperial gallon at $1.80 to the £ sterling. At the same exchange rate the total motoring expense was £382. It should be remembered that the car was a full four-seater and any motorist planning to visit the USA could hardly do better at that time than this excellent and relatively cheap arrangement offered by Avis through American Express. Any number of daily vouchers (minimum 7) could be purchased in the UK; they need not have been used on consecutive days, nor for the same car, and afforded a very flexible means of seeing something of the new world at a competitive price. No need to blind across a dozen states like me – just meander or fly from place to place using different key cities as starting and finishing points. It was a long time since I had enjoyed driving so much – my wife's normal annual mileage in four days. Not a 'Cannonball Run', but a jolly good 'Cutlass Slash' – and I now know how big is America.

103 *Brief encounter with the Bonneville Salt Flats, Utah, scene of many World Record attempts*

104 *Downfall of many a speeder – airplane painted on hard shoulder to mark end of measured distance for spotter plane, Utah – August 1981*

Like I said . . .

We insular-minded Britons write letters in English to hoteliers in foreign countries taking it for granted that they will reply in our language – and not their own.

Manfully, even the most humble innkeeper will do his damnedest best to comply – often with results which cannot fail to raise a smile.

With great respect to the writer I treasure the following letter from the proprietor of an Auberge near Reims to my request for two twin-bedded rooms:

'I can reserve for you: two rooms with one bed for two persons, but no two rooms with two beds for one person.'

Motoring the world over

In 1948 I was appointed to two jobs. A Chartered Accountant by training, I became an executive in a ship-owning company; and, a Vintage Bentley enthusiast by inclination, I assumed the cloak of the President of the Bentley Drivers Club on the death of Woolf Barnato. To these two offices I owe a great deal. The former provided the wherewithal to indulge my hobby of motoring and the opportunity to travel to many parts of the world. The latter contributed greatly to the pleasure Con and I have derived from the many friendships formed with like-minded enthusiasts, and nowhere has this kinship been more evident than on our visits to foreign parts. However romantic the names of foreign cities may sound, one's enjoyment can be minimal if you are a stranger in town. To be friendless in a foreign country usually induces a loneliness which cultivates dislike for the place and, unless one meets the 'natives' on their own ground – and, preferably, in their own homes – it is not possible to gain a meaningful impression of life as it is lived there.

Fortunately for us, enthusiasm for interesting cars transcends all national and social boundaries, and in countries all over the world we have been welcomed into family circles where an instant rapport has been engendered by the common interest in motor cars and motoring for its own sake. Holidays have been planned to include such meetings and most business trips have permitted an evening's or week-end's diversion into this wonderful world of motoring enthusiasts affording opportunities to drive interesting cars, many of them not readily available in the UK.

I find that I have driven cars in forty different countries or territories – excluding such technical qualifiers as Gibraltar and Monaco.

On one of my visits to New York – in November 1958 – I borrowed the latest Jaguar saloon from Briggs Cunningham and drove to Washington with that extrovert motoring enthusiast James Tilling, whom I had met by chance on 6th Avenue. I had not been to the capital city before and wanted to spend a day unashamedly rubber-necking. Everything went according to plan and we enjoyed the excursion – except for two incidents!

The first one was when I ran out of petrol in the rush-hour traffic on one of Washington's bridges. (In my defence I reckon J.T. shares the blame for this contretemps, having misdirected me, when looking for a filling station, into a lane of traffic from which I could not extricate myself to regain the right road without covering several circuitous miles.) There I was – stationary and causing a solid and impatient traffic hold-up. Almostly instantly a police patrol man riding a motor-cycle and sidecar was on the spot and took charge. Without demur he told the driver of the car behind to push me off the bridge bumper to bumper. This he did, fortunately with no damage to the Jag. Was my face red?

The second incident occurred when we were bowling along an almost deserted twin-track highway in New Jersey on the way back to New York. I said to James, 'What do these radar speed traps look like?' He said he didn't know. Scarcely were the words off his lips when I knew the answer – I was caught in one and was told to follow the Highway Patrolman to the Court House where I paid a summary fine of $25.

It was in 1963 that I realized we had motored in most of Europe and, if we wished to explore further afield, it would be necessary to fly to the area and start motoring when we got there. Our first target was the Middle East and, much as I would have liked to have driven there and back, the time needed was just not available. So we planned the first of our do-it-yourself 'fly and drive' holidays. We flew to Istanbul and were fortunate in having a car and English-speaking driver placed at our disposal. Having visited the sights in the city we drove along the Bosphorus towards the border with Russia and for part of the way were in company with one of 'our' tankers on its way into the Black Sea to load. On a subsequent business trip to 'Constantinople' I enquired about old cars and a

Motoring the world over 219

105 *The Mercedes in which Shevket Pasha was shot on 11 June 1913. The car is now in the Military Museum in Istanbul*

colleague remembered having seen one in the Military Museum. Needless to say, I was soon there making a bee-line for this car. It turned out to be a Mercedes in which a Turk, Shevket Pasha, had been shot in 1913. The bullet-holed glass was still in the windows. It was not a runner, one cylinder block being missing, and the non-original 'LACRE' radiator fooled me until the similarity to my own car was pointed out to me.

From Istanbul we flew to Beirut in the Lebanon and rented an Opel to see the surrounding country and the fabulous ruins at Baalbeck. We then drove via Damascus the 270 miles to Jerusalem and certainly felt very adventurous crossing the Syrian desert in searing heat. We had a good look at Jerash on the way and then visited the Dead Sea, and all the Biblical sites in Jerusalem and Bethlehem, but had to forego a hoped-for trip to Petra for lack of time. The drive back to Beirut was uneventful and after a night's rest we went by air to Cairo and checked in at the Hilton.

In Egypt we were greatly indebted to the Egyptian head of our shipping agents for driving us around in his Mark IX Jaguar. Not only did we see the Pyramids and the Sphinx, but spent a night at Suez and then drove the whole length of the Suez Canal to Port Said before returning to Cairo. It was extremely interesting driving alongside the canal passing a convoy of ships in transit. The terrain was such that on some occasions an approaching vessel looked as if it was on the road. Con had her moments when we visited the National Stud and she was mounted on a purebred Arab for a few swift laps round the paddock.

Reluctantly leaving Egypt we flew to Athens, where once again our motoring was of the chauffeured variety. Plenty to see in this part of Greece and we made the most of it before leaving for home.

I would like to drive to the Middle East – the signpost outside Damascus pointing across hundreds of miles of desert to 'Baghdad' at-

106 *The Mark IX Jaguar by the pyramids of Egypt*
107 *Approaching vessels on the Suez Canal gave the illusion of being on the road*

108 *Lenin's 1922 Silver Ghost Rolls-Royce in
the V.I. Lenin Central Museum, Moscow*

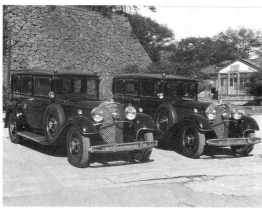

109 *Two Mercedes owned by HIM The Emperor
of Japan lined up for the author's delectation
in the Palace Grounds in Tokyo*
110 *Guy Slaughter's Straight 8 1930 Packard
Phaeton in Hawaii*

tracted me – but such has been the changing
political situation in that part of the world
that it has been scarcely possible to plan a trip
with any certainty of being able to execute it.

Immediately after our daughter Carol's wedding in October 1964, Con and I embarked upon
a trip round the world by air. It occupied 33
days and, although that may sound a bit rushed,
we found time to see what we wanted to and time
to relax, due to meticulous planning beforehand.

Our first stop was Moscow, but the only
motoring we were able to do here was in taxis
provided by Intourist. There were very few
private cars, but they were all clean, it being an
offence to drive a dirty vehicle. The main aven-
ues in the city were wider than any I have seen
and on some roads the central reservations
marked out in white lines on the road surface
were so wide as to eliminate the need for left
turns, cars being able to make U-turns in the
centre of the avenue and then turn right.

In the course of a visit to the V.I. Lenin
Central Museum, I did seek out the 1922 Rolls-
Royce Silver Ghost used by Lenin. On my re-
turn home I wrote asking for some information
about the car and received a reply from the
Deputy Director as follows:

'In answer to your enquiry, we send you
details of the Rolls-Royce used by V.I.
Lenin. Engine No: 207H, chassis no: 17KC,*
Coachwork: torpedo, no. of cylinders: 6,
diameter of cylinders: 114 mm.

'By order of the Council of Peoples' Com-
missars of the Russian Soviet Federated
Socialist Republic, a number of such vehicles
were obtained. The motor car at Gorky was
the same series, but it was transferred to the
Putilovsky Works for use on snow-covered
roads and in places where roads did not
exist.'

The Director of the Polytechnic Museum
admitted to there being some cars at a garage
outside Moscow, but said that they were in a
terrible state and so was the building, and for

*This must have been 17KG.

this reason it would not be possible to see them. I gathered that they were all Soviet vehicles except one, which may have been either a Steyr or Stoewer. He did, however, take me into the basement of the Museum and there (amidst displaced busts and statues of Stalin) were three vehicles, one a 1902 NAG, a 1924 AMO and a 1927 NAMI. The AMO was a lorry and seems to have been the first Soviet vehicle built. The NAMI was also a Russian vehicle, but rather a dull-looking saloon.

Whilst Con was seeing art treasures, I was strolling towards the British Embassy when I saw a convoy of big, black (ZIM?) limousines approaching and sweep swiftly through a gate in the Kremlin wall. Little did I realize at the time that I was probably witnessing history of the USSR in the making, for on that day Kruschev was removed from office.

Next stop was New Delhi, and we were very excited at the prospect of seeing something, however little, of the teeming sub-continent of India. It seems to be a quirk of air time-tables that all flights in and out of Delhi happen in the small hours of the morning – and so it was with us. The inconvenient hour did not stop Johnny Marshall, Rolls-Royce Aero Engine Service representative in India, and his wife, Bobbie, from turning out to meet us and whisk us to the Ashoka Hotel. After a day's sightseeing we left the city in Johnny's Ford station-wagon to see the Taj Mahal at Agra, and to stay overnight with his friend the Maharajah of Bharatpur. My mind was turning to all those magnificent Rolls-Royces, Hispano-Suizas, etc. bought by the dozen in more affluent days and now said to be standing unused and unloved on vast estates. I knew that the Maharajah had a Rolls or two, but did not know what they were. On arrival at Moti Mahal, the Maharajah's palace, I lost no time in enquiring about cars, but found only a couple of interest. One was a 1926 20 hp Windover Cabriolet with a polished aluminium saloon body which the Maharajah's mother had bought new and the other was a well-used

Phantom II Hooper Limousine, which followed us to a duck shoot full of servants and bearers. His Highness was charming and we treasure this glimpse of the magnificence that once was India.

(Lest it be thought that ironmongery always takes precedence over beauty and even wonders of the world, I hasten to say that the Taj Mahal lived up to all the pictures and descriptions.)

After a stop-over at Bangkok we went straight to Tokyo. Our motoring in Japan was limited to taxi rides in the notoriously congested capital city – more than usually throttled by the additional traffic caused by the Olympic Games.·

We did, however, have an astonishing piece of good fortune. I had told our Japanese guide – a charming young lady named Keiko – that I would like to see the Emperor's cars! She opened her eyes in incredulity and said that the Palace grounds were open only on one day each year and then not the Palace itself. Clearly I had asked for the Moon. Imagine my surprise, therefore, next morning when the smiling Keiko arrived at the hotel to say she had arranged through the Emperor's chauffeur for me to visit the Imperial garages! There I first saw the moderns – a Phantom V Rolls-Royce and an S3 Bentley in current use. Then the chauffeur produced a pre-war Mercedes in immaculate condition with the engine running beautifully. He indicated that there was another similar car and showed me a third, adding that a fourth was away being 'fixed'. They were the Type Nurburg, first produced in 1930 and in limited numbers thereafter until 1938 against special orders. The three cars seen in the Palace left the factory in March 1932 and January 1934.

After a short stay in Hong Kong, during which we were driven around the colony in a Mercedes placed at our disposal by business associates, we made the long overnight flight to Sydney to spend the week-end in Australia. Forewarned of our arrival, John ('Jumbo') Goddard invited all members of the Bentley Drivers Club living in New South Wales and – on the off-chance – Victoria to a party at his home. The response to his invitation was astonishing and resulted in an 80 per cent turn-out of those living in NSW. This was not all – members came from other parts of the Continent – some by Bentley; some in other cars and some by air. The distances travelled by Members to meet me as President of the Bentley Drivers Club were quite something and the effort, time and cost involved speak themselves for the high regard for the Marque.

Among those travelling long distances by road were Doug Jarvis from Adelaide (1,000 miles); Malcolm MacDonald from Brisbane (600 miles); Ian McColl and Albert Gladwin from Melbourne (600 miles); Jim Ryrie from Michelago (250 miles) and Ted Lobb from Grenfel (250 miles). Campbell Jaquet drove from Rowena – a mere 430 miles – in his fine Vanden Plas Saloon 8-litre. This car – one of the only two of this model in Australia – provided me with first class transport during a well filled 48-hour stay in Sydney. Bill Hands completed a rebuild of his open VdP 3 litre just in time to set off for Sydney – 600 miles away – without any time for a trial run. He had minor troubles on the way, but turned up at John's place in good shape.

The 'Oscar' for enthusiasm went to Arthur Vance – no millionaire and no youngster – who flew from Perth to Sydney for the week-end especially to be present at the meeting – a distance of 2,128 miles each way. Arthur Vance's pilgrimage (no lesser word suffices to describe his journey) was accepted by all as the seal on this spontaneous evocation of respect and regard for W.O. and his Bentleys.

All too soon we were winging our way to New Zealand. Con and I had accepted a very kind invitation to stay with the late 'Max' and Eilidh Maxwell-Stewart in Wellington. They met us at the airport in their R-Type Continental which I had been instrumental in purchasing for Max in England earlier in the year, and which he had collected personally and used for a holiday here before shipping home.

Again a gathering of Bentley enthusiasts was arranged – this time at the newly-opened Motor Museum of Len Southward. The Museum was most interesting and contained a wealth of motoring miscellany in addition to a collection of Veteran and Vintage cars, including Len's 3-litre awaiting restoration.

The next two days were spent in touring northwards to Auckland (530 miles) in the Continental and I revelled in the opportunity to drive this car in conditions which approached a motorist's paradise. Few cars and fast well-surfaced roads through scenery reminiscent of Wales, Scotland and occasionally Switzerland.

Whilst we were checking in at Auckland airport and digesting the news that our departure would be delayed by 3 hours, the distinctive burble of Vintage Bentleys announced the arrival of A.B. Seccombe and his daughter in his beautifully turned-out open Speed Six, followed by his son driving his $4\frac{1}{2}$. These were soon joined by N.C. Adams' 3-litre and R.S. Mills' $4\frac{1}{2}$-litre Park Ward Saloon. Also present were several other Vintage car enthusiasts. The waiting hours were spent happily – albeit in an uncomfortable and 'dry' airport lounge – talking Bentleys. The party gradually dispersed, but a few stayed until the bitter end to see us off to Fiji around midnight.

After a very short night in bed at Nandi I hired a Holden and we set off for the 70-mile drive along the beautiful, unspoiled coastal road to Koru Levu. The couple of days complete rest here was enough for me, but Con would have stayed a good deal longer and often talks of Fiji as the place she would most like to go back to. At the end of a two-hour drive to the airport in the dark, during which we saw scarcely a soul or habitation, we left Nandi for Hawaii.

On arrival at Honolulu – you've guessed it – we were met by Guy Slaughter, the owner of a $4\frac{1}{2}$-litre Bentley, and his wife Betty, who placed the traditional leis round our necks in welcome. In the car park was the only Vintage Bentley for at least 2,000 miles in any direction and a Vintage

Packard Club Sedan to transport us and our luggage to the Hotel.

As far as was known there were only about half a dozen enthusiasts in the Islands and you can imagine how the three I met welcomed a personal contact with one closely connected with the cult in the UK. The inhabitants appeared to have little appreciation of Vintage cars and their lack of knowledge was quite surprising – it took quite a thick skin to drive around in an old car at the receiving end of laughs, jibes about 'Model T's' and countless daft questions and suggestions.

The afternoon was spent in motoring round the island of Oahu in the open Bentley, which Guy had finished putting together with new big ends only the previous day. It ran like a bird and we enjoyed our sightseeing trip immensely. That evening we dined with one of the few Vintage car owners in Hawaii – Judson Ihrig – whose garage housed a PII Rolls-Royce, a 1926 37.2 hp Hispano-Suiza, a 1913 EMF and a small Vintage Rolls. Another enthusiast in Hawaii – then without any Vintage machinery – was Warren Kernaghan who had owned until recently the 12-cylinder Packard used in the film 'South Pacific'.

Our second day in Hawaii included a 100-mile drive round the main island in a most elegant Straight 8 1930 Packard Phaeton from Guy's stable.

From Honolulu to San Francisco where we found awaiting us at the hotel, a letter from a Club Member, Jay Heumann, inviting us to spend the following day with him and his wife. This turned out to be a guided tour of San Francisco in his R-Type Continental with lunch and dinner included. This hospitality we accepted appreciatively and spent a most pleasant day sightseeing. Not far behind the Golden Gate Bridge and the giant redwood trees ranked Jay's 4¼-litre (MX series) Bentley. This car had been completely rebuilt by Jay and it did him great credit. Incidentally, Jay really has mastered the change down into bottom gear on

his Continental – he had to, living in a City where nearly all the streets are steeper than any encountered in this country. Con and I agreed that San Francisco would be our choice if we had to live in the States.

An invitation to visit the almost legendary Harrah Automobile Collection caused me to dent our itinerary between San Francisco and Los Angeles and thus we arrived at Reno at 11 o'clock one morning with a bare five hours to do less than justice to this unique car museum. We were met by Bud Catlett, the Purchasing Supervisor of the Collection, who devoted his day to showing us the cars and answering innumerable questions. It would be quite impossible to give an adequate description of Mr (Bill) Harrah's collection in anything less than a volume, but I will give just a few facts and figures as a bare framework in which one's imagination may wander.

There were then 940 cars, about 300 of which were on display, the majority having been restored in the plant which was the backbone of the collection. This plant covered 5 acres and, in addition to two large showrooms, included a large workshop area and separate buildings for coachwork, upholstery, plating and sandblasting. In these shops were employed 70 craftsmen and there did not seem to be a single job arising in rebuilding cars which they could not tackle – I saw radiators, wheels and lamps being repaired and, where necessary made from scratch, for veteran, vintage and classic cars undergoing restoration.

Bill Harrah had brought out on the occasion of my visit, a Supercharged 4½-litre Bentley awaiting its turn for face-lifting and an 8-litre bought from an owner in the Eastern United States. I also saw another 8-litre recently bought from Briggs Cunningham and a 100 mph 3-litre. We were joined at lunch in the staff cafeteria by Bill who, once his natural reserve had been overcome, enjoyed a stimulating discussion on motor-cars in general and Bentleys in particular.

After the breath-taking tour of the showrooms and workshops we visited and lingered in the library. Yes – this, too, defied description. Thousands of volumes covering every aspect of motoring and a research staff – all maintained to one end – the authentic and true-to-original restoration of cars in the collection.

And so to our last port of call, Los Angeles, where Briggs Cunningham met us at the airport and, drove us to his new home at Newport Beach where we were to spend the next two and a half days. I had asked Briggs if he would arrange a meeting of Club members in the area and if those attending might then see his collection of cars. He did more than this. Briggs wrote personally to all the members resident in California and neighbouring States inviting them to a lunch at his home and to see the cars afterwards. So great was the response that the venue of the lunch was moved to the garage itself.

The Saturday of the Club party arrived and much effort had gone into cleaning up the cars and especially sprucing up the Bentleys. In the morning I enjoyed driving around in, successively, the ex-Pierre Marechal Speed Six; the ex-Peter Bell 8-litre; the Eddie Hall TT $4\frac{1}{4}$ and my old Phantom III Rolls-Royce. We parked the three Bentleys and three others ($4\frac{1}{2}$-litre Supercharged; $4\frac{1}{4}$-litre Overdrive and 'R' Type Continental) outside the 'warehouse' containing the remaining 40 or 50 cars in the collection and awaited the arrival of the guests.

First to arrive was Norman Brooks from San Diego without his 8-litre, which was still undergoing coachwork restoration at the hands of an unhurried craftsman. He was closely followed by Arthur Rippey who flew in from Denver, a thousand miles away, thus providing further evidence, if any were needed, of the enthusiasm of we car-minded people. Members began arriving thick and fast. Amherst Villiers (designer of *the* Blower) took time off from rebuilding a Supercharged $4\frac{1}{2}$-litre – subsequently owned by Phil Hill – to join the party.

Briggs and Laura had set up a U-shaped lunch table for 40 in the garage and we sat down to the groaning board in the presence of as fine a selection of cars as one could wish for. This very happy occasion concluded with a vote of thanks to Briggs and Laura for arranging the meeting and for their generous hospitality. The guests reluctantly departed in ones and twos as the air was shattered by the Bentleys being driven back under cover.

In January 1967 Con and I decided to see something of Africa and my carefully planned itinerary enabled us to visit countries in East and South Africa in a three-week round trip.

After a most worthwhile visit to Murchison Park in Uganda and an unpleasant experience at the hands (and rifle-butt) of a guard outside the palace of the deposed Kabaka, we flew to Nairobi. There were only four Club members living in Kenya at the time and I had written to each of them suggesting getting together one evening, perhaps in Nairobi. The response was prompt and enthusiastic. In fact, each one had suggested different ways of making the most of our short visit to Kenya and extended invitations to us to stay a day or two with them, which, unfortunately, my closely planned itinerary would not permit. Eventually, we all lunched at Nakuru, 100 miles from Nairobi, on Sunday, 22 January, a private room at the Stag's Head echoing to Bentley talk for a couple of hours or so; but first let me go back to our arrival in Nairobi. At the airport we were met by Ken Rhys-Maitland – Dental Officer in the RAF then stationed in Kenya – and his wife, Joan.

There were no Bentleys in Nairobi, but Ken took me to see a 1913 London-Edinburgh Silver Ghost being restored by its owner Willy Balabanoff.

The drive to Nakuru was pleasant enough and the first car I saw in the main street was a very clean and standard open $4\frac{1}{2}$. This belonged to John Jeeves and was the only Bentley present. Stewart Hamilton had burned a lot of midnight oil in an effort to get his Standard 6½ on parade, but was beaten by drain tubes which had been incorrectly threaded. These two, together with Ken Rhys-Maitland who had accompanied me from Nairobi, represented a 75 per cent turnout of the whole membership of the country, plus an erstwhile member, Roddy Williams, who had a 3/4½ at home – in bits hanging on the wall, as far as I can gather. Those present were exhorting him to 'build up' or 'part up'. Another non-member present with his Mk VI was Stephen Hempstead, who also owned a 1915 Alpine Silver Ghost. Thereafter, some of us, including John Jeeves in his 4½, went to the nearby lake famous for being the home of flamingoes said to number up to two million at times. There were so many that the edge of the lake was fringed in pink as far as the eye could see, and the level lake shore invited driving antics.

In Mombasa I rented a 'bread-and-butter' car and drove several miles into the bush to see what Kenya was really like. I found that only a mile or two off the main road the land was free from all the trappings of so-called civilization, the people going about their daily life in the villages as they must have done for centuries. Now I know why it is necessary for makers of cars intended for East African markets to drive them through dust-bowls to ensure that they are leak-proof! I noticed that the most popular makes of cars were those which had done well in successive Safari Rallies.

Only one Member was living in Dar es Salaam, our next port of call – Francis Spencer – a temporary immigrant from the UK and a dyed-in-the-wool Vintage Bentley enthusiast.

He took me off in a taxi to the house of a friend, 6 miles out of town, to show me his Bentley. We arrived at this house amid palm trees and as I followed him round to the back I was surprised to see under a lean-to a bodyless 3-litre chassis in an advanced stage of rebuild.

The car was then complete mechanically, as was demonstrated to me when I went for a ride

111 *John Jeeves (centre) with his 4½-litre Bentley in Nakuru, Kenya*

112 *Francis Spencer's 3-litre Bentley in Dar es Salaam*
113 *Briggs Cunningham's 275GTB4 Ferrari and his wife Laura's mother-of-pearl Lamborghini Miura at Costa Mesa*

on the bonnetless machine, standing on the chassis frame and gear-box with the driver seated in a bare, bucket seat. The body work was to be started soon and an entirely new body fabricated.

Francis had recently discovered in Dar es Salaam a Vintage $4\frac{1}{2}$ Bentley with a Mk VI radiator owned by a Mr William Boddy. The log book showed Chassis No XF 3517 and Engine No XF 3515 which belong to the 1929 Paris Show car. It had a VdP body, was running on one set of ignition and had a Fordson dynamo. The replacement parts used from time to time looked distinctly agricultural. The front brakes had been converted to hydraulics using lorry parts. The Tanzanian Registration No was IR 1231 and it had been imported before the War.

We then went to Livingstone and found the Victoria Falls to be one of the most impressive sights we have ever seen and afterwards headed south to Johannesburg, where our visit would coincide with the Annual Dinner of the local members of the BDC.

Whilst Con's hair was having attention in readiness for the dinner, I was taken to Jeffs Watson's lovely home in his drophead Mk VI Bentley. I saw his very nice, standard VdP $4\frac{1}{2}$, which was driven during the rest of the week-end by Jeffs' eldest son, Roy, who, incidentally, had recently rebuilt a Tiger Moth from scrap and raced it with satisfactory results. Jeff had a collection of Veteran and Edwardian cars, and being restored in the garage were a Type 35 Bugatti (with a Type 38 engine) and a curved-dash Oldsmobile.

In the evening we were collected at the hotel by Gordon Strauss in his well-preserved, high-mileage, early Mk VI and taken to the venue for dinner. This was, in fact, the most off-beat imaginable – a prison and the waiters were inmates. Sounds awful, doesn't it? Well, it wasn't. The establishment was a rehabilitation centre for first offenders – an open prison at which they were taught trades and vocations with a view to keeping them out of trouble when they were released. It catered for both black and white and was seemingly doing a good job. For our part, the table, the service and the food were beyond criticism and the room could have been the banqueting room of any provincial English hotel.

Before we sat down to dinner I was able to meet and talk to all the members present – no less than 18. Some of these had driven several hundred miles to be there, Waldie Greyvensteyn from Bloemfontein probably scoring top marks in this respect. The party, including families, numbered 46 in all. The usual toasts were proposed and the meaningful words spoken on the subject of the Club, 'W.O.' and Bentleys generally, reflected exactly the same sincerity of admiration and feeling as on similar occasions in the UK.

Gordon Fisher presented to me a handsome, inscribed copper tray as a memento of the occasion. I replied suitably, I hope, and the party dissolved for conversation. As always, I was impressed with the enthusiasm and the detailed technical knowledge of these chaps who did miracles in maintaining their Bentleys far from the comparatively easy sources of spares and technical know-how available to UK members. Anyone overhearing the post-prandial conversation in Johannesburg would have thought himself at a Club meeting in the 'local' at home.

At Cape Town we were met by Luccio Labia from whom I had acquired my Mercedes. He showed us round and then lent me his Alfa-Romeo for the duration of our stay. Two members of the Bentley Drivers Club, Tony White and Rudi Reitz, on hearing of our 48-hour stay in Cape Town, contacted all Members within reasonable distance and arranged a meeting. Thanks to the generous hospitality of Tony and his wife, this took the form of a supper party at their home. Driven there from our hotel by Rudi Reitz we were greeted, as we entered the drive of the White house, by the sight of the two open $4\frac{1}{2}$s of the Rohr brothers, Bert and

Ralph, standing side by side, with Cecil Harris's S-Type discreetly parked in the shade. In all 12 members attended, Rudy Reitz having driven nearly 300 miles from George. Dr Clarke came from Worcester, 70 miles away, to which town he had recently moved from Livingstone in Zambia. (The Secretary of the Club had notified Tony White of this change of address specially for the purpose of the gathering and, when Tony telephoned John Clarke from out of the blue and said, 'Are you a member of the Bentley Drivers Club?' the surprised medico replied, 'Yes, but how the hell did you know?')

We soon repaired to the garage where Tony White's Standard 6½ awaited commencement of the complete rebuild scheduled for it. Alongside it Barry Morton was rebuilding his 4½ from the ground up and was in the middle of mounting a replica VdP body imported from England in kit form.

Our Cape Town visit terminated on a very happy note when Cecil and Ann Harris insisted on picking us up at the Mount Nelson Hotel at 6.15 am (!) and driving us to the Airport in their S1 Bentley.

This was the start of our journey home, but we had yet one more country to visit – Rhodesia.

Not many members were then living in Rhodesia, but a tentative enquiry about the possibility of a get-together to E.J.L. ('Charles') Griffith brought a speedy response with a promise to meet us at the airport and to arrange a dinner in Salisbury. I had known Charles in the immediate post-war years before he left the UK and well remembered his prowess in competition in a Blower Bentley in those days.

He met us on arrival in a more pedestrian, but well-maintained 3½-litre saloon and drove us to the City centre, where I picked up a Hertz car to leave at once for the Vumba Mountains 180 miles away. Charles' last remark as we left Salisbury was: 'If you are in trouble in Umtali, chief 'Itala-swinger' Jack Sanderson – a reference to VSCC Silverstone meetings years ago – is with Meikle's Garage there.' I wasn't in

trouble in Umtali, but I did call on Jack – happily married with a growing family – and he did not need much persuading to drive 20 miles over a mountain road (187 bends) to dine with us at Leopard Rock that night.

I found motoring in Rhodesia a joy – perhaps the best of any country I had visited. The road from Salisbury to Umtali (160 miles) was surfaced all the way, gently curving and undulating and interesting – and traffic-free! I needed only 160 minutes to cover the 160 miles in a 'cooking' Cortina in which I rarely exceeded 65 mph, and never 70.

It was thus no hardship to leave the Vumba three days later to drive to Salisbury in time to catch an 11 am hair appointment for Con in preparation for the evening party. The afternoon was spent at Charles' house where his chain-driven Frazer Nash and other automotive projects occupied some time.

Four Club members – Charles, T.E. Barlow Pye and his son, J.B. Pye, who had flown in from Ndola in neighbouring Zambia, and C.A.L. Meredith were present at the dinner party in the Ambassador Hotel. Several other Bentley owners were there. Also Joan Rowland, a niece of W.O.

Again, we spent a most pleasant evening and the kindness and hospitality extended to us was further evidence that the interest of Members in Bentleys transcends not only social, financial and geographical boundaries, but also thrives with complete indifference to political barriers.

Altogether, during our trip, we met no less than 40 Club members. Each one of them – and the wives of the married ones – contributed something to our enjoyment which cannot be assessed in material terms.

In June 1968 in the course of a business trip to Australia and back in the short space of 13 days I managed to contact Club members in several places. Over the Pole to Tokyo via Alaska – no BDC members there – then via Hongkong and Manila to Sydney. John Goddard was here, instead of there, but a telephone call to Jack Jeffery brought forth an invitation to dine at his house and a visit to his garage – then devoid of Bentleys, but boasting a fine Mercedes-Benz.

In the course of a 24-hour visit to Melbourne, 460 miles away, Gregor Rusden managed to gather together a party of Members and Bentley enthusiasts at his home where I spent a very pleasant evening. I was impressed by the perseverance and tenacity of these Australian Bentley lovers who rebuild and maintain their cars under difficulties scarcely imaginable to those who are within two-day postal delivery of most spare parts and a local call away from expert knowledge and advice.

Next stop was Honolulu, to refuel and pass through US Customs. An air mail warning of my passage to Guy Slaughter brought him hotfoot from his place of work at Pearl Harbour to the airport in his $4\frac{1}{2}$. We spent a pleasant hour in the Coffee Shop – it was breakfast time – talking of matters Bentley and Vintagery generally. Five hours and 2,400 miles later I landed at Los Angeles to be met by Briggs and Laura Cunningham who whisked me away to Bruce Fagan's apartment. Here we were joined by Bill Anderson and John Milchick and later adjourned to a Beverly Hills restaurant for dinner and talked about – you've guessed – Bentleys and ancillary subjects until nigh on midnight, when Briggs drove me south to his home at Newport Beach.

Early next morning I was in Briggs' Automobile Museum at nearby Costa Mesa relishing once again his wonderful collection of cars. I then drove his 275 GTB4 Ferrari and Laura's Lamborghini Miura, before being driven to LA to catch the 1 pm flight to New York. On arrival I picked up a Hertz Ford Galaxie and drove out to spend a night in Bernardsville, New Jersey, with daughter Carol and her family.

I flew to Bermuda the next morning and, after lunch with friends at the Mid-Ocean Club and three business meetings in Hamilton, I took a taxi out to Stanley Sears's home for tea. (Guess what we talked about!)

Charles Noble, owner of no less than four supercharged $4\frac{1}{2}$-litre Bentleys, was awaiting my arrival at J.F. Kennedy Airport having driven out from the City especially to spend an hour with me between flights and – yes – we talked Bentleys until about 1 am. Such is the dedication of Bentley enthusiasts.

A visit to Mexico for the Olympic Games in 1968 provided an opportunity to taste the joys and hazards of driving in Central America. On the way there we stopped off in New York to visit Carol and Roger, and our grandchildren, in New Jersey, and again in Washington where I enjoyed driving Con around the capital city this being her first visit there, in a Mustang belonging to Mr Hertz.

We were met at Mexico City Airport by Porfirio ('Sunny') Diaz, who owned the only Vintage Bentley in the country. It was an 8-litre, particularly interesting in that it was the only one fitted with American coachwork when new, a roadster body by Murphy. It was not in good shape. The engine was dismantled pending rebuilding and motive power was provided by an International diesel truck engine – sounded rather like a Vintage Bentley, I must admit, but not like an 8-litre. I drove it with some trepidation as the ancient tyres had that rather tired 'dried-up mud' appearance. Another unusual feature of this Bentley was the wooden-spoked wheels. When Sunny acquired the car it had no wheels at all; it was only by good fortune that he found four wheels off a Mercedes in a breaker's yard which fitted the splined hubs (This 8-litre and all the bits were subsequently acquired by Don Weber of Texas and underwent a once-and-for-all restoration at the premises of Hofmann & Mountfort at Henley-on-Thames where the car and pieces were delivered in huge crates from Mexico.)

Whilst in Mexico City we visited some of the nearby ruins in our rented Ford Galaxie, the

114 *Stanley Sears gives the author a ride during a visit to Bermuda*

115 *The author with Sunny Diaz and his 8-litre Bentley in Mexico City*
116 *Arthur G. Rippey and the Mk VI Bentley in his museum at Denver, Colorado*

pyramids at San Juan Teotihuacan impressing us perhaps most of all. The relics we saw in the City itself and in the Museum of Anthropology whetted our appetite for the planned excursions to Uxmal and Chichen-Itza from our next stopping-place, Merida in Yucatan. Motoring in this part of Mexico was very enjoyable and exploring the Mayan ruins filled us with awe and admiration for their creators – tinged with disgust at the barbarity of some of their ways.

We continued our journey by air to Kingston, Jamaica and rented a car to drive across the island to Ocho Rios where we were to stay a few days. There was some unrest and labour trouble in Kingston and not long after leaving the town an attempt was made by a Jamaican driving an old banger to run me off the road; I can only think he took exception to being overtaken by a more modern car and retaliated in anger.

In May 1969 we were fortunate enough to be on the belated maiden voyage of 'Queen Elizabeth II' from Southampton to New York. A contingent of old Rolls-Royces and their owners were on board at the start of a tour in the United States, so motoring talk was predominant throughout the trip. After visiting New Orleans and Williamsburg – where I rented cars locally – we joined up again with the RR party in Washington and rode with them to attend a reception at the British Embassy. Afterwards, everyone was entertained to dinner by members of the Rolls-Royce Owners Club (of America) in the Smithsonian Institute. Films were shown of the previous year's Rolls-Royce and Bentley Pageant at Goodwood and I was called upon to make impromptu remarks each time a Bentley appeared on the screen – a task I performed indifferently, I'm afraid, not having seen the film before, but it was made intelligible and enjoyable by John Dymock-Maunsell's commentary, for he had organized the event and knew nearly every car.

In June 1971, bidden to attend the opening of a mammoth dry-dock in Lisbon, we flew to

Faro, borrowed a Toyota from Sr Hertz and spent an interesting week in the Algarve before allowing business to raise its ugly head. This was my first experience of Japanese motoring and the car provided perfectly adequate transport. We took the attractive inland road to Lisbon and whilst staying there revisited Cascais, Guincho and Sintra, which we had first seen in the Mk VI in 1959, and, of course, drove over the magnificent new bridge spanning the Tagus.

In February 1972 Con and I decided to get away from the English winter for a week's sunshine in Tunisia. Whilst staying at Hammamet we hired a car and drove southwards 100 miles or so to see Kairouan and Sousse. We then spent a few days with our old friends the Scheels at Carthage, during which Ditlev took us for a long drive in his Opel Diplomat to the fantastic, but perhaps not so well-known, ruined city at Dougga.

Oil business took me to Colorado and California in May 1972 and I decided to take a few days holiday to see the Indianapolis '500' Race on the way home. First call was on Arthur G. Rippey in Denver, Colorado, who had flown nearly 1,000 miles to Los Angeles to meet me when Briggs Cunningham gave the lunch party in his 'garage' in 1964, and I was glad of the opportunity to repay the courtesy. On his retirement from business at the end of 1966, Mr Rippey sold his original collection of Veteran and Vintage cars, but then found it possible to indulge his hobby once more by running a purchase-and-sale business alongside his museum. The collection was not a large one and included a majority (I think) of post-Vintage and post-World War II cars. My first choice would be the 1933 Chrysler Custom Imperial with Le Baron phaeton coachwork.

After an overnight stop in LA, a non-stop flight in a DC-10 took me to West Palm Beach in Florida where I stayed overnight with Bill Spear. There were no longer any Bentleys in his stable, but I seized the opportunity to drive his 3-litre BMW (named the 'Bavaria' in the States by the manufacturers to dispel the prevalent impression that it was a British car!), Wankel-engined Mazda and his latest acquisition – a Dino Ferrari.

I made a side trip to the Bahamas to inspect some land I had misguidedly purchased some years before, and then flew from Nassau to Toronto where I had been invited to a private preview of a collection of about 50 Veteran, Vintage and Classic cars to be unveiled to the world at large three weeks later. This collection had been put together quietly during the previous year by selected purchases made for the sponsors, Rothmans of Pall Mall Canada Ltd, through 'The Craven Foundation'. The shopping list was compiled by an advisory Committee of enthusiasts in the field of Veteran and Classic cars in Canada and a prominent part was played by Ralph Turner whose personal Speed Six was well-known in those parts. Many desirable cars had been acquired, including an 8-litre Bentley costing £15,000 which I was privileged to be the first to drive on the road there. I rode as a passenger in a 'J' Duesenberg and fifty-one thousand dollars-worth of Packard – an immaculate, dual-cowl phaeton '734' model of 1930; also a rare 1930 Ruxton and a Graham.

Later that week, having completed business matters in New York, I flew in to Indianapolis to see the '500' on the following day. I had been looking forward to seeing the famous race at Indianapolis. I felt my education in the motor-racing field was lacking until I had seen this race – once! I knew that it was unique and surrounded with a lot of bally-hoo, but the speeds were fantastic and my impression from films and photographs – which actually concentrated on spectacular crashes – was that the event was becoming too dangerous. The start was spectacular and I saw one heart-stopping crash in which the car returned to the paddock as a crumpled ball of metal dangling from the crane of a rescue track but, mercifully, the driver survived. As the race progressed and cars spread out it became less enthralling and for many laps it was frankly boring. The speed of the cars did not appear to be near the 200 mph mark and certainly the whole thing looked relatively safe to me. The protection for the spectators is so good that the track tends to provide 'slot-racing' with the result that when a driver runs out of road, he is, in fact, bounced straight back on to it in the path of following cars. As there is no verge between the outer edge of the track and the barrier, the following drivers have less chance of avoiding a car in trouble, and are, therefore, more at risk from the misdoings and mishaps of others than would be the case on most European circuits.

Right after the race I flew to Detroit and was the guest of Dick Mertz, President of the Rolls-Royce Owners Club of America who very kindly took me to the Ford Museum at Dearborn, and allowed me to drive his immaculate Phantom III. A direct VC 10 flight to London terminated that trip.

In March 1973 I seized the opportunity to visit the Chinese Peoples' Republic in connection with the British Industrial Technology Exhibition in Peking. After flying to Stuttgart, and driving from there to Athens (reported elsewhere), I decided to stop off for a week-end in Bangkok on the way to Hong Kong, the jumping-off point for Pekin. In anticipation of my stop-over I wrote to 'Bira' (Prince Birabongse Bhanubandh) asking if H.M. King Bhumibol of Thailand owned any old cars and, if so, could he arrange for me to see them?

Soon after checking in at the Intercontinental Hotel, I called him at his apartment in the Dhusi Thani Hotel to learn that he did not know whether his Royal cousin had any old cars or not. 'Bira' was busily engaged running his own airline and had lost interest in motor racing and motoring. Nevertheless, he readily agreed on a voyage of discovery and first took me to the garages at the King's residence, Chitrlada Palace, where three cars, one Veteran and two

117 *The author out in Toronto with Ralph Turner on the first trip in Canada of the 8-litre Bentley recently added to the Craven Collection*

118 *Mike Mosley's car returning to the Paddock as a crumpled ball of metal during the Indianapolis '500' in 1972*

Vintage, were to be seen among the fleet of modern cars.

The Veteran, a beautifully kept – presumably restored – four-cylinder Renault four-seater tonneau with a fringed canopy was pushed out into the open so that I could take photographs. The two Vintage vehicles, not in pristine condition, but apparently complete and in workmanlike shape, were a Hotchkiss and a Voisin.

The former had a Saoutchik body, and the latter coachwork by Ottin of Lyon.

My appetite thus whetted, and 'Bira' and his beautiful wife now infected by my enthusiasm avidly searching for identification plates in dusty and oily darkness, we were then piloted by a couple of Royal Mews employees to another palace the name and whereabouts of which I failed to note. On arrival we drove past many modern cars and several immaculate post-war Delahayes which, I believe, the King himself had acquired during the time he lived in Paris, and perceived promise of better things to come as two Rolls-Royces came into sight.

On blocks was a Silver Ghost (chassis No. 108AG) with an enclosed drive cabriolet body by Hooper. This car was supplied to H.E. Buri Navarash on 4 October 1921. I noticed that it was fitted with apparently original Dunlop Limousine 895 × 150 tyres. Its later sister was a Phantom III (chassis no. 3DL 158) with a limousine de ville body by H.J. Mulliner finished in the Royal deep cream. It was immaculate and was driven out of its garage as silently and smoothly as any PIII I have known. The records show that this car was shipped from Southampton on 21 August 1939 to HRH Prince Aditya Dhipya Arbha in Bangkok. The radiator shutters were fixed in the open position, presumably to cope with the tropical climate.

Next to the Rolls-Royce a pair of (to me) less interesting cars stood on blocks, a Mercedes with rear wheels hanging grotesquely on their swing-axles and a Daimler with a Charlesworth body. My failure to pursue further investigation of these cars was due to a glimpse of a group of large radiators visible in a series of open-fronted garages further down the road. Impatiently approaching this Aladdin's Cave, my eyes popped out of my head when I realized that the five giants from left to right were a Cadillac, a Pierce-Arrow, a Mercedes, a Hispano-Suiza and a Voisin! The Pierce-Arrow, a 1930 or 1931 Straight Eight with a phaeton

body was unusual in having bracket lamps instead of the traditional ones faired into the front mudguards. The Mercedes was a six-cylinder supercharged car of 1929, almost certainly a Type 630B. The chassis had been sent by train from the factory in Stuttgart to Paris in July 1929 where the coachbuilders, Saoutchik, fitted a touring body.

The Hispano-Suiza was the well-known H6B 37.2 hp six-cylinder car of 1927. And last but by no means least, the V12 Voisin. Time was getting short and I did not look for identifying information on this car, but my attention was captured by an interesting feature: an extra radiator under the bonnet. Was this for water or oil, and was it a standard feature or a tropical extra?

I left the Royal mews with mixed feelings. Gratification that examples of these Grandes Marques still existed; sorrow that the prevailing climatic conditions must have wrought severe but not irreparable damage; regret that there was no prospect of the cars passing into the hands of enthusiasts able and prepared to restore them to new condition – the latter sentiment tempered by the knowledge that any self-seeking dealer contemplating a trip to Thailand with a view to making a kill would be more likely to be on the receiving end of Royal disapproval – for the King never sells anything.

The best hope was that something may be done to restore the cars and put them on exhibition in Bangkok – a course of action which I enjoined 'Bira' to commend to His Majesty.

I dodged about a bit in Japan and then flew from Hong Kong to Pekin in a chartered BOAC VC 10 on the first-ever direct airline flight between these two cities. Of motoring in 'Red' China, there was virtually none. Lots of trucks, seemingly millions of bicycles, some taxis, motor-coaches and Chinese-built cars used by Government officials and employees, but the only private cars to be seen were those of foreign diplomatic staff. The roads were wide and motorized traffic sparse. The biggest hazard

119 *'DL' Series Rolls-Royce Phantom III limousine de ville by H.J. Mulliner*

120 *Prince Birabongse Bhanubandh with the 1909/10 Renault*

were the ubiquitous cyclists – who were not required to carry lights at night – causing drivers of the few taxis and other vehicles to blow their horns incessantly.

There were 900 Brits. in Peking on this occasion and the Chinese certainly made us welcome. It was, for me, a never-to-be-forgotten experience to stand upon the Great Wall of China and I left the country feeling that, given political stability, it had a great future. It seemed to be developing slowly and surely, and if the will to continue was maintained there was a great opportunity to raise the standard of living, at the same time avoiding the pitfalls which have plagued Western civilization. I am conscious that any views I express about China, based as they are upon a week in two cities without any knowledge of the language, are virtually value-less, but I know what I saw – and that is an apparently healthy and contented people work-ing hard. Nevertheless, I must confess to a feeling of freedom regained as I got off the train from Canton and walked across the border bridge to Lo Wu into the New Territories of Hong Kong. I continued the same day by air to Tokyo and across the Pacific to Los Angeles.

And so to California where I found that Acton Cochrane had once again risen to the occasion by arranging not one but two Bentley meetings on the same day – a concours in the afternoon and a dinner in the evening. Accord-ingly, Barry Hon called for me at the Beverly Hilton early on Saturday morning and I drove his S1 Continental out to the Santa Anita Park Racecourse (horses, not cars) on the outskirts of Los Angeles. Here I found myself in unfamiliar surroundings when asked to be in the Winner's Circle to welcome the winning horse and jockey of a race named 'The Rolls-Royce and Bentley

Owners Purse' in honour of the two clubs. I then presented the prizes to winners of the Rolls-Royce and Bentley Concours.

In the evening the basement hall of the elegant Bank of America Building outside the dining-room was graced by the presence of three Bentleys, a gesture I appreciated very much.

I was pleased to be able to reciprocate in some measure by showing my films of the Club visits to Le Mans and Aubusson, thereby bringing to life the photographs of Bentleys seen in the pages of the Club's magazine by the many who might never be able to come to the UK to see the cars themselves.

A fitting close to this day was when, at some-where approaching midnight, the Speed Six driven by Dave Clark, and the Blower $4\frac{1}{2}$ driven by Phil Hill, had a drag race down Flower Street, in the heart of the financial district. As the Club's local scribe, Don Taylor, put it – 'The Bentley Burble and the Blower whine echoed and re-echoed from the walls of glass and steel that were only a quarter their age, or even less . . . The Perfect Epilogue.'

Brief stays in Toronto and New York, where I renewed motoring friendships, ended this, my third circumnavigation of the World.

California
In January 1975, during one of my transatlantic business trips, I was fortunate to be able to experience a couple of interesting drives. In Los Angeles Phil Hill called for me at my hotel at 9 am sharp in one of his beautiful Packards – a 1938 12-cylinder saloon considered a worthy rival to the Rolls-Royce Phantom III – and took me to various locations in Santa Monica to see his collection of cars. At the last place of call Phil brought out his supercharged $4\frac{1}{2}$-litre Bentley and we proceeded southwards on the San Diego Freeway to attend a meeting of Bentley Drivers Club members at Briggs Cunningham's museum in Costa Mesa. I was privileged to drive the Blower and recalled that I had driven this very car $23\frac{1}{2}$ years previously, when I took it to

123 *A 'Red Flag' limousine in Peking, manufactured in Changchun No 1 Factory, which produced between fifty and a hundred cars a year for official use. The limousine had a 5.65 litre engine, a weight of $2\frac{3}{8}$ tons, and was understood to come with varying degrees of armour-plating and bullet-proof glass*

Kensington Gardens for the then owner, Charles Langlands, who had had it since new. I then borrowed 'my' P III out of Briggs collection and took up a position on a bridge over a nearby freeway to take photographs of Phil's and other Bentleys passing underneath. Altogether a day of nostalgic motoring.

In September 1977, after a week of business meetings in Bermuda and New York, Con and I flew to Los Angeles to visit Briggs Cunningham in Newport Beach. With his customary generosity he lent us his 450SE Mercedes for a touring holiday in California. The first day we drove northwards through Los Angeles and Bakersfield into the Sequoia National Park to visit Giant Forest, where the magnificence of the great trees quite overawed us. After overnighting in Fresno at the Hilton (kept awake by the noise of the ventilating fan in the multi-storeyed car-park opposite) we made for Yosemite National Park and were fortunate to have secured reservations at the Ahwahnee Hotel right inside the valley. Then we turned westwards to Pebble Beach, where we spent a night at the Del Monte Lodge – a peaceful haven on non-concours occasions. Paul and Emily Woudenberg hosted a party for us in their nearby home, where other Bentley enthusiasts had gathered to greet us.

Then we commenced the run southwards along the scenic Pacific Coast road past Big Sur, making an expedient night stop at San Luis Bay Inn at Avila Beach for the virtually mandatory visit for tourists to Hearst's Castle at San Simeon. The last resting-place on this trip was the luxurious Beverly Wilshire Hotel in Beverly Hills, where Gerry and June Baxter joined us for dinner. When I reluctantly surrendered to Briggs his Mercedes-Benz we had covered 1,193 miles in the week and the petrol consumption worked out at 16 miles per (US) gallon, i.e. 19.2 miles per Imperial gallon.

On the way home an overnight stop for business meetings in Toronto brought BDC members Hugh Young and Ralph Turner to the airport to meet us and subsequently take us to

124 *Giant sequoia dwarfs Briggs Cunningham's 450SE Mercedes-Benz – September 1977*

meet other like-minded enthusiasts at dinner. Little over 24 hours after our arrival we were airborne again for London, with another rewarding holiday in the family album.

An opportunity arose in August 1979 to sample some quintessential American motoring – using a station wagon for the purpose it was designed to fulfil, i.e. the transportation of a number of passengers and a large quantity of luggage. The occasion was the happy coincidence during the same week in August of three important motoring events in California, namely the Laguna Seca Race Meeting, the Pebble Beach Concours d'Elegance and the National Meet of the Rolls-Royce Owners Club at Monterey.

The weekend would attract Bentleys from all over the United States and some from Canada;

125 *Why we needed a full-size station-wagon –*
August 1979

126 *Driving the Clénet at Santa Barbara,*
California – August 1979

but few owners in Europe had the time and money at their disposal to enable them to take their cars across the Atlantic and then across America. In the event this feat was accomplished by three intrepid owners of Vintage Bentleys who sent their cars by sea to New York and then drove by circuitous routes to the West Coast. These were the Medcalf brothers, Bill and Jim, (with members of their families) in their Speed Six and 4½-litre respectively, and the globe-trotting Bob May in his Speed Six. Bill and Bob had driven

over 14,000 miles each by the time they reached New York on the way home; and Jim shipped his Bentley home from San Francisco with a mere 5,500 miles of American motoring to his credit. The enthusiasts gathered on the Monterey peninsula were unstinting in their admiration for these demonstrations of roadworthiness by cars with about half-a-century of motoring behind them.

Con and I went to San Francisco by air accompanied by a party of members of the Bentley Drivers Club and took with us, as guests of the Club, Margaret Bentley, 84-year old widow of 'W.O.', and Barbara Fell, long-serving Secretary of the Club. On arrival in San Francisco I picked up the afore-mentioned estate car (sorry, station wagon) from Avis. It was a Chevrolet Caprice and was to be our transportation for some 1,500 miles – and it served us very well. Our itinerary took us to Yosemite, Monterey, Santa Barbara, Disneyland, and to Briggs Cunningham's Automotive Museum at Costa Mesa. I was privileged to drive Briggs' 8-litre Bentley on to the prize-winners' dais at Pebble Beach and again to lead the parade of Bentleys round the circuit at Laguna Seca. Whilst staying at Santa Barbara I visited the Clénet works and drove one of the current models. Not exactly the sort of car, this, that I would choose for commuting – although one was regularly parked in a street off Park Lane in the early 1980s – nor would I feel comfortable entering the paddock at Vintage Silverstone in one. Not surprising really, for it is designed to appeal to the extrovert Californian's craving for something different – open-car motoring with all the features and amenities of the current top-of-the-range American sedan. And in this I think it succeeds. It does not aspire to be a sports-car, except perhaps in looks, nor does it pretend to be a clone of any respected predecessor. It was based on a new Lincoln Continental Mk. V chassis and running gear, from which the body had been removed and disposed of to the spare parts trade. This procedure was less costly than buying only the parts required from Ford and meant that the company avoided being defined as a manufacturer in the eyes of certain Government agencies. About three feet was cut out of the chassis, the better to move the engine back by that amount. The engine was a 400 cu.in. (6½-litres) V8. The chassis was strengthened by boxing-in and additional cross-members. As to the next step, I quote from Henry N. Manney III writing in *Road and Track*:

> In the meantime, Clénet's spies have been scouring the countryside for worn-out Sprites/Midgets (no great task) and they are whisked off into the gas chamber and their bodies taken off. These choice items then are sawed in half just before the firewall, neatened up, the welds re-done, reinforced by plates over the floor and gently modified into the form Clénet wants, by a Lebanese body man who has the best steel-drum band beat this side of Trinidad.

(Tongue in cheek Manney enquired why the discarded Lincoln bodies were not then mounted on the Spridget chassis and learnt that the stiffening involved would make the finished product nearly as heavy as the Eiffel Tower and just about as fast from 0-60!)

It offered a pleasant way of proceeding along the sunlit, speed-limited freeways of the West Coast – provided one could get away from the smog. I once met a married couple at a meeting of the Rolls-Royce Owners Club who had 'his' and 'hers' versions – one open and the other closed!

Altogether a memorable trip, bringing Bentley enthusiasts together from widely separated places, many of whom had known Barbara Fell for years in correspondence or at the end of a telephone, but were meeting her for the first time. Margaret Bentley greatly enjoyed her first visit to America and her gracious and enthusiastic presence enhanced the pleasure of all who met her.

Morocco

The promise of warm sunshine tempted us to North Africa in January 1982.

Superb roads, sparse traffic and striking sce-

127 *Margaret Bentley with Phil Hill and his 4½-litre supercharged Bentley at his works in Santa Monica – August 1979*

nery, sum up my impression of a thousand miles driving during a week's holiday in and around Marrakesh in southern Morocco.

On arrival at Inezgane Airport, Agadir, in the warm winter sunshine, I collected a pre-booked Avis rental car – a Renault 12 – and set off inland for Marrakesh. The 'new' road (P511) went north-west to join the road from Essaouiara (formerly Mogador) (P10) at Chichaoua then east to Marrakesh. The road had an excellent surface and, apart from a gentle climb over the Maachou Pass, was straight and level. The absence of other vehicles was a refreshing experience, but the traditional four-legged transport prevalent in villages called for diligence and prompt reactions. The 162-mile journey from Agadir to Marrakesh was comfortably completed in three hours.

Our destination was the Mamounia Hotel made world-famous by its choice as a winter resort by Winston Churchill. Suffice it to say that we could not find a single thing to criticize during our stay. It is true that the hotel was by no means full, but the service was impeccable and equalled any I had met in the world – truly an oasis of elegant living of a bygone age with all modern facilities, in, to northern European eyes, an environment of poverty and squalor. Marrakesh

128 *Signpost to Timbuktu in Zagora – note temporary plastic windscreen on rented Renault – January 1982*

is in the middle of the Houaz plain and the snow-capped High Atlas mountains form a beautiful backdrop whichever way one looks. The thought of the Sahara Desert beginning less than 300 miles away to the south tempted me to forego the sybaritic surroundings of the Mamounia to drive over the mountains for an overnight stay in Zagora. The road (P31) passed through only one town of any size, Ouarzazate, 125 miles from Marrakesh on the other side of the High Atlas mountain range which we crossed by the Tichka Pass (6,200 ft.) The road had an excellent surface and in the mountains was as well-engineered as any in Europe. It had been cut into the mountainside and the absence of retaining walls on the drop side could have worried nervous passengers. Zagora lies 100 miles further to the south-east along the 'Road of the Kasbahs' – fortified villages – and the total distance of 225 miles from Marrakesh occupied six hours of driving time. Whilst picnicking on the roadside in the mountains a small boy appeared from nowhere and offered us a piece of rock. It was

brown and rough just as it had been picked up off the mountain, but the underside was crystalline and shining purple. It was, of course, a chunk of amethyst and was seemingly deemed a fair exchange for a contribution from our picnic basket.

Three miles short of our destination my windscreen was shattered by a stone thrown up by a passing car. I drove slowly into Zagora and, when I stopped to find the way to the hotel, selected a likely-looking lad from the customary clutch of youngsters offering their services. He said 'No problem' when he saw the shattered screen and took me to a workshop in a row of shabby shops. Although it was 6 pm the *garagiste* said he would remove the glass, fit a plastic screen for the equivalent of £13 and clean out the car ready for collection in two hours – and so he did. (Where in the UK could one find such service?) Incidentally, a telephone call to Avis on return to Marrakesh resulted in them collecting the car from the hotel and returning it a few hours later with a proper glass screen fitted.

The hotel in Zagora was pretty basic and the heating was not turned on until 7 pm, but it was adequate for an overnight stay. Zagora used to be the end of the road, beyond which were only *pistes* more suitable for cross-country vehicles than ordinary cars, but the *piste* was then a well-surfaced single track road as far as Mhamid, 55 miles to the south, where the caravans assembled to cross the Sahara. Regrettably we had insufficient time to go that far, but I was inveigled by Con's desire to see the sun rise over the Sahara into getting up at 5.30 am and setting off in the dark (with the aforesaid lad as a guide) some 17 miles into the desert near Tamgroute to witness the dawn. Standing in the sand dunes was extremely cold and uncannily silent, but the sunrise was indeed an experience worth waiting for.

After breakfast we retraced our route to Marrakesh, stopping for lunch at Ouarzazate and arriving back at the Mamounia in time for tea.

It was a most rewarding two-day excursion.

One afternoon we spent three hours driving out (and back) to the ski resort of Oukaimeden, 47 miles to the south of Marrakesh and at an elevation of 7,740 ft in the High Atlas. The road approaching the distant snow-capped mountains was at first straight and level before following the fertile Ourika valley. It then climbed in a spectacular manner, giving magnificent views at every turn. Oukaimeden was for keen skiers, the accommodation being limited, but there were everywhere signs of development in progress. The ski-lift up to 10,500 ft was claimed to be the highest in the world.

On the return journey to Marrakesh I made to turn left on to a steep unsurfaced track to Tahanaout, but gave up in deference to the protests of my passengers.

After six days of blue skies and warm sunny days (and cold nights) we returned to Agadir from Marrakesh by the same route as that followed on arrival, having abandoned my plan to travel by the 'old' road via Taroudant over the Test Pass (5,815 ft) for the comfort of my fellow-travellers surrounded by excess baggage, to stay overnight before flying home.

One had to admire the determination with which the community had rebuilt Agadir after its destruction by an earthquake in 1960. The sensible policy of anti-seismic precautions had necessitated a predominance of ferro-concrete and the town did not truly represent Morocco. For those seeking sun, sea and sand, Agidorm – sorry, Agadir – doubtless had its attractions. It was developing fast for the tourist, but we did not take to it, and our disenchantment was not dispelled when we woke up to find a hot wind, the *chegri*, blowing strongly from the south and carrying sand in the air from the Sahara. I saw two cars in Agadir bearing English plates which means that the owners had driven at least 550 miles from Tangier plus whatever mileage they covered in Europe from their disembarkation port in France or Spain.

There is no doubt in my mind that any motorist not relishing the 1,400 mile flog across Europe each way to cross the Straits of Gibraltar would find a fly/drive holiday in Morocco a worthwhile change from Continental Europe.

Grand Canyon via Japan and Hawaii

In the course of a journey round the world in June/July 1982, following a business trip to Japan to participate in the naming ceremonies of two tankers, Con and I had some interesting motoring experiences.

In Tokyo I telephoned Bentley Drivers Club member Kohji Nakauchi, owner of an R-type Continental Bentley then in the UK, and we spent an interesting hour together, during which he referred to the collection of cars owned by Mr Yoshiyuki Hayashi, which included two Vintage Bentleys – a blower 4½-litre and a 'T.T.' 3-litre. I had seen the blower car (EU 919 ex-Klein) at Laguna Seca in 1979, but had not met the owner. I was puzzled by the reference to a 1922 T.T. Bentley. It was with great pleasure, therefore, that I received a call from Shotaro Kubayashi, editor of that superb Japanese monthly *Car Graphic*, offering to take me out to Gotemba, about 70 miles from Tokyo, to see Mr Hayashi's cars. The collection, which was not open to the public, was housed in a new purpose-built 'garage' holding about 40 cars. These included the W125 Grand Prix Mercedes, P3 Alfa-Romeo and Type 35B Bugatti, all acquired from Neil Corner. There were about a dozen Mercedes, several Alfas, Bugattis, and many other interesting cars. Altogether an enviable selection, superbly displayed.

The 'T.T.' 3-litre Bentley turned out to be the replica built by Cyril Wadsworth over a period of eight years using contemporary parts and painstakingly fabricating the missing bits. Cyril went to a great deal of trouble to produce a car similar in all respects to the actual race cars, and nothing was too much bother in his search for authenticity. The car is a lasting tribute to his industry and represents in concrete form one of the milestones of Bentley history which could otherwise have been seen only photographically.

My next surprise was when one of the executives of the shipyard in Tokyo said, 'I saw a Bentley in a coffee shop the other day'! I hope I disguised my incredulity when I asked if he could take me to see it. He did – and sure enough, there in a side street in Tokyo was the 'Bentley Coffee Shop' with a 4¼-litre Park Ward Saloon in the window taking up a good deal of floor space. It was in good condition, and a peep under the bonnet revealed it to be Chassis No. B 106 LS, then with the UK registration number CAJ 92. The proprietor of the establishment was not on the premises so I could not ascertain the background to this incongruous combination. May the Orient continue to yield up its (Bentley) secrets.

Stopping over in Hawaii, we renewed our acquaintance with Guy Slaughter, who drives his 4½-litre Bentley in and around Honolulu – two-and-a-half thousand miles from his nearest fellow-owner in California. In Maui I rented an Avis car (an Omega, I think) for local motoring, and in Los Angeles a Ford Fairlane for the same purpose, but the most interesting motoring was yet to come. Flying from San Diego, where we had been staying with Briggs Cunningham, to Phoenix, Arizona, I picked up a Chevrolet Camaro and drove northward on the desert road to Flagstaff and then westwards along the South Rim of the Grand Canyon to the Thunderbird Lodge where we were to spend a couple of nights. I had some problem with the car engine whilst staying in the canyon village – I can't remember whether it was poor starting or running-on when switched off – the latter I think, but the Avis man there told me that it was a common problem because of the altitude, which surprised me as the terrain was only 7,000 feet above sea level. We drove to several of the signposted viewpoints and always marvelled at the new vista before us. One

129 *Bentley in a coffee-shop in Tokyo – June 1982*

felt truly humbled by the grandeur of nature in this famous National Park.

We left the Canyon reluctantly for our next stopping-place – Las Vegas – passing the impressive Hoover Dam into Nevada. 'Why Las Vegas?', you may ask. Well, I suppose everyone should visit there – *once* in a lifetime! The distance from Grand Canyon Village to Las

130 *Chevrolet Camaro between Phoenix, Arizona and the Grand Canyon – July 1982*

Vegas was 278 miles and took 5 hours 53 minutes including stops for sustenance, petrol, and sight-seeing totalling 56 minutes. I turned in the car at Las Vegas airport, having covered 660 miles since leaving Phoenix, and flew straight home via Los Angeles.

We had been away from home for three weeks and a day, plus another bonus day crossing the International Date Line. A total of 14 flights totalling 21,892 miles and we were airborne for a total of 42 hours 52 minutes. And Con doesn't like flying!

Western Canada and California

As Con's inclinations are equestrian rather than mechanical I usually manage to inject something of four-legged interest on our joint motoring travels. The month of July 1984 presented a couple of equine opportunities in the shape of the famous Calgary Stampede and the equestrian Olympics in Los Angeles and San Diego. These could be combined with a long-cherished wish to drive through the Rockies, so out came the maps of Western Canada for the first time and those of California for the umpteenth time.

I chose Edmonton in Alberta as our 'gateway' – as the airlines say – to Canada, and as the start of our motoring, in a rented car, of course. In this regard I was very fortunate. When I was getting nowhere in the Air Canada office in London, enquiring if they operated a Fly/Drive package, the gentleman awaiting attention behind me introduced himself as Ted Tilden, President of Tilden Rent-a-car, the biggest operator in Canada. He had overheard my requirements and at once undertook to arrange for me to pick up a car in Edmonton and leave it in Vancouver with no drop-off charge. On our arrival in Edmonton I discovered that I had left the keys to our luggage at home. I enlisted the help of Canadian Customs at the airport who produced a biscuit tin full of keys and within a few minutes all our bags were unlocked. (Intending smugglers be warned!)

The next morning, 9 July, a virtually new Chrysler Fifth Avenue was delivered to the Weston Hotel where we had gone to ground after a non-stop Air Canada flight from London. We set off westwards across the flat farmland towards the mountains and Jasper Park, 180 miles away. We spent two days at Jasper Park Lodge in one of the delightful lakeside cottages, and knew we were really in Canada when we met a bear roaming in the woods during a pre-dinner stroll round the lake. From here we were to drive along the Icefield Parkway stopping for a night at Château Lake Louise. The mountain scenery was magnificent – everything was so big and spacious and seemed to make even the Alps look small in comparison. I think I lost a few Canadian friends when I described the Château Lake Louise Hotel as looking like a jail outside and a provincial English hotel inside. Beautifully situated but, as one of the few hotels in this part of Alberta, it was invaded each day by coachloads of passing tourists, and the lobby had constant streams of people passing through, reminiscent of a railway terminus. (I banged my head on a low parking sign and had to seek first-aid treatment – perhaps that coloured my perception of the place.)

We pottered happily down the remainder of the Parkway, passing Banff, to which we were to return later, into Calgary. An account of the festivities during Stampede Week would be out of place in a motoring book. Suffice it to say that the whole town goes Western – bank managers go about their daily business in cowboy gear with fancy boots and ten-gallon (well, five-gallon, or should it be $22\frac{3}{4}$-litre) hats; hotel reception areas decorated to look like ranch-houses; and Indians riding horseback through the streets in their colourful dress and feathered head-dress. The chuckwagon races – four horses galloping ahead of four-wheeled vehicles made the chicane at Silverstone look like a church parade.

Having soaked up the atmosphere in Calgary and seen much of the action we retraced our route to Banff (79 miles away). We would have chosen to stay at the famous Banff Springs Hotel, but it seems that reservations have to be made a year or more in advance – mostly by the operators of coach tours – so we stayed at the comfortable Banff Park Lodge.

Next, we set out for the drive of over 500 miles to Vancouver, making night-stops at Revelstoke and Kamloops. No rush on this trip; the scenery meriting leisurely appreciation. I was fascinated by the spiral railway tunnels west of Lake Louise, where a pair of tunnels describe a figure of eight, the loops of the '8' being entirely within a couple of mountains. If one happens to be there when one of the tremendously long freight trains comes along, it is possible to see the locomotive emerge from one portal while the end of the train disappears into the other. The rushing Fraser River ran near the road for many miles, the road, railways and river having to share the same canyons through the mountains, and the white water tumbling through Hell's Gate was an awesome sight, never mind crossing in the aerial tram; and the thought of rafting . . .! Another stirring sight was the huge logging trucks, speeding down the mountain roads.

We checked in at the Westin Bayshore in Vancouver having taken three days to cover the 534 miles from Banff. The Chrysler had proved itself a very good choice for the journey and I turned it in at the Tilden depot having driven 2,157 kilometres (1340 miles). I found driving in Western Canada most enjoyable – good roads, comparatively little traffic, good driving manners and superb scenery.

The next day – 20 July – was my 70th birthday and a surprise lunch party had been arranged by Hugh Young and fellow-enthusiasts. It was hosted by Rolls-Royce represented by John Craig, head of the company's Pacific Rim operations, whom I first met in 1948, when he was competing in the Brighton Speed Trials in an XK120 Jaguar and I was the chap putting the timing spoon under his front wheel. Thirty-two BDC members and wives gathered on this occasion and appropriate toasts, responses and presentations were made, adding to a memorable day. John and Vera Craig took us on a compre-

hensive tour of the city and surrounding country and delivered us to the quayside to board a Twin Otter seaplane for Victoria where Hugh Young, who lives there, had booked us in at the Empress Hotel. After a day in which Hugh demonstrated the charm of his chosen domicile and we were further entertained by fellow-enthusiasts, we left Canada on the good ship *Princess Marguerite* for Seattle, four and a half hours away across the border in the State of Washington.

Although we spent less than 24 hours in Seattle, Gordon Apker found time to take us to his home to see his fine collection of cars, which included a Vintage Bentley I had known in England when owned by none other than Hugh Young, then resident in the UK. It was a Corsica-bodied Speed Six close-coupled saloon in top concours-winning condition.

From Seattle/Tacoma we flew to Reno to see how the Harrah Museum was developing under new ownership. I collected a Buick Century Limited from Avis, and the Olympic Games having sucked into the Los Angeles area all available rental cars from miles around I was charged more than double the normal tariff. I am pleased to report that it provided very satisfactory transport for the remainder of our holiday. We drove up to Lake Tahoe on the Nevada/California border; the State line runs through the centre of the town which results in gambling being catered for on the Nevada side by many casinos, but prohibited on the California side. Our short stay on the shore of this beautiful lake was the more enjoyable because, quite by chance, Jay and Sally Heumann were living in their summerhouse nearby.

Our next objective was the Ahwahnee Hotel in Yosemite Valley. This was the first time we had approached it from the Nevada side over the Tioga Pass (9,945 ft) – a 200-mile drive from desert to wooded mountain country. I know of few places that can equal – and none that can surpass – the grandeur of Yosemite National Park, viewed either from the valley floor or looking down from Glacier Point, thousands of feet vertically above the hotel, but over 30 miles away by road.

After a restful stay here we had a fair day's motoring – about 370 miles – to Santa Barbara on the Pacific Coast where we stayed when Margaret Bentley was with us in 1979. This time, however, we were to stay a few miles inland at the San Ysidro Ranch, selected from the *Relais et Chateaux* book on which we have always been able to rely. We were very comfortable in our guest cottage in the secluded grounds, but did not find the much-vaunted cuisine to our liking – tiny artistic creations of nouveau cuisine rather than even modest portions of palatable food.

From Santa Barbara we continued south for 230 miles to stay with Briggs and Laura Cunningham at Rancho Santa Fe near San Diego. The cross-country events of the equestrian Olympics were held a few miles away during our stay and, combined with a trip to the main stadium in Los Angeles for the show-jumping competition, made an acceptable four-legged leavening to a considerable four-wheeled content on this holiday.

We reluctantly started our journey home, driving to Los Angeles airport where I turned in the Buick which had served us well for 1,464 miles; and flying home via Edmonton.

This holiday was a rather special one marking my retirement from business and lasted nearly a month – rather longer than usual, and enjoyable enough to leave us both wishing to visit Western Canada again.

'State-hopping in the USA'

Having nearly completed my first year's retirement from business – a state which I entered with some misgivings as to how I (and my wife Con) would cope with the withdrawal symptoms – I was pleased to find that I (i.e. we) had adjusted very comfortably and I could sum up the situation in the words 'every day's a Saturday'. The reason was, of course, that I had plenty to occupy my increased leisure hours. The main deprivation arising from no longer holding an executive position in the shipping industry was the cessation of world-wide travel which for three decades had given me immense pleasure and afforded opportunities to meet fellow motoring enthusiasts and to make friends in many countries. Now, any excursions outside the UK had to be made at my own expense, without any assistance from an employer or the Inland Revenue. Thus it was that I seized the opportunity of a special cheap return fare of £110 to Detroit (offered briefly by PanAm to mark the inauguration of a direct non-stop service) to cross the Atlantic. I spent some time planning how to make the best use of my relatively inexpensive landfall in Detroit by making additional internal flights to visit motoring friends spread all over the United States and to return home within the 15 days stipulated by the special fare. The outcome was that I left Heathrow on the last day of May 1985 with the following planned itinerary ahead of me – Detroit/New York/San Antonio/Dallas/San Francisco/Monterey/San Diego/Los Angeles/New York/Detroit and home.

Although I was flying on to New York without stopping over in Detroit, I decided to delay my onward flight by a few hours to pay a return visit to the Ford Museum at Dearborn, the object being to have another stare at the Bugatti Royale in the collection. I was not disappointed – even if the cab fare from the airport to the museum and back was nearly half the cost of my flight from London to Detroit! I knew that the organizers of the prestigious annual *concours d'elegance* at Pebble Beach, California, were tackling the onerous task of trying to assemble the whole of the world's surviving production of Bugatti Royales, six in all, on the West Coast in August. Enquiries in the curator's office revealed only that the possibility of sending their car was under consideration. (It is now common knowledge that this magnificent coming-together of these famous Bugattis was achieved.)

I stayed overnight in New York, catching up on some much-needed sleep before flying the next day to San Antonio in Texas, where I was met by Don and Mimi Weber, and Ed and Jan Swearingen; I was to stay with Ed and Jan for a couple of nights. Ed, having sold his 4½-litre supercharged Bentley to Tom Perkins of San Francisco, was (and as far as I know still is) concentrating on building a 3/8-litre Special which he planned to bring to the UK to race. Knowing something of Ed's brilliance in the field of engineering and technical innovation, I feel sure that he will make even the fastest and most successful of the British drivers sit up and take notice – possibly of his disappearing rear number-plate. I was taken next day to Kerrville, 60 miles away, to visit an automobile museum owned by Bob Atwell. Among an interesting collection of Rolls-Royces and Classic American cars were two Vintage Bentleys. One was a 3-litre (chassis no. 650, engine no. 652) with an unusual sports tourer body by Viotti of Italy. The other Bentley was a 4½-litre (chassis no. PB 3541).

Dallas was my next overnight stop and I had written to Bill Chadwick, an expatriate Englishman representing the Bentley Drivers Club in that part of the US, to tell him of my proposed visit. Not only did he meet me at Dallas/Fort Worth airport, but he drove me to my hotel and thence to the office of the organizers of the Great American Race, where I had an interesting talk with LeRoi 'Tex' Smith, Public Relations Director, about that year's forthcoming event and future plans. All my efforts to raise sponsorship to enter my 8-litre and the Speed Sixes of several other Club members came to naught, and the only Vintage Bentley from the UK taking part was the Speed Six of Peter Agg. Dick Burdick of Texas was also to take part in a much-modified 3-litre and has distinguished himself in this demanding event which, although not a race, is a long distance time-speed rally for cars built before 1936. Dick was the outright winner in 1989 and 1990, pocketing a substantial share of the £138,000 prize money at the end of a gruelling run of 4,000 miles over 12 days.

Bill invited local Bentley enthusiasts to his

house that evening and eight of them accepted. We enjoyed the sight of Bill's (ex Barry Eastick) 8-litre and Ted Elkins (one-time Basil Mountfort) 4½-litre standing on the Chadwick lawn before going out to dine.

And so on to San Francisco the next morning where I was met by Jules (Jay) Heumann; truly, to know him is the 'Open Sesame' to the desirable car collections in Northern California, for he is co-chairman of the Pebble Beach *Concours d'Elegance*. He is a car enthusiast in his own right, having owned at one time a self-restored concours-winning 4¼-litre Bentley, two R-type Continentals, and several Hispano-Suizas on which marque he is a leading authority.

I had asked Jay to arrange, if possible, for me to meet Bob Cole, who had recently become the owner of the famous 'Blue Train' Speed Six and he whisked me of to join Bob, Lorin Tryon and Russell Head for lunch at Burlingame. I told Bob that the immediate reaction in the UK on learning the result of the auction was to wonder, 'who was this guy who was willing to pay over quarter-of-a-million pounds for the car to put it into a sweet shop?' – for it had been reported that it was destined for the 'Candy Store'! Now let's get this straight: the Candy Store is the name given to a beautifully restored 1920s Packard showroom jointly owned by 30 dyed-in-the-wool enthusiasts and houses a changing population of about 50 superb cars from the collections of the participating individuals. Jay is President of the Candy Store and Bob Cole is a member, contributing several Jaguars and other makes to the display. The name Candy Store was a light-hearted choice of its founders because it conjured up the same vision of joyful anticipation as the 'sweet shop' did when they were small boys.

Bob's acquisition of the 'Blue Train' Speed Six was a long-cherished dream and he was in Hawaii when a friend called him to say that the car was in a forthcoming Sotheby's sale. He admits that he did not start out with the intention of paying such a high price for it and related an amusing account of the stress of bidding across the world by telephone. Hearing the bids go up, at first by £5,000 increments and then slowing down to £1,000 steps, he was working hard with his computer converting pounds to dollars and figuring out which cars he would have to sell to go any higher. Bob was delighted to have secured this Bentley and told me that when it arrived in California he received two unsolicited offers to buy it at the same price. It was beyond one's wildest dreams that the price paid would scarcely have bought a clapped-out Speed Six a few years later.

Bob is no spit-and-polish-only enthusiast; he was driving the Speed Six with zest and enjoyment. He even found a train to play with! The *San Francisco Chronicle* reported: 'As Southern Pacific's Peninsula commuter train came abreast yesterday of a custom-built Bentley, owner Bob Cole dropped the coupé into low gear and the race was on. The re-enactment of a famous car-versus-train race held 54 years ago ended 21 minutes 23 seconds after it began in San Francisco, when the Bentley pulled up at Burlingame station more than two minutes before the twin-engine four-car train'. The 'Blue Train' Bentley has definitely found a good home.

After a post-prandial drool over the delectable cars in the Candy Store, Jay drove me over the Golden Gate Bridge to visit Tom Perkins' collection. The latter's penchant for super-charged cars was evidenced by the sight of a room full of Mercedes, Alfa-Romeos, Bugattis and the ex-Swearingen blown 4½-litre Bentley. The only unblown car I recall seeing in the collection was the ex-Peter Hampton 12-cylinder Hispano-Suiza, in which Tom had just completed a week-long tour with other aficionados of the Stork.

After a 48-hour side trip to Monterey to visit Gerry and June Baxter I was back in San Francisco once again, being driven by Jay Heumann to see another car collection – this time the 'Blackhawk Collection' of Ken Behring in the Ramon Valley, some 40 miles from S.F. These cars, numbering about 200, were housed in four warehouses and were destined to provide the

basis of a museum then in the planning stage, but now one of the most striking edifices ever built to show off a collection of cars; something not to be missed by enthusiasts visiting northern California. Most of the cars were of American manufacture, but they had recently been augmented by several examples of European makes. There were no Vintage Bentleys, but I saw a 4¼-litre Gurney Nutting saloon (chassis no. B73GP) and a Mk. VI 4¼-litre Park Ward saloon (B410FV). There were indeed some unusual cars, including a Bucciali, and a 1924 Daimler with a Rolls-Royce-looking radiator and a large, open touring body made entirely of German silver – think of the polishing – and weighing over five tons. It was built for the Maharajah of Riwa. I had a short ride in a 'J' Duesenberg and was not impressed. The truck-like impression of this car which I gained in Canada some years previously was not dispelled.

Briggs Cunningham met me at my next port of call, Orange County, and, after a nostalgic walk round his museum, we drove out to his new home at Rancho Santa Fe, near San Diego. That evening found us both at Cy Conrad's home in La Jolla, admiring his Bentleys and other cars. Of particular interest was his resurrected 4½-litre, the acquisition and restoration of which was a saga of persistence and endeavour. It was a worthy stable-companion to his 3-litre (RC32) and does Cy and his wife, Yvonne, great credit.

A call to Barry Hon at Laguna Beach brought forth an invitation to lunch the following day at the newly-opened Ritz-Carlton, where pride of place outside the main entrance was given to his very nice Vanden Plas tourer 4¼-litre Bentley (B42KT) which I had been privileged to drive there. Barry has had this car for many years and actually found a new – yes, new – engine for it in a New York Rolls-Royce dealer's showroom.

An overnight stop in Los Angeles enabled me to visit Gary Wales in Woodland Hills to find that he, too, had been unable to find sponsorship for an entry in the Great American Race – and he was the previous year's winner in his 3½-litre

Bentley (B141FC). I drove this car to a nearby restaurant for lunch and Gary drove back – in about half the time. He certainly pushes this motor along and, seemingly, its rapid progress produced more excited interest than citations from the local Highway Patrol. Of more personal interest to me was to see and drive Gary's 4½-litre Bentley, for this was the well-known three-seater owned until 1977 by a good friend of mine, Arnold Stenhouse of Kingston-upon-Thames. Another Vintage Bentley in the Wales 'parking lot' was a recently-acquired 4/6½-litre (i.e. a 4-litre chassis with a Speed Six engine). It had an unusual body of unknown origin and when found by Gary in New Jersey was in deplorable state, having provided a home for squirrels, whose droppings and discarded nut shells were still in the car. The roof lining was in tatters and the whole had suffered the ravages of time. Gary told me that it went like a bomb and was scheduled for a ground-up restoration. Since then it has formed the basis of a unique car, which Gary calls the 'Bentley Royale', a very special 11.4-litre, 16-cylinder Bentley! In fact, it has two 8-cylinder versions of the Rolls-Royce B80 industrial engine side by side, one of them turned back to front, geared together at both ends. I have not heard whether this device has yet moved under its own power, but one can be sure that nothing will be spared in the way of expense and technical expertise to ensure that the finished car will command admiration, if not always approval, from fellow-enthusiasts.

After a brief stop-over in New York I left for home via Detroit and felt that I had extracted the maximum pleasure from my economy trip. It served to confirm what I had known for over 40 years – that the camaraderie and mutual interest among owners of desirable motorcars is the same all over the world.

131 *Briggs Cunningham at the wheel of Barry Hon's 4¼-litre Bentley – owner and author riding shot-gun – May 1985*

Florida

In October 1986 I stopped off in Florida, on the way home from a visit to California, to visit Bentley Drivers Club members in St Petersburg and to attend a dinner given by them in Tampa.

Losing three hours on clock time crossing the country eastwards necessitated an overnight stop in Miami. As my flight across the state to the Gulf Coast was not until late afternoon the following day, I seized the opportunity to fulfil a long-cherished wish, rented a Chevrolet Monte Carlo and drove the 160 miles to Key West, the most southerly city in the continental United States. This road, US 1, links a string of islands (called Keys) stretching 113 miles, by a series of 42 bridges. It is a unique sight and well worth the trip. After a quick lunch I did not stop in Key West, but flew back to Miami to catch the plane to Tampa. (It was not for another four years, when a cruise ship made an unscheduled call at Key West, that I realized what an interesting place it is.) The next day I was whisked to Anna Maria over the remarkable Sunshine Skyway Bridge to visit Dale Powers to see the spare parts operation he ran under the aegis of Appleyard Rippon for pre-1955 Rolls-Royce and Bentley cars – and to see his 4½-litre and 8-litre Bentleys. The latter was an H.J. Mulliner Sedanca de Ville of which few still remain, and provided us with

132 *At Key West, Florida, the most southerly city in the continental United States, in a rented Chevrolet Monte Carlo – October 1986*

appropriate transport to lunch at 'Fast Fred's'. My remark about it being the first time I had ridden in an 8-litre with power-steering (sorry, Powers steering) was met with the derision it deserved. Thanks to Fred Kenfield for providing his S1 Continental as a 'taxi' during my stay.

Round the world again – not by car
In August 1987 a special class for 8-litre Bentleys was included in the programme of the Pebble Beach *Concours d'Elegance* and I was invited to judge, assisted by Hugh Young and Tony Thompson. It was an invitation not to be lightly declined and I started planning a holiday to include this occasion. My problem was that Con – having been spoiled by first-class air travel when accompanying me on business trips – did not take kindly to flying long distances in economy class. I considered that it was just 'not' on to pay first-class return fares to California, and that the only way the cost of first-class travel could be justified was by means of a round-the-world ticket. Con accepted (I nearly wrote 'swallowed') this assertion, so we arranged to go the other way around – via Singapore, Hong Kong and Honolulu – a distance of 16,308 miles, arriving in San Francisco by the back door as it were. We managed to steal 24 hours to visit Yosemite again and were lucky to secure a cabin at the Ahwahnee Hotel. I rented a Chrysler LeBaron – not a proper LeBaron, you understand, but a modern eponymous version – to provide our means of transport on this occasion – a mere 568 miles.

We stayed at The Lodge at Pebble Beach, where we had a room overlooking the lawn on which the *concours* cars were displayed. Nine Bentleys were entered in the 8-litre class and the high standard of turn-out made judging a demanding task. The winner was Ted Reich's

Vanden Plas tourer; Sam Ornstein's Mulliner saloon and Donald Williams Smith & Cane Boat-tail two-seater were placed second and third respectively. Four other Bentleys were taking part in classes for 'European Classics' – the $4\frac{1}{4}$-litres of Gary Moore, and Lee and Marlene Zuker; the 3-litre of Robert Atwell; and the $4\frac{1}{2}$-litre of Mr and Mrs John Pearcy.

Briggs Cunningham had disposed of his museum collection at the end of 1986 to Miles Collier, but not all the cars had yet been transported across the continent to Florida, so the opportunity was taken to send the 8-litre to Pebble Beach for the *concours*. For the first time Briggs had no interesting cars of his own and, reluctantly recognizing the limitations of his physical shape, travelled the journey of over 400 miles each way in the unfamiliar luxury rear compartment of a chauffeur-driven stretch limo. I ferried the 8-litre around Monterey, and eventually drove it on to the dais with Briggs as passenger to receive (on behalf of Miles) from Con the Montagu of Beaulieu Trophy for the best car of British origin.

I had the pleasure of driving Barry Hon's 1904 Mercedes 40/45 along the coast road with Austen Clarke riding shotgun, but had to give it up sooner than I would have wished as I was frozen in my Californian attire!

133 *Author driving Miles Collier's 8-litre Bentley on to the prize-giving platform at the Pebble Beach Concours d'Elegance with former owner Briggs Cunningham as passenger. Author's wife is presenting the award – August 1987*

134 *Driving Barry Hon's 1904 Mercedes at Pebble Beach, California – August 1987*

Having done our flying so far by the excellent Singapore Airlines we were now transferred to Air Canada for the journey home via Calgary where I rented a Cadillac. We spent a few days visiting Banff and Jasper, which we had so enjoyed so much on our previous visit. An interesting landmark near Lake Louise was the Great Divide on the Alberta/British Columbia border. This is the Continental Watershed, where all waters flow either west to the Pacific or east to the Atlantic. After driving around for 800 miles we flew home, totting up a mileage of 21,698 miles on our circumnavigation of the globe – and Con still doesn't like flying!

United States again

In April 1988 I made another of my whirlwind tours of the United States, visiting Houston, Miami, San Diego, San Francisco, New York, and Washington DC in a couple of weeks.

Miami was a staging-post for a visit to Naples on the Mexican Gulf coast of Florida, to see progress on the museum being built by Miles Collier to house the Briggs Cunningham collection, which he had acquired, and his own collection of cars, mostly Porsches. I rented a Buick and made the 200-mile round trip in a day – a boring run across the Everglades, subjected, of course, to the nationwide limit of 55 mph. On the return run a locally-registered Rolls-Royce Silver Cloud III passed me, going like the clappers, so I tucked in behind and followed the rest of the way to Miami rather quicker than I would have otherwise driven.

The Collier Automotive Museum, which was officially opened on 19 November 1988, is a striking windowless, air-conditioned building occupying 50,000 sq. ft of floor space, with complete restoration facilities, stores and technical library. Fifty-two cars from Briggs' museum were transported nearly 2,500 miles across the continent and augmented by Miles' personal collection of racing cars to make a fine museum. Miles, whose father drove the Cadillac saloon for Briggs at Le Mans in 1950, is mainly interested in

135 *With rented Cadillac at the Great Divide on the Alberta–British Columbia border, Canada – August 1987*

racing and sport-racing cars, of which there were many among Briggs' cars and, although he accepts that there is a place in the museum for examples of the classic marques which Briggs gathered together over half-a-century, has disposed of some, including the now world famous Bugatti Royale. (Briggs says that this car must by now have done more miles in the air – between auctions – than it ever did on the road!) The collection includes many mouth-watering cars – five Bentleys: 8-litre, $4\frac{1}{2}$-litre supercharged, Speed Six, 3-litre and the Eddie Hall $4\frac{1}{4}$-litre T.T.; four Mercedes (remember the 1914 Grand Prix car); seven Cunninghams; three Hispano-Suizas, etc. The Porsche section comprises one of the largest and most important assemblages outside the manufacturer's museum in Stuttgart, ranging from the 1958 Behra Formula 2 car to the 1980 Interscope Indianapolis race car. A much treasured addition to the museum is the 1958 Vanwall Formula I car, previously in the Donington collection. Any enthusiast finding himself or herself in Miami should set aside a day for a

visit – a comfortable two-and-a-half hour drive away. However, a telephone ([813]643 5252) to ascertain opening days and hours could save a wasted journey. In Washington DC I spent some time with Bob Meyer, a member of the Bentley Drivers Club who, for 21 years until his retirement, was Curator of Aero Propulsion at the Smithsonian Institute, searching in the Institute's store of items not currently on exhibition for BR1 and BR2 rotary aero engines designed by W.O. in the first World War.

. . . and again

In the Spring of 1989 my thoughts were turning to what had by then become virtually an annual whistle-stop tour of the United States. Learning that the Bugatti Royale which I had seen auctioned in the Albert Hall was to be auctioned again in Las Vegas on Sunday, 23 April I arranged my itinerary to include that event. I arrived there two days before the sale. This gave me time to soak up the atmosphere of an American auction and to visit the Imperial

Palace collection of some 200 cars. This is located on the fifth floor of the Imperial Palace Hotel car-parking facility, and provides a peaceful haven from the glitz of 'The Strip'. The majority of cars were of American origin, but there were some examples of European makes, and I understand that the exhibits are changed from time to time. I also took the opportunity of driving out into the surrounding desert – an experience rarely open to us Europeans and certainly not in our continent. The hype, showmanship and circus ambience pervading this auction was a startling revelation to one accustomed to the almost ecclesiastical serenity of our friends Sotheby's, Christie's and Brooks' over here. The Royale did not sell and resumed its flying career back to Europe.

Next day, in San Francisco, I called upon J. Heumann – my infallible guide to car collections in northern California – and on this occasion he took me to see the Behring Museum at Danville, 30 miles east of San Francisco, where the 'Blackhawk Collection' was now housed in a strikingly modern, new purpose-built museum. It contains some 150 cars dating from 1897 to 1987 – backed up by another 100 or so in store and thus enabling exhibits to be changed from time to time. As one would expect, the museum included some superb examples of the very best cars in the world – Rolls-Royce, Hispano-Suiza, Bugatti, Duesenberg, etc. A worthwhile deviation for enthusiasts finding time to spare when in the Bay Area. (Telephone for an appointment [415] 838-0728 and have twenty bucks ready for the admission charge.)

The next few days I spent with Briggs Cunningham near San Diego, and was privileged to be taken by Barry Hon in his helicopter to see the private car collection of General Lyon. This included *the* first Bugatti (L-EB 10) made in 1908/9 and a car that brought back memories of my first motoring venture into Europe – the SSK Mercedes-Benz which belonged to Gerry Crozier in the '50s. The Corsica coupé body was black when I knew the car, but was now white.

My next stop was Chicago to see old friends and meet new ones at a lunch arranged by the local members of the Bentley Drivers Club at the Windermere Country Club. One incident which occured during this visit to the Windy City I cannot forget. Bill Boone had kindly met me at the airport and drove me to my hotel – the Marriott Downtown – the entrance drive to which is quite restricted. Bill pulled in the approach behind a brand-new white Lincoln Continental sedan which was disgorging its driver and passengers, and waited his turn to move up to the door. Then a car 'jockey' jumped into the Lincoln to take it to the valet parking area and the next thing we heard was the engine revs shoot up as the car leaped forward to demolish a marble wall and distinctly modify its front end. We could not conceive how such an accident could happen, and did not wait around until the owner was told what had befallen his pristine automobile.

Then back to Heathrow by TWA 747 which, assisted by a tail-wind of 96 mph, made the flight in 6 hours 39 minutes – 3,950 miles = 594 mph. (Can't this chap leave times and distances alone even when flying!)

And that is about the sum total of my globe-trotting experiences in the world of motoring. South America has been on my list as a 'must' for some time and I hope I shall be able to visit that part of the world whilst I am still 'young' and fit enough to enjoy it.

Meantime, I consider myself very fortunate to have travelled so widely and thus been afforded the privilege of meeting fellow enthusiasts on their home ground. For my part, the hospitality and friendship which has been extended to me in so many places overseas has been more than adequate reward for work I have put into the Club over the years. It is not too much to say that life has been enriched beyond measure by friendships formed all over the world.

My sincere thanks go to all concerned.

Postscript – about me

A respected motoring journalist reviewing the original edition of *Motoring My Way* wrote: 'If a criticism may be directed at this extremely readable, fascinating motorist's record, it is that one wants to know more about the author himself. It is not until page 174 that one gets a brief mention of his background. Becoming humility perhaps; but one could go along with him so much better if one knew him.'

So, if only to satisfy one reader, and perhaps to answer the question which may arise in the minds of other readers: 'What sort of chap is this who finds an absorbing interest in what, to the majority, is just a convenient (and smelly) means of transportation?', I have appended this chapter.

I was born in Huddersfield, Yorkshire, on 20 July 1914, and moved to south London in 1922 when my father was transferred to the London office of the insurance company for which he worked. I won a scholarship to the John Ruskin School in Croydon, where I matriculated, and left in 1930 at the age of 16 to go straight into articles with a small firm of Chartered Accountants in the City of London. For the next five years I received no pay – just the return in monthly instalments of the premium paid by my father – and passed the Final Examination of the Institute of Chartered Accountants in November 1935, being admitted in February 1936 at the age of 21, and reputed to be the youngest ACA in the country.

I started my career the following month as a qualified audit clerk with a different firm of Chartered Accountants, at a salary of £250 per annum, and taught book-keeping at evening classes at the Croydon Polytechnic. After a spell with another firm, I found myself the Managing Clerk of yet another firm in the City, on the outbreak of World War Two.

I married Con on the day before we entered the war – 2 September 1939 – and to this day she takes a dim view when I say it was the fact that her father had a Chrysler Straight Eight that clinched it! In August 1942, following a special *Daily Telegraph* crossword puzzle time-test, I was recruited to the Foreign Office, and after a six-month course at a house in Bedford – known locally as the 'Spy School' – I was posted to Bletchley Park (Government Code and Cipher School) and spent the remainder of the war working on cryptanalysis.

On 16 November 1943 our daughter, Carol Ann, was born and destined for a life of 'motoring madness'.

On being released from War Service in September 1945, I joined a firm of accountants, but after just more than a year made a break with the cloistered environment of the professional office and entered the hurly-burly of commerce. After a couple of years experience gained in the model manufacturing industry, and a

transport and removal business, I became Company Secretary and the first employee of a new shipowning company – London & Overseas Freighters Ltd. I remained there for the rest of my working life, becoming Managing Director in March 1976, and later Joint Chairman, before retiring in 1984 at the age of 70. I enjoyed my job very much and looked forward to Monday mornings!

In addition to the many overseas trips arising in connection with shipbuilding contracts, finance, ship launchings and trials, there were a number of out-of-the-ordinary experiences collected along the way: a Channel trip on the American nuclear-powered ship *NS Savannah*; a helicopter visit to a North Sea drilling platform; a week in Istanbul investigating a fraudulent agent; commuting between Government offices in Washington DC and a longshoremen's union in New York refusing to load a ship because it had called at a Cuban port; a voyage from New York to Newfoundland on the QE2 (chartered for the occasion) for the start-up of a new refinery and subsequently a visit to that island to attend court proceedings in connection with the insolvency of the charterer(!); attending a British Technology Exhibition in Beijing in the time of Mao; standing at ground zero where the atom bomb fell in Nagasaki; sitting in the basement of the Ministry of Foreign Trade in Moscow dictating to a telex operator, etc.

My introduction to motor-racing was in 1934 when I accompanied my father to Brooklands to see the British Empire Trophy Race. Thereafter Con and I were regular spectators there by virtue of a five-shilling (25p) ticket bought at Waterloo, which covered both the return train journey to Weybridge and admission to the track.

At the opening meeting of the Crystal Palace circuit in 1937 I noticed in the programme that the Chief Timekeeper, Roland King-Farlow, was a Chartered Accountant. I hastened round to his office in the City on the following Monday to offer my services and was welcomed into his time-keeping team. I did lap-scoring at Brooklands and Donington and, after the war, set up and organized scoreboard systems at Goodwood and Silverstone from the very first meetings. The only bright spot on the motoring scene during the war years which comes to mind is the Chessington Rally in July 1941, when members of the Vintage Sport-Car Club managed to field some delectable cars.

After the cessation of hostilities I lost no time in throwing myself into motoring activity. My involvement with the Bentley Drivers Club and the large part it played in my life will be self-evident to readers of this book. I was appointed Honorary Secretary on its revival in October 1945; became President three years

136 *Terence Cuneo at work on the portrait of the author in the summer of 1980*

137 *Portrait of the author by Terence Cuneo, commissioned by Bentley Drivers Club members on his retirement from the Presidency in August 1980*

later on the death of Woolf Barnato and, after more than 30 years in that office, was honoured by being made Patron of the Club, a position previously filled by 'W.O.' until his death in August 1971. The transition from President to Patron was marked by the Club commissioning Terence Cuneo to paint a portrait of me sitting in my 8-litre Bentley. (I now describe the function of the Patron as being interference without responsibility.)

I was appointed an International Timekeeper by the RAC in January 1946; was a founder member of the Steering Wheel Club in Mayfair; and became increasingly involved in motor sport. I helped the Cambridge University Automobile Club organize what I believed to have been the first race meeting after the war at Gransden Lodge in July 1947, and was Clerk of the Course on that occasion. In 1950 I took a team of lap-scorers and timekeepers to Le Mans and took care of that aspect for Briggs Cunningham's team, continuing to do so for the ensuing five years. In 1951 I edited the first four quarterly issues of *Autocourse*, and attended most of the important races in Europe in this capacity. In February 1953 I was appointed to the Competitions Committee of the RAC to fill the vacancy left on the death of John Cobb.

Nine months later we moved house – a mile down the road to our present abode. Russell Brockbank amusingly illustrated our change of address card. There was an enforced period of inactivity for six months when I became a TB patient at King Edward VII Hospital at Midhurst, fortunately being restored to health without undergoing surgery and emerging in February 1956 with a new set of values as far as health is concerned.

I passed the driving test of the Institute of Advanced Motorists in July 1956 and, with a membership number of 38, am now its 'senior' – well, longest-lasting – member. We had a short holiday in Madeira in September that year flying to Funchal via Lisbon by Aquila Sunderland flying-boat, and made our first visit to the United States on the *Queen Mary* in April 1957. I distinguished myself in August 1958 by selling Con's MGA to a confidence trickster for a dud cheque – a real genuine Vintage-looking chap he was, too, whiskers and all!

I took a driving test in New York, in 1959 (I think), UK and International licences not being acceptable in the US at the time. In the '60s our social life took off and we were able to enjoy a good deal of travel. Daughter Carol married Roger Salter in October of 1964, following which we made our first trip round the world taking in the Equestrian Olympics in Tokyo. I bought a 3½-litre Bentley which had belonged to Gavin Maxwell for Carol and Roger – since rebuilt by Roger and well-known in Bentley and Rolls-Royce circles. I was a Founder Member of the Brooklands Society when it was formed in October 1967. Just after the war I had exposed – to no avail I'm afraid – the 'plot' to sell Brooklands to Vickers, thus ending its existence as a motor racing track.

We have acquired a taste for cruising (in large ships) and have made several voyages in the Caribbean and the Far East. I have been able to indulge my liking for travelling in famous trains and now have three in my 'collection' – the Japanese Bullet; the Orient Express; and the South African Blue Train.

In 1979 we celebrated our 40th Wedding Anniversary with a day out in Paris with our progeny, flying out from Hurn in a chartered Cessna Citation, and in 1989 marked our Golden Wedding by taking a small party of family and friends to Jersey for a weekend.

In addition to my keen interest in motoring and travel, I am a serious, amateur photographer. It has enabled me to record my experiences with a succession of Leicas and to process the results in my own darkroom. This book would have been dull without access to my library of thousands of negatives.

I enjoy air travel. My first experience was by way of a 21st birthday present in 1935, of a return flight from Croydon to Ostend and a weekend with Con's family in Knocke. The plane was a Fokker VII with (if a I remember correctly) a corrugated metal fuselage and wicker seats. My first flight across the Atlantic was in 1956. In those days BOAC was using Boeing Stratocruisers which had folding berths and a downstairs bar. It took seventeen and three-quarter hours to New York, including a refuelling stop at Shannon or Gander. I see from my diaries that I have flown across the Atlantic over 80 times, including three mind-boggling (still) Concorde trips, and round the world four times. And I guess that's about it.

Index